BARGAIN H
IN
COLUMBUS

A comprehensive shopper's guide to savings and values
in Columbus and Central Ohio

BY DEBBIE KERI-BROWN

LOTUS PRESS
WESTERVILLE, OHIO

DISCLAIMER

The information contained in this book is a result of my own efforts and identifies prices, brand names and other details which were evident at the time of my visit to the business. Other references were extracted from advertisements and additional sources. Whenever possible, management was spoken with in order to gain further insight into the business's operation. Listings in this book, regardless of how worded, do not necessarily imply or state an endorsement by the author, Lotus Press or its employees or assigns. Businesses/services have not paid a fee to be listed in this book, and listings are not necessarily with the prior consent or knowledge of the business/service. Listings reflect the opinions and observations of the author. While every attempt has been made to ensure accuracy and provide current, objective information, neither the author, Lotus Press or its employees or assigns will be held responsible for any or all omissions, typographical errors or erroneous information. As business/service policies, hours of operation, type of stock etc. have a tendency to change as needed, I strongly recommend that you call ahead to those places you intend to patronize.

Bargain Hunting In Columbus. Copyright © 1992 by Debbie Keri-Brown. Printed and bound in the United States of America. All rights reserved. No part of this book may be reproduced or transmitted, without permission in writing from the publisher, in any form or by any means, electronic or mechanical, including photocopying, recording or by any informational storage or retrieval system, except by a reviewer who may quote brief passages in a review to be printed in a magazine or a newspaper- For information, contact: Lotus Press, POB 8446, Westerville, Ohio 43081-8446.

First printing, 1992.

Library Of Congress Cataloging-in-Publication Data

Keri-Brown, Debbie, 1953-
    Bargain hunting in Columbus : a comprehensive shopper's guide to
    savings and values in Columbus and central Ohio / Debbie Keri-Brown.
    p.   cm.
    Includes index.
    ISBN 0-9629590-6-5 : $12.95
        1. Shopping--Ohio--Columbus--Guide-books. 2. Columbus (Ohio)-
    Description--Guide-books. I. Title.
    TX336 . 5. 032C655 1991   91-31118
    380. 1'45'0002577157--dc20   CIP

DEDICATION

This book is dedicated to my parents and grandparents who started me on my journey. To my Aunt Marilyn and other relatives who unknowingly became a source of inspiration. To my children, Jason and Janelle, who have been dragged around town on my shopping excursions when they would have much rather been home playing on the computer.

To my husband, Dave for his love, support and encouragement through my many sleepless nights. And to God for providing me with the insight and perseverance to accomplish this enormous task, especially during my recent illness.

ACKNOWLEDGEMENT

I would like to thank my editor, David St. John, for his assistance. In spite of my frequent requests to cut corners, he kept me on track and encouraged me to write the best work possible. To Steven W. Justice for his eye-catching cover art. And to Jason, Janelle, Andrea and Ryan for their valuable contributions.

TABLE OF CONTENTS

v

vi

PREFACE

As far back as I can remember, I have always loved to shop for bargains. I recall the frequent exhilaration I felt as a child every time I came across an unexpected "find".....and it still continues. I have many relatives who are somehow connected to the New York Garment Center district, and this is how my interest in shopping began. My dad, an accountant, still maintains his practice which includes many Korean owned manufacturers as well as others. In fact, he is the executive director of the *Greater New York And New Jersey Korean Garment Manufacturers' Association*. He has recently been described by the New York Post as the "spokesman for the economic trends in the garment industry".

My grandfather helped to set up many of the prominent manufacturers by selling them industrial sized sewing machines. He also owned and operated several garment factories. My grandmother was a stylist for an international design house and as a benefit, she received many couture clothes for free. In fact, she owned so many formal clothes that she used to wear cocktail dresses when she went to the grocery store! Numerous other relatives have been involved in the New York Garment district in other capacities. As I was growing up, my dad frequently took my sisters, mom and I behind the scenes to the manufacturing operations where the garments were made. It was a thrill to see the workers in action and the rows upon rows of finished garments awaiting shipment to the retail stores. My dad pointed out that, "this manufacturer makes clothes under such and such designer labels, and he also makes other merchandise for lower priced lines". "Hmm, an interesting fact I thought." I acquired a wealth of knowledge and many additions to my wardrobe from those frequent factory visits. The lively conversations I had with my relatives also provided me with food for thought.

My aunt Marilyn always delighted me with her stories of how she frequently travelled to New York City by bus from Wilkes Barre, Pennsylvania as a personal shopper for some of the more affluent residents of that city who wanted special baked goods and other items which were not available in their home town. She really enjoyed those shopping experiences. It's no wonder that she was supportive of my idea for a book on shopping!

My mother always made certain that my sisters and I had new clothes when school began each September and intermittently throughout the year. After I came of age to shop on my own, my parents would give me money to buy clothing and I would come home with a shopping bag full of things for a mere $20, unlike my sister, Bonnie, who would only buy 1 or 2 items. She was loyal to designer brands and as hard as I tried to convince her that she wasn't always getting good value for her money, she was stubborn and did not want to listen. My parents were delighted about my bargain hunting escapades and would not fail to tell all of the relatives, plus their friends, every chance they had. Soon my friends began asking me where to find certain items cheaply. I began to keep a card file and referred to it whenever necessary. Over the years, I continued to search out bargains and have thoroughly enjoyed my experiences.

In 1980, my husband was relocated to Columbus through American Electric Power and I found myself in the middle of the Midwest with he and my 2 children. In 1981, we opened up a women's clothing store and a gallery, Potpourri Boutique and Fantasy Designs Gallery, in the Ohio Center, now called the Columbus Convention Center.. This was really a dream come true. I could use my knowledge of buying at fair prices with my fashion flair, and my familiarity with the New York Garment district to dress Columbus women in style. At the time I opened the store, there were only a few places in Columbus where you could purchase fashion forward accessories and clothing at a reasonable price. The women would "ooh" and "ahh" at the styles and were especially delighted at the colorful selection of jewelry in the showcases. They all had experienced difficulty finding jewelry to coordinate with their clothes. Would you believe that it was hard to find purple, red or even yellow earrings back then? Business was good and I was having a great time merchandising, selling and best of all......buying. It wasn't uncommon for me to spend $20,000-$30,000 in a snap over a 2 day buying spree in New York, I knew how and where to go to find those great bargains. My customers appreciated the exceptional values they were able to find in my store. The retail experience provided me with new insights about manufacturing, buying, selling and consumer behavior.

At about the same time that my store opened, I began to volunteer for the Central Ohio Radio Reading Service by reading magazines over the air to people who are print handicapped. I proposed a new weekly show to the program coordinator, Ellen Bernhardt, in which I would host a program that would address entertainment, community services, special events and bargain shopping in Columbus. I would always try to mention sources which were free or reasonably priced, as many of the station's listeners were on a limited budget. The idea sounded great to me, but it was difficult at first, to convince her that I was the right person for the job. After all, I had only been in Columbus for 1 1/2 years. I guess I must have been very persuasive and she saw that the proposed program would fill a void on the station. Not only did she allow me to host the program as I had proposed, but I have been hosting it for 10 years! The program was named after my store and called, Columbus Potpourri. The title also reflected the fact that it would contain much diverse information about Columbus. I continued to search out bargain information for the show and found that either some of what I found, was not appropriate for the listeners or that I didn't have enough time to mention it on the program. I managed to save all those newspaper clippings and notes, not realizing that one day I would write a book on bargain hunting.

After my divorce in 1986, and the subsequent closing of my store, I limited my shopping experiences to personal use only. Along the way, I managed to keep mental notes of Columbus' best shopping spots and still saved all of those newspaper clippings. In 1990, I began to teach a class through the Ohio State University's Creative Activities Program entitled, *Bargain Hunting In Columbus,* and have taught it through many adult education programs and at libraries throughout the city. At last, I had found a way in which to share all of the information I had accumulated! The course participants were literally begging for more bargain leads as a follow up to the class. Since I obviously could not fit any more information into that exciting 2 hour program, I chose another option. As a result of that demand, I felt that the time was right to publish a book. As I look through the pages of *Bargain Hunting In Columbus,* I stare in awe at the overwhelming number of businesses in the area where you can obtain free or low cost entertainment, services, clothing, art and more! Columbus has so much to offer and it is right under your nose.

In July of 1990, I married my current husband, Dave, who has been a constant source of love, encouragement and support. Everyone should be so fortunate to have a spouse as wonderful as he. I am also blessed to have married a man who enjoys shopping. In writing *Bargain Hunting In Columbus,* I felt that it was equally necessary to provide you with tips on how to shop, as it was to suggest places which offer excellent values.

HOW I RESEARCHED INFORMATION FOR THIS BOOK

You'll be surprised to know that many of my leads have been generated by looking through newspapers-the *Columbus Dispatch* and all of the community papers. That is why I strongly recommend that you read them and let them become part of your daily routine. Of course, I have had my share of times when I accidentally stumbled upon a shop while on one of my bargain hunting escapades, leads from friends and those which I received while instructing *Bargain Hunting* classes throughout Columbus. Other leads have come through mailings from local organizations, to be used on a radio show I host for the Central Ohio Radio Reading Service. Some of my research was conducted at the main branch of the Columbus Metropolitan Library, a valuable community resource.

When I visited a potential bargain business, it was done incognito- I didn't tell the staff why I was there. Instead, I tried to absorb all that I could from staff comments plus my own observations. Afterwards, I either identified myself and defined my purpose, or called back to speak with the owner/manager. In some cases, I was surprised at the difference in the information that I received as compared to what I was initially told. One store owner, who shall remain unnamed, told me that his entire inventory is discounted 40-60% as a result of making special purchases. When I tried to clarify this over the phone, I was told that he was just having a brief sale and that he wasn't discounting his merchandise. I was surprised at how many upscale businesses which were discounting their stock or selling it at a good value for one reason or another, didn't want to be associated with a book on bargain hunting. "We don't want THOSE sort of people" or "Our customers would frown on us if we were associated with your book, or "Even though I'm telling you for your own knowledge, I can't have you print that we buy overstocks from a famous New York store because our customers would think that the merchandise is not as good as it really is" were common complaints. Being the excellent sales person that I am, I convinced all but a few that it was to their benefit to be in the book (they weren't being charged to be listed anyway). Today's shopper is not hesitant to be a bargain hunter. The shopper of the 1990's is more value conscious than ever, but is also demanding quality products. And you'd be surprised how many arrive in Cadillacs and Jaguars to their favorite bargain and value priced stores!

Some store owners or managers were reluctant to share certain inside information on their business or did not want me mention brands which they carry or percentages of discounts which they offer. For this reason, you will note that some of the descriptions appear very generic and lacking in detail. This book is not intended to tell you where to purchase budget or inferior merchandise at low prices. Rather, it is intended to provide you with the names and addresses of businesses where you can buy or obtain moderate to designer quality merchandise or a service, at a discount, or a good value. So, price alone, has not been the sole factor for inclusion in *Bargain Hunting In Columbus*.

HOW TO USE THIS BOOK

I personally feel comfortable shopping at upscale stores, garage sales, flea markets and no frills businesses, and I'll go almost anywhere to find a bargain. If you feel uncomfortable about shopping in a certain type of environment, either turn your head the other way and head on to more comfortable territory, or practice some of the visualization techniques described in the *Keeping A Positive Attitude* section of the introduction so that you can overcome your fear or dislike of certain environments. In conducting the research for this book, I have tried to provide a wide variety of offerings. I amassed so much information, that I couldn't fit it all into this book. So, there will be a quarterly newsletter which you can subscribe to for $9 annually. It will provide you with more shopping tips, updates on listings in this book and new bargain sources I have found. The first issue will be mailed in January, 1992. See the order form at the back of this book. You'll find that some stores are categorized into unlikely chapters. For instance, Pearls of Wisdom bookstore is filed under the entertainment chapter. The reason is that it doesn't discount books. It offers free and low cost entertainment options. Where a business offers values in several categories, it has been cross referenced into each and is indicated at the end of each chapter under a subheading of *Also See*.

All listings are in the 614 area code, and are located within Ohio, unless otherwise noted. The description of businesses in other parts of the state are categorized according to the type of merchandise which they sell and are mixed in with all other listings for that category. Do you want to take a bargain hunting day trip outside of Columbus? Another chapter in the book called *Bargain Hunting Day Trips,* provides you with a listing of those out of town businesses. There is no consistency in the length of the description provided for each entry in this book. As you read you'll find businesses such as Phar Mor which will have an enormous description, while others will have small write-ups. Please be aware that the length of the description has absolutely no reflection on how good a business is or how great a bargain you will receive there. Some businesses specialize in just one type of product and so their description can be quite concise.

Lotus Press has also published a pocket sized bargain hunting directory which categorizes the listings in this book by zip codes. The directory is small enough to fit into the glove compartment of your car or even your briefcase. It will enable you to have a portable listing of the bargain sources mentioned in *Bargain Hunting In Columbus,* as I doubt you'll be carrying the book itself around with you at all times. The booklet will also have a space where you can attach swatches of fabric so you'll be able to match up accessories. See the order form at the back of this book.

If you know of any businesses/services which would be suitable for inclusion in the newsletter or in future editions of this book, please drop me a note and provide me as much information as possible so that I can properly pursue your lead. I appreciate hearing about your experiences at the places listed in this book and welcome all comments and suggestions. I can be contacted at: Lotus Press, POB 8446, Westerville, Ohio, 43081-8446

INTRODUCTION

BEING A PREPARED SHOPPER

The most important part of bargain hunting is being a prepared shopper. This can be accomplished in many ways. Keep a list with you at all times of what you need (including sizes), and what it is supposed to match. For example, you might need a purple sweater to match your purple plaid skirt, or a black and white tie to match your pin striped suit. It's also helpful to keep some small swatches, even threads of the clothes you want to match accessories to (belt, tie, hose, shoes, shirt, jewelry, scarf). This way, when you come across an irresistible item, you'll know if it can coordinate with something you already own. And, if you don't think that great wearable will match anything you own, you'd be surprised to learn that very often people can match up an intended purchase to an item they already have in their closet at home.

Dress appropriately for the shopping experience, from tip to toe. High heels are a definite mistake walking on gravel at an outdoor flea market, and they are not the best choice for a long day of shopping. Do not bundle up in too many layers of clothes and accessories. You will be discouraged from trying things on if there is too much to remove or if it is too difficult to remove it. For this reason, jump suits are a definite taboo. If you dress too warm for an indoor experience, you will get too hot and uncomfortable to shop. And who wants to schlepp around a coat over their arms when you are shopping? The opposite applies too: do not underdress for the weather.

Bring a large shopping bag or several. Stores do not always have them available and at some flea markets, you are lucky to get a bag with your purchase. If you have made several small purchases a shopping bag is especially helpful.

Whenever possible, do not shop with people whose attitude or behavior will inhibit you from finding a bargain and purchasing it.

Of utmost importance is to keep a mental note of the prices, amenities and quality of items you have seen elsewhere. This way, when you come across something which you feel may be a bargain, you can make a mental comparison and an informed decision.

DETERMINING IF YOUR FIND IS TRULY A BARGAIN

The most important issue is that you need to be an informed shopper. Spend time leisurely reviewing prices, brand names, fiber contents of clothing/products, quality of construction/components, warranties, even store return policies. On certain items like appliances, televisions, cars etc., you may want to do some advance reading in the current issue of *Consumer Reports,* and maybe even check the *Better Business Bureau's* various magazines and books before committing to certain purchases. Both will provide you with excellent tips on buying certain items. The *Consumer Reports* publication will provide you with detailed information on specific makes and models. If you do not care to make the investment in a purchase of both books, you can borrow them from the library. Another option is to call up your favorite library branch and ask the librarian to read you the necessary information from both or either book. As long as you are only seeking some limited information, the librarian would be delighted to read it to you. By staying informed, you will be better able to make an educated decision.

Decide if the item you are intending to purchase is something you need now or realistically will need in the future. Will the shelf life expire before you are able to use it? Are all of the parts working or is it damaged in any way? If so, what steps are necessary and at what cost and time are needed to repair it? One year I went crazy buying pharmaceutical items on sale, only to find that I should have anticipated that I would never be able to use all of it before the expiration date. My legitimate bargains turned out to be a financial loss as I had to discard my many unused purchases.

If you are making a purchase for someone and you are not sure if it will appeal to him or her, you will be stuck with the merchandise if the store does not accept returns. Always verify the store's return policy even if you think you will never need to return the item.

When you examine the quality of a product there are obvious things you should check for. Again, both the *Consumer Reports* book and the *Better Business Bureau's* publications can provide you with many sorts of tips on a variety of products. As with clothing, however, check the fiber content. A garment which needs frequent dry cleaning may not really be worth the bargain price in the long run.

Forget the word sale and objectively evaluate the price, value, quality, warranties, expiration date (if applicable), return policies and fiber content.

KEEPING A POSITIVE ATTITUDE

Having a positive attitude is also very important. If you convince yourself before you leave your home that you will not find anything on your shopping excursion or that you will have a lousy time, you probably will. Expect to find what you are looking for. Expect to have a pleasant experience. Here is a very powerful mental exercise you can practice. The process is called visualization and you can say several affirmations I have developed or create your own. The affirmations,, which are positive statements, should indicate the conditions which you want to achieve, but should be stated in the present tense as if they are already happening. Affirmations generally begin with the words "I have, I am, I feel or I accept". First, get comfortable: Either lay down in bed or sit upright in your favorite chair, and clear your mind of all thoughts. If soft instrumental music will relax you,, by all means turn it on. Check the records, tapes, CDs section in this book for sources. You can also find some for free loan at area libraries. Here are a few affirmations to get you started: "I release the old ways of thinking and make way for the new. I am open and willing to change my negative feelings about shopping. I am able to find what I need. I am able to enjoy the shopping experience (or, I am able to tolerate the shopping experience). I am easily achieving my goals".

Next, imagine yourself entering a relaxed state, and becoming relaxed. Imagine yourself going through the process at home of preparing to go shopping. What would you be doing? Gather your belongings, put on your coat, get into the car and drive to your destination. Imagine yourself enjoying the experience. Imagine yourself going up and down the aisles and finding those bargains. If you are looking for a specific item, imagine yourself finding it, touching it, examining it and trying it on or testing it out if necessary. Continue with this mental imagery through the process of paying for the merchandise, driving home, unpacking your purchase and putting it away. Since some of you might have to release many years of negative thought patterns about shopping, don't be disheartened if you don't feel and experience an immediate change. I suggest that you spend 5 minutes a day for several days before embarking on a shopping excursion. For a more in-depth approach to the process of visualization, pick up a copy of *Creative Visualization* by Shakti Gawain at any of the book sources listed in *Bargain Hunting In Columbus.*

SHOULD YOU BUY YOUR ACCESSORIES FIRST OR YOUR CLOTHES?

When I owned my store, I encountered a frequent phenomenon which was very disturbing. Most people are of the mindset that you purchase your clothing before you purchase your accessories (tie, belt, hose, jewelry etc.). I don't know when or how this mindset developed, but this is one way to miss out on owning a delightful accessory and maybe even at a good price. Why can't you buy that fabulous necklace even though you may not have anything to match? Of course you can do it! I'll bet that you can find something in your closet to coordinate with it.

IS IT REALLY ON SALE?

Approach the word sale with caution. Retailers have learned that consumers want to buy things on sale. Very often, they will inflate the retail price and then put the item on sale, so in essence, you are paying about the same or a tiny bit less than the real price the product should be. Very often, retailers do not expect to sell merchandise at the price they have it marked. They will take a large markup over their wholesale cost and run a big sale with supposedly great savings, expecting to make "a killing" during the special sale. Be wary of sales. Be a comparison shopper and stay alert so you can make an informed decision. In so doing, do not overlook legitimate sales.

Also, don't be discouraged from buying something which is not on sale. It could be a great value but not reduced. Remove the "on sale" mindset which you might have. Let me recount a personal experience. I was in the *Anderson's General Store* and stopped by an area to admire some solid oak bathroom accessories: tissue box covers, soap dishes and the like. The items were not on sale, but were priced about 20 to 30% lower than the discounted price on more famous brands at area discount stores. The workmanship was excellent, the color was perfect and it was something which I needed. I purchased several items. When I returned home, I told my husband about my bargains. He suggested that I return them and wait until they go on sale. After carefully explaining the situation to him, he decided I was right. By the way, there are some items which, for whatever reason, never go on sale.

PRODUCT LABELS

Product labels do not always mean what you think they mean. In an effort to mislead consumers, some manufacturers will lead you to believe that (1) the product is made from some material it is not or (2) that it is manufactured by a company other than the true manufacturer. Let me explain.

I have seen some supposedly crystal vases and bowls which, at first glance, appeared to indicate the word "crystal" on the outside of the box or the word "cristal" (note the spelling) in a descriptive phrase on the product's outer packaging, leading me to believe that the box contained genuine crystal. I received one such vase as a wedding gift. When I opened the box, the vase had a yellowish sticker affixed to it which read 24% PbO. I had never heard of that formula on a vase so I did some checking in the library and found out that this is the formula for Lead Oxide which is a highly refractive type of glass (it shines brilliantly when exposed to light) that is used most often in optical apparatus. This was not genuine lead crystal!

In another instance, I had received a factory boxed salad bowl which, at first glance, appeared to be identified as crystal on the outside of the box. A closer look at the packaging led me to discover that there were several glass colors written on the box clearly stating, color: (*) crystal ,( ) ruby. The manufacturer had used the word crystal to identify the color of the glassware and not the material from which it was created. Only by opening the box and examining its contents would you discover that it was not true crystal. This was an obvious attempt, to mislead you, the consumer. The product was also priced ridiculously lower than a true crystal bowl would have been and the quality of the packaging was less than desirable. It is not to say that you cannot find true crystal at a bargain price, but just be wary when you encounter this sort of a situation.

A friend of mine showed me a lovely necklace she had purchased for about $10 which was made of black and gold colored beads. The necklace, which was imported from India, had a hang tag which read "color: onyx". She thought that she was purchasing a necklace made out of genuine black onyx semi-precious stones and was ecstatic at her apparent "find". I really hated to burst her bubble, but when I explained to her what the manufacturer had done, she felt quite disturbed. Those little black beads were none other than coco wood heishi which were dyed black. Just as was the case with the "crystal" bowl, the word "onyx" was used to denote a color and not a material.

Oftentimes, manufacturers will give a name to a product line which is very similar to the name of a more expensive line of similar products. Again, this is usually being done to mislead you into believing that you are getting a top name, quality product. Unfortunately, in many cases, all you are getting is inferior merchandise.

I DON'T WANT TO MISLEAD YOU

Up until this point, I have been explaining about all of the questionable tactics which manufacturers and storeowners use to pull the wool over your eyes. While I want to make you aware that these problems exist, I also want you to know that there are retailers and manufacturers who would never consider these tactics. There are many honest, truly caring companies/businesses which strive to treat you fairly. I commend those companies which pride themselves in achieving this.

TIPS WHEN PURCHASING FINE JEWELRY

I have purchased some excellent pieces of jewelry simply because the seller was not aware that he was parting with something which was actually more valuable than he had thought. If you are considering purchasing some jewelry, check the clasp and backing for the following markings which mean the type of metal indicated; 900 or 925 means sterling silver, S means silver, 800 means silver, 14Kt means 14 Karat gold, 585 means 14 Karat gold and 14K HG means 14Karat Hamilton gold electroplate.

I purchased a thin, flat gold linked bracelet, marked 585, for twenty five cents at a flea market simply because the vendor was not aware that this Italian marking meant 14 Karat gold. You should also be aware that some gold or silver may not be marked. While it is more common that silver may not be identified as such, I own a beautiful handmade gold bracelet which does not bear any markings. Be certain to purchase any fine jewelry from a reputable dealer who is willing to stand by his products and offer you a written guarantee.

Here is a handy tip which I learned from my grandmother. She taught me that if I left my silver jewelry in aluminum foil when it was not being worn, that it would prevent it from tarnishing.

Another good tip which you should be aware of is that you should not spray perfume, hairspray or deodorant on yourself while wearing costume or fine jewelry. Always let the spray dry first before putting on your jewelry. The chemicals in the sprays can damage the finish on your favorite accessory.

FLOOR MODELS, DAMAGED MERCHANDISE, AS IS AND MORE

For heaven's sake, do not turn up your nose and walk away from something which might be labelled as damaged, "as is" or irregular.

When you come across something which is supposedly damaged, assess the extent and nature of the imperfection. Certain bakery thrift stores sell some merchandise which is not suitable for regular supermarket distribution. When a retailer is purchasing first quality products, he expects, as does his customers, that the merchandise is in perfect condition and meets all standards set forth on the labels. A baked goods shipment which is a bit underweight will not pass inspection in the plant, so it is sent to a thrift store to be sold.

The quality is the same as that found in the supermarkets. On food items, other irregularities may include slightly crushed boxes, close to or past expiration date. None of these so called irregularities should pose a problem for the consumer, with the exception of the expiration dates, unless the item is perishable. I have purchased cookies weeks past the printed "sell by" date on the package and have still found them to be fresh.

Furniture and appliances which have cosmetic scratches can generally be touched up quite easily and inexpensively using special paints and crayons found in your local hardware store. Also, depending on the location of the cosmetic damage, it may be hardly noticeable when you set up the item at home. I purchased a beautiful bedroom suite in New York from a dealer who dealt in slightly damaged merchandise at bargain prices. The suite had obvious flaws which had been touched up quite well. It also had distressed marks all over the surface which added to its charm. The store owner told me that the furniture was not originally intended to have a distressed surface, but as a way of making the scratches and nicks less noticeable, one of his staff members distressed all of the furniture to make the surface look more uniform.

When an electrical appliance, television or other item is sold "as is" there could be some minor cosmetic flaws or some possible malfunction which you will not be able to detect until you have used it for a few days. Before purchasing an "as is" item, check with the salesman and find our what is wrong with the product and what sort of a warranty would be available. It is also important to find out about the store's return policy in the event that you are not satisfied. As a personal choice, I try to stay away from purchasing floor samples on which children have been allowed free rein. I would feel more comfortable purchasing a floor model refrigerator than a boom box. However, there are big savings which are possible when purchasing floor models. Weigh the pros and cons of each.

Damaged merchandise should be clearly identified as such. Clothing manufacturers have various ways of identifying damaged merchandise. Let me state here that not all damaged merchandise is inferior. There are all degrees of damages. From a slight pull to an inconspicuous spot, to an unsightly grease stain where it counts, they all should catch your attention so that you are aware of them. I have taken the time to stitch loose seams or tears after having purchased a wearable and have even hidden tears and discolorations under appliques and fabric paints which come in tubes.

Storekeepers and manufacturers attempt to identify their damaged garments in one or more of these ways:
1. By using a piece of masking tape on top of the damage.
2. By cutting a slit through the manufacturer's label which is usually found on the neckline or by the waistline.
3. By stamping the sewn in label with a red, often undecipherable mark, "Irregular".
4. By stamping the word "Irregular" on a hang tag or a price tag.

Sometimes garments which have become damaged in the store are not identified as such. When this happens, and if you are interested in purchasing the item, ask the store manager if he can reduce the price for you. After all, it is damaged. If the price is reduced, is it to be sold "as is" with no return policy?

Also notice where the price tag has been attached to the garment. The appropriate place is through a seam or label so that it will not make an unsightly hole. If it appears as if a potential problem hole has been created by the price tag, bring this to the manager's attention and nicely suggest that the stock people be a little more cautious in the future. If you decide that you want to purchase that item, ask for some money off the price and explain why. Do not be surprised if you occasionally will not get a reduced price. I am not implying that you should nit pick and drive the store managers insane, but when the situation warrants it, there is no reason to remain tight lipped.

CONSIGNMENT, RESALE, THRIFT AND PAWN SHOPS

An abundance of these have popped up over the years selling varying qualities of clothes, toys, children's accessories, cameras, musical instruments and the like. In writing this book, I have included only those which offer upscale products. These are gently used and sometimes you will even find some new items. The savings can vary from 30-80% off "if new" prices. Consignment items belong to the original owner until such time as they are sold by the store. If they do not sell, the owner is obligated to pick up the merchandise or it will be donated to charity. Resale shops purchase items from the owners and sell them in their business. The merchandise is immediately owned by the shop. If it does not sell, the business will generally donate it to a charity. Thrift shops sell merchandise which has been donated to them. Pawn shops loan money to people in exchange for collateral such as gold jewelry, musical instruments, cameras, watches etc. If a client chooses not to repay a loan or is unable to, the merchandise is sold. Most of it is used. You will also find antiques and collectibles as well.

SHOPPING WITH COUPONS

Did you know that over 20 billion coupons are distributed annually by manufacturers, yet only 4% are redeemed. Many people feel that coupon clipping can be boring, frustrating and time consuming. If you take the time, you can usually save $40 or more per month on your grocery bill. Organize your coupons by subject and take them with you whenever you go to the grocery store. Cub Foods, the Grandview and Lane Road libraries offer coupon exchanges in which you can leave coupons you no longer need and/or take those which you want to redeem. There are no membership fees. Another option is the *Coupon Clearing House* where you can order coupons through the mail for a nominal fee. Check the index to locate these businesses in this book.

MERCHANDISE DISPLAY

Inventory in most stores is set up to encourage you to make a purchase. In supermarkets especially, most shoppers circulate around the outermost aisles. As a result, the stores have their most profitable items such as produce, meat and high priced gourmet goods, in these areas. Stock clerks usually place the most expensive and profitable items at eye level. So, look high and low on those shelves for values.

Some of the bargain places mentioned in this book, have done little to make their stock appealing. Messy, disorganized shelves and racks, simplistic display stands and even basic decors can be found. Do not be discouraged! If you want to find the great bargains, be prepared to weather the storm! One such store, whose name I cannot mention, but is generically described in this book, sells 2 piece Neiman-Marcus silk suits for $40 (which have not been steamed pressed and which look quite wrinkled) and haphazardly arranges some of its stock. On a recent visit, I saw a designer crystal vase on a shelf next to a budget quality household item. Be persistent and go in with your bargain hunting antennas fully extended. These places offer wonderful values.

Also keep in mind that most everything looks like junk in a store which sells low quality merchandise or which doesn't maintain its stock in an appealing fashion. So be sure to look selectively through a store's inventory so you don't bypass some wonderful bargains. Use the visualization technique to imagine yourself wearing the intended purchase or placing it in your home or office. This will help you to gain a better perspective on whether or not this item is something which you will really enjoy. Also keep in mind that some stores which sell budget quality merchandise, occasionally get moderate to designer quality goods. Read the description of Family Dollar in this book. This is a classic example of an occasion when I saw Paolo Gucci (formerly with THE GUCCI business) earrings for $5, regularly $35. That was hardly typical of the type of stock in their store. Yet, it was there.

VARIATIONS IN INVENTORY

Very often, a business which has several locations, will vary some of its inventory from store to store, based on what sells best in different parts of town. Another reason for variations in inventory, is that there may not be enough of a particular style or color to be distributed to each branch. My suggestion to you is to check out as many of the business's other locations as possible. This is especially true if you have decided that you do not like a particular store's merchandise. You might find that one of their other sites offers more to suit your taste. Sometimes, the difference between the stores" offerings is like night and day. Another important tip is to try shopping at a store several times before you make the decision that you don't like it.

TIMING YOUR SHOPPING

Don't be embarrassed to ask the staff of your favorite stores when their new merchandise will be put on the shelves or racks. Some stores have certain days and times set aside for this. On the other hand, deliveries to some stores are so sporadic, that the store may not know when their next shipment will arrive. Armed with the timing information, you will be able to select the cream of the crop.

CREATIVE SHOPPING TIPS

It's okay to use an item in a way other than originally intended. I purchased a lovely miniature mirror with a handpainted porcelain figure on the reverse, removed its handle and inserted a gold chain through the loop at the top. I realize that I may have played havoc on its original value, but I loved it and wanted to wear it. That $10 purchase is the most eye-catching accessory in my wardrobe. I have purchased old buttons at flea markets and randomly sewn them on sweaters, and even used an old child's potty trainer as a planter! Antique kitchen implements can be used to adorn you walls. Old jewelry can be restrung or used in wearable art collage jewelry (see chapter on classes for instruction offered by the author of this book).

There is another way to add pizzazz to your Ho-hum apparel purchases. A simple shirt, dress or denim jacket can be embellished with glitzy doo-dads and fabric paints, adding considerable value to the garment. Look carefully at the clothes in your favorite stores and try to copy some of the embellishment techniques. Go to your closest craft shop and pick up ideas and products which can be used to add intrigue and excitement to your garments and home furnishings, at a fraction of the cost of hand decorated store bought merchandise. Sign up for a class to learn these skills or take out a book at the library. The chapter on classes in this book offers a listing of value priced instruction.

PERSONAL FAVORITES

There are so many businesses/services which I love, but here is a list of some of my personal favorites. Each provides excellent values as evidenced by their inclusion in this book, in addition to having merchandise or program availability which is consistent in quality and abundance of selection. I have tried to explain the additional reasons why they stand above the crowd.

ALL FOR ONE: Everything's only $1? Excellent selection of inventory and merchandising techniques for a store of this type.

BERWICK CORNER OUTLET: The ever changing inventory is full of chic surprises.

CAFE ON 5: Delicious food and cozy atmosphere.

CI BON: Unusual furniture and accessories in tastefully decorated vignettes.

COLUMBUS METROPOLITAN LIBRARY, MAIN BRANCH (INCLUDING THE LIBRARY STORE): I can't imagine why it took a divorce to turn me on to the library. Now, we're best friends. It can satisfy your every need (well almost) from business to personal. Best of all, most of the services are free. It welcomes people from all walks of life and all ethnic backgrounds to share its treasures within. It certainly must be the end of the rainbow. The bookstore provides excellent values on all types of books especially used reference books not otherwise available through traditional used bookstores.

COLUMBUS RECREATION AND PARKS DEPARTMENT PROGRAMS (MUSIC IN THE AIR, COLUMBUS CULTURAL ARTS CENTER, KIDS DISCOVER COLUMBUS, LASER LIGHT SHOW, ARTICIPATION, GOLDEN HOBBY SHOP, COMMUNITY AND SENIOR CENTERS, PARKS, POOLS, KIDSPEAK AND SPECIAL EVENTS): Fine examples of your tax dollars at work. The Columbus Recreation And Parks Department programs should be part of your life.

COMMUNITY MEDIATION SERVICE: It's hard to believe that this quality service is free. Professionalism and courteous, knowledgeable assistance is provided.

COMPUTER SUCCESS: Friendly, courteous and knowledgeable staff treat kids as well as adults as valued customers. Inventory changes daily offering a wide selection.

DESIGNER SHOE WAREHOUSE: Has the most diverse and unusual selection of quality women's shoes in Central Ohio

DOLL HOUSE: Breathtaking bundles of joy, especially the porcelain dolls.

ECLECTIC FASHION ALTERNATIVES: At long last, Columbus has a high fashion menswear consignment shop, and a top notch one at that.

ENTERTAINMENT 91/92/93 BOOKS: Excellent opportunity to dine at some of the top establishments in the city, in addition to great savings on entertainment and services. Everyone should own a copy of this book.

FESTIVAL OF THE TREES: You don't have to celebrate Christmas to appreciate the splendor and creativity of these tastefully decorated trees and wreaths, and the entire festival ambience. Even Scrooge could get into the holiday spirit here.

FRANKLIN COUNTY METRO PARKS: Nature's splendor at its finest plus some very interesting and relaxing programs.

GREATER COLUMBUS ANTIQUE MALL: This is such a fun place to shop!. Your first experience will leave you awestruck. Don't miss an inch of the mall.

HALF PRICE BOOKS, RECORDS, MAGAZINES: The inventory changes frequently to provide one of the best used selections in Columbus.

RAY JOHNSON'S: When I die and go to heaven, I hope there will be spring rolls (the store's specialty seafood egg rolls) waiting for me as I enter.

MADISON'S GRAND FINALE: The store features an excellent selection of quality accessories and apparel (in a full range of sizes) in a well merchandised environment. Friendly, knowledgeable staff treat you royally as they do in Madison's full price stores.

NICKLEBY'S BOOKSTORE CAFE: Cozy, friendly atmosphere, wonderful selection of full priced books, delicious food and an abundance of quality, free entertainment and programs.

OHIO VILLAGE, OHIO HISTORICAL CENTER AND COLONEL CRAWFORD INN: Delightful, intriguing, entertaining and enriching quality programs of days gone by. Truly a delight for the senses.

ONE MORE TIME: Large selection of gently used, high fashion apparel and accessories at low, low prices. Excellent source to consign your unwanted wearables and earn some extra money to purchase others.

PEPPERCORN DUCK CLUB: When I die and go to heaven, I hope that the Ultra Chocolatta Bar will be there for dessert after the spring roll.

ROUSCH HARDWARE: They treat you like family.

SCHOTTENSTEIN'S: Great values on a wide selection of products for all your needs.

SUPER SAVER 8 CINEMAS: What a great light show!

TUESDAY MORNING: Unusual selection of high quality merchandise.

WINTERFAIR: Unsurpassed excellence of handmade crafts for discriminating tastes.

APPLIANCES/ COMPUTERS/ SOFTWARE

APPLIANCES

AL'S VACUUM
4252 E. Main St., Columbus, 43213, 236-0707

First quality Hoover, Eureka, Panasonic and Royal vacuum cleaners are sold at 25-30% off regular retail prices. Repairs are also value priced. Gives exchanges. M-F 9:30-5:30, Sat 9:30-4. Accepts checks, MC, Visa & AmExp.

AUDIO EXCHANGE
3500 N. High St., Columbus, 43214, 263-4600

This retailer sells top quality brands of used audio and video equipment such as VCRs, CD players, tape decks, receivers, televisions, stereos and other products by such brands as Pioneer, Magnavox, JVC, Nikoh and Infinity. Savings are about 25-50% off the "if new" prices. Their high level of merchandise turnover offers a constant influx of additional inventory. You can also expect to save about 5-10% off manufacturers suggested retail prices on a limited inventory of new items. Most of the inventory comes with a 30 day warranty. Gives exchanges. M-F 12-7, Sat 12-5. Accepts checks, MC & Visa.

BLACK AND DECKER U.S.A., INC.
3975 E. Livingston Ave., Columbus, 43227, 237-0461

First quality, blemished, unclaimed and discontinued small appliances as well as house and garden tools by Black And Decker, are available at savings of 20-40% off regular retail prices. You can also purchase parts and accessories for Black and Decker products at this manufacturer's outlet store. Gives refunds. M-F 8-5, Sat 9-2. Accepts checks, MC, Visa & Discover.

BLANCHARD VACUUM CLEANERS
1071 S. High St., Columbus, 43206, 443-9479

The most popular brands of new vacuum cleaners are available at savings of 10-30%. Used models which start at $29, are sold at 30-50% less than the manufacturers' list price for new merchandise. A selection of reconditioned vacuum cleaners is available at about 75% less than "if new". Warranties vary depending on the product. Gives exchanges. M-F 9-5:30, Sat 9-12. Accepts checks, MC & Visa.

HOLTON T.V.
6334 Huntley Rd., Columbus, 43229, 846-4445

Super savings are to be found from this hotel, hospital and business liquidator of televisions. You will find factory rebuilt and used console and table top models at savings of 50-80% off regular retail prices "if new". On a recent visit, I saw a 5" Sony color television for $59.95 and a 19" Zenith television with VHF for $79.95. The store reserves the right to limit quantities. A 90 day warranty is in effect on purchases of used or reconditioned merchandise. Extended warranties for 2-5 years, which cover parts and service, are available at a cost of $15-$75. You can purchase a lifetime picture tube warranty for $19.95. The store also offers free estimates on repairs of televisions. camcorders, computer monitors, stereo systems, Nintendos and car audio systems. Repair prices are very reasonable. Return policy varies with product. M-F 9-8, Sat 9-5. Accepts checks, MC, Visa, AmExp & Discover.

HOOVER COMPANY FACTORY OUTLET STORE
2100 Morse Center, Columbus, 43229, 848-4110

This is Columbus' only Hoover factory owned and operated sales and service center. Over 50 models are on display including uprights, shampooers, quick brooms and hand cleaners. Save 30-50% off the new price on reconditioned floor sample vacuums. The store has frequent factory authorized sales and every day low prices. A one year warranty is offered on new as well as reconditioned merchandise. Gives exchanges. M-F 8-6, Sat 9-5. Accepts checks, MC & Visa.

HYPERSTORE
1070 Morse Rd., Columbus, 43229, 885-1655

This no frills warehouse type business features 40,000 square feet of electronics, stereos, audio-visual equipment, large and small appliances, televisions, camcorders, computers, office equipment (typewriters, fax machines and copiers) as well as car audio systems at savings of 10-30% below manufacturers' suggested retail prices. It is the largest electronics and appliance showroom in Ohio, with over 8 miles of savings under one roof. All major brands are offered including Canon, GE, Panasonic, Sharp, TDK, Maytag, JBL, Smith Corona, Black and Decker, Memorex, KLH and others. Floor samples are not marked as such, but are identified by large red and yellow price tags. The floor sample prices are excellent buys, priced lower than their everyday low prices, but you will not be entitled to the same warranty that you would get if it were new. The salespeople are not working on a commissioned basis which means that you'll get an honest, no pressure sales pitch. The store features the largest car audio display in Columbus and offers free car stereo installation. Offers a free extended warranty on every purchase and free next day delivery, 7 days per week. Several financing options are available. Open a Hyperstore charge account and you'll get $5 off your first purchase. Gives refunds. M-Sat 10-10, Sun 11-6. Accepts checks, MC, Visa & Discover.

MENDELSON'S ELECTRONICS AND INDUSTRIAL SALVAGE
340 E. 1st St., Dayton, 45402, (513) 461-3525

Wow! Over 150,000 square feet of new and used electronic, computer and electrical components, hardware, telephone wire and related items can be found here. This is the largest electronic and industrial surplus store in the world. Savings are 30-90% off regular retail and "if new" prices. The store also sells used office furniture at savings of 30-60% off "if new" prices. This shopping adventure is well worth the trip. All sales are final. M-Sat 8:30-5. Accepts checks, MC & Visa.

NORTHLAND SEWING MACHINE CENTER
1973 Morse Rd., Columbus, 43229, 267-5026

New sewing machines by Viking, Singer and White are discounted 20-40%. About 5 times per year, this business offers further savings on buyouts of new overstocks and unclaimed sewing machines at savings of up to 60%. Offers full warranties and 90 days same as cash financing to qualified buyers. Gives refunds within 72 hours. M and Th 9:30-9; T,W,F,and Sat 9:30-5:30. Accepts checks, MC Visa & Discover.

RADIO SHACK OUTLET STORE
4343 Williams Rd., Groveport, 43125, 836-3060

Demonstration, as-is, overstocks and box damaged products are available at savings of 20-80% off their regular retail prices. You'll find calculators, telephones, electronic toys and games, answering machines, radios, stereos and more. Many products are available with a warranty. The annual tent sale is held in May and features similar discounts on a much larger variety of merchandise. All of the Radio Shacks in town have a free battery club. Pick up an identification card at any branch, and you'll be entitled to 1 free battery of your choice per month. No purchase is required. Gives exchanges. M-Sat 10-9, Sun 10-6. Accepts checks, MC & Visa.

STARR SURPLUS
1044 N. High St., Columbus, 43201, 294-1117

Surplus electronics components from the government and industry, such as capacitors, resistors, vacuum tubes and relays, are available at savings of about 50%. The stock is displayed somewhat haphazardly, but if you enjoy rummaging, the savings are well worth the effort. Aside from the address, the only identification on the outside of the store is the name, "Nic's". All sales are final. M-Sat 11-5. Accepts cash only.

SUN TV

2175 Morse Rd., Columbus, 43229, 475-2410
4815 E. Main St., Columbus, 43213, 866-0150
4250 W. Broad St., Columbus, 43228, 276-7247
6655 Sawmill Rd., Dublin, 43017, 761-0900
1375 W. Lane Ave., Columbus, 43221, 486-4351
1824 W. Henderson Rd., Columbus, 43220, 459-3200
1583 Alum Creek Dr. (Outlet Store), Columbus, 43207, 445-8294
674 Hebron Rd., Newark, 43055, 822-2191
1038 N. Bridge St., Chillicothe, 45601, 775-8409
2360 W. 4 St., Mansfield, 44901, (419) 747-2400
3528 Maple Ave., Zanesville, 43701, 455-2909

Save 10-20% off manufacturers' suggested retail prices on an extensive selection of brand name televisions, large and small appliances, computers as well as audio and stereo equipment. The back of the Alum Creek Drive location is the warehouse outlet where savings are up to 40% off discontinued, overstocks and scratch and dent merchandise from all of their stores. The Sawmill Road store offers free one hour computer classes on Tuesday and Thursday from 6:30-7:30PM. This introductory demonstration will teach you the basics of working on an IBM compatible computer. Neither reservations nor a purchase are necessary. Gives refunds except on outlet merchandise. Gives refunds. M-Th and Sat 10-9:30, F 10-12 midnight, Sun 11-6. Accepts checks, MC, Visa & Discover.

VACU-MEDICS PLUS

320 S. State St., Westerville, 43081, 882-8400

Every 4 weeks the owner rotates 4 different sales which are for vacuum cleaner, sewing machine, clock, lamp and small appliance repairs. Even his regular priced repair work is about 20-30% lower than most other businesses. He usually charges $24.50 to clean, oil and adjust a sewing machine, but during the sale, you can have it done for only $9.95-$14.95. The price elsewhere ranges from about $27-$35. Vacuums can be tuned up during a non-sale time for $24.95 or $14.95 during the sale. All work is guaranteed. His sales are usually advertised in the Westerville area newspapers. The business also offers a pick-up service. M-F 9:30-7, Sat 9:30-3. Accepts checks, MC & Visa.

ALSO SEE

Aurora, Berwick Corner Outlet, Columbus. Police Property Auction, Darby Sales, Extravaganza, Franklin Co. Sheriff's Dept., Globe Furniture Rental, Kitchen Collection, Lazarus Final Countdown, Office America, J.C. Penney Outlet, Sam's Club, Schottenstein's, Sears Outlet, Service Merchandise, and Uncle Sam's Pawn Shop

COMPUTERS/SOFTWARE

AMERICA RENTS
2100 Morse Rd., Columbus, 43229, 436-9644
82 N. Wilson Rd., Columbus, 43204, 279-7774
3146 S. Hamilton Rd., Columbus, 43232, 864-4478
789 Hebron Rd., Hebron, 43025, 522-8441

Thousands of videos are available for rental at a cost of 49 cents per day. New releases can be rented for $1.99 the first day and 99 cents each additional day. Two day Nintendo game rentals are 49 cents, 99 cents or $1.99 per day. There is no membership fee. M-Sat 10-9. Accepts checks and cash only.

BLOCKBUSTER VIDEO
3730 E. Broad St., Columbus, 43213, 235-2200
3637 W. Broad St., Columbus, 43228, 351-9100
3350 Cleveland Ave., Columnbus, 43224, 263-1010
2760 E. Dublin-Granville Rd., Columbus, 43231, 794-2901
1111 Fountain La., Columbus, 43213, 863-1557
2260 W. Henderson Rd., Columbus, 43220, 442-1660
5070 N. High St., Columbus, 43214, 885-1600
1725 Northwest Blvd., Columbus, 43212, 481-8688
6520 Sawmill Rd., Columbus, 43235, 792-6400
6323 Tussing Rd., Reynoldsburg, 43068, 759-0055
1209 Hill Rd., Pickerington, 43147, 759-7878
3191 Maple Ave., Zanesville, 43701, 453-4114
616 Hebron Rd., Heath, 43056, 522-2233

Has a series of free loan, community service videos for adults and children on such topics as back pain, say no to drugs, the facts of life, arthritis, how to plan a fire escape from your home, divorce and other topics. There are about 30 different videos and the selection varies from store to store. It is necessary to have a Blockbuster Video membership card in order to borrow these videos. Membership is free if you have a driver's license and a major credit card. . However, if you do not have both of these, a one time $3 membership fee will be assessed, but the videos can still be borrowed for free. The stores also sell previously rented Nintendo tapes, which are missing the instructions, for only $14.95 each. These are usually $20-$40 "if new". A selection of previously rented videos is also available for $9.95. When these movies first came out, the videos were selling for $25-$80. M-Sat 10-9, Sun 10-5. Accepts checks, MC, Visa, AmExp & Discover.

COLUMBUS METROPOLITAN LIBRARY
96 S. Grant Ave., Columbus, 43215, 645-2000

The library is more than just books. The media production center in the audio visual department is a great place to transfer your home movies onto video tape at a cost of only $5. If you were to have this professionally done through a private company, you could expect to pay $20-$30. The equipment enables you to transfer 8MM film, 16MM film or slides to video format or to repair 8 MM and 16MM film as well as video and audio cassettes. The equipment may be used at no cost by anyone who is aged 18 and older.

However, you must provide the supplies, which you can obtain at low cost from the library if you choose. If you are not familiar with the equipment, you may schedule a free instructional session prior to use. You can also obtain free on site use of a tracing machine, 16MM video or audio cassette duplicator, badge maker, comb binder equipment and deep throated staplers. The library also provides free on site rentals of their IBM PC computers and their extensive selection of business and educational software. The cost to rent a typewriter for on site use is 25 cents for 15 minutes. An enormous selection of videos on every subject from cooking, sports, crafts, performing arts, car repair, gardening, physical fitness as well as entertaining videos for adults and kids, are also available for free loan. The second floor maintains 20,000 pieces of sheet music for free loan upon presentation of your library card. A large selection of CDs and audio cassettes for enjoyment and personal growth, including business and managerial subjects, are also available for free loan. The Grantsmanship Center houses a large collection of books on how and where to obtain grants for individuals, businesses and nonprofit organizations. The Center For Discovery, the children's section, features the largest toy lending library in Ohio with over 2000 puzzles, puppets and other developmental toys for loan. The Center For Discovery maintains its own mailing list of kids programs. Call to be added. The library has free slide programs, story times, book discussions, puppet shows, craft sessions, musical performances and other diversions for all ages. Call to be added to the mailing list for *Novel Events* which provides information on programs at each of the branches. The library has a used bookstore offering fantastic bargains. Refer to the write-up in the chapter on books. I think very highly of the library.. Some of the research for this book was completed there. The Columbus Metropolitan Library is one of my personal favorites. M-Th 9-8, F 9-6.(Sun,. 12-5 Sept.-May only).

COMPUSED
5992 A Westerville Rd., Westerville, 43081, 898-1088

Computer consignment store for used Apples and IBMs can save you 30-50% off new prices. The inventory also consists of liquidations and buyouts. Laptop computers, monitors, software with business and entertainment applications, as well as accessories are available. The inventory is tested to ensure proper functioning. All sales are final. M-F 10-9, Sat 10-5, Sun 12-5. Accepts checks, MC & Visa.

COMPUTER BARGAIN CENTERS OF AMERICA
4412 Cleveland Ave., Columbus, 43224, 478-8148

Central Ohio's largest reconditioned PC supplier sells IBMs and IBM compatibles at savings of 40-60% off "if new" prices. New software and accessories are discounted about 20%. The business buys and sells nationwide. Offers a 90 day warranty. Satisfaction guaranteed. M-Sat 10-7, Sun 12-5. Accepts checks, MC & Visa.

COMPUTER SUCCESS
5025 Olentangy River Rd., Bethel Ctr. Shpng. Ctr., Columbus, 43214, 457-2983

Save 20-80% on new and used computers, accessories and software by Nintendo, Sega, IBM, Atari, Panasonic, Amiga, Commodore, Star and others. The software is available in both business, personal and entertainment applications, and also includes a group of imported ones from Europe and the Orient. You'll find a large selection of merchandise which changes almost daily. Trade-ins are accepted or the business can purchase your items outright. The store also rents Neo-Geo and Super Famicon systems and games. It also rents Genesis games which have come mostly from Japan. (Instructions are in English). The staff is very friendly, patient and knowledgeable. This short but sweet description describes this flourishing business in a nutshell. Run, don't walk to Computer Success. It offers the best prices in Columbus on these products and has earned the distinction of being one of my (and certainly my children's) personal favorites. Gives exchanges. Offers warranties. M-F 11-8, Sat 11-7 and Sun 12-5. Accepts checks, MC, Visa & Discover.

ELECTRONICS BOUTIQUE
179 Columbus City Center, Columbus, 43215, 224-7638
2720 Eastland Mall, Columbus, 43232, 863-0908
1475 Upper Valley Pike, Springfield, 45501, (513) 324-1142

Has a large assortment of business, educational and computer game software for Nintendo, Sega, Genesis, Turbografix, IBM, Atari, Amiga, Commodore 64 and Apple which is discounted 10-50% off manufacturers' suggested retail prices. Their frequent purchaser plan, "Inner Circle Club", entitles you to a $25 store gift certificate upon submission of $250 worth of store receipts. Some restrictions apply. Sign up for their mailing list and receive advance notice of sales and special savings coupons. Gives refunds on unopened items. M-Sat 10-9, Sun 12-5. Accepts checks, MC, Visa, AmExp & Discover.

KINKO'S KOPIES
4499 Kenny Rd., Columbus, 43220, 451-9640
18 E. 15 Ave., Columbus, 43201, 294-7485
147 N. High St., Columbus, 43215, 621-1100
604 Schrock Rd., Columbus, 43229, 898-0000
2656 Brice Rd., Reynoldsburg, 43068, 575-0800

All locations offer a $10 per hour rental of a Macintosh computer, plus 95 cents per print for laser output. If you can't afford to purchase a Macintosh for personal use, this is an excellent way to utilize its extensive capabilities to create brochures, resumes, and letters for business or personal applications. You can save between 30-50% off the cost of having these items created by a photocopy/printing center or a freelance designer. Training is not provided, so you will need to come prepared with your skills. Computers are available on a first come, first serve basis. Reservations are not accepted. Kinko's also has a number of programs available at no additional charge such as Pagemaker 4.0, Microsoft Works 4.0, Madras, Superpaint, Macwrite and others. Every July, Kinko's features their annual 3 cent copy sale for a 2 week period. Hours vary from store to store. The Kenny Road and E. 15 Avenue locations are open 24 hours a day, 7 days a week. Accepts checks, MC & Visa.

MICRO CENTER
1555 W. Lane Ave., Lane Avenue Shpng. Ctr., Columbus, 43221, 481-8041
85 Westerville Plaza, Westerville, 43081, 794-4400

Find new IBM, Macintosh, Apple, Epsom and Laser brands of computers, in addition to software, floppy disks, books, paper and related items, at savings of 10-40% off manufacturers' suggested retail prices. Bargain tables can be found throughout the store, which offer savings of 50-90% off used, demonstrator and reconditioned merchandise as well as selected books. The Lane Avenue location offers an extensive selection of computer classes, some of which are free. Sign up for their mailing list. Gives refunds. M-F 10-9, Sat 10-6. Accepts checks, MC, Visa, Apple and IBM charges.

SOFTWARE ETC.
Columbus City Center #199D, Columbus, 43215, 224-8731

Educational, business and entertaining software for adults and children, to be used on the Amiga, Commodore, Macintosh and IBM computers, is discounted 10-30% off regular retail prices. Don't miss the large selection of software which is priced at $10 and under. This includes discontinued, overstock and closeout merchandise for adults and children. Gives refunds on unopened packages and exchanges on defective merchandise. M-Th 10-8, F and Sat 10-6, Sun 12-5. Accepts checks, MC & Visa.

VIDEO GAMES EXPRESS
5480 Westerville Rd., Westerville, 43081, 794-1888

Purchase used computer and gaming magazines for 25-50% off the cover price. Used Nintendo, Sega, Atari 2600, Gameboy, Neogeo, Turbo Graft and Genesis electronic game cartridges and systems are available at 30-50% off the original new selling price. New games and systems are discounted 10-15%. A 30 day store warranty is offered on used items and a 90 day manufacturer's warranty is available on new merchandise. On Monday, Tuesday or Wednesday, you can rent 1 video game or a movie for $1.89 and get 1 free rental. M-Sat 11-8. Accepts checks, MC & Visa.

WALDEN SOFTWARE
1686 Northland Mallway, Columbus, 43229, 263-2332

Use your Walden Books *Preferred Member Card*, or purchase one here for $5 annually, which will provide you with special savings at both stores. At the software business, your card will entitle you to 5% off the price of sale items, and 10% off their already low prices on non-sale items (excluding magazines). Most of the software is typically discounted 5-25%, with many in-store specials at higher savings. Sells IBM, Amiga, Commodore, Macintosh and Lotus programs for educational, entertainment and business use for adults and children. Gives refunds on unopened packages. M-Sat 10-9, Sunl 12-5. Accepts checks, MC, Visa, AmExp & Discover.

ALSO SEE

Columbus Metropolitan Library, Extravaganza, Greater Columbus Fantastic Camera Show And Computer Swap, Grandview Heights Public Library, Hyperstore, Meijer, Office America, Phar Mor, Pine Factory, Radio Shack Outlet Store, Sam's Club, Sear's Outlet, Service Merchandise, Summer Tech, Sun TV, Tag Sales, Toronto Business Equipment, Toys 'R Us, Uncle Sam's Pawn Shop, Upper Arlington Public Library

ARTS AND CRAFTS/ PHOTOGRAPHY/ CAMERAS

ARTS AND CRAFTS

ART FAIRS AND FESTIVALS
see Ohio Arts Council listing in this chapter

ARTIST'S WORKSHOP
2583 1/2 N. High St., Columbus, 43202, 262-2589
44 S. Washington, Columbus, 43215, 224-1993

Utrecht brand art supplies such as gesso, acrylics, oil paints and watercolors, are sold at 40-60% less than similar products by other manufacturers. The owner indicated that many of the Utrecht supplies are better quality than the popular brands. Gives refunds same day of purchase. M-F 10-6, Sat 10:30-5, Sun 12-5 (N. High St. only). Accepts checks, MC & Visa.

BENZLE PORCELAIN COMPANY
41 W. Bridge St., Dublin, 43017, 792-6325

Curtis and Suzan Benzle are internationally recognized porcelain artists who create bowls, lights and 22 Karat liquid gold trimmed jewelry, all of which are available in their store. This location also doubles as a working studio in which the delicate creations are made as well as sold. The store has recently set up a small section in which seconds, discontinued styles and prototypes are priced at 50% off the regular retail prices of $10-$175. Return policy varies. Tu-Sat 11-5, Th 11-7. Accepts checks and cash only.

BYZANTIUM
245 King Ave., Columbus, 43201, 291-3130

A large selection of beads from around the world is sold here by the piece for those who are interested in making their own earrings, necklaces and bracelets or using them as embellishments on clothing and other objects. The beads are available in clay, wood, shells, semi-precious stones, glass, Fimo, bone, horn and other materials. A large selection of trade and other ethnic beads, a full line of findings and other supplies, in addition to instructional books, can also be found. Staff members are always available to provide assistance in creating wearables, which can be done on the tables in the store, in the comfort of your own home. The beads are fairly priced, but provide the opportunity to save 50-80% off the price of this do-it-yourself jewelry as compared to finished jewelry in other stores. Byzantium also features an unusual selection of handmade necklaces and earrings incorporating beads. The earrings are particularly value priced at $4-$6 per pair. The Central Ohio Bead Society meets monthly at Byzantium and presents discussions, workshops and demonstrations of interest to bead lovers. Annual dues are $10 per family, which entitles you to a monthly newsletter and a 20% discount at Byzantium on purchases over $20. The Bead Society sponsors an annual Bead Bazaar and Jewelry Jamboree in the fall. Don't miss the bead museum in Byzantium which offers a small, but interesting selection of antique jewelry and other items incorporating beads. Stop by the adjacent King Avenue Coffee House where you'll find a large selection of teas and vegetarian foods. Gives refunds. M-Sat 12-7, Sun,. 1-5. Accepts checks, MC & Visa.

CRAFTS 'N THINGS
6095 Mc Naughten Center, Columbus, 43232, 861-4164
5668 Columbus Square, Columbus, 43231, 890-5348

Ceramcoat and Folkart brand acrylic paints are priced at 99 cents on Thursdays, regularly $1.99. These full line arts and crafts stores have a frequent purchaser plan in which you can buy a key ring for $1 and each time you make a purchase, the ring will be validated. When you accumulate $100 in purchases, you will be entitled to $20 in free merchandise. Both locations offer craft classes from $5-$25. Call to be added to their mailing list. Gives refunds. M-F 10-9, Sat 10-6. Accepts checks, MC & Visa.

COLUMBUS CLAY COMPANY
1049 W. Fifth Avenue, Columbus, 43212, 294-1114

Ceramic materials such as glazes and clays are available at savings of about 20% from this manufacturer. New and used pottery equipment such as kilns and wheels are sold at savings of 10-30% less than new prices. Return policy varies. M-F 9-5. Accepts checks, MC & Visa.

COMMERCIAL, INC.
198 E. Gay St., Columbus, 43215, 228-3238

A full line of art and drafting supplies are discounted 10% off manufacturers' suggested retail prices to students, businesses, professionals as well as the general public. You'll find illustration board, Windsor-Newton paints, mat board etc. Gives exchanges on unopened packages. M-F 8:30-5, Sat 9:30-1. Accepts checks, MC & Visa.

DANIEL SMITH, INC.
4130 First Ave. S., Seattle, Washington, 98134-2302, 1-800-426-7923

Call to be on their mailing list to receive a bimonthly brochure of artist's materials. The catalogue includes an in-depth feature article each month on a particular art technique such as metallic watercolor painting, basic metallic leafing or portable fresco painting. Artist's supplies and tools are generously described and include suggestions for use. Savings are 10-30% off regular retail prices through this mail order source. Gives exchanges. M-F 8:30-6. Accepts checks, MC & Visa.

DICK BLICK ART MATERIALS
6510 Riverside Dr., Village Sq. Shpng. Ctr., Dublin, 43017, 791-1900

Save about 10-25% off manufacturer's suggested list prices on fine arts supplies such as watercolor paper, foamboard, paints, pastels and more at this full service store. Many of their own brand of paints and related products are about 15-35% less than comparable products by other companies. Gives refunds. M-Th. 10-7, F and Sat 10-5, Sun 12-4. Accepts checks, MC, Visa & AmExp.

EKSTROM ARTS
located in Northwest Columbus, 889-8950

Save about 30% on custom framing at this business. The owner, being an artist himself, has an eye for helping you to select the best frame and mat combinations for your artwork. Hours are by appointment. Accepts checks and cash only.

FRAME WAREHOUSE
7502 E. Main St., Reynoldsburg, 43068, 861-4582

Thousands of ready made frames in all shapes and sizes are in stock at this no frills store. Savings are off regular retail prices on signed and numbered limited edition prints, posters and photography by Ansel Adams, Nagel and others as well as custom and ready made frames. If you call ahead, the business can often arrange to custom frame your artwork while you wait. The inventory consists of overstocks, special purchases, and discontinued goods, all at savings of 40-60% off regular retail prices. Gives exchanges only. M-F 9-5, Sat 9-4. Accepts checks, MC, Visa & Discover.

FRANK'S NURSERY AND CRAFTS
5500 W. Broad St., Columbus, 43228, 870-7772
3333 Refugee Rd., Columbus, 43232, 231-3998
6380 Tussing Rd., Consumer Sq. E., Reynoldsburg, 43068, 863-3322
7141 E. Broad St., Columbus, 43213, 861-6767
1700 E. Dublin Granville Rd., Columbus, 43229, 891-1313
4261 W. Dublin Granville Rd., Dublin, 43017, 889-0330

These full service craft and nursery stores have a large clearance section of craft items at a remote corner of their business where discontinued, past season and overstocked items are reduced 30-80%. Pick up a free copy of the "Monthly Gardener", a flyer developed by the company's horticulture education department. The flyers can usually be found at the checkout area. They are filled with planting and pruning tips; holiday and seasonal decorating ideas using plants, vines and baskets; types of feed which are appropriate for different types of birds; how to set up a feeding station and more. Pick up a free copy of Frank's spring gardening guide which is a 25 page booklet that provides helpful tips on such topics as pruning, weed control and soil preparation. During the Christmas season, the stores offer a free 12 page booklet, Guide To A Beautiful Christmas, which includes suggestions on buying an artificial or fresh cut tree, how to decorate your tree, care of poinsettias and other topics. Gives refunds. M-Sat 9-9, Sun 9-6. Accepts checks, MC, Visa & Discover.

KOVAL KNIVES
460D Schrock Rd., POB 26155, Columbus, 43229, 888-6486

This is the only store of its kind east of the Mississippi and one of only five similar type stores in the country. The business sells component parts and kits for the hobbyist or professional, with which to make cutlery and hunting knives. The store also sells supplies for repairs. The owner said that a hunting knife kit which sells for $25.95 here, is sold as a finished product in stores for $75-$100. Savings amount to about 50-80% when you make the knives yourself from Koval's supplies, as compared to store bought knives. You can pick up a large mail order catalogue in the store for $4. Gives refunds. M,Tu, W, F 9-4; Th 9-7. Accepts checks, MC & Visa.

LEE WARDS
2745 Northland Plaza Dr., Columbus, 43231, 794-1083
110 N. Wilson Rd., Great Western Shpng. Ctr.,Columbus, 43204, 276-0100

Consistently has the lowest prices in the city on an extensive line of crafts including yarns, painting supplies, floral supplies and general craft items for adults and children. Prices average 10-25% lower than the competitors. The stock is all first quality, current merchandise, and also includes some buyouts at savings up to 60% off regular retail prices. Watch the newspapers for their frequent sales which offer additional values. Lee Wards offers large jars of cooking spices for 99 cents apiece which are about 25-50% less than those of popular brands found in the super markets. On major holidays, they feature 33% off any item in the store if your purchase is accompanied by a newspaper coupon. Sign up for their mailing list to receive advance notice of sales and special percentage off coupons. Lee Wards will meet all competitors' prices on like items if you present the ad. The stores also offer a variety of craft classes for adults and children such as painting, cartooning, and knitting. You will be entitled to a 10% discount on class supplies purchased in the store. Once a month, the businesses offer a special value priced class for only $5. Classes generally run $6-$25 depending on the number of weeks. Pick up a class schedule in the store as these are not mailed. In June, the stores feature a Super Sidewalk Sale where savings are 30-60% off discontinued, overstock, end of season and special purchase items. Gives refunds. M-Sat 9:30-9, Sun 10-6. Accepts checks, MC & Visa.

M.J. ORIGINALS
749 N. High St., Columbus, 43215, 291-2787

Limited edition prints are discounted 10-70% off suggested retail prices. While the store maintains an inventory of these, it is well known for its ability to search for works which it does not carry. These are obtained through a variety of sources so the discount will vary greatly. The store also stocks an unusual selection of handmade jewelry and small craft items at typical gallery prices. Gives exchanges. M-Sat 11-7, Sun 1-5. Accepts checks and cash only.

OHIO ARTS COUNCIL
727 E. Main St., Columbus, 43205, 466-2613

Call to be added to the mailing list to receive the free quarterly magazine, Artspace. It includes feature stories about the visual,. literary and performing arts around the state, issues of national importance such as private funding for the arts, and a description of upcoming major arts events. The publication can be enjoyed by artists and arts supporters alike. The Ohio Arts Council sells copies of the Art Fairs And Festivals Guide for only $2 which lists all of the events statewide. The book is updated annually by the Ohio Arts And Crafts Guild and is a valuable resource if you are interested in purchasing handmade fine arts or arts and crafts. In most cases, you will be able to save 20-50% off typical gallery prices by purchasing directly from the artist, as the gallery's markup is thereby eliminated. OAC maintains an artists' slide bank as a low cost service to practicing artists. For only $5, 20 slides and your resume will be maintained on file for review by gallery curators and other individuals. Many leads and sales have been generated from this slide bank. Call to request an application. M-F 8:30-5.

P.M. GALLERY
726 N. High St., Columbus, 43215, 299-0860

This long established Short North gallery offers discounts on custom framing to artists who wish to frame their creations. In this case, savings will be 10% off the retail price on the frame, mat and glass if you let the gallery assemble it for you. Another option is that if you are ambitious and would like to frame the artwork yourself, you will be charged 10% above the gallery's cost which is roughly equivalent to 40% off the regular retail prices. Additional savings are available for the purchase of several custom frames of the exact size, shape and color. You may ask the gallery for details. The store also offers a unique selection of fine arts and crafts, some of which are bargain hunters' delights. Gives exchanges only. Tu, W, F and Sat 11-6; Sun 12-5. During the first Saturday of each month (for the Gallery Hop), the store is open from 11-10. Accepts checks, MC, Visa, AmExp & Discover.

PHILATELIC CENTER, U.S.POSTAL SERVICE
850 Twin Rivers Dr., Columbus, 43215, 469-4223

You will pay the face value for regular issue and commemorative stamps, envelopes and postcards at this store which is operated by the post office. As independent stamp and coin dealers add a markup to their inventory above the price they pay for it, your savings can amount to 10-30% at the Philatelic Center. The shop also sells low cost stamp gift packets with varying themes. All sales are final. M-F 9-4:30. Closed from 1:30-2:30 for lunch. Accepts checks and cash.

QUALITY ART AND FRAME OUTLET
6561 E. Livingston Ave., Reynoldsburg, 43068, 759-9922

Save 20-30% on custom framing and original artwork. This full service business also features quality restoration work at savings of about 50% off comparable prices at other galleries, according to the owner. Gives exchanges on artwork. M-F 10-7, Sat 10-5. Accepts checks, MC & Visa.

STAR BEACON PRODUCTS
1104 W. Goodale Blvd., Columbus, 43215, 294-4657

Health and beauty products in addition to general variety merchandise such as light bulbs, office supplies, inexpensive gift items, toys, infant products by Evenflo such as nipples and teething rings in addition to party supplies are available at savings of 30-75% off regular retail prices. This wholesaler, who sells to flea market vendors, fundraisers as well as the general public, also offers a wide selection of arts and crafts supplies at similar savings such as construction paper, calligraphy sets, exacto knives, drawing pads, tempera paints, origami paper and more. Although you can purchase small or large qualities, the higher discounts are for bulk sales. During the Christmas season, the store features holiday supplies and an expanded toy selection at similar savings. The merchandise consists of first quality manufacturers overstocks, discontinued items as well as liquidations. This is also a great place to purchase party favors and stocking stuffers. Gives refunds. M-F 9-5, Sat 9-12. Accepts checks, MC & Visa.

SU SAN'S SPECIALITIES
252-6557

This business is open by appointment only. The friendly owners represent 35 different lines of yarns, most of which are not available at retail in Columbus. The brands offered include Silk City, Classic Elite, Berocco, Ironstone Warehouse, Glimakra, Plymouth Yarns and others. Additionally, you'll find yarns from small companies such as Green Mountain Spinnery, Davidson's Old Mill and a small selection of handspun yarns by local artists. There's alpaca, mohair, linens, cottons, pigtail, silk, wool, blends, glitzy lurex, knubby and textured yarns, all in a rainbow of classic and contemporary fashion colors. Savings are 20-35% off regular retail prices. Mill ends are available at greater savings, usually 30-60%. Hard to find, flame retardant baby yarns, are available in several color options. Unspun yarns for spinners can also be found at similar savings. Su San's sells high end merchandise discounted to the level of affordability. Looms and other weaving equipment can be obtained by special order and are discounted 10-20%. If you've never had a love affair with yarns, this is definitely the place to begin. You'll keep coming back for more. Gives exchanges. Accepts checks, MC & Visa.

ARLENE TEAL
262-6190

If you like contemporary found object art, this artist offers an exciting and whimsical selection at value prices. Her pieces are usually one-of-a kind and are made to be hung on the wall. The materials include fiber, buttons, shells, wood, plastics, metal, glass and other found objects in combination with paints. Techniques include collage, assemblage and unusual arrangements of materials. Arlene is an extremely talented artist who creates unusual works from the simplest of objects. Call her to find out when and where her next exhibition will be held.

TRACY ART AND FRAME
3127 N. High St., Columbus, 43202, 263-0196

Low overhead allows this professional framing store to have a low markup on framing supplies. You'll save about 10% on custom framing as compared to other stores. This business also prides itself on offering a variety of matting options which are not readily available elsewhere, such as marblized paper matting, french matting and unusual mat shapes. The manager says that the store will frame anything. M-Sat 9-6. Accepts checks, MC & Visa.

VILLAGE FRAMERS
1388 King Ave., Columbus, 43212, 486-7419

Value priced custom framing and ready assembled frames are available at this business. The prices are about 10-15% lower than at other stores which offer framing services. The Village Framers also offers low prices on art and frame restorations. Gives exchanges. Accepts checks, MC & Visa.

ALSO SEE

Allen's Coin Shop, Aurora Farms Factory Outlet, Business Equipment Electronics, Ci Bon, Create-A-Craft Spectacular, De'Romeo's Exclusives, Doll House, Educable 25, Embroiderer's Guild, Experienced Possessions, Greater Columbus. Antique Mall, Hancock Fabrics, Kitchen Place, Lake Erie Factory Outlet, Majestic Paint Store, Miniatures Unlimited, Model Home Furniture and Accessories Sale, My Cousin's Closet, Odd Lots, Office America, J.C. Penney Portfolio, Ritchey's, Sofa Express Outlet, Special Events/Sale Index, Starr Beacon, Tag Sales, WOSU Channel 34, Waterford Hall, and Woodworking World

PHOTOGRAPHY/CAMERAS

COLUMBUS CAMERA GROUP
55 E. Blake Ave., Columbus, 43202, 267-0686

Used cameras, related equipment and accessories, for the novice or professional photographer, are available at savings of 20-60% off "if new" prices. The store also stocks a limited amount of new buyout merchandise at similar savings. All popular brands can be found including Pentax, Minolta, Olympus, Polaroid and Kodak. The store also stocks some cameras for kids, antique and collectible photographic equipment in addition to picture frames. Film processing is priced below that of full price competitors. Extended warranties are available. Gives refunds. M-Sat 9-7. Accepts checks, MC, Visa & AmExp.

K MART
5436 Westerville Rd., Westerville, 43081, 890-1440
3463 S. High St., Columbus, 43207, 491-7312
5005 Olentangy River Rd., Columbus, 43214, 459-2150
3100 S. Hamilton Rd., Columbus, 43232, 868-0410
3616 E. Broad St., Columbus, 43213, 231-3577
3800 W. Broad St., Columbus, 43228, 276-5282
300 S. Hamilton Rd., Columbus, 43213, 476-0940
1284 Brice Rd., Reynoldsburg, 43068, 864-4714
2400 Stringtown Rd., Grove City, 43123, 875-9800

K Mart is well know throughout the retail industry as a discounter which sells merchandise at a low markup. Take into account their tremendous buying power and its easy to see how they can sell many products for 20-50% less than at other stores. Watches by Timex, Halston, Gruen, Gloria Vanderbilt, Valentino, Adolfo, Seiko, Pierre Cardin, Jules Jurgensen and Pulsar, some with diamonds, are discounted 25-60%. Values are up to $325. You'll find men's, women's and children's styles as dressy or casual timepieces. The stores are filled with many popular name brand products in addition to K Mart brands or "unbranded" products (such as canned foods, automotive supplies and light bulbs) at even greater savings than a branded comparable item. Read the fine print on the labels or the cartons to find the words "made for K Mart". Uniroyal makes K Mart tires in all grades, which are sold at very reasonable prices. Follow the newspapers for their frequent sales, especially the dollar days sales which offer substantial savings throughout the stores. A photographer comes to most of the stores about 4 times per year for 5 days at a time, and offers excellent prices on photo packages for adults and children. For example, you could get one package which contains 55 color pictures in assorted sizes for only $14.95. Inquire at the stores for dates, or follow the newspapers. The book section, called the *Readers' Market,* offers savings of 5% on magazines and 10-30% off all current and overstock books for adults and children. K Mart is a general merchandise store which sells a full line of budget to moderate quality housewares, hardware, automotive, health and beauty, clothes, arts and crafts as well as books at value prices. Gives refunds. M-Sat 9:30-9:30. Sun 10-6. Accepts checks, MC, Visa & AmExp.

MCALISTER CAMERA COMPANY
1454 W. Lane Ave., Columbus, 43221, 488-1865
594 W. Schrock Rd., Columbus, 43229, 794-1865
6610 Sawmill Rd.,Columbus, 43235, 766-1865

About 75% of the stock is available at savings of about 10-40% off regular retail prices. You will find all of the popular brands of cameras and camcorders including Pentax and Nikon. This store also stocks children's cameras at similar savings, which start at $39. A variety of services are offered including film processing and video duplication at standard retail prices. Financing is available. Provides layaway. Gives refunds. M-F 10-8, Sat 10-5, Sun 12-5. Accepts checks, MC & Visa.

MIDWEST PHOTO EXCHANGE
200 Crestview, Columbus, 43202, 261-1264

Save 40-80% off previously owned and 20-50% off new cameras and photographic supplies. Amateur as well as professional photographers will find something to satisfy their needs. Film processing is one of the lowest in town. The extensive selection of popular brands such as Minolta, Pentax, Nikon, Olympus, Kodak, Polaroid and others is found in 3,000 square feet of selling space of mostly adult, but some children's merchandise. The business allows trade-ins and will also purchase your cameras and equipment outright. Collectors will appreciate the extensive selection of hard to find antiques. A camera repair service is also available at substantial savings. The owner indicted that his customers come from throughout the Midwest. Offers an unconditional 30 day warranty. M-F 10-6, Sat 10-4. Accepts checks, MC & Visa.

SEARS PORTRAIT STUDIO
2765 Eastland Mall, Columbus, 43232, 868-7169
1811 Morse Rd., Northland Mall, Columbus, 43229, 261-4230
441 W. Broad St. Westland Mall, Columbus, 43228, 275-2230

The regular price on the portrait package ranges from $26.95-$29.95 and includes a minimum of 38 color pictures in a variety of sizes. Sears regularly features discount coupons in the *Columbus Dispatch* and various direct mail sources which provide a savings of 50% off these low prices. I was told by a staff person at the portrait studio, that even if you can't find a discount coupon, simply come to Sears and you will be able to participate in one of their regular specials which offers similar savings. The portrait packages are equally suited for adults and families as they are for infants. Children of any age may register for a free membership in the birthday club, which entitles them to a free 8x10 color photo as a gift from Sears each year. M-Sat 10-8, Sun12-6. Accepts checks, MC, Visa & Discover.

ALSO SEE

Columbus Metropolitan Library, Columbus Police Department Auction, Drug Emporium, Drug World, Franklin County Metro Parks, Giant Columbus Fantastic Camera Show And Computer Swap, Harts, Home Video Club, K Mart, Lazarus Final Countdown, Ohio Camera Collectors Society Show And Sale, OSU Department Of Photography And Cinema, J.C. Penney Outlet, Schottenstein's, Sears Outlet, Service Merchandise, Uncle Sam's Pawn Shop

AUTOMOTIVE

AAA
90 E. Wilson Bridge Rd., Worthington, 43085, 431-7901
5755 Maple Canyon Ave., Columbus, 43229, 899-1222
4701 Reed Rd., Columbus, 43220, 457-2614
4601 Leap Ct., Hilliard, 43026, 771-5777
42 N. Sandusky St., Delaware, 43015, 1-800-233-9265
23513 U.S. 23 S., Circleville, 43113, 477-2506

Your annual fee of $30-$45 entitles you to a $2 savings of the price of adult evening admission to all Columbus, Heath and Newark AMC Theaters (advance purchase required); 10-20% off at out of town attractions such as Kings Island, The Beach, Dollywood, Busch Gardens and others; 10-30% savings on hotel rooms at Ramada Inn, Comfort Inn, Clarion Inn and others. Membership also entitles you to fee free American Express travellers checks, discounts on Hertz/Avis car rentals, 10-20% off travel products, 10-30% off the price of cruises and 10% off recreational vehicle rentals. Their newest benefit is the *Auto Pricing Service,* which will provide you with fast, accurate estimates on new and used cars in terms of the dealer invoice cost, retail price, current trade-in and a printout by mail. The cost is $9.95 for one vehicle with quantity discounts available. Certain restrictions apply. Of course, your membership provides you with road service, towing and other related services. Another excellent benefit if the availability of free trip-tiks (routed maps to your next vacation spot) and free tour books which provide you with information on lodging, restaurants and interesting things to do once you arrive at your intended destination..M-F 8:30-5.

ALL TUNE AND LUBE
6115 Cleveland Ave., Columbus, 43231, 794-0445

This business offers a free oil change, lube and filter, regularly $21, with the purchase of a complete engine tune up ($34.90 for 4 cylinder cars, $39.90 for 6 cylinder or $44.90 for 8 cylinder). Free brake inspections are offered at any time. Several more branches of this business are scheduled to open in Columbus in 1991 at sites which were undetermined at the time this book went to press. M-F 8-6, Sat 8-4. Accepts checks, MC, Visa & AmExp.

AUTOWORKS
3254 Cleveland Ave., Columbus, 43224, 261-1121
2800 N. High St., Columbus, 43202, 263-1525
3003 E. Livingston Ave., Columbus, 43209, 231-2078
166 S. Hamilton Rd., Columbus, 43213, 863-0804
4305 Eastland Sq. Dr., Columbus, 43232, 866-6146
2655 W. Broad St., Columbus, 43204, 278-9494
1034 Harrisburg Pike, Columbus, 43223, 276-5213
649 Central Center Plaza, Chillicothe, 45601, 773-1155
1186 N. Court St., Circleville, 43113, 477-3307
73 London Rd., Delaware, 43015, 363-9484
93 N. Stygler Rd., Gahanna, 43230, 471-5584
613 W. Wheeling St., Lancaster, 43130, 654-1757
226 Lafayette Rd., London, 43140, 852-5153
1049 Mt. Vernon Rd., Newark, 43055, 366-7357
7113 E. Main St., Reynoldsburg, 43068, 866-6475
11 Cherri Park Sq., Westerville, 43081, 899-1884
205 Sunrise Center, Zanesville, 43701, 454-2564
1423 Maysville Pike, Zanesville, 43701, 454-8539
627 Hebron Rd., Heath, 43056, 522-3118
1790 E.Dublin Granville Rd., Columbus, 43229, 794-1259

This national chain of over 900 stores sells auto parts and related supplies such as spark plugs, radiator sealant, seat covers, brake pads, oil filters, batteries and other necessities in popular brands, as well as their own brand, "Flag". Bargains in these businesses will be on their "Flag" products which will save you about 50% off the price of a comparable branded item. They will match any competitor's price. Gives refunds. M-F 8:30-8, Sat 8:30-7, Sun 10-6. Accepts checks, MC, Visa & Discover.

BP GAS STATIONS
over 50 area gas stations

Pickup a free brochure at participating BP (formerly Sohio) Gas Stations, called *Gas Saving Tips From That BP Guy*. You'll find it right near the cashier. The booklet provides ways in which you can reduce your gasoline consumption through proper car maintenance and fuel selection. This amounts to extra money in your pocket in the long run. Open 24 hours a day, 7 days a week.

BATTERY MANUFACTURER'S OUTLET
1220 W. Broad St., Columbus, 43222, 272-1007

You'll find an enormous selection of automotive, truck, motorcycle, tractor, golf cart and aircraft batteries at savings of 10-50% off regular retail prices. A complete line of automotive accessories is also available, but at full retail price. The inventory consists of first quality overstocks, liquidations and current merchandise from such companies as Delco and East Penn. . Gives exchanges. M-F 8-6, Sat 9-3. Accepts MC & Visa,.

CONSUMER REPORTS, AUTO PRICE SERVICE
POB 8005, Novi, Michigan, 48376

When a new car dealer is offering you a supposed discount of $200-$300, this may not be the best price at which you can purchase the car. When the difference between the sticker price and what the car actually costs the dealer is as much as $1600, and you know exactly what the dealer paid, you will be in a better position to negotiate a deal. When you send in $11 for 1 car, $20 for 2 cars or $27 for 3 cars ($5 for each additional car), Consumer Reports will send you a computer printout comparing the list price and the dealer's cost for the car you are interested in purchasing, including every factory installed option. You'll also get a listing of the optional equipment recommended for the car, if any, by the *Consumer Reports Auto Test Division,* plus a recent report on how to best negotiate with the dealer. This service is especially valuable in negotiating prices on domestic models, as discounts are usually greater on imports. Domestic models come with a longer list of factory options, while some imports have none. In all cases, prices are for factory installed, not dealer installed, options. When ordering your computer printout, simply list the make, model and exact style of each car you are considering. Then mail your request with your check.

D.JAY'S TIRE AND AUTO SERVICE CENTER
863 S. Hamilton Rd., Whitehall, 43213, 237-7631

Why pay $14-$20 when you can have a chassis lube, oil change and oil filter for only $11.95? The owner will also provide you with a coupon valid for a $1.25 rebate on any 5 quart system, which lowers your final cost to $10.70. M-F 8-7, Sat 8-6. Accepts checks, MC, Visa & Discover.

DUNLOP TIRE DISCOUNTERS
1397 W. Mound St., Columbus, 43223, 461-8196

Sells overstocks of top quality Dunlop brands of tires at a savings of 10-25% off manufacturer's suggested retail prices. Also sells Spartan brand, a lesser quality tire, which is manufactured for Dunlop by the B.F. Goodrich Company, at similar savings. This factory outlet also offers full service automotive repairs at typical shop prices, but will mount tires purchased here at no cost. Automotive supplies by Monroe, Wagner and Moog are available at about a 10% savings. Gives exchanges. M-F 7:30-6, Sat 8-3. Accepts checks, MC & Visa.

EDISON
1529 McKinley Ave., Columbus, 43222, 274-1118

Rear view mirrors, hubcaps, batteries, doors and most car parts are available at this dealer which sells used parts from salvaged cars. Save about 50-90% off the new prices. The owner stressed that it is important to bring in the part which needs to be replaced in order to accurately match it up with a part in stock. (Also check the yellow pages for other auto salvage stores). Gives exchanges and a 30 day warranty. Accepts MC & Visa.

HUBCAP ANNIE
4423 E. Main St., Columbus, 43213, 237-7778

New and used hubcaps, 20,000 to be exact, are in stock, ranging from current years and makes to those dating back to the 1940's. Used OEM's (original equipment from the manufacturers) are priced at 30-70% lower than you would expect to pay for the hubcap if it were new. New replacement hubcaps are priced at about 10-30% off comparable caps in other retail stores. Gives exchanges only. M-F 9AM-5:30PM, Sat 10-3. Accepts checks, MC & Visa.

IRON PONY ACCESSORIES
5309 Westerville Rd., Columbus, 43231, 891-2461
2040 Eakin Rd., Columbus, 43223, 272-1165

First quality, liquidations and blemished stock of motorcycle parts, accessories and clothes are available at savings of 10-15% off manufacturers' list prices. Gives exchanges only. Gives exchanges. M-F 10-8, Sat 10-5, Sun 12-5. From October to February, the hours are shortened. Accepts checks, MC, Visa & Discover.

MEINEKE DISCOUNT MUFFLERS
2446 E. Dublin Granville Rd., Columbus, 43229, 882-6549
3720 Refugee Rd., Columbus, 43232, 237-2904
6854 Sawmill Rd., Columbus, 43235, 792-2108

This chain of close to 1,000 stores nationwide, each individually owned and operated, can offer you savings of about 20-30% off the cost of replacing your muffler elsewhere. Mufflers sold under their private label, "Everlast", are made by the same company which manufacturers brands such as Maremont and Gabriel. The company also makes mufflers for stores such as Sears and K Mart. Warranties vary according to the type of muffler you purchase. M-Sat 8-6. Accepts checks, MC & Visa.

NATIONAL TIRE WHOLESALE
5840 Scarborough Blvd., Columbus, 43232, 863-6222
6700 Schrock Ct., Columbus, 43229, 846-8001
655 N. Wilson Rd., Columbus, 43204, 274-5500

Goodyear, Michelin, Pirelli, B.F. Goodrich and other popular and private brands of first quality tires are sold at 10-50% savings off manufacturers' list prices and comparable retail prices. General automotive repairs are also available at value prices. Gives refunds. M-F 7:30AM-8PM, Sat 8-5, Sun 10-3. Accepts checks, MC, Visa, AmExp, Discover & Sears charges.

ODD LOTS
2837 Winchester Pike, Berwick Plaza, Columbus, 43232, 231-0065
3459 Cleveland Ave., Northern Lights Shpng. Ctr., Columbus, 43224, 263-1704
3755 S. High St., Great Southern,Columbus, 43207, 491-5934
657 Harrisburg Pike, Central Pt., Columbus, 43223, 274-3119
68 N. Wilson Rd., Great Western, Columbus, 43204,274-5650
221 Graceland Blvd., Columbus, 43214, 888-3007
920 S. Hamilton Rd., Columbus, 43213, 866-6527
1900 Brice Rd., Reynoldsburg, 43068, 864-8991
2855 Olentangy River Rd., University City Shpng.Ctr.,Columbus, 43202, 262-1223
340 S. Hamilton Rd., Gahanna, 43230, 471-1713
635 Hebron Rd., Southgate Shpng. Ctr., Heath, 43056, 522-8404
1281 N. Memorial Dr., Lancaster, 43130, 654-2447

4075 Hoover Rd., Grove City, 43123, 871-2749
1071 Mt. Vernon Rd., Newark, 43055, 366-7915
137 E. William St., Delaware, 43015, 363-7310

Closeouts, buyouts, discontinued goods, overstock and bankruptcy purchases result in a constantly changing inventory of automotive supplies, housewares, packaged and canned foods, toys, tools, hardware, gifts, linens, sporting goods, socks, office supplies and arts and crafts materials. The quality varies from budget to moderate. Savings are 30-75% off regular retail prices. On a recent visit, I purchased Columbia-Minerva yarns for 39 cents a skein (regularly $2.29), Playskool brand tools and Maybelline cosmetics for 89 cents (regularly $3.99). Don't be discouraged by the no frills environment. This is truly a bargain hunter's delight. In cities over 60 miles out of Columbus, Odd Lots is called Big Lots. You'll find these stores in Marysville, Chillicothe Circleville and other Ohio cities. Gives refunds. M-Sat 9-9, Sun 12-6. Accepts checks, MC, Visa & Discover.

SEARS

The *Sears Auto Discount Service Club* charges a $50 annual fee. You'll receive discount coupons for auto services at Sears as well as cashback bonus options on certain car repairs done at repair shops other than Sears! Another benefit is free detailed new auto summaries, including performance reports, expert evaluations and recommendations, as well as retail and dealer cost pricing. This will greatly help you when purchasing a new car. Customized used car summaries are also available at no cost. When you call 1-800-999-7545 Monday-Saturday from 9-5 to inquire about this program, you will get a "hard sell" technique from the staff person who will tell you that he cannot send you information to review before you make a commitment to participate. He will also tell you about the money back guarantee in case you are not satisfied. While this hardly seems a fair way to deal with customers, trust Sears. I have been a member of this club for about 2 years and have saved about $275 off my auto repair bills. Sears is a nationwide chain which offers advance notice of sales in its stores to its charge card holders as well as occasional extra savings on purchases during certain sales. The *Sears Charge Bonus Club* allows you to earn a cashback bonus based on the amount of your annual purchases. You will get a free gift such as an umbrella or a set of knives upon completion of a credit application in any of their stores. For only $9.95 annually, seniors aged 50 and older, can join the *Mature Outlook Club*. Benefits include $100 in *Sears Money* good in any Sears store or catalogue for merchandise or services, automatic membership in the *Travel Alert Club* providing savings of 35-50% on last minute tours and cruises, a free subscription to *Mature Outlook Magazine* and the *Mature Outlook Newsletter*, hotel and car rental discounts, discounts on optical needs at Sears Optical departments, free travel accident insurance and more. . Your spouse's membership is included at no additional cost. To join the *Mature Outlook Club,* call 1-800-336-6330. Also see the chapter on photography for Sears photography studio.

TIRE AMERICA
4481 Kingsland, Columbus, 43232, 864-5000
4475 W. Broad St.,Columbus, 43228, 272-2227
4800 Sinclair Rd., Columbus, 43229, 436-1303
1327 Brandywine Blvd., Colony Sq. Mall, Zanesville, 43701, 452-0007
3575 Maple Ave., Zanesville, 43701, 452-0007

Purchase Patriot, Dunlop, Goodyear, Michelin, B.F. Goodrich, Century and Pirelli brands of tires here at savings of 35% off regular retail prices. Automotive parts such as shocks and struts are sold at similar savings. Alignments and other services are provided at savings of about 15-20% lower than at other service centers. Has 90 days same as cash financing available to qualified buyers. Tire America features a 125% price guarantee. Gives exchanges. M and Tu 8-5, W-F 8-8, Sat 8-5, Sun 10-3. Accepts checks, MC, Visa, Discover & Sears.

WESTERN AUTO OUTLET STORE
1675 U.S. Route 42 S., Delaware, 43015, 363-2612

This manufacturer's outlet store sells brand name auto parts, appliances, electronics, bicycles, televisions and appliances. It is attached to their distribution center which ships merchandise to 430 stores across the country. *Western Auto* is owned by *Sears*, and you can find some of their "Craftsmen" tools and "Die-Hard" brand batteries here. The inventory consists of new, discontinued and some scratch 'n dent merchandise. Savings are about 20-30% off comparable items on a large portion of their inventory. Gives refunds. M-F 9-7, Sat 9-5, Sun 10-5. Accepts checks, MC, Visa, AmExp, Discover, Sears & Western Auto charges.

ALSO SEE

Ameritech Pages Plus, City of Columbus. Police Dept., Columbus Spring Swap, Consumer Information Ctr., Extravaganza, Franklin Co. Sheriffs, Hyperstore K Mart, John Kalmbaugh Insurance, Ohio Auto Auction, Only $1, Rideshare, Sam's Club, Warehouse Club

---

The *Bargain Hunting Zip Code Directory* fits into the glove compartment of your car and provides you with a geographic listing of the businesses in this book. See order form at the back of the index.

BARGAIN HUNTING DAY TRIPS

The information in this chapter was extracted from the subject listings in this book. It has been compiled to provide you with the opportunity to take a bargain hunting day trip outside of Columbus, and be able to easily locate those businesses within a certain geographic area. . To find a description of the businesses, first check the index at the back of this book to find the page numbers on which they are listed. You might also be interested in purchasing the pocket zip code directory which geographically categorizes all of the listings in this book by their zip code. This handy guide book easily fits into the glove compartment of your car and is invaluable when you accidentally find yourself in a certain part of town or are planning to visit a particular area and would like to shop in several stores in that community. See the order form at the back of this book for further information.

AKRON/CANTON AREA
Aurora Farms Factory Outlets, Carter's Factory Outlet, Regalware Factory Outlet, Ecko Outlet Store, Yankee Peddler Arts And Crafts Festival

CHILLICOTHE/CIRCLEVILLE AREA
Odd Lots, Consumer Credit Counseling Service, Jo-Ann Fabrics, Frisch's Big Boy, Autoworks, Ponderosa, Sun TV, Carrington's, Topping Outlet Store, Circleville Pumpkin Show, Feast Of The Flowering Moon

CINCINNATI AREA
Kitchen Collection, Polly Flinders, Candlelite Outlet, Shapely Outlet Center, Outlets Limited, Leshner Outlet, Fostoria Factory Outlet, Loehman's

CLEVELAND AREA
Cricketeer For Her, Loehmann's, American Commodore Tuxedo, Ohio Mills, Richman Brothers Outlet Store

DAYTON AREA
Mendleson's Electronics And Industrial Salvage, Ceaser's Creek Flea Market, Paneltown And More, Baggerie, Miamisburg Starving Artists Show

GRANVILLE/NEWARK/HEATH AREA
Granville Recreation Commission, Denison University, Columbus Polo Club, Finish Line, Majestic Paint Center, Lenscrafters, One Price $7, Ten Below, Color Tile, Grandma's Country Ruffles, Lechter's, Sally Beauty Supply, Sofa Express, Capezio Footwear, Value City Department Store, Blockbuster Video, Color Tile, Only $1, Linens And Wares, Odd Lots, Aldi, Bobbi Gee, Licking County Bicycle Club, Wallpaper Outlet, Dawes Arboretum, Treasure Trunk, Newark Golf Company Factory outlet, Mack Mattress Outlet, Weathervane Playhouse, Licking County Players, Value City Department Store, Sun TV, Jo-Ann Fabrics, Another Glance II, Clothing Go Round, Arcade Art Affair, Health And Harmony Fair

LANCASTER AREA
Leslie Charles Collections, Capezio Footwear, Klosterman's Baking Company, Only $1, Consumer Credit Counseling Service of Central Ohio, Linens And Wares, Kitchen Collection, Dots, Bobbi Gee, Odd Lots, Value City Department Store, Sally Beauty Supply, Ten Below, Lens Crafters, Furniture Liquidation Center, Brooks Shoe Factory Outlet, Lithopolis Fine Arts Association, State Parks Family Fun Pack, Lancaster Festival

LIMA AREA
Kidswear House, Lancaster Colony

MANSFIELD AREA
Backstrom, Bobbi Gee, Dots, North American Knitting Company, Wallpaper Outlet, Only $1, Consumer Credit Counseling Service, One Price $7, Value City, Record And Tape Outlet, T.J. Maxx, Mansfield Flea Market, Sally Beauty Supply, Perfect Seat, Bed Factory, Trio Foods, Kids Quarters, Coupon Clearing House, Lake Erie Factory Outlets

MARION AREA
Odd Lots, Baldauf Do-It-Center, Jo-Ann Fabrics, Kaybee Toys And Hobby, Consumer Credit Counseling Service

OTHER OHIO CITIES NOT LISTED
Capezio Footwear (New Philadelphia), Fostoria Factory Outlet (Cambridge), Washington Courthouse Flea Market (Washington C.H.), Middleton Doll Factory Outlet (Belpre and Marietta), U.S. Shoe Factory Outlet (Ripley)

SPRINGFIELD/MARYSVILLE AREA
Bobbi Gee, Dots, Springfield Arts Council, Klosterman's Baking Company, Odd Lots, Clothing Wearhouse, Springfield Antiques Show And Flea Market, Panel Town And More, Sally Beauty Supply, Value City Furniture, Electronics Boutique, Hancock Fabrics, Denny's, Blue Jacket, McGraw's Showcase Fabrics, Der Dutchman, Dutch Kitchen, Big Lots, Paper Factory, Madison Commons Factory Direct Stores, Urbana Flea Market, Jo-Ann Fabrics, Autoworks, Famous Sportswear, Majestic Paint Store, Famous Sportswear, Bargain Days, Yellow Springs Street Fair

SUNBURY AREA
Stork Exchange, Big Walnut Skate Club, Sunbury Flea Market

TOLEDO AREA
Fashion Factory Outlet, Libbey Glass Factory Outlet Store

ZANESVILLE AREA
Ohio Pottery West, Blockbuster Video, Hartstone Pottery, Value City Department Store, Ten Below, Grandma's Country Ruffles, D.E. Jones, Autoworks, Tire America, Family Dollar, Sun TV, Fostoria Factory Outlet, Robinson-Ransbottom Pottery,, Salt Fork Arts And Crafts Festival,

BOOKS/MAGAZINES/ NEWSLETTERS

BARGAIN BITS
C/O Columbus Monthly Magazine, 171 E. Livingston Ave., Columbus, 43215

A monthly column on special sales and values in the Columbus area is featured in this magazine. Writers/shoppers Ann Seren and Maggie Kozelek, feature 4 businesses or services each month. The column occasionally includes write-ups on products/services which do not necessarily provide values, but might be considered unusual or new to the Columbus area.

BARGAIN HUNTING IN COLUMBUS NEWSLETTER
C/O Lotus Press, POB 8446, Westerville, 43081-8446

If you would like to keep informed of updates to this book, *Bargain Hunting In Columbus*, then subscribe to the quarterly newsletter at a cost of $9 annually. It will provide information on new stores opening, more shopping tips, businesses closing, mail order bargains, additional services which provide valuable free and low cost assistance, other special event and special sales bargains and more! As the book will not be revised for two years, this is an excellent way to stay abreast of new developments. See order form at the back of this book.

BARGAIN HUNTING IN COLUMBUS ZIP CODE DIRECTORY
C/O Lotus Press, POB 8446, Westerville, 43081-8446

This companion booklet to *Bargain Hunting In Columbus*, provides you with a geographical listing, by zip code, of all of the businesses listed in the book. It is an invaluable tool when you are planning to be in a certain area or when you unexpectedly find yourself in a certain part of town, in that it will enable you to visit several places within a limited geographic area. The zip code booklet also contains a space where you can attach fabric swatches so you'll be able to match up accessories, and charts on which you can write down items you need, special occasions such as birthdays, sizes and color preferences of family members. While the book lists the zip codes after each listing in the particular subject areas, the booklet categorizes these listings by community. The zip code booklet can easily fit into the glove compartment of your car. You should be aware that it is not a replacement for the book. The zip code directory is available at a cost of $2.50 to those people who have purchased a copy of *Bargain Hunting In Columbus*. See the order form at the back of this book.

BOOK CITY
891 S. Hamilton Rd., Columbus, 43213, 231-3756

Save 40-50% off the cover price on a large selection of used books. The store specializes in adult paper back novels, but also features a small selection of children's and young adult's books. The business also offers the opportunity for you to trade your unwanted books for those in their inventory at a 2 for 1 plus 10 cents arrangement. Inquire for details. All sales are final. M-F 10-8, Sat 10-6, Sun 12-5. Accepts checks and cash only.

BOOK LOFT OF GERMAN VILLAGE
631 S. 3 St., Columbus, 43206, 464-1774

Thousands of first quality, discontinued and publishers' overstocks as well as hurt books, are sold at savings of 30-95% off the cover price. Current best sellers, other new titles as well as special orders are available at 10% off the cover price. This store will beat any competitor's price by 10% for like merchandise. 27 rooms are brimming with books in every subject, for adults and children. Check the basement area for a large selection of hurt books at substantial savings. The store is so large, 1 city block long to be exact, that you'll appreciate the free maps to guide you through the maze. The spring and summer times are the most beautiful at this store as their courtyard is all abloom with impatiens. There's benches to sit on and browse through your new purchase, or bring a sack lunch and relax. Return policy varies. M-Sat 10-9, Sun 10-6. Accepts checks, MC,Visa, AmExp & Discover.

BOOK RACK
1115 Worthington Woods Blvd., Worthington, 43085, 846-0036

Thousands of gently used current paperbacks, in 25 different categories, are available at half off the cover price. A selection of in-stock new books, as well as special orders, are available at a 20% discount. You'll find non-fiction, romance, historicals, fiction, westerns, science fiction, mysteries, best sellers and 17 other categories for adults, young adults and children. You may also choose to trade in your unwanted books for those in the store at 1/4 the cover price, which will be issued as a store credit towards future purchases. Books purchased in the store are always accepted for trade, providing that they are in saleable condition. This store offers a unique opportunity to rent newly released hardbacks at a cost of $2 per week or $3.50 for 2 weeks. This is a substantial savings off the cost of purchasing the books for about $15-$25. On my recent visit, I saw the following rental books: Nancy Reagan, the Unauthorized Biography, Follow The Wind and about 7 other titles. Twice a year, in the spring and the fall, the store features their semi-annual half off sale where you can save 50% off their already low prices. The Book Rack is a franchised business with 187 stores in 37 states. Gives exchanges. M and Th 10-8, Tu, W, F and Sat 10-6, Sunday 12-3. Accepts checks and cash only.

BOOK WAREHOUSE
5899 Scarborough Mallway, Columbus, 43232, 860-9025

Books in every subject, for adults and children, can be found in this large store which sells publishers' overstocks and some out of print books. Savings are 50-90% off the original cover price. Classical cassette tapes are similarly discounted. Full time certified teachers are entitled to an additional 10% discount. This store is the largest of the chain's 37 sites throughout the United States. Gives exchanges only. M-Sat 10-9, Sun 12-5. Accepts checks, MC, Visa, Discover & Diners Club.

BORDERS BOOKSTORE
4545 Kenny Rd., Columbus, 43220, 451-2292

Most hardcover books are sold at 10% off the cover price, and New York Times hardcover best sellers are discounted 30%. Monthly staff selections in both the adult and children's areas are also discounted 30%. The hurt books section at the store's entrance, offers savings of 60-80% off the cover price. The bargain book area of closeouts and overstocks, features savings of 30-50%. The store has free children's programs every Saturday at 11AM including storytimes, author visits, holiday parties and crafts. Children aged 12 and under can register to be a member of the Borders Birthday Club. Each year on their birthday, they will receive a birthday card and a gift certificate valid for $3 towards a purchase in the store. A variety of free adult programs are held each month in the Victorian reading room, which is open to the public at all times, such as book discussions, art talks, the Great Decisions series on foreign policy, a weekly classics discussion group, seminars on wine tasting and health as well as demonstrations. On the last Friday of every month at 8:30PM, Borders features a free women's coffee house in which the issues and challenges of contemporary women will be discussed in an open forum atmosphere. The store also features a new parent' book registry in which your friends and relatives will be able to purchase books for your library and not duplicate what you currently have. Free gift wrapping is available upon request. Call to be added to their mailing list. Gives refunds. M-W 9-9, Th-Sat 9-11, Sun 11-8. Accepts checks, MC, Visa & Discover.

CENTRAL CITY COMICS
1460 Bethel Rd., Columbus, 43220, 459-5045
2440 E. Dublin-Granville Rd., Columbus, 43229, 523-2800
4347 E. Main St., Columbus, 43213, 231-1620

Models, tee shirts, magazines, art prints and yes, comics, can be found here. Consider joining their subscription service at a one time cost of $10 for a family or an individual. Your lifetime deluxe membership includes 20% off back issue comics, 10% off new comics on the rack, a free subscription to Central City News, free activation of the Gaming Guild Option (a $5 value which provides you with a 10% discount on all fantasy gaming merchandise such as books), plus 20% off new comics which are set aside for you monthly according to a preference list you are asked to complete. There is no obligation to purchase a minimum amount of merchandise. Simply buy what you need. Another discount option here is the Gaming Guild Program which provides you with a 10% discount on all gaming merchandise such as books and dice. Figurines are expected to be stocked in the near future. The one time membership fee of $5 is good for a lifetime. Gives refunds. M-Sat 11-9, Sun 12-6. Accepts checks, MC & Visa.

COLUMBUS DISPATCH AND OTHER NEWSPAPERS
461-5100 (Dispatch)

If you are not a daily subscriber to the city's only major newspaper, I urge you to do so. The weekly subscription rate for home delivery is $2.45, a savings of 65 cents off the newsstand price or a savings of $33.90 per year. The paper will keep you informed of sales and special offerings, many of which are not readily obtainable through other means. Thursday's Weekender section offers the latest information on special events and happenings for the weekend. Sunday's Arts In Ohio section has many upcoming programs which are advertised, and described throughout the section. Due to the short deadlines required to submit information to the Arts Datebook calendar as well as the rest of the Dispatch, many events are listed which may not appear in other publications. The food section of Wednesday's Dispatch includes recipes, cookbook reviews, plus coupons and grocery shopping tips which will stretch your food dollar. Throughout the paper, the many special columns and features will help you stay informed of news events as well as many opportunities for savings. A subscription to *The Suburban News Papers* is $1 per month and provides you with an issue each week. *This Week Newspapers* are delivered to your home at no cost. *Columbus Alive* is distributed free of charge at area bookstores and many other sites in town and provides you with current information on entertainment, sales and quality news reporting. I urge you to read all newspapers, periodicals and publications you can get your hands on. That is the best way to stay informed.

CONSUMER INFORMATION CENTER
Department DF, Pueblo, Colorado, 81009

Send a check for $2.25 for a copy of the booklet, *Can I Really Get Cheap Or Free Public Land?* The publication offers tips on how to buy public land through auctions and competitive bidding, as well as a listing of other availabilities. These include office buildings, small lots and industrial complexes located throughout the country. You may also request a free copy of the brochure, *Sales Of Federal Surplus Real Estate...*Request a free copy of the *Consumer Information Catalogue* which lists a variety of free and low cost pamphlets/booklets such as *Gas Mileage Guide, Tips For Energy Savers, Starting And Managing A Home Business, Your Trip Abroad, Food Additives, How To Adopt A Wild Horse Or Burro and more.*

CONSUMER REPORTS TRAVEL LETTER
POB 51366, Boulder, Colorado, 80322-1366

If you're a frequent traveller, you are probably aware that the person in the next plane seat or the couple in the adjacent hotel room may have paid much less than you did. In the confusing world of travel pricing, how can you stay abreast of the current options, prices and benefits? This monthly newsletter, by the well respected publishers of Consumer Reports, will provide you with helpful tips. The annual subscription rate is $37, and comes with a satisfaction guarantee.

B. DALTON BOOKSELLER
771 Bethel Rd., Olentangy Plaza, Columbus, 43214, 459-9191
2753 Eastland Mall, Columbus, 43232, 861-6860
520 S. State St., Westerville, 43081, 890-8277
193 Columbus City Ctr. Dr., Columbus, 43215, 228-4581
5091 E. Main St., Columbus, 43213, 861-5505

Membership in the Booksavers Club costs $5 annually and provides you with several benefits. You'll get a 10% discount on all regular priced and sale books, in addition to magazines, a free subscription to the Just Browsing (flyer on new books in their stores and those available by mail order) and the opportunity to purchase selected super saver books at a 50% discount. Gives refunds. M-Sat 10-9, Sun 12-5. Accepts checks, MC & Visa.

DISCOUNT PAPERBACK CENTER
1646 N. High St., Columbus, 43201, 291-5136

Current and back issues of comics, magazines, paperbacks, hardbacks, adult magazines and the latest releases of Comics Weekly can be found in this unpretentious store. You can save 10-20% off the cover price of new publications and 30-50% off used merchandise. Although this store specializes in science fiction and fantasy publications, you will find an assortment of subjects mainly for adults. There is a limited amount of children's books. Gives exchanges only. M-F 10:30-6:30, Sat 11-6, Sun 12-5. Accepts checks, MC & Visa.

FOUL PLAY
6072 Busch Blvd., Columbus, 43229, 848-KLUE (5583)

Mystery, suspense and horror novels line the shelves of Ohio's premier mystery bookstore. New books are sold at regular retail prices, but the large selection of used books is available at 50% off the cover price. Gives exchanges only. M-Sat 10-9, Sun 11-5. Accepts checks, MC, Visa, AmExp & Discover.

HALF PRICE BOOKS, RECORDS, MAGAZINES
2100 Morse Rd., Columbus, 43229, 847-3866
2660 Bethel Rd., Carriage Place Shopping Center, Columbus, 43220, 457-6333

Save 50% off and more on new and used books, magazines, records and tapes. The inventory consists of manufacturers overstocks, discontinued merchandise, as well as used items in all subjects for adults, teens as well as children. The inventory changes frequently, so stop in whenever possible. The store offers a 5% discount on your next purchase if you return their bag. The discount may not be used with other discounts or coupons. The store has earned the distinction of being one of my personal favorites. Gives exchanges only. M-Sat 9-9, Sun 12-6. Accepts checks, MC & Visa.

HAUSFRAU HAVEN
769 S. 3 St., Columbus, 43206, 443-3680

What do you do with those taped books you no longer need? Trade them in, of course! This whimsical German Village gift shop has recently begun a taped book exchange and is looking for eager people to participate at no cost. Simply bring in a tape you no longer need and exchange it for one at the store. You can keep exchanging tapes indefinitely. As this is a relatively new program, it has gotten off to a slow start. However, Fred and Howard, the owners, are anxious to have this free service take off and so am I, as I feel that this is a wonderful gesture on the part of these fellows. M, Tu, Th, F 10-6:30; W,Sat, Sun 10-5.

INTERNATIONAL TRAVEL NEWS
201 Lathrop Way, Suite D, Sacremento, Ca. 95815

If you're looking for tips and bargains relating to travel abroad, purchase a year's subscription to this newsletter for $15. You'll learn about the best priced places to stay, where to eat and where to shop around the world.

KAREN WICKLIFFE BOOKS
2579 N. High St., Columbus, 43202, 263-2903

Used and rare books, 40,000 titles to be exact, line the shelves of Columbus' largest used book dealer. The store features titles in all subject areas. Most of the books are sold for 20-50% off the cover price, with the exception of rare books. Gives exchanges. M-Sat 11:30-5:30. Accepts checks and cash only.

THE LIBRARY STORE
96 S. Grant Ave., Columbus, 43215, 645-2617

Housed within the Main Library, this small store is truly a bargain hunters paradise, brimming with business, entertainment, crafts, children's, fiction and nonfiction books at rock bottom prices. The books consist of library discards as well as donations. Most of the books are priced at $1-$2 with values up to $50. Encyclopedias and other reference books are priced at $5-$15 with values up to $200. Small paperbacks are priced at 50 cents. Be prepared to spend some time in this store to browse thoroughly, as the books are not arranged by subject. The store does such a high volume, that the shelves are restocked daily. It has earned the distinction of being one of my personal favorites. All sales are final. M, Tu and Th 10-8; W, F and Sat 10-5; Sun 1-5. Accepts checks, MC & Visa.

LITTLE PROFESSOR BOOKSTORES
155 Worthington Sq., Worthington, 43085, 846-4319
6490 Sawmill Rd.,Sawmill Place, Dublin, 43017, 766-7775
1657 W. Lane Ave., Lane Ave. Shpng. Ctr., Columbus, 43221, 486-5238

Each month, 12 books are chosen as the "staff selections" which are then sold at 20% off the cover price. As are the New York Times bestsellers. Every July, the stores have an annual library buyout booksale, where hardcover books are sold for $1.79 each or 10 for $12.99. Their annual pre-season calendar sale, offers 30% savings on August purchases, 20% off September purchases and 10% off October purchases,. The calendars resume their regular retail price until February when they are reduced 50%. Little Professor will gift wrap your purchase for free. The Worthington Square site features a panelled library, fireplace and couches for relaxation. Special programs are held in this area as well, including regular meetings of their poets guild. The guild critiques members' works and learns about the various aspects of the writer's craft. Sign up for their mailing list to stay posted on the many free programs such as pre-school storytimes, author visits and booksignings, musical performances and informative discussions at all area stores. Gives refunds. M-Sat 10-9, Sun 12-5. Accepts checks, MC & Visa

MAGAZINE SUBSCRIPTIONS

By subscribing to your favorite magazine or publication, you can save 20-60% off the single copy, newsstand price. On the other hand, you can read your favorite adult or children's magazines for free at the library branch nearest your home or office. Some magazines may also be borrowed on your library card. The largest selection of magazines can be found at the main branch of the Columbus Metropolitan Library at 96 South Grant Avenue, downtown. The last time I visited the library, I read over $60 worth of magazines there!

NEWSSTAND
3309 E. Broad St., Columbus, 43213, 236-5632

Save 10-20% off the top ten books on the Publisher's Weekly best sellers list. About 20% of the inventory consists of bargain books in a special section of the store at savings of 40-80% off the cover price. Adult and children's remaindered books from other stores are found in this area. Gives exchanges only. M-F 7:30AM-10PM, Sat 9-9, Sun 7:30-8PM. Accepts checks, MC, Visa & AmExp.

OUTREACH CHRISTIAN BOOKS
4352 Indianola Ave., Columbus, 43214, 268-2008

Christian oriented games, books and bibles are discounted 25%. Records, cassettes and CDs are sold at a 20% savings off regular retail prices. Gives exchanges only on defective items. M-Sat 10-8, Sun 11:30-5. Accepts checks, MC & Visa.

PENGWYN BOOKS, LTD.
2500 N. High St., Columbus, 43202, 267-6711

Thousands of used, rare and curious books are offered in all subjects. Savings are 30-50% off the cover price on used items. Check out the clearance tables where books are priced at 29 cents to $3.98. Gives exchanges only. M-Sun 11-7. Accepts checks, MC Visa & Discover.

READMOR BOOKSTORES
1649 Morse Rd., Northland Lazarus, Columbus, 43229,265-1459
4141 W. Broad St., Westland Lazarus, Columbus, 43228, 278-4972
131 N. High St., Columbus, 43215, 464-3092
2677 S. Hamilton Rd., Eastland Lazarus, Columbus, 43232, 860-1594
141 S. High St.,downtown Lazarus, Columbus, 43215, 463-3327

The top 10 books on the New York Times best sellers' list are discounted 25% off the cover price. In the fall, you can purchase the following year's calendar for 30% off and in February, calendars are reduced 40-50% off. Frequent sales feature a buy one book and get a second of equal or lesser value for half price (usually held during the first weeks of November, April and July). Your wallet will get a great boost if you accumulate $100 in purchases because Readmor will give you a coupon worth $20 towards you next purchase. This frequent shopper's card will be stamped in $5 increments until you accumulate the designated amount, which means that you don't have to save your receipts. There is no membership fee to participate. Gives refunds. M-Sat 10-9, Sun 12-5. North High St. hours are shorter. Accepts checks, MC and Visa.

ROY WILLIS, BOOKSELLER
195 Thurman Ave., Columbus, 43206, 443-4004

Thousands of used, rare and collectible books are available. in all subjects. The store features a large selection of art, mystery, horror, science fiction and fantasy books in addition to small antiques and collectibles. Savings on many used books are about 20-50% off the cover price. All sales are final. M-F 11-6, Sat 11-5:30. Accepts checks and cash only.

UPPER ARLINGTON PUBLIC LIBRARY
2800 Tremont Rd., Columbus, 43221, 486-9621
1945 Lane Rd., Columbus, 43220, 459-0273

The Tremont Road location has a daily book sale in the audio-visual department containing about 300 books in a variety of subjects,. The prices range from 50 cents to $2. I recently picked up a hard back copy of Trader Vic's Bartending Guide for $2 which would have cost about $15 if new. The Friends Of The Library also offer a used book sale in the lobby every Wednesday from 9:30-5, every Saturday from 9:30-3 and every Sunday from 1-5. The Lane Road Library has a small selection of used books and magazines, from 25 cents to $1, on a cart as you enter the library. The Lane Road branch also hosts a mystery club for adults which meets at 1PM on the last Thursday of each month. This brown bag lunch program includes a presentation on a crime related topic or a discussion of favorite mysteries. The Tremont Library also offers free, in-house rental of Macintosh and IBM computers to library cardholders. The Lane Road branch features free rental of IBM compatible and Apple II E computers. A variety of programs for adults and kids with business and entertainment applications, may also be used. Anyone is eligible for a free library card. The Friends also distribute free copies of "Holiday Happiness", an annual booklet containing about 15 pages of holiday recipes. They are available during December while supplies last. As is the case with most area libraries, the Arlington branches offer many free and low cost lectures, seminars, book discussions, poetry readings, performances and craft workshops each month for adults and children. Some previous programs have been "Hand And Nail Care", "Life Without Guilt", "Creative Bow Making And Gift Wrapping Ideas", "Pigging Out In Columbus" and more. The Tremont Road branch features an annual musical series, Eine Kleine Nachmusik, which presents free monthly performances from September to June with local as well as regional talent. This branch also rents slide projectors for $5 per day and $1 per day to rent a screen. The equipment may be taken off site. M-F 10:30-8:30, Sat 9-6, (Sun 1-6 at the Tremont branch only.). Accepts checks and cash only.

U.S. GOVERNMENT BOOKSTORE
200 N. High St., Columbus, 43215, 469-6884

This bookstore maintains an inventory of posters, pamphlets and books developed through the efforts of the government printing office, most of which are not available through other retail outlets. Prices range from 50 cents to $35 and include a wide range of subjects such as business, agriculture, science, energy and consumerism. You can also pickup a free copy of the consumer information catalogue which lists some of the publications offered. Did you know that more than 19,000 titles are available through mail order including more than 600 subscription services?. Gives exchanges only. M-F 9-4. Accepts checks, MC & Visa.

VILLAGE BOOK SHOP
2424 W. Dublin Granville Rd., Worthington, 43085, 889-2674

Publishers' overstocks, out of print and closeout books in all subjects, are available at savings of 10-90% off the cover price. You'll find over 2 million books for adults, young adults and children, most of which are new, plus a small selection of used books and magazines. This business is housed in an old church. There's also an upper level which is a bit hard to find, so ask if you can't locate it. The owner indicated that this is the largest remainder bookstore in the country, outside of New York City. Gives refunds. M-Sun 10-10. Accepts checks, MC & Visa.

VOLUNTEERS OF AMERICA
2511 Summit St., Columbus, 43202, 262-3384

The upstairs level houses all of the books, records and tapes collected citywide by this nonprofit organization. Used paperbacks and hardbacks cost 50 cents-$2, records and tapes cost 50 cents. All sales are final.. M-Sat 9-4:30. Accepts checks, MC, Visa & Discover.

WTTE CHANNEL 28 KIDS CLUB
6130 Sunbury Rd., Westerville, 43081, 895-2800

Sign up your child for the free monthly newsletter which provides discount coupons and freebies for entertainment, services, food and other desirables. The newsletter also includes stories and games. Your child will receive a special mailing for his/her birthday, which includes additional coupons for special surprises. Children up to age 15 can participate. M-F 9-5.

WORTHINGTON PUBLIC LIBRARY
805 Hartford St., Worthington, 43085, 885-3185

The library offers a self serve used book, video, magazine, cassette and compact disc area called the *Bargain Place* which is in the lower level. Prices are 25 cents for magazines or paperback books; 50 cents for hardcover books, cassettes and record albums and $1 for CDs and videos. The merchandise consists of items no longer needed by the library as well as patron donations. The Bargain Place features mostly novels. Correct change is needed. A dollar bill changer is located within the building. The library also offers free adult book discussions on Wednesdays at 7PM and Thursdays at 10:30AM. All sales are final. M-Th 9-9, F and Sat 9-6,(Sun 1-5 Sept.-May).

ALSO SEE

AAA, Arts Midwest Jazzletter, Cafe On Five, Columbus Bookfair, Columbus Dispatch, Drowsy Dragon, Extravaganza, Field Publications, K Mart, Microcenter, Nearly New Shop, Nickleby's Bookstore Cafe, Office America, Ohio Periodical Distributors, OSU Friends Of The Library Booksale, Pearls Of Wisdom, Riverside Hospital Health Education Library, Sam's Club, Software Etc., WDLR Radio and Warehouse Club

CLASSES

ALOHA BRIDGE CENTER
1367 Community Park Drive, Columbus, 43229, 890-1459

Free beginning bridge classes are offered on Mondays at 2PM and Wednesdays at 8:30AM. Free intermediate level bridge classes are offered on Mondays at noon and Wednesdays at 7PM. Answering machine is on at all times.

CAPITAL UNIVERSITY
2199 E. Main St., Columbus,. 43209, 236-6200

Senior citizens aged 60 and over may enroll in selected university courses at no cost on a space available basis in the *Senior Audit Program.* Books and lab fees, if needed, must paid by the senior. Call M-F 9-5.

COLUMBUS PUBLIC SCHOOLS, DEPT. OF COMMUNITY EDUCATION
365-6000

Several free and low cost non-credit programs are available to the public. The Career Transitions seminars assist unemployed, underemployed or dislocated workers to learn skills which will assist in attaining gainful employment. The free course meets for 10 hours a week for 2 weeks. Call 365-5239 to register. The Displaced Homemaker program assists newly divorced, separated or those in the process and/or single females to make the transition from homemaking to wage earning. The free course emphasizes the development of coping as well as marketable skills. Call 365-5136. The GOALS Program (graduation, occupation and living skills) assists young single and/or expectant parents to work towards earning a high school diploma or GED, to understand child development and to seek training for employment. For information on this program, call 365-5140. ONOW (orientation to non-traditional occupations for women)) assists women who want to prepare to enter a non-traditional job, an adult vocational program or apprenticeship training. Topics range from math and blueprint reading to hand tool use and physical fitness. The fee is $15. Call 365-5239 for information. The ongoing courses are offered from September through May, in several week sessions, at various schools in the city.

COLUMBUS CULTURAL ARTS CENTER
139 W. Main St., Columbus, 43215, 645-7047

Housed in one of the earliest arsenals existent in Ohio, this multifaceted arts facility offers free and low cost programs in the visual, performing and literary arts for adults and children. 48 exhibitions are featured annually, in four galleries within the building. Adult studio classes are offered year round in 8 week sessions and include weaving, drawing, painting, bronze casting, stone carving, ceramics, sculpture, metalsmithing, and copper enameling. The fee for the 8 week term is $19 for classes meeting once per week and $38 for those meeting twice per week. Supply fees are extra. Each month, the Center offers a changing menu of workshops such as basketry, papermaking, Fimo jewelry, collage, handcoloring black and white photographs and more. Most are priced at $7-$30. The free, weekly Conversations And Coffee series presents practicing artists discussing their works, often accompanied by a slide presentation or a demonstration. Lectures, performances, poetry readings and many children's programs offer exciting opportunities for learning and experiencing the arts. Special events and festivals are planned such as the Festival Of American Culture which will celebrate the decade of the 1950's in August 1991, and the 1960's in August 1992. Admission to the building and its exhibits is free. The instructional staff are top in their fields, with several educators being nationally recognized. Comraderie is high among participants whose creativity truly flourishes in this environment. The building can be rented for private functions at a cost of $10 per hour for up to 99 people or $20 per hour for 100 or more people. If you have some spare time and would like to volunteer, call the Arts Center, as there are many opportunities for short and long term commitments. Sign up for their mailing list to stay posted on these wonderful programs for beginning, intermediate and advanced level individuals of all ages. Classes fill early, so don't delay in registering. This facility has earned the distinction of being one of my personal favorites. The Columbus Cultural Arts Center is operated by the City of Columbus, Recreation And Parks Department. Issues credits on class cancellations. M-F 8AM-5PM, M-Th. 7PM-9:30PM, Sat and Sun 1-5. Accepts checks, MC & Visa.

COLUMBUS FOLK DANCERS
St. Stephen's Episcopal Church, 30 W. Woodruff, Columbus, 43210, 268-1698

These weekly sessions offer instruction from 8-8:30PM on Wednesdays, followed by dancing and fun. The annual membership fee is $15 which permits you free admission to the programs. Non-members are admitted for only $1 per session. The group consists of college aged individuals through seniors who dance Balkan as well as English Country dances. All skill levels are welcome. Call anytime.

COLUMBUS RECREATION AND SENIOR CENTERS
City of Columbus, Recreation And Parks Dept., 645-3300

27 recreation facilities citywide offer free and very low cost art classes, athletic and recreational programs for adults and youths. Recently, these centers have taken on a focus in which each has the general programs described, in addition to specializing in a particular area such as photography, printmaking, martial arts, skateboarding, fabric art, outdoor and environmental education, international cultures, vocal and choral music, cooking, ceramics and other areas. The 8 senior centers offer a variety of programs in the visual, literary and performing arts, lectures, seminars, bus trips and other programs of interest to this age group. Most programs are free but there is a nominal $2 annual

membership fee. Call the general phone number for the Recreation and Parks Department listed above for more information. (Communities in the surrounding areas have senior centers which also offer value priced programs. Check your phone book for a listing)

DAVIS DISCOVERY CENTER
549 Franklin Ave., Columbus, 43215, 645-7469

Quality, free after school, weekend, summer and school break programs are offered for youths aged 4-18 in music, dance and drama, stage combat, magic and theater illusion. special effects makeup for the stage and more. Housed within the old Players Theater building, the Davis Discovery Center provides excellent opportunities for kids to grow through the arts, under the direction of trained professionals. Some classes culminate in free public performances at the Center as well as at sites within the community. The Davis Discovery Center has a Children's Drama Company, the Park Playhouse Teen Community Theater, the Columbus Honors Band, a Dance troupe in addition to the other offerings mentioned. Sign up for their mailing list. This facility has earned the distinction of being one of my personal favorites.

DAWES ARBORETUM
7770 Jacksontown Rd., S.E., Newark, 43055, 323-2355

This botanical delight offers free and low cost (usually $5-$8) programs for the family on nature and horticulture related topics. Discussions and slide programs on Victorian graveyards, pest identification and control, gardens of Europe and plant habitats, as well as workshops on composting, bonsai, perennial landscaping and brick patios have been offered. Children's programs include films, hikes and crafts workshops. . Also offers a master gardener's certificate program. M-F 8-5, Sat and Sun 1-5. Accepts checks and cash.

DELAWARE COUNTY METRO PARKS
363-2934

Offers a free nature lovers lecture series from June-November each year at the Perkins Observatory, 3199 Columbus Pike. The once per month programs are held on weekday evenings and Saturday mornings. Past topics have included beekeeping, attracting wildlife to your yard and trees in the urban environment. At this time, there are no metro parks in Delaware county, but this organization has been looking for some suitable land. Call M-F 9-5

EDUCABLE CHANNEL 25
36 W. Gay St., Suite 301, Columbus, 43215, 469-8825

A changing sampler of quality programming is available on this cable television station. Big Bear stores will sponsor the kitchen show, "A Matter Of Taste" during 1991 and 1992. This 20 part series will survey a wide variety of basic and gourmet foods and their on camera preparation. Emphasis will be placed on the design and presentation of finished dishes. The programs air on Tuesdays at 12 noon and Sundays at 3:30PM. Some other scheduled instructional programs at the time this book went to press include bridge basics, business communication skills, Chinese brush painting, watercolor instruction, home gardening Japanese language instruction and needlecraft. Call to receive their free program guide.

FAMILY LIFE EDUCATION PROGRAM
365-5136

The Columbus City Schools offer free adult classes in living skills, preparation for parenthood and parenting education during the school year at various sites throughout the city. The classes are held in day and evening times. The *Living Skills* course meets weekly and covers stress management and self esteem, consumer education, community resources, budgeting and financial management, clothing construction and care, mending/alterations, buying clothes economically, parenting issues, food and nutrition topics etc. The *Parents To Be* course meets for 4 sessions and is most beneficial when taken during the last 3 months of pregnancy. It is also appropriate for adoptive parents. The class is held at the Columbus Health Department clinic sites. Topics addressed include parental physical and emotional adjustment, infant care, infant health and illness as well as community resources. The *Parenting* course covers the growth and development of children, safety and nutritional needs of children, raising pre-teens and how to help your child learn. These are 6 week classes for 2 hours per week. The classes are open to anyone in the community, without regard to income or community of residence. A free daytime childcare option is also available through prior arrangement. Call M-F 9-5.

HARDING HOSPITAL
See phone numbers below.

Offers free lectures 2-3 times per year through the Harding-Evans Foundation such as with Judith Viorst, author of "Necessary Losses". Programs are usually held at the Worthington High School. Contact Eleanor Jones at the Foundation at 785-7426 to sign up for the mailing list. Harding's outpatient services department offers a variety of family mental health programs during the year, usually in the winter, spring and fall. The fee averages about $10 for the series. Call Charlene Restivo at 848-9900 to be added to the mailing list. M-F 9-5.

DEBBIE KERI-BROWN
The author of *Bargain Hunting In Columbus,* Debbie Keri-Brown, teaches a variety of classes in the community at most of the adult eduction and parks and recreation programs in the suburbs. Most of the programs offer instruction in wearable art. Classes include bead stringing and design, paper beads, wire wrapping jewelry, ito-mari holiday ornaments, decorated papers, hot glue jewelry, sweat shirt painting, Bargain Hunting In Columbus, Egyptian jewelry making and others. Please contact your local adult education program.

LEARNING GUILD
OSU-Continuing Education Dept., 1050 Charlock Rd., Columbus, 292-8571

This interdisciplinary program in the arts and humanities provides noncredit, adult opportunities for learning. Varied program formats such as dinner lectures, seminars, tours, exhibits and performances are centered around a single theme, generally with a multicultural focus. Past themes have included China, Russia, archeology, philosophy, literature, history and political science with about 15 programs planned for each theme. The events are educational as well as entertaining. Prices range from free to about $30 per program, with many being $10 and under. Call to be added to their mailing list.

OSU-OFFICE OF WOMEN'S SERVICES
408 Ohio Union, 1739 N. High St., Columbus, 43210, 292-8473

You don't have to be a student or an employee of the university to participate in these free and low cost programs held on campus and at various sites within the community. Call to be added to their mailing list to learn about their lectures, performances and workshops of interest to women which deal mostly with personal growth, assault prevention, career and arts issues. M-F 9-5.

OSU PROGRAM 60
1050 Charlock Rd., Room 152 Mount Hall, Columbus, 43210, 292-8860

Ohio residents aged 60 and over, may attend classes on a non-credit basis for free. Book or lab fees are extra where needed. Some classes require pre-requisites. Registration is held in January, March, June and September. *Program 60* is administered by the Office of Continuing Education. In 1973, the Ohio Legislature passed a law requiring state funded colleges and universities to open their classrooms to seniors at no charge on a space available basis. M-F 9-5.

OSU SCHOOL OF MUSIC
156 W. 19 Ave., Columbus, 43210, 292-0404

The division of music history (292-9451) offers a free public series, *Lectures In Musicology* in the winter, spring and fall. The series is held on Wednesdays at 4PM in the music library of Sullivant Hall, 1813 N. High Street. Previous topics have included, *A Clash Of Two Cultural Paradigms In Russian Music Of The 17th Century, Liszt's Les Preludes Who Told The Truth? Draft Of Inspiration: Perspectives On The Nature Of Musical Composition From Lully To Stravinsky.* Call to sign up for their mailing list. M-F 9-4:30

RIVERSIDE METHODIST HOSPITAL FOUNDATION
3535 Olentangy River Rd., Columbus, 43214, 261-4430

Several times during the year, the Foundation sponsors free or low cost lectures/presentations (about $5-$6) with nationally recognized health care and wellness professionals. In the past, guests have been Dr. Bernie Siegel, Dr. Cheepak Chopra and others. Programs are held at the hospital or other sites in the community. Call to be added to their mailing list.

SENIOR FREE AUDIT PROGRAM
Otterbein College, N. Grove and W. College Ave., Westerville, 43081, 898-1356

Seniors aged 65 and over may enroll in college courses at no cost, except for book and lab fees where applicable. Participation is on a space available basis for the non credit classes. M-F 8-5.

SUMMER TECH
221-3228

The Columbus Public Schools will be entering their ninth year in 1991 with this program for pre-schoolers through adults, which offers special low cost instruction in business, classroom and home applications of the Apple II, IBM or Macintosh computer. There are about fifty courses which include programming, desktop publishing and classes especially designed for elementary school aged children. Courses include ten hours of instruction during one week sessions which are held from early July through early August at Brookhaven, Eastmoor, Fort Hayes and Whetstone High Schools in addition to the Northwest Career Center and at 52 Starling Street. The fees are $25-$40 per course. Golden Apple Pass holders ,aged 60 and over, receive a 10% discount. M-F 8:30-5.

UPPER ARLINGTON OLDER ADULTS EDUCATIONAL NETWORK
486-9511

Offers an annual seminar series from October through March addressing issues of importance to older adults. The programs are held at various sites within Upper Arlington during day and evening hours. Topics addressed have included: long term care insurance, combating holiday stress and loneliness and veterans' reminiscences of wartime involvement. The series is sponsored by 5 local health and community organizations such as: First Community Village, Upper Arlington Commission On Aging, Upper Arlington Public Library, Northwest Counseling Older Adult Services and the Upper Arlington Senior Center. This free series is open to the general public. Flyers are available at the Upper Arlington Public Library. M-F 9-4.

WOSU CHANNEL 34
2400 Olentangy River Rd., Columbus, 43210, 292-4510

This public television station offers several weekly instructional classes. On Saturdays at 8AM, you can watch, *The Joy Of Painting*. On Tuesdays, *Sewing With Nancy*, provides sewing tips such as how to apply facings and pockets, sewing with knits etc. The *Frugal Gourmet*, teaches you low cost cooking recipes every Thursday at 8:30PM. Auction 34, the station's annual fundraising event, is held from late April through early May. Viewers have the opportunity to bid on a variety of items and services such as artwork, trips, jewelry, meals at restaurants, household items etc., often saving 20-40% off the regular retail price. Check with your accountant as you may be able to deduct your purchase as a donation on your income taxes. All sales are final. M-F 9-5.

ALSO SEE

B.A.B.I.E.S. Club, Backstrom, Byzantium, Builder's Square, Central Ohio Home And Garden Show, Columbus Coal And Lime Company, Columbus Metropolitan Libraries, Columbus Museum Of Art, Columbus Sports-Vacation And Travel Show, Columbus Swim Center, Columbus Zoo, Cover To Cover Bookstore, Delaware County Cultural Arts Center, Design Materials, Downtown Dance Club, Dress Barn, Dress Barn Woman, Educable Channel 25, Fabric Farms, Forever Green Foliage Co., Franklin Co. Cooperative Extension Service, Franklin Co. Metro Parks, Frugal Fox, Golden Hobby Shop, Hancock Fabrics, Henri Bendel, Katz and Dawgs, Lee Wards, Majestic Paint Stores, Martin Luther King Center, Microcenter, Milo Artists Colony, Nancy's Fabrics, Nickleby's Bookstore Cafe, ODNR-Division Of Watercraft, Ohio Historical Society, OSU Department of Architecture, Ohio Tuition Trust Authority, Panel Town And More, Pearls Of Wisdom, St. Ann's Hospital, Sports-Vacation And Travel Show, Sun TV, Upper Arlington Cultural Arts Commission, Upper Arlington Public Library, Volunteer Administrator's Network, Wallpaper 4-U, Wallpapers To Go, Wines Inc., Woodworking World and Worthy Citizen Card

CLOTHING

Invest a few dollars in a clothes shaver. It's one of those battery operated gizmos which shaves those unsightly little balls off your clothes. Jo-Ann Fabrics usually has them for $5-$10. This will keep your garments looking fresh and like new. It can also help you to make excellent purchases on clothes which have been reduced because they've become too fuzzy on the store's racks.

Each manufacturer cuts their clothes and shoes differently. So don't be stubborn about trying on something which is several sizes larger or smaller than you usually wear. Another reason to check the racks in other sizes is that some people will misplace clothes they have tried on into the wrong size on the rack. Another tip is to search the racks for clothing in the opposite sex's department. Many fashions are made nowadays so that men and women could be equally flattered in certain styles. I have found that on the clearance racks in the men's department, there always seems to be an abundance of colored garments, possibly considered to be feminine, in addition to patterns which are unpopular with men.

AIR WAVES
6575 Huntley Rd., Columbus, 43229, 841-4100

Four times a year, you can enjoy their sale of overruns and misprinted tee shirts, sweatshirts, jackets and caps. This custom printing operation does airbrushing and silk screening work. You'll find savings of 40-60% on items for adults and youths. All sales are final. Accepts checks, MC & Visa. M-F 8-5.

ALTERNATIVE SHOP
1806 W. 5 Ave., Columbus, 43212, 486-0225

Consignment men's, women's and children's clothing as well as bridal wear, can be found at this store at savings of about 30-75% off "if new" prices. You'll also find a limited amount of accessories. Provides layaway. All sales final except 24 approval policy. M-F 8:30-6, Sat 9-5 Accepts checks, MC & Visa.

AMERICAN COMMODORE TUXEDO OUTLET STORE
5147 Warrensville Center Rd., Maple Hts., 44137,
(216) 663-6688
5847 Smith Rd., Brookpark, 44142, (216) 676-6050

New and used formal wear can be purchased here for up to 80% off regular retail prices. You can find shirts, tuxedos, shoes, ties, pants, tails, vests and related items. Tuxedos are $99 and up, shirts are $4 and up, ties are 50 cents and up. The stores offer a selection of moderate as well as designer lines such as Pierre Cardin, Bill Blass and Stephen St. Clair. The Maple Heights location is open Saturday from 10-5 and provides the largest selection between the two stores. The Brookpark store is open Monday-Friday 12-8 and Saturday 10-6. All sales are final. Accepts checks, MC, Visa, AmExp & Discover.

AMY STOUDT
7671 New Market Center Way, Columbus, 43235, 764-2935
5828 Scarborough Mallway, Columbus, 43232, 868-5523

Moderate to better priced large sized women's clothing is available at sizeable savings (no pun intended). The first quality merchandise includes suits, dresses, casual and special occasion wear by popular companies such as Miss Russ and Oleg Cassini. You'll also find accessories such as hats, jewelry, belts, lingerie and handbags. The inventory in the store is discounted about 20-25% off regular retail prices. Provides layaways. Refunds with receipt. M-Sat 10-9, Sun 12-5. Accepts checks, MC, Visa & Discover.

ANNE'S COLLECTION OUTLET STORE
1879 Henderson Rd., Columbus, 43220, 457-1942

If classic women's fashions with a trendy flair sounds like your type of stuff, run, don't walk, to the outlet store for this national catalogue company. Choose from shoes, jewelry, purses as well as clothes in dressy and casual styles for missy and petite sizes. Companies such as Maggy London, Marissa Christina, Jennifer Reed, Anne Klein, Bally Shoes and Carlo Falchi purses can be found here. The first quality current catalogue items are priced at 20-30% off retail prices, the previous catalogue (some still current season) merchandise is 40-50% off. Watch for their semi-annual warehouse sales, in January and July, where savings are 50% off current catalogue prices and up to 80% off past season items. Sales are final on items marked down 50%. Exchanges offered on other merchandise. M-Th 10-8:30, F and Sat 10-6. Accepts checks, MC, Visa & AmExp.

ANOTHER GLANCE
2390 E. Main St., Bexley, 43209, 237-0636
1232 N. 21 St., Newark, 43055, 366-6716

Upscale gently used evening wear, silk, satin and beaded garments in sizes 3-42, are sold here at savings of 30-50% less than if they were purchased new. Never worn salesman's samples and remainders from area boutiques and specialty shops are also available at savings of 40-60% off regular retail prices. Accessories such as jewelry, purses and belts can be found at similar savings. Moderate to designer quality brands you will find here include J.H. Collectibles, Liz Claiborne, Forenza, Dawn Joy, Anne Klein, Louis Vuitton, Gucci and others. Sign up for a free membership in their *Clothes-A-Holics Unanimous Club*, which is a frequent purchaser plan. You'll get a card which will be stamped each time you purchase $10 worth of merchandise. When you have accumulated 20 punches (and you've spent $200), you will be entitled to $20 in free merchandise from the store. The Newark location features a large selection of bridal gowns and veils in addition to the other merchandise described above, and is well worth the trip. Sign up for their mailing list to stay posted on their sales and fun special promotions. All sales final. M-Sat 10-6. Accepts checks, MC & Visa.

AURORA FARMS FACTORY OUTLETS
549 S. Chillicothe Rd., Aurora, 44202, (216) 562-2000 or 1-(800) 837-2001

You can enjoy a delightful atmosphere at Ohio's first factory outlet center where 30 stores offer savings of up to 70% off name brand merchandise. All of the stores are factory owned and operated and include such merchandise as craft items, clothing for the family, cosmetics, paper products, gift items and furniture. Some of the stores you'll find include Aileen, Crazy Horse, Gitano, Hanes Activewear, Harve Benard, Izod, Jonathan Logan, Jones New York, Van Heusen, Bass Shoes, L'eggs And Hanes, Carter's, Toy Liquidators, Corning/Revere, American Tourister, Wallet Works, Ribbon Outlet, Sequels Book Outlet and others. Aurora Farms features many special events throughout the year including sidewalk sales (which offer greater savings), arts and crafts festivals and classic car shows. Every Wednesday and Sunday from 8-4 year round, they feature a large farmer's market and flea market with free admission, in another section of this 60 acre complex. It is Ohio's largest and oldest flea market. Aurora Farms is close to Sea World and the Geauga Lake Theme Park, 4 miles north of Ohio Turnpike exit 13. It is about 2 1/2 hours from Columbus. Return policy varies with each store. M-W 10-6, Th-Sat 10-9, Sun 10-5. Accepts checks, MC & Visa.

AVALON
1434 N. High St., Columbus, 43201, 294-9722

This vintage clothing store seasonally features beaded sweaters from the 1950's, in addition to cocktail dresses, shoes, hats, sweaters and other wearables. It specializes in used denims at about $18, regularly $60 if new. The vintage sportcoats from the 1960's are an exceptionally good buy at $20. The inventory is a combination of military surplus, used and vintage items as well as sportswear and accessories. This fun, energizing atmosphere is sure to please men and women alike. A large portion of the merchandise is unused, although vintage, as a result of being warehoused for many years. You'll find fairly priced, unique wearables in top shape. Provides layaways with $50 minimum. Gives exchanges. M-F 10-8, Sat and Sun 12-5. Accepts checks, MC, Visa & AmExp.

JOSEPH A. BANK CLOTHIERS
270 Worthington Sq. Mall, Worthington, 43085, 785-1070

These classic, high quality men's suits and slacks are sold exclusively through their own stores and national catalogues and are manufactured in their own factories. The quality is comparable to that of designer fashions by Hart Schaffner and Marx and Ralph Lauren but you'll pay about 20-30% less. This amounts to a savings of about $75-$150 on a suit. Their factory also makes women's clothing which is available at similar savings, but also sells other quality brands at full retail price. If you have discriminating tastes and appreciate exquisite fabric, construction and styling, this is the place for you. Gives refunds. M-Sat 10-9, Sun 12-5. Accepts checks, MC & Visa.

BEARLY WORN CLOTHES FOR KIDS
557 Hill Rd. N., Pickerington 43147, 833-0909

Quality resale clothing for children in sizes newborn to 14, plus toys and related accessories such as car seats, are offered at savings of 50-75% less than if you were to purchase these new. The savings depends on whether the merchandise is slightly used or never worn. Some of the brands the store carries include Martha Miniatures, Brian Dresses, Health-Tex and Oshkosh. Grandmothers can obtain a free "grandmother's discount card" which entitles them to a 10% discount off all purchases. Gives refunds for clothing within 7 days of purchase. M-Sat 10-5. Accepts MC, Visa and checks.

BETTER CLOTHES AND BARGAINS
9226 Dublin Rd., Powell, 43065, 889-1520

Women's upscale and designer clothing, jewelry and related accessories are available at this recently opened business. You'll find current season, new merchandise at 30% off manufacturers' suggested retail prices and gently used consigned items at least 50% below "if new" prices. The new stock consists of salesmen's samples and special purchases. The business is located next to Experienced Possessions, an upscale home furnishings consignment shop which is also listed in this book. The store is just north of Muirfield and is closer to Dublin than it is to Powell. Gives exchanges on new merchandise. Used items are final sale. Tu-Sat 10-6, Sun 12-4. Accepts checks and cash.

BOBBI GEE
613 Hebron Rd., Southgate Shpng. Ctr., Heath, 43056, 522-4488
1113 Park Ave. W., Mansfield, 44906, (419)529-9750
1733 N. Memorial Dr., Lancaster, 43130, 653-3727
2984 Derr Rd., Springfield, 45503, (513) 390-6188

First quality overstocks in men's and women's contemporary apparel, are available at savings of 20-40% off manufacturers' suggested retail prices. You'll find moderate to better quality casual and career wear by such brands as L'eau Vive, Gitano, L.A. Gear and Palmettos. Men's wear is priced at $26.97 and under and women's wear is priced at $24.97 and under. The stores also offer a small selection of women's accessories. This chain is planning to open 100 mores sites in Ohio within the next 4 years. Gives refunds. M-Sat 10-9, Sun 12-5. Accepts checks, MC, Visa & Discover.

BON WORTH OUTLET
5810 Scarborough Mallway, Columbus, 43232, 575-1032

Sizes from 6-46 can be found at this manufacturer's outlet whose factory is in Hendersonville, North Carolina. Mix and match separates in traditional and basic styles are available at savings of 30-40% lower than comparable quality merchandise from other manufacturers. The store is owned and operated by the manufacturer. The inventory bears the Bon Worth label and is not sold at unaffiliated businesses. Provides layaway. Gives refunds. M-Sat 10-9, Sun 12-5. Accepts checks, MC & Visa.

BURLINGTON COAT FACTORY WAREHOUSE
270 Graceland Blvd., Columbus 43214, 885-2628
6426 Tussing Rd., Consumer Sq. E., Reynoldsburg, 43068, 863-3791

Find current, first quality casual, sport and career wear for men, women and children at savings of 20-40% off regular retail prices. Petite, regular and large sizes are available by nationally recognized moderate to designer quality brands such as Carole Little, J.H. Collectibles, Pierre Cardin and Ocean Pacific. Purses, hosiery, lingerie, fashion jewelry and shoes are also available. The linen department sells towels, comforters, sheets, bathroom accessories and pillows at savings of 20-70% off suggested retail prices. Nationally recognized brands are featured. The Graceland location has a baby room which stocks quality furniture, clothes, accessories and carriages by all popular brands such as Fisher-Price, Graco, Gerry Century and others. Savings are 10-40% off regular retail prices. Gives exchanges only. M-Sat 10-9, Sun 11-6. Accepts checks, MC, Visa, AmExp & Discover.

CAPERS
7680 New Market Center Way, Columbus, 43235, 889-5724

You will find contemporary styled moderate to better priced casual fashions for junior guys and gals. Most of the inventory is sold under the Julabee and Lindsay Gray labels, in this manufacturer's outlet store. The merchandise is first quality. Savings are about 20-40% off prices for comparable products from other manufacturers. Capers also has stores in Lima, Sandusky and Findlay, Ohio. Provides layaways. Gives refunds. M-Sat 10-9, Sun 12-5. Accepts checks, MC, Visa, AmExp and Discover.

CARTER'S FACTORY OUTLET
1733 Pearl Rd., Brunswick, 44212, (216) 225-0900
549 S. Chillicothe Rd., Aurora Farms Factory Outlets,   Aurora, 44202, (216)562-9030

This children's wear factory outlet features brands by Carter's and Bugle Boy at savings of 15-20% off regular retail prices on first quality merchandise and 50% off retail on irregular goods. Gives refunds. Gives discount to seniors. M-Sat 10-6, Sun 1-5. Accepts checks, MC & Visa.

CASUAL MALE BIG AND TALL
7617 New Market Centerway, Columbus, 43235, 764-9165

Save 20-40% off casual slacks, shirts, shorts and tee shirts for large and tall men. The contemporary clothes are found in sizes 1x-4x, 17 1/2-22 and 40-52. Gives refunds. M-Sat 10-9, Sun 12-5. Accepts checks, MC & Visa.

CHAPEL BELLES BRIDAL WORLD
2680 Courtright Rd., Columbus, 43232, 863-0999

A full line of bridal gowns, prom dresses, bridesmaid's dresses and mother of the bride dresses in sizes 4-44, are available at savings of 15-20% off suggested retail prices. Flower girl dresses are also available at similar savings. The first quality merchandise includes brand names such as Jordan, Lisette, Barry J, Alfred Angelo, Jasmine, Jessica McClintock and others. Allow 2-12 weeks for delivery. Provides layaway. M, T, Th. 10-8, W 12-5, F & Sat 10-5. Accepts checks, MC & Visa.

THE CLOTHES STORE
1198 Kenny Center, Columbus, 43220, 459-0846

This moderate to better priced women's clothing discounter, offers savings of 20-50% off regular retail prices. Most of the inventory is traditionally styled, but you can find some contemporary merchandise as well. Suits, sweaters, skirts and pants are available in mostly casual, but some dressy, styles. Brands such as Counterparts, Misty Harbor, Rhoda Lee, Forecaster, Evan Picone, Russ, Liz Claiborne, Cos Cob and Campus Casuals can be found. I recently purchased a wool blazer here for $49.99, regularly $100. Gives refunds. M-Sat 10-6, Sun 12-6. Accepts checks, MC, Visa & Discover.

CLOTHING CORNER OUTLET
4734 E. Main St., Columbus, 43213, 864-7044

Save 50-60% on first quality women's apparel in sizes 4-18. Occasionally larger sizes are carried. Sportswear and dresses from such popular manufacturers as Liz Claiborne and Peter Popovich can be found here. The store also stocks quality boutique type infant and children's clothes by such brands as Oshkosh, Martha's Miniatures and Tickle Me at 50-75% savings. The inventory consists of end of the season merchandise, manufacturer closeouts, as well as buyouts from boutiques and other stores which are going out of business. The children's clothing is exceptional. Don't miss this store! Gives refunds. Th-F 11-6, Sat 10-5, Sun 12-5. Accepts checks and cash only.

CLOTHING GO ROUND (FORMERLY CLOSET CLASSICS)
265 S. 21 St., Newark, 43055, 344-8082

Moderate to better quality children's clothing is available at this resale shop in sizes newborn to 16. You'll also find a small selection of maternity clothes and children's accessories such as car seats and walkers. Savings are about 30-60% off "if new" prices on the gently used merchandise. This business is in an older home across form the entrance to the Indian Mound State Park. All sales are final. Tu-F 10-5, Sat 10-4. Accepts checks and cash only.

CLOTHING WAREHOUSE
3971 Hoover Rd., Grove City, 43123, 875-0977
1920 Mitchell Blvd., Springfield, 45502, (513) 399-3648

First quality, moderate to designer quality women's apparel by Skyr, Gordon of Philadelphia, Act I, Breckinridge, Albert Nippon, Maggy Boutique, Joanie Char and others is available in sizes 6-44. You'll find casual and formal wear as samples, overstocks and special purchases from salesmen. manufacturers and boutiques. Savings are 20-60% off regular retail prices. The inventory is priced at $15-$80 with most being under $50. You will find simple polyester garments to high fashion exclusive boutique items in casual, career and after five wear. The Springfield site carries similar merchandise in addition to men's clothes, tennis clothes and occasionally children's wear. Look throughout the whole store as this business initially gives the appearance of offering only traditional styles. On my recent visit, I purchased a polyester/cotton knit skirt/top set that was highly embellished with lace, sequins and appliques, for only $39 which I will wear to a friend's wedding. Gives exchanges only. M-W 10-6, Th and F 10-7, Sat 10-5, Sun 12-5. Accepts checks, MC & Visa.

CRICKETEER FOR HER
4600 Tiedman Rd., Brooklyn, 44144, (216) 941-3323

First quality women's suits and casual attire are available at savings of 50% off regular retail prices at this manufacturer's outlet store. Gives exchanges only. W 11-6, Th and F 11-9, Sat 9-5, Sun 12-6. Accepts checks, MC & Visa.

DAN HOWARD'S MATERNITY FACTORY OUTLET
2100 Morse Rd., Columbus, 43229, 846-1955

Quality contemporary maternity wear is available at savings of 20-50% of manufacturer's suggested retail prices and comparable prices for similar merchandise in other stores. This factory direct business operates 90 stores throughout the country and sells 80% of their stock as merchandise which was made in their factories, and 20% of their stock as private label goods made by other manufacturers for these stores. All of the inventory bears the Dan Howard Maternity label. The first quality stock is available in sizes 4-20 and includes casual and career wear, lingerie and bathing suits. Gives refunds on non-sale items. Accepts checks, MC, Visa, AmExp & Discover. M,Tu,F,Sat 10-6; W, Th 10-9, Sun 12-5.

DEJA VU
11 N. State St., Westerville, 43081, 890-1130

Quality branded men's, women's and children's clothing (to size 22) and accessories are offered here at savings of 30-60% below "if new" prices. This consignment shop offers fashions from Gloria Vanderbilt, J.,H Collectibles, Halston, Polly Flinders, Mariea Kim, Izod, Oshkosh, Calvin Klein and others. Some new salesmen's samples of Europa Skiwear are offered at savings of about 50% off retail. All sales are final unless a 24 hour approval is requested. M-F 10-8, Sat 10-6. Accepts checks, MC & Visa.

DE'ROMEO'S EXCLUSIVES
1097 Mt. Vernon Ave., Columbus, 43203, 253-9001
Another site in the same area will be opened in the summer of 1991

De'Romeo is a talented artist who creates custom airbrushed and silkscreened designs on tee-shirts, sweatshirts and other articles of clothing. While he specializes in whimsical African-American images, he can create most any design for you from a magazine picture or a snapshot. Or, you can leave it to his imagination. He has some finished items in the store and an ample supply of clothing blanks waiting to be painted. Or, you can supply your own clothes for him to design upon. The cost is $20 to paint the front of your tee-shirt or sweatshirt, $45 to paint both the front and back of your denim jacket or $35 to paint just the back of your denim jacket. Glitzy embellishments such as rhinestones or studs are extra. These prices are applicable when you supply the garment. Add a few dollars extra for using his clothes. De'Romeo can generally have your work completed within two days. M-Sat 11-8, Sun 12-5. Accepts checks, MC & Visa.

DOTS
3467 Cleveland Ave., Columbus, 43224, 447-8855
4103 W. Broad St., Columbus, 43228, 272-2225
1017 Bechtle Ave., Springfield, 45501, (513) 322-3687
596 N. Lexington-Springmill Rd., Mansfield, 44901,(419) 529-6465
1733 N. Memorial, Lancaster, 43130, 653-3727

Junior, missy and plus sized women's apparel is sold at $10 and under. The stock consists of first quality overstocks of budget to moderate quality casual and dressy wear in addition to lingerie and accessories. Gives refunds. M-Sat 10-9, Sun 12-5. Accepts checks, MC & Visa.

DRESS BARN
7624 New Market Center Way, Columbus, 43235, 764-0557
5610 Cleveland Ave., Columbus, 43231, 882-5533
3654 Soldano Blvd.,Consumer Sq. W., Columbus 43228,279-2935
6464 Tussing Ave., Reynoldsburg, 43068, 863-0041

Save 20-50% off current, first quality fashion merchandise by such popular manufacturers as Jonathan Martin, Dawn Joy, Carole Little, Liz Claiborne, Jennifer Reed and others. You will find moderate to better quality career and casual attire in addition to accessories. Ask about the free in store wardrobe seminars. Provides layaway. Gives refunds. M-Sat 10-9, Sun 12-5. Accepts checks, MC, Visa, AmExp & Discover

DRESS BARN WOMAN
7624 New Market Center Way, Columbus, 43235, 764-0557
5610 Cleveland Ave., Columbus, 43231, 882-5533
3654 Soldano Blvd.,Consumer Sq. W., Columbus 43228,279-2935
6464 Tussing Ave., Reynoldsburg, 43068, 863-0041

The fashion conscious large sized woman can find savings of 20-50% off regular retail prices on a large selection of career and casual wear and accessories. Sizes range from 14-24. The selections are moderate to better quality. Inquire about their free in store wardrobe seminars. Provides layaway. Gives refunds. M-Sat 10-9, Sun 12-5. Accepts checks, MC, Visa, AmExp & Discover.

E.S.P. FASHIONS
C/O Emmanuel Sutton (Peaches), 475-3335, 475-3753

Custom designed clothes for the fashion conscious woman in regular and large sizes are available from this friendly designer. She can also design clothes for teens and people with disabilities. Peaches has an assortment of fabrics or you may supply her with your favorite store bought material. The craftsmanship is excellent and the prices are very reasonable. Dresses begin at $25. Peaches also makes house calls. By appointment only. Accepts checks and cash only.

EAGLE CLOTHES
7645 New Market Center Way, Columbus 43235, 766-6329

This is the outlet for the Eagle Clothing company which has been in the manufacturing business for over 75 years. Eagle brand suits are sold in some of the finest specialty and department stores across the country. You'll find first quality, moderate to designer labels of other manufacturers, in addition to their own merchandise, at savings of 20-50% off retail. The store runs frequent sales where savings are even greater. On a recent trip here, my husband purchased a $25 silk tie for $12.50 and an Oleg Cassini raincoat with a zip out lining for $159 regularly $260. Brands stocked include Egon Von Furstenburg, Botany 500 and others. Gives refunds. Discount to seniors. M-Sat 10-9, Sun 12-6. Accepts checks, MC, Visa & AmExp.

ECLECTIC FASHION ALTERNATIVES
3139 N. High St., Columbus, 43202, 267-2900

Upscale men's consignment shop sells Hickey Freeman, Botany 500, Armani, Boss, Ferre, Corneliani and other quality brands of suits, slacks, sportswear, shirts, sweaters and silk ties. There is also a large selection of European Designer merchandise from Gianni, a Short North men's store. The regular price on the merchandise would be about $50-$1000, but here, the prices are about $7-$225. So, savings can amount to about 50-85%. The merchandise is in top shape and the decor is simplistic chic. The store will also accept your consigned, gently used clothes. On a recent visit, I almost purchased an Ultrasuede sportcoat for my husband for only $50, but was disappointed when I found out that it was not his size. If you are seeking contemporary, better quality and designer men's wear, this shop is not to be missed. This store has earned the distinction of being one of my personal favorites. All sales are final. M-Sat 11-6. Accepts checks and cash only.

THE ENCORE SHOP
1811 W. 5 Ave., Columbus, 43212, 486-5647

Men's, women's and children's gently used clothing is available at this upscale consignment shop. A limited amount of new salesmen's samples, as well as used toys and women's accessories, is also available. Savings are about 30-80% off "if new" or manufacturers suggested retail prices. Some brands I have found here include Jones New York, Evan Picone, Izod and Polly Flinders. Offers a 24 hour approval policy on purchases. Tu-F 10-6, Sat 10-5. Accepts checks and cash only.

FAMOUS SPORTSWEAR
2060 Hardy Pkwy., Grove City, 43123, 875-8180
23 S. Main St., London, 43140, 1-852-2957

Overstocks,.misprints and erroneously colored designs are sold by this factory outlet which is in the custom screen printing business. You'll find college, fraternity and business logos, as well as decorative designs emblazened on windbreakers, tee shirts, sweatshirts, caps and anything which is printable. There are items for men, women and children. Savings are 30-60% off the price of comparable products. In mid September, the business features a gigantic, 2 day tent sale at the Grove City location. You should note that some of these items are not generally offered for sale through typical retail operations. All sales are final. M-F 8-5. Accepts checks, MC & Visa.

FASHION FACTORY OUTLET
2543 Reynolds Plaza, Sylvania, 43560, (419) 882-8073

Sells first quality closeouts of famous maker women's clothing such as Kenneth, Evan Picone, Campus Casuals and Misty Harbor. Savings are 40-70% off regular retail prices. Gives refunds. M-Sat 10-9, Sun 12-6. Accepts checks, MC & Visa

FASHIONS 4 KIDS
5835 Scarborough Mall, Columbus, 43232, 575-0122
7208 New Market Center Way, Columbus, 43235, 792-2715

Salesmen's samples comprise a large portion of the inventory at these stores and are marked at 40-50% off regular retail prices. The stores specialize in pageant and party dresses, but also sell casual clothes at similar savings. The boutique type garments are certainly eyecatchers. You can find infant through size 16 for boys and girls. Some of the brands offered include Martha Miniatures, Weather Tamer, Pazaaz, Ruth Of California, Miss Nannette and Donmoor. The merchandise is all first quality. Gives refunds. M-F 10-9, Sat 10-7. Accepts checks, MC, Visa, AmExp & Discover. (Also see We're 4 Kids in this chapter)

$5 AND $10 APPAREL
3350 Cleveland Ave., Columbus, 43224, 267-6501
3493 Great Western Blvd., Columbus, 43204, 274-4811
189 S. High St., Columbus, 43215, 221-9575
59 W. Schrock Rd., Westerville, 43081, 523-1028
3700 E. Broad St., Town and Country Shpng. Ctr., Columbus, 43213, 237-8888

Moderate to better quality misses, junior and large size women's apparel is available at savings of 30-60% off regular retail prices. You'll find casual and career styles in such popular brands as Pierre Cardin, Details, L.A. Gear, Barrie Stevens and Outback Red (The Limited's private brand) in sizes 6-22. The merchandise consists of first quality overstocks, discontinued and special purchases. Gives refunds. M-Sat 10-9, Sun 12-5. Accepts checks, MC & Visa.

5,10, 15, 20 PLACE
63 Graceland Blvd., Columbus, 43214, 436-4026
3644 Fishinger Blvd., Market At Mill Run, Hilliard, 43026, 876-2176
3841 East Broad Street, Town and Country Shpg. Ctr., Columbus, 43213, 237-6764

Everything in this store is priced at $5, $10, $15 or $20 with some accessories priced at 2 or 3 items for $5. Junior and missy first quality(and some irregular) merchandise is available at savings of 20-60% off regular retail prices. The merchandise is current season goods. The inventory consists of overstocks, overruns and discontinued items. You will find such brands as Forenza and Outback Red (the Limited's private labels),Pasta, One Step Up and others. In addition to clothes, you'll find jewelry, panties, barrettes, socks and occasionally purses and tote bags. This 53 store chain is a division of Paul Harris. Provides layaway. Gives refunds. M-Sat 10-9, Sun 12-5. Accepts checks, MC, Visa & Discover.

THE GAP OUTLET STORE
3433 Mineola Pike, Florence, Ky., 41042, (606) 283-1100

Customer returns, irregulars and overstock items from Hemisphere, Banana Republic, The Gap and The Gap Kids stores can be found at savings of 30-60% off regular retail prices. Florence, Kentucky is only 20 minutes from Cincinnati. Gives refunds. M-W 9-6, Th and F 9-9, Sat 10-4. Accepts checks, Mc & Visa.

GENERAL MERCHANDISE SALES
13690 E. Broad St., Pataskala, 43062, 927-7073

6,000 square feet of surplus military type goods includes coveralls, heavy duty socks, sleeping bags, mess kits, books and what-not. The new and used quality merchandise is available at savings of about 10-40% off comparable retail prices. Gives exchanges. M-Sat 10-7, Sun 12-5. Accepts checks, MC, Visa & Discover.

GENTRY SHOPS
1000 Morse Rd.,Gentry Plaza, Columbus 43229, 436-2288
2716 Brice Rd., Brice Pk. Shpg. Ctr., Reynoldsburg, 43068, 759-0077

Gentlemen in all shapes and sizes can save 30-50% off dress and sport attire and accessories in popular and designer brands. Suits, ties, belts, socks, sweaters, shirts and jackets are offered in sizes up to 52 and include regular, short, long, extra long, big man and athletic cuts. Tailors are on premises who offer prompt alterations at a nominal cost. On a recent visit, I spotted an all weather trench coat with a zip out lining for $159 regularly $265, a wool fisherman's sweater for $45 regularly $95, handmade Italian silk ties for $22 regularly $45 and a worsted wool suit for $205 regularly $435. The Brice Road location has a permanent backroom sale at all times, in which merchandise from all of their stores is greatly reduced. You'll save 50-80%. Due to the nature of this clearance area, a particular style may not be available in all sizes, but there is an enormous selection from which to choose. This off priced retailer buys tail end inventory from manufacturers, which is a small amount of merchandise considered to be remaining stock that hasn't been sold to other stores. Some of the labels have been removed from garments. Their annual March warehouse sale, often held at the Ohio State Fairgrounds, offers savings are up to 70% off regular retail prices. Provides layaway. Gives refunds on unaltered garments. M-Sat 10-9:30, Sun 12-6. Accepts checks, MC, Visa, AmExp & Discover.

GRAND FINALE
1-800-637-7714

Please note: this is not the same as Madison's Grand Finale. Save 10-60% off regular retail prices on quality, discontinued clothing, accessories and gift items previously offered in the Horchow Collection and Trifles catalogues. A one year's subscription to the Grand Finale catalogue costs $3, which will entitle you 6 issues plus a $5 gift certificate to use on your next purchase. However, if you make at least one purchase, you will get the next year's subscription for free. You will find Gucci, Spode, Horchow, Wedgewood, Reed and Barton, Christian Dior, Lane, Perry Ellis, Adrienne Vittadini plus other brands represented. Gives refunds. M-F 9-5. Accepts checks, MC, Visa & AmExp.

HAND MOTION
3990 Fisher Rd., Columbus, 43228, 279-8050

First quality overstocks of better screen printed tee shirts and sweatshirts are available through this custom screen printer. You'll also find a small selection of slight misprints. Tee shirts are priced at $3 and sweatshirts are priced at $5 regardless of whether it is an adult or child's article of clothing.   The designs include corporate names, festival advertisements and the like. The selection is small but worth the trip. All sales are final. M-F 9-5. Accepts checks and cash only.

HANES, L'EGGS FACTORY OUTLET
Showcase of Savings, POB 748, Rural Hall, N C. 27098

This mail order factory outlet can save you 50% off the price of regular and large sized pantyhose which is slightly imperfect due to color variations from their standard hues, or a slight change in the panty knit. None of the imperfections will affect the durability of the hose. Knee highs, control top, support, ultra sheer and other types are available. Write to request a free flyer. Accepts checks, MC & Visa.

HIT OR MISS
2025 Henderson Rd., Columbus, 43220, 451-0628
7648 New Market Center Way, Columbus, 43235, 766-0981
4428 Crossroads Ctr., Crossroads Shpg. Ctr., Columbus, 43232, 864-3967
2707 Northland Plaza Dr., Columbus, 43229, 523-1786
3760 E. Broad St., Town and Country Shpg,. Ctr., Columbus, 43213, 237-8090
121 N. High St., Columbus, 43215, 461-0550

Moderate to better quality missy, junior and petite fashions are value priced at savings of 20-50% off regular retail prices. You'll find such brands as Sasson, Kasper, Jonathan Martin, Leau Vive, Nilani and others. Accessories are similarly discounted. The store stocks casual and career wear. Provides layaway. Gives refunds. M-Sat 10-9, Sun 12-5. Accepts checks, MC, Visa, AmExp & Discover.

HUNTINGTON CLOTHIERS
1285 Alum Creek Dr., Columbus, 43209, 252-4422

Traditional styling in quality men's apparel, is available at this retail store and mail order outlet. Dress shorts, suits, ties, trousers, sweaters, belts, outerwear as well as formalwear and related items, are available in such sought after fabrics as Oxford cloth and Pinpoint Oxford in 100% cotton and 60/40 blends, Egyptian cotton broadcloth, worsted wool blends, wool gabardine, silk, camel hair, alpaca, shetlands, Belgian linen and silk/wool blends. The store carries such brands as Ruff Hewn, Boston Traders and Huntington Clothiers. Savings are about 15-45% on first quality goods. The store has a *Rear Door Clearance Sale* in an adjacent warehouse on a quarterly basis in which savings are up to 90%. The merchandise there consists of overstocks, overruns and some irregular goods. *Rear Door Store* sales are final. Call to be added to their mailing list. Retail store hours are M-F 10-6, Sat 10-5, Sun 12-5. Accepts checks, MC, Visa, AmExp & Diners Club.

JUST FOR KIDS
30 E. Liberty St., Powell, 43065, 846-1333

Sells gently used consigned toys and clothing for sizes infant-14. The quality merchandise includes such popular brands as Oshkosh, Ocean Pacific and Fisher-Price. This business also offers rentals of baby equipment such as car seats and high chairs. Has a 24 hour approval policy on returns. M-Sat 10-6. Accepts checks and cash only.

KIDS MART
871 Bethel Rd., Columbus, 43214, 451-0665

Funky children's clothing and accessories are sold at 20-60% off regular retail prices. You'll find first quality merchandise by Health-Tex, Hobie, Gitano, Ocean Pacific and other popular brands. Gives refunds. M-Sat 10-9, Sun 12-5. Accepts checks, MC, Visa, AmExp & Discover.

KIDS QUARTERS
37 E. Main St., Shelby, 44875, (419) 342-4453

Gently used children's clothes in sizes newborn to 12 are available at this resale shop. You'll also find used children's furniture, bedding, bottles, toys, shoes and related accessories. Top quality brands such as Martha's Miniatures, Little Tykes, Fisher-Price,

Jenny Lind, Cosco and others are available. Savings are about 50-70% off "if new" prices. Shelby is about 15 minutes north of Mansfield. Gives refunds. Tu-F 9-5, Sat 10-3. Accepts checks and cash only.

KIDS R US
4360 W. Broad St., Columbus, 43228, 274-7766
1700 Morse Rd., Columbus 43229, 841-1600
2560 S. Hamilton Rd., Columbus, 43232, 759-9422
6525 Sawmill Rd., Dublin, 43017, 793-0405

The world's largest clothing store for kids features sizes newborn to 20 in regular, chubby and husky sizes. First quality, name brands such as Hanes, Levi's, Bugle Boy, Health-Tex, Oshkosh, Ocean Pacific, French Toast, Le Tigre, Justin Charles and others are offered at savings of 20-50% off suggested retail prices. Don't overlook their socks, hairclips, backpacks and other necessities at similar savings. Provides layaway. Gives refunds. M-Sat 10-9, Sun 10:30-5. Accepts checks, MC, Visa, AmExp & Discover.

KIDSWARE HOUSE
122 N. Broadway, Spencerville, 45887, (419) 647-4063

This outlet store is owned and operated by Maristan Manufacturing, which produces the Allison Scott For Spencerville line of children's wear. Savings are 10-25% off regular retail prices on merchandise in sizes infant to 14. Play sets regularly $20-$24 are about $16-$20 here. Gives exchanges only. M, T, W, F, Sat 9:30-5; Th 9:30-12 noon, Sun 9:30-1. Accepts checks, MC & Visa.

KUPPENHEIMER
2886 S. Hamilton Rd., Columbus, 43232, 864-4122
2203 Morse Rd., Columbus, 43229, 471-7677
6238 Sawmill Rd., Dublin, 43017, 793-9901

You can find quality men's suits, slacks and sport coats here in all fabrics ranging from wools, wool blends, poplin, silk blends and more. Savings are about 20% less than what you would expect to pay for a comparable product elsewhere. The Kuppenheimer label only appears in retail stores bearing its name. However, the company designs and manufactures career apparel for Delta Airlines, the Shriners and Realtors. Pick up a free copy of the flyer which shows several different ways to knot a tie such as the Half Windsor, the Four In Hand and the Bow Tie. Offers rock bottom prices on alterations of garments purchased in their stores. Or, you can bring in your clothes from another store and let them alter it for you. If you choose this latter option, you will pay double the alteration price, which is still 25% lower than having the alteration done elsewhere. Gives refunds,. M-F 10-9, Sat 9-9, Sun 12-5. Accepts checks, MC, Visa, & Discover.

L J FASHIONS
76 Parsons Ave., Columbus, 43215, 224-4761

High fashion women's business, special occasion and casual wear can be found in this off the beaten path boutique. The current season, first quality merchandise from American and European designers, is sold at about 25-30% below regular retail prices. There are many one of a kind items. Sizes range from 6-22. The clothes are very distinctive and unlike most which I have encountered in Columbus. A limited selection of men's and women's accessories is also available at similar savings. The owner is an extremely friendly and accommodating salesman. Provides layaway. Gives exchanges only. M-Sat 12-8. Accepts checks, MC & Visa.

LOEHMAN'S
2755 Southern Chardon Rd., Willoughby Hills, 44094, (216) 944-0633
11974 Lebanon Rd., Sharonville, 45241, (513) 563-4111

This is the original off-price ladies clothing store, which started in Brooklyn, New York, over 50 years ago. This nationwide chain features a simplistic atmosphere in which fashion aficionados can save 30-50% and more off regular retail prices. Many of the manufacturers' labels have been removed, but don't let that disturb you. The quality workmanship of their offerings is very obvious. You will find sizes ranging from 2-16, in casual and elegant apparel, and a large selection of purses, belts, jewelry and related accessories. Moderate to couture manufacturers' inventory is represented here. Patience is a virtue and it will definitely pay off here as you sort through the racks and shelves of merchandise. Gives exchanges only. M, Tu and Sat 10-5:30, W-F 10-9, Sun 12-5. Accepts checks, Mc, Visa and AmExp.

MADISON COMMONS FACTORY DIRECT STORES
I-70 and State Rte. 29, W. Jefferson (scheduled to open in April 1992)

The newest outlet center to open in Central Ohio will feature 50 manufacturer direct stores such as American Tourister, Aileen, Gitano, Bass, Van Heusen, Izod, Jordache, West Point Pepperell, the Paper Factory, Kids Express, Aussie Outback, S&K Famous Brands, Geoffrey Beane, Bugle Boy, Sweatshirt Factory, Old Mill, Rolane Lingerie, Capezio Shoes, Socks Galore, Prestige Fragrances(division of Revlon), Boston Traders, Ribbon Outlet, Mikasa, Wallet Works, Wemco Ties, Banister Shoes, Miki's Designer Separates, Cape Isle Knitters, Warner-Olga, Hathaway, Hanes L'eggs, Kitchen Collection, Westport (division of the Dress Barn), Toy Liquidators and others. At the time I spoke with the developer, I was told that he is in the process of negotiating leases with several upscale businesses, but could not mention names until the leases are signed. The strip type shopping center will feature 222,000 square feet and measures 1/2 mile from end to end. Savings will be 30-80%. Follow the newspapers or subscribe to the Bargain Hunting In Columbus Newsletter (see section on books) to learn more about this exciting shopping experience.

MADISON'S GRAND FINALE
2819 Festival Lane, the Festival At Sawmill Shpng. Ctr., Dublin, 43017, 764-1757

Clearance merchandise from 23 stores is consolidated at this business which is owned and operated by Madison's. You'll find upscale and designer contemporary women's fashions in sizes 4-18, in casual, career and evening wear. Accessories including belts, jewelry, purses and scarves are also available. A small selection of men's shirts and ties an also be found. You'll recognize the famous brands such as Carole Little For St. Tropez West, Adrienne Vittadini, Gregge Sport, Patty O'Neill, Liz Claiborne, Oscar de la Renta, Jennifer Reed, Anne Klein and others. The first quality merchandise is available at savings of 40-60% off regular retail prices. You'll also be delighted at the store's full range of sizes in each style, the neatly maintained stock as well as the courteous and fashion conscious sales staff. This store has earned the distinction of being one of my personal favorites. All sales are final. M-Sat 10-9, Sun 12-6. Accepts checks, MC, Visa & Madison's charges.

MAMA BEAR'S MATERNITY
36 W. Columbus St., Pickerington, 43147, 833-2327

Current season, upscale maternity clothing is available at this resale shop. The prices are about 50-75% lower than if you were to purchase the merchandise new. Dresses, suits, pants and shirts are available in Motherhood, JCKU, Mothercare, Recreations, Puccini and other quality brands. There is a limited amount of new merchandise available at similar savings which is obtained from store buyouts. As an added surprise, the store will buy back the clothes from you after you have finished using them, provided that they are in salable condition. This is the only shop in Central Ohio to exclusively sell maternity clothes. Over 800 pieces are in stock at all times. Gives refunds. T, Th, F, Sat10-5, W 10-7. Accepts checks, MC, Visa & Discover.

MARED CONSIGNMENTS
3510 N. High St., Columbus, 43214, 267-6181

Gently used women's apparel and accessories are available at this consignment store at savings of 30-50% off "if new" prices. The store also sells salesmen's samples and end of the season merchandise from boutiques across the state at similar savings. The moderate to haute couture quality casual, career, wedding and formal wear is available in such brands as Albert Nippon, Ann Taylor, Diane Von Furstenburg, Oleg Cassini, Adrienne Vittadini, Ultrasuede, Anne Klein and others. It is not unusual to find dresses valued at $800-$1000 here for a fraction of the price. You'll find costume and fine jewelry, shoes, hats, gloves, purses, evening bags, scarves and belts. All sales are final. M,Tu,Th,F 11-6; W 11-7; Sat 10-4. Accepts checks, MC, Visa & AmExp.

MARSHALL'S
805 Bethel Rd, Columbus, 43214, 451-5486
2300 S. Hamilton Rd., Columbus, 43232, 863-0189
2681 Northland Plaza, Columbus, 43231, 794-1017

The inventory consists largely of manufacturer's overruns and special purchases of men's, women's and children's apparel and accessories, shoes for the family, linens, designer fragrances for men and women, giftware, lingerie and leather goods at savings of 20-60% off regular retail prices. You'll find missy, junior, petite, large and pre-teen sizes. Moderate to designer quality can be found in such brands as Chaus, Diane Von Furstenburg, John Henry, Liz Claiborne, Adolfo, Pierre Cardin Jasmine, 9 West, Bass, Stacy Adams. Bugle Boy and others. While most of the inventory is first quality, the irregulars are clearly marked. Provides layaway. Gives refunds. M-Sat 9:30-9:30, Sun 12-6. Accepts checks, MC, Visa AmExp and Discover.

MONA LISA
55 S. High St., Dublin, 43017, 764-0509

Gently used women's apparel is available at savings of 50-80% off "if new" prices. This consignment shop sells upscale and designer merchandise in sizes 4-18, by such popular brands as Liz Claiborne and Nilani. All sales are final. Tu 10:30-7:30; M, W-Sat 10-5:30. Accepts checks and cash only.

MOSTLY KIDS STUFF
3087 W. Broad St., Columbus, 43204, 272-2887

New and used children's clothing in sizes newborn to 14, is sold at 50% off the regular retail price. New Polly Flinders dresses, Health-Tex, Brian and Oshkosh brands are often available here. New and used cribs, car seats and bedding can also be found at savings of about 20-30% off. Provides layaway. Gives exchanges only. M-Th 12-6, F 1-6, Sat 12-7. Accepts checks.

NEARLY NEW SHOP
3667 E. Broad St., Columbus, 43213, 231-7861

This nonprofit resale shop offers clothing, books, toys and housewares at savings of 60-95% off "if new" prices. While the inventory is a mixture of quality, the careful shopper will not overlook an inch of this store. On a recent visit, I spotted a curly lamb jacket for $40, a genuine Gucci cosmetic bag for $5, an ultra-suede dress for $40, and a stuffed animal in khaki attire for $3. Provides layaway. All sales are final. M-Sat 10-6. Accepts checks, MC, Visa , AmExp & Discover.

$9.99 STOCKROOM
7680 New Market Center Way, Columbus, 43235, 889-5724

This is their only location in Columbus. The majority of the missy and junior clothes are priced at $9.99 with values to $32, a savings of about 20-50% off regular retail prices. The merchandise is first quality, contemporary casualwear and related separates suitable for work or play. My recent purchase included a metallic marblized button down shirt and matching pants, and a tie-dyed tee-shirt and matching leggings, each priced at $9.99. This business also operates stores in Lima, Sandusky and Findlay, Ohio. Gives refunds. M-Sat 10-9, Sun 12-5. Accepts checks, Mc, Visa, AmExp & Discover.

NINTH STREET BRIDAL CLEARANCE CENTER
Scarborough Mallway, Columbus, 43232, 863-1010

Wedding and formal gowns are priced at $10-$39 and veils at $19. This is the clearance site for the Ninth Street Wedding and Formal Outlet mentioned directly below this description. The prices at this outlet reflect a savings of 75-95% off retail prices. All sales are final. Accepts, checks, MC & Visa. Sat only 12-4.

NINTH STREET WEDDING AND FORMAL OUTLET
5843 Scarborough Mallway, Columbus, 43232, 863-1010

Moderate to better quality bridal gowns, prom dresses, veils, formal and special occasion wear are offered at savings of 40-60% off regular retail prices. The inventory consists of manufacturers' closeouts, showroom samples and store buyouts in sizes 6-22 1/2. Some petite garments are also available. Brands offered include Priscilla, Alfred Angelo, Milady and Piccione. Also see the listing above for their clearance center. Gives exchanges only. M-Sat 10-9, Sun 12-5. Accepts checks, MC & Visa.

NORTH AMERICAN KNITTING COMPANY
490 Dewey Ave., Mansfield, 44901, (419) 524-1112

Upscale and designer knitted women's clothing are available at this manufacturer's outlet. The company creates merchandise for Castleberry, Pendleton, Andrea Jovine and other quality brands. The stock consists of first quality, samples, prior season, irregular and seconds in sizes 4-20. Some petite sizes are also offered. Savings are 50% and more off regular retail prices. U.P.S. delivery and phone orders are also available. Tu-Th 12-5, Sat 9-12 once per month during special sales. Write to the company to be added to their mailing list as the sales are by invitation only. All sales are final.

NOW AND THEN CLASSICS
3575 E. Livingston Ave., Livingston Ct. Flea Market, Booth #105, Columbus, 43227, no phone

A small, but unique selection of handmade sequin/beaded pins are priced at $5-$35, with most being in the $12-$20 range. These very decorative wearables can be pinned onto most any type of dress or sweater to add instant glitz! and come in a range of abstract, geometric, floral and other motifs, with clusters of dangling seed beads at the bottom. The value lies in the pin's versatility. It allows you to instantly transform an ordinary garment into a fancy party wearable. If you've priced glitzy sweaters and dresses, you know how costly these can be. Your minimal investment in one of these pins, will enable you to have many such items at whim, simply by pinning on the glitz! The business also offers a small, but unusual selection of vintage clothes and accessories, many of which are embellished with beads or sequins. These are available at regular vintage shop prices. The owner, Julia, is a friendly and accommodating salesperson who is eager to please. Gives exchanges. F and Sat 12-7, Sun 1-5. Accepts checks and cash only.

NU LOOK FACTORY OUTLET
5080 Sinclair Rd., Columbus, 43229, 885-4936

This manufacturer owned and operated store sells first quality men's suits, sportcoats and slacks at savings of about 30-50% less than the same products in other stores. Nu Look makes suits for Lazarus, J.C. Penney's and other department and speciality stores across the country with that store's own labels sewn into the garments. At Nu Look, these same garments, 200,000 in 142 different styles, have the Gino Capelli, Barryton and Elmhurst labels. You'll find wool, wool blends, silk and polyester fabrics in traditional and contemporary styles. Sizes 36-52, short to extra long, are available. The alteration department offers value prices on repairs of clothes purchased in the store as well as those men's and women's garments which were purchased elsewhere. The prices include $4.50 to cuff pants, $4-$6 for hems, $6 to take in the waist and the seat. Other types of alterations are also available. The tailor is open Monday-Friday from 11-6 and can be reached at 436-2135. Store hours are M-F 10-7, Sat 10-6. Accepts checks, MC & Visa.

OHIO KNITTING MILLS
4735 W. 150 St., Cleveland, 44135, (216) 881-4646 or (216) 267-1295

This manufacturer of better updated sweaters, creates private label merchandise for department stores and national mail order catalogues. Savings are 70-80% off retail prices of $60-$110. There's junior, missy and large sized women's clothes and some men's, in natural, cotton and novelty fibers. Gives exchanges. M-Sat 10-5. Accepts checksMC ,Visa.

OLD MILL LADIES SPORTSWEAR OUTLET
7588 New Market Center Way, Columbus, 43235, 889-9552

Missy, petite and large women's sportswear in sizes 4-18, is offered at savings of 20%-30% off regular retail prices. You'll find first quality Country Suburbans and Weathervane brands in addition to others. This factory outlet store carries mostly updated classical styles, in a variety of fabrics, for casual and career wear. Offers layaways. Gives refunds. M-Sat 10-9, Sun 12-5. Accepts checks, MC & Visa.

ONCE UPON A CHILD
55 S. High St., Dublin, 43017, 761-8488
320 S. State St., Westerville, 43081, 899-6654
1903 Northwest Blvd., Columbus, 43212,488-8806
2378 E. Main St.,Bexley, 43209, 236-5550
897 High St., Worthington, 43085, 885-0885
471 Morrison Rd., Gahanna, 43230, 337-0200

Quality used children's toys, accessories and clothes are available here at savings of 30-70% below "if new" prices. Brands such as Oshkosh, Ocean Pacific, Health-Tex, Youthland, Rothschild and more, in sizes newborn to 14, fill these stores. Occasionally some new merchandise is sold at similar savings. Gives exchanges only. Tu-Sat 11-4. Accepts checks and cash.

ONE MORE TIME
1521 W. 5 Ave., Columbus 43212, 486-0031

Gently used quality clothes are sold at savings of 40-70% off department store prices "if new". Some new garments and accessories are also available at similar savings. It's not unusual to find a leather skirt, an ultrasuede suit, or other designer garments by such brands as Nippon, Tahari and Liz Claiborne. This store sells mostly high fashion apparel although you'll find quite a few classic styles as well. Sizes carried are 4-46. A limited amount of maternity and men's clothes are also available at similar savings. Don't miss the $5 rack in the center of the store. This upscale women's consignment shop also sells accessories such as jewelry, belts and purses and a small selection of gift items. The store features its annual sidewalk sale in early August, where savings are 75% and more. Don't miss this store! It has earned the distinction of being one of my personal favorites. All sales are final. T-F 12-6, Sat 10-6. Accepts checks, MC, Visa & Discover.

ONE PRICE $7
6452 Tussing Rd., Consumer Square, Reynoldsburg, 43068, 868-1818
3445 Cleveland Ave., Northern Lights Shpng. Ctr., Columbus, 43224, 267-3200
3892 E. Broad St., Town & Country Shpng. Ctr., Columbus, 43213, 236-5200
959 Hebron Rd., Crosscreek Shpng. Ctr., Heath, 43056,522-2927
1246 Park Ave., Kingsgate Mall, Mansfield, 44901, (419) 529-2133
3898 Linden Ave., Dayton, 45432, (513) 256-9841
4394 Eastgate Sq. Dr., Cincinnati, 45245, (513) 753-5506

Everything in this store is priced at $7 each or several items for $7. You'll find moderate and some better quality junior, missy and large size women's apparel, as well as hair accessories, socks 5/$7, fashion jewelry 3/$7, sunglasses 3/$7, by such brands as Gitano, Cherokee, Prima Class and Carmel. A limited selection of children's apparel, in sizes 4-

14, is also available. The inventory is first quality and includes mostly casual wear. Prices are about 30-60% less than manufacturer's suggested retail prices. Gives refunds. M-Sat 10-9, Sun 12-6. Accepts checks, MC & Visa.

OUR GANG SHOP
2681 E. Main St., Columbus, 43209, 231-1773

This New York style retailer sells salesman's samples and other stock at 20-60% off regular retail prices. Also check out their clearance racks for out of season merchandise at substantial savings. They specialize in casual and school clothes in sizes infant through teens, and also offer a selection of funky accessories. The merchandise is all current season and first quality. You'll find such brands as E.J. Gitano, Spumoni, Gino Venucci , Marcel and others. Sizes carried in the store are newborn to 20 and even some junior/pre-teen clothes. Gives exchanges only. M-Sat 10-6. Accepts checks, MC & Visa.

OUTLETS LIMITED MALL
5300 Kings Island Dr., Mason, 45034, (513) 398-5532

26 factory outlet stores sell housewares, toys, apparel, shoes and cosmetics at savings of 20-60% off regular retail prices. You'll find the Dress Barn, Famous Footwear, Toy Liquidators, Children's Outlet, Julie's, Linens 'N Things, Prestige Fragrances, Van Heusen, Old Mill, Totes, Hit Or Miss and others. Mason, Ohio is north of Cincinnati, take exit 25 (Kings Island-Mason) off I 71. Return policy and charge acceptance varies from store to store. M-Sat 10-9, Sun 12-5.

J.C. PENNEY OUTLET
2361 Park Crescent Dr., E., Columbus, 43232, 868-0250
8770 Colerain Ave., Cincinnati, 45251, (513) 385-9700

Customer returns, overstocks and past season merchandise from the stores and catalogues are available at savings of 20-80%. You will find furniture, shoes, clothes for the family (including chubby, husky, petite, tall and large sizes in additional to bridal and formal wear), linens, sporting goods, lingerie and gift items. The back corner of the store features an area of customer returns which offer the greatest savings. The J.C. Penney Outlet is the top tourist attraction in Ohio! Gives refunds. M-Sat 10-9, Sun 10-6. Accepts checks, MC, Visa, AmExp & Penney's charge.

POLLY FLINDERS OUTLET
234 E. 8 St., Cincinnati, 45202, (513) 621-3222
Shapely Outlet Center, 2430 E. Kemper Rd., suite 10, Cincinnati, 45241,
(513) 771-7414

This quality children's clothing manufacturer is well known for its darling smocked dresses. Savings are 40-60% off regular retail prices on first quality overstocked merchandise and seconds. A limited amount of children's accessories can be found here at similar savings. Gives exchanges only. M-Sat 10-9, Sun 12-6. Accepts checks, MC, Visa & Discover.

RICHMAN BROTHERS OUTLET STORE
6885 Southland Dr., Middleburg Hts., 44130, (216) 843-6840

Merchandise from over 300 stores throughout the United States ends up in this outlet. You will find first quality current season (but from a previous year) men's and ladies' apparel such as suits, coats, dresses and more. Savings are 50% off regular retail prices. Their only other outlet store in the country is in New Orleans. Gives refunds. M-Sat 10-9, Sun 12-5. Accepts checks, MC, Visa, AmExp & Discover.

S & K FAMOUS BRANDS
2643 Northland Plaza Dr., Columbus, 43231, 794-2407
767 Bethel Rd., Olentangy Plaza, Columbus, 43214, 442-3944
7655 New Market Center Way, Columbus, 43235,764-7435
2078 E. Dorothy Lane, Kettering, 45420, (513) 293-4248

Moderate to better quality menswear is sold at about 30-50% off comparable retail prices. Much of the inventory has the Deansgate and Granby Club labels, which are the store's own brands. S & K is able to sell their quality products so low because they are made by nationally recognized manufacturers who do not sew in the exclusive labels, but instead have S&K's private labels sewn in. These clothes are sold in upscale department and specialty stores throughout the United States under famous brands. Membership in the Premier Club is free and guarantees free alterations for the life of your suit. You just need to pay your initial alteration fee when the suit is purchased. By the way, alterations are budget priced. The store will also alter your clothes which were purchased elsewhere for an additional $2, which still makes their fees lower than in many other businesses. I noticed some Botany 500 and Adolfo suits in the store on my last visit, which were about 30% less than the suggested retail price. You'll find suits, sportcoats, slacks as well as casual wear for gentlemen with discriminating tastes. This chain also operates stores in Milan and Toledo. Gives refunds. M-Sat 10-9, Sun 12-6. Accepts checks, MC & Visa.

SALESMEN'S SAMPLE SALES

Look through the classified ads section at the back of the Columbus Dispatch and the community newspapers to find these great sales. Salespeople who represent different lines of adult and children's clothes, giftware, and purses in budget to designer quality, need to find a way to dispose of these products after their selling season is over, as they have already paid for all of their samples. Sometimes the no longer needed samples are placed in area consignment shops (see other listings for these stores in this chapter), or sold at these salesmen's sales. Savings are generally 40-75% off regular retail prices. Don't expect to find nickle and dime prices typical of other types of garage/home sales. You should be aware that a salesperson's selling season typically ends about 2 months before the merchandise is shipped to the stores which placed the orders. So the merchandise at these sample sales is always suitable for the current or upcoming season. Often, there is a limited size range in garments. When you go to these sales, ask the salesperson if he/she maintains a mailing list, as many do. Scan the newspapers regularly as these sales are held year round. One such group of sales is offered by a person who carries several better and designer children's clothing lines which are sold at boutiques and specialty department stores throughout the country. I can't mention brand names in print, as many ads will reveal. The wholesale prices to you are about $10.50-$45, but the garments retail for about $23-$100. You need to come to her sale in order to be added to her mailing list. The phone number for these boutique sample sales is 965-5555.

SAMPLES ON THE CORNER
2270 E. Main St., Bexley, 43209, 231-0063

Fashion conscious shoppers should run, not walk, to this business which sells handpainted denim jackets, tee shirts, silks, dresses and other items, many of which are also embellished with embroidery, leather and lots of glitzy doodads. This is the factory outlet store for a handpainted clothing business which sells to the top boutiques and department stores throughout the United States. The merchandise consists of overstocks, samples and past season goods from the Sport Deco line, in addition to designer salesmen's samples of other lines of clothing. Savings are about 30-50% off regular retail prices. If you have discriminating taste and understand the value and workmanship of a denim jacket which normally retails for $250, then you'll be delighted at the values here. You'll find women's and children's wear at this fun shop. All sales are final. M-F 10-4:30 and occasional Saturdays. Accepts checks and cash only.

LINDA SAMS
861-2611

Linda creates one-of-a-kind wearable art clothing utilizing surface design techniques such as hand painting and embellishment with buttons, lace etc. As an alternative, she can incorporate a piece of your handpainted artist's canvas onto the garment. She can also sew clear plastic onto the garment, leaving one side unsewn so you can insert small sketches, photographs or the like and change them at whim. Her distinctive, fashion forward garments are made from a variety of quality materials, or denim, and are designed to compliment your personality. Linda can make clothes for men, women and children in regular and large sizes. She will come to your home to measure and discuss your clothing interests and she can generally work within anyone's budget. A complete 3 piece outfit can cost about $100-$300, a jacket can cost about $60-$150, dresses cost about $40-$200. Prices will greatly vary depending on how much embellishment is added to the garment, if any, the intricacy of the design, the type of fabric used and other factors, which explains the range of prices stated.. Linda's clothes will be modelled 4 times per month on her own television show, *Linda's Studio*, which will air on the ACTV cable 21 station. Her prices are about 30-50% less than comparable quality items found in upscale boutiques and specialty stores. Call anytime to set up an appointment.

SAVINGS ZONE
2831 Festival Lane, the Festival At Sawmill Shpng. Ctr., Dublin, 43017, 791-8033

Save 40-70% off quality misses and junior sportswear in casual, dressy and career styles. at this off-price retailer. Belts, hair clips, purses, jewelry and scarves are also available at similar savings. On a recent visit, I saw Erika, Jordache, Gloria Vanderbilt, Forenza (the Limited's private label), Jennifer Reed, Victoria Jones, Esprit, Anne Klein and Gantos brands of clothing in addition to Nina Ricci, Macy's New York, Ann Taylor and Van Cleef And Arpels brands of costume jewelry. This business is owned by the company which operates the Ten Below chain of apparel stores. However, this is their upscale division. The merchandise consists of first quality overstocks,, discontinued goods and special purchases. You'll love the contemporary styles, all of which are displayed in an appealing manner. Gives refunds. M-Sat 10-9, Sun 12-6. Accepts checks, MC & Visa

SCHOTTENSTEIN'S
3251 Westerville Rd., Columbus, 43224, 471-4711
6055 E. Main St., Columbus, 43213, 755-9200
34 North Boulevard, Columbus, 43204, 278-6000
1887 Parsons Ave., Columbus, 43207, 443-0171

This mini department store offers moderate to couture merchandise at savings of 20-90% off regular retail prices. Brands such as Adrienne Vittadini, Stanley Blacker and Anne Klein run rampant in the designer section. You can purchase a cordless phone for $39.99 regularly $90, luggage for $19.99-$39.99 regularly $60-$130, wallpaper for $1.99 regularly $12.95-$24.95, children;s Health-Tex separates at $2.99-$4.99 regularly $6-$21. Other merchandise includes clothes for the family (including large and maternity sizes), furs, lingerie, small appliances, bicycles, fishing/golf and other sporting goods, toys, gardening supplies, lamps, patio furniture, watches, health and beauty aids, fine jewelry, cameras, housewares and giftware. All widths of shoes are offered for the family in dressy and casual styles by such brands as Giorgio Brutini, Reebok, Bally, Evan Picone and Joan And David. The linen department offers savings of 20-90% off suggested retail prices on first quality and irregular merchandise by Utica, Stevens and other popular brands. The pharmacy department offers similar savings on brand name cosmetics, snacks, personal grooming items and seasonal merchandise. The inventory consists of first quality, irregulars, seconds, buyouts and liquidations. This store has earned the distinction of being one of my personal favorites. Gives refunds. M-Th. 10-9, F 10-7, Sun 10-8. Closed on Saturday. Accepts checks, MC, Visa, AmExp, Discover & Schottenstein's charges.

SEARS OUTLET
4545 Fisher Rd., Columbus, 43228, 272-3001

Customer returns, overstocks, past season and some irregular merchandise from Sears stores and catalogues are available at savings of 20-80% off regular retail prices. You will find toys, clothing for the entire family, shoes, housewares, linens, gifts, cameras, watches, tools, power gardening equipment, sporting goods, lamps, furniture, jewelry, audio and stereo equipment as well as computers and electronic games. Gives refunds. M-W 10-6, Th-Sat 10-9, Sun 12-5. Accepts checks, Discover & Sears charges.

SEEK-N-SAVE CONSIGNMENT SHOPPE
3165 N. High St., Columbus 43202, 267-0645

Men's and women's casual and dressy vintage clothes are available at this consignment shop. Prices are about 20-30% less than a comparable quality new garment which you would find in a department store. Although the extensive collection of vintage jewelry and accessories is priced at market rates, this is one of the largest selections of period accessories in Central Ohio. The owner is a friendly and knowledgeable salesperson who is anxious to please. All sales are final. M-F 11-7, Sat 11-6. Accepts checks, MC & Visa.

SHAPELY OUTLET CENTER
2430 E. Kemper Rd., Cincinnati, 45241, (513) 771-9828

13 factory outlets sell first quality fashions, shoes and linens at savings of 30-60% off regular retail prices. You'll find Your Wedding Connection, Fashion Factory Outlet, Anne's Son Shoes, Cut Rate Hair Salon, Old Mill, Polly Flinders, Cotton Mills Store, Something Special, Newport Sportswear, Best Selection, Julie's and The Head Factory

Outlet. The Shapely Factory Outlet store sells Leslie Fay, Kasper, Sasoon, Outlander and Breckinridge brands of better women's apparel in petite through large woman sizes. Take the Masteller exit off the I-275 bypass to get to this store.

SIZES UNLIMITED
207-211 Graceland Blvd., Columbus, 43214, 436-2150
3499 Cleveland Ave., Northern Lights Shpng. Ctr., Columbus, 43224, 262-8581
3827 S. High St., Great Southern Shpng. Ctr., Columbus, 43207, 497-1039
4125 W. Broad St., Columbus, 43228, 274-0885

Large size women's clothing is available at savings of 20-50% off regular retail prices. You'll find first quality casual and career wear by Sasson, Chaus and other companies in sizes up to 52. Gives refunds. M-Sat 10-9, Sun 12-5. Accepts checks, MC & Visa.

STORK EXCHANGE
484 W. Cherry St., Sunbury, 43074, 965-4411

Upscale clothes, toys, cribs and other accessories for children are available at savings of 30-50% off suggested retail and "if new" prices. You'll find Polly Flinders, Carriage Boutique, Martha's Miniatures, Oshkosh, Childcraft, Evenflo, Sears and Penney's brands. The store stocks new salesmen's samples as well as gently used merchandise, in sizes newborn to 14. Gives refunds. M, Tu, Th-Sat 10-6; W 10-8. Accepts checks and cash.

T.J. MAXX
4117 W. Broad St., Columbus 43228, 272-1141
1871 W. Henderson Rd., Columbus, 43220, 451-9924
5929 E. Main St., Columbus, 43213, 864-7005
2210 Morse Rd., Columbus, 43229, 476, 1964
1193 Park Ave. W., Mansfield, 44901, (419) 529-6724

Moderate to designer quality fashions for men, women and children, in addition to giftware, linens, lingerie, shoes, luggage, designer fragrances, leather goods and purses, accessories as well as fine gold and silver jewelry are sold at 20-60% off regular retail prices. The inventory consists of first quality manufacturers' overstocks and some past season merchandise. A small quantity of irregular goods is clearly marked. Provides layaways. Gives refunds. M-Sat 10-9, Sun 12-5. Accepts checks, MC & Visa.

TANGO'S
6120 Busch Blvd., the Continent, Columbus, 43229, 436-6511

Free spirited, women's fashions are available at this off-price retailer. You will find dressy and casual separates and dresses with a contemporary appeal, at savings of about 20-50% off comparable retail prices. The merchandise is moderate to better quality. Tango's is owned by the same people who own Justine's and the former Melons stores. You will find a definite Melons echo here. The store also sells fashion accessories such as costume jewelry and belts at similar savings. Gives refunds. M-Sat 10-9, Sun 12-5. Accepts checks, MC & Visa.

TAN YER HIDE
400 Dublin Avenue, suite 1019, Columbus, 43215, 221-9936

Suede and leather lingerie, bathing suits, skirts, tops and pants are available from this manufacturer at savings of 50% off regular retail prices. You'll find novelty patterns such as leopard prints, as well as hot fashion and basic colors, in sizes small, medium, and large. Most of the stock is for women, with a few items for men. The wholesale prices you can expect to pay here are about $10-$50., representing a savings of 50-60% less than regular retail prices. Tan Yer Hide sells quality garments to boutiques and specialty stores across the country. All sales are final. M-F 9-5, by appointment only. Absolutely no walk-ins.! Accepts checks and cash only.

TEES-N-U
2489 N. High St., Columbus, 43202, 262-6965 (the phone number will change shortly)

You can purchase airbrushed tee shirts with adult and children's novelty designs such as whimsical characters, sunsets, animals, flowers and other images. The cost of the stock designs on their garments is $12.50 and includes free name personalization. Special orders are also available from this artist, at a cost of about $20-$25 on tee shirts, sweatshirts or blouses, and about $30-$40 on denim jackets. Rhinestones and studs are available at an extra fee depending on the amount used. Similar types of hand airbrushed garments are sold at area boutiques, but the prices here will save you about 20-60%. All sales are final. M-Sat 10-6. Accepts checks and cash only.

TEN BELOW
4268 Eastland Sq. Dr., Columbus, 43232, 759-9319
3718 Fishinger Blvd., Hilliard, 43026, 876-0200
57 Graceland Blvd., Columbus, 43214, 785-1600
3831 S. High St., Columbus, 43207, 491-6161
6007 E. Main St., Columbus, 43213, 759-0035
4641 Morse Center Rd., Columbus, 43229, 847-9422
2637 Northland Plaza Dr., Columbus, 43231, 882-7502
6642 Sawmill Rd., Columbus, 43235, 889-5085
3650 Soldano Blvd., Consumer Sq. W., Columbus, 43223,
863 Bethel Rd., Olentangy Plaza, Columbus, 43214,442-1885
771 S 30 St.,Indian Mound Mall, Heath 43056, 522-5667
1139 Columbus Pike, Rt. 23, Delaware, 43015, 363-0969
1635 River Valley Circle S, Lancaster 43130, 653-2911
3575 Maple Ave. #520, Colony Sq. Mall, Zanesville, 43701. 452-7648
U.S. Route 23, Circleville, 43113, 474-2390
1475-Marion-Waldo Rd., Marion, 433-1, 389-4099
436 1/2 Lexington, Mansfield, 44901, (419) 756-3985

Two former Gold Circle executives operate this local chain of women's apparel and accessories stores in which 95% of the inventory is priced at $10 and under. Manufacturers' overstocks and cancelled orders comprise the budget and moderately priced items in such brands as Sasson, Gitano, Miss Lizz, Erika, Bonjour, Counterparts and others. The store carries missy, junior and large sizes, in addition to accessories such as earrings, socks, scarves and purses. Gives refunds. M-Sat 10-9, Sun 12-5. Accepts checks, MC & Visa.,

TOPPING OUTLET STORE
5002 E. Main St., Ashville, 43101, 1-983-3757

Save 20% on western wear and accessories including leather vests, shirts, Stetson hats, saddles, belts, T-shirts and boots for adults and children.   Navajo and Zuni turquoise jewelry is similarly discounted.   Brands offered include Justin Walker, Lee, Dan Post, Wrangler and others.   Gold and diamond jewelry as well as repairs are offered at a 20-30% savings. Gives exchanges only. M-Sat 9-8, Sun 11-7. Accepts checks, MC &Visa.

TRADER TOTS
1390 Grandview Ave., Columbus, 43212, 488-8687

Resale children's clothes, toys and equipment as well as maternity clothes can be found here at prices 50-80% lower than new. Toys are priced 40-60% lower than new prices. Accessories such as cribs, strollers and car seats are about 50% less than new items. The quality, upscale merchandise includes such popular brands as Fisher-Price, Health-Tex, Oshkosh, Polly Flinders, Carters, Brian dresses, Recreations, Harvey Seller, Ninth Moon and Lady In Waiting. Provides layaway. Gives a 24 hour approval policy. M and Tu 10-6, W 10-8, Th-Sat 10-6. Accepts checks, MC, Visa & Discover.

TREASURE TRUNK
1183 W. Church St., Newark, 43055, 344-7232

Upscale consignment shop sells quality children's clothes in size newborn to pre-teen size 16. You'll find Gunne Sax, Oshkosh, Buster Brown, Health Tex, Polly Flinders, Brian and other brands. A small selection of toys, shoes and maternity wear is also available. Savings are about 50-60% less than "if new". Gives a 24 hour approval on returns. M-F 10-5, Sat 10-4. Accepts checks and cash only.

2X NICE
3971 Broadway, Grove City, 43123, 875-9543

Upscale consignment shop for children's clothes in sizes newborn to 14. You'll find Brian, Polly Flinders, Oshkosh, Health Tex and other brands at savings of 40-60% off "if new" prices. All sales are final. M-Sat 10-6. Accepts checks and cash only.

UHLMAN'S CLEARANCE CENTER
71 Graceland Blvd., Columbus, 43214, 431-8880

Merchandise from 34 Midwest stores, as well as from their key suppliers, is consolidated under one roof. You'll save 35-70% off fashions for men, women and children as well as lingerie, ladies shoes, purses, jewelry, belts, linens and gift items. On the first Wednesday of each month, seniors can save 20% off all purchases. The stock consists of surplus inventory, end of season styles and end sizes. While most of the inventory is first quality, some imperfects are also available. You'll find such brands as Jones New York, Campus Casuals, Pendleton, Ocean Pacific, Oshkosh, Norton McNaughton, Leslie Fay, Bugle Boy, Carter's, Martex, Fieldcrest and Russ in petite, regular and large sizes. Gives refunds. M-Sat 10-9, Sun 12-5. Accepts checks, MC, Visa, AmExp & Uhlman's charge.

V.O. ORIGINALS
POB 1324, Columbus, 43201, 291-4681

Fashion designer, Voszi, will design and sew a unique fashion garment for you using her fabric or yours. Most of her jackets, dresses, tops etc., have tie or Velcro closures or slip over the head, making them additionally suitable for the elderly or people with disabilities. Her fabrics range from simple to ornate, cotton to linen, and styles are funky to casual chic. The quality is excellent and the prices are very low. She'll design a "wear me anywhere" overcoat or a dress for your favorite occasion. Hard to find sizes are welcome. Dresses range from about $35-$70, tops range from $15-$40. Although prices vary according to style and fabric used, you can expect to save 30-60% off the price of comparable store bought goods. She will see you by appointment only. She also maintains an inventory of garments to buy off the rack, including some clearance merchandise. All sales are final. However, if not satisfied with the fit of a garment, she will fix it for you. Accepts checks.

VALUE CITY DEPARTMENT STORES
725 Hebron Rd., Heath, 43025, 522-8125
721 N. Memorial Dr., Lancaster, 43130, 653-5280
701 Main St., Zanesville, 43701, 452-5435
1280 Lexington Ave., Mansfield, 44901, (419) 756-7000

Outside of the Columbus area, Value City Furniture operates mini department stores. Owned and operated by Schottenstein's, these businesses offer a larger selection of seconds and irregular merchandise than the Columbus Schottenstein's stores. The stock includes budget to moderate quality goods. A few designer items are also available. Keep your bargain hunting antennas fully extended here as you might bypass the great bargains which are mixed in with some undesirables. The stores sell housewares, shoes, apparel for the family, luggage, leather goods, fine jewelry, linens and toys. Gives refunds. M-Th 10-9, F and Sat 10-9:30, Sun 11-7. Accepts checks, MC, Visa and Discover.

VAN DYNE-CROTTY COMPANY
1543 Frebis Ave., Columbus, 43206, 444-6838

Used men's uniforms including overalls, jackets, lab coats, shirts and pants are available at savings of about 50-60% less than "if new". All sales are final. M-Th 8-5, F 8-6, Sat 8-4. Accepts checks and cash only.

WE'RE 4 KIDS
324 S. Hamilton Rd., Hunters Ridge Mall, Gahanna, 43230, 476-1794

See Fashions 4 Kids description in this chapter.

WE THREE
74 Mill St., Gahanna, 43230, 471-1567

Gently used children's clothing and toys, as well as women's clothes are sold at savings up to 75% off "if new" prices. You'll find popular brands such as Polly Flinders, Oshkosh and Brian dresses as well as Fisher-Price and Little Tykes toys. Savings are 50% and more on nursery nic-naks and crafts at this upscale shop. On a recent visit, I saw a wool Harve

Benard suit for only $25 and other wearables by Evan Picone, Liz Claiborne and other sought after brands. Check the back room for additional merchandise. The store also carries a value priced line of imported greeting cards. Provides layaway. All sales are final. M-Sat 10-6. Accepts checks.

WRIGHT PLACE
143 E. Main St., Columbus, 43215, 228-0550

Check out the bargain basement of this dance and theater wear shop, where you'll find savings of 30-70% on discontinued and seasonal items such as dance wear, canvas and dance shoes, appliqued sweatshirts, theatrical makeup and anything relating to the performing arts and exercise. The stock is for adults and children. All sales are final. M 10-7, Tu-Sat 10-6. Accepts checks, MC, Visa, AmExp & Discover.

ALSO SEE

Acorn Warehouse Sale, Angie's Tailor, Bargain Days (Weiss' Department Store), Bellepointe, Berwick Corner Outlet, Cia's Annual Clearance Sale, D.E. Jones, Dean's Discount Outlet, Department Of Defense, Dunham's Sporting Goods, Eddie Bauer Warehouse Sale, Extravaganza, Family Dollar, Golden Hobby Shop, Greater Columbus Antique Mall, Henri Bendel, Home And Garden Line, Just For Feet, Lake Erie Factory Outlet, Liquidations Now, Odd Lots, Only $1, Paul's Marine, Sam's Club, South High Drive-In Theater, Springfield Antique Show And Flea Market, Starr Cleaners, State Discount, Sunbury Flea Market, SuSan's Specialities, Suzanne's Suede And Leather, Tag Sales, Talbott's Semi-Annual Sale, Totes Outlet, Tuesday Morning, Value City Department Stores, WDLR Radio, Walker's April Fool's Sale, WarehouseClub

CLUBS/ MEMBERSHIPS/ CHARGES

CLUBS/MEMBERSHIPS

By becoming a member of an art or special interest club/organization, you will have the opportunity to participate in many free and low cost lectures, workshops, field trips etc. , many of which are only open to members of that group. Even if you don't have any art skills to speak of, or do not have any background in a particular field, membership in a group or club as a patron/enthusiast will enable you to learn more about that field of interest through the group's programs. Membership also provides you with the opportunity to interact with kindred spirits. Many groups provide other benefits such as discounts in organizational operated gift shops; discounts at other local, statewide and even nationally affiliated facilities; health care group plans; a free subscription to their newsletter and other opportunities.. Some clubs restrict members to those who fall within a certain category like seniors, divorced individuals etc. Check with your accountant, as these membership dues might be tax deductible under certain circumstances. Most groups have a $10-$30 annual membership fee.

THE B.A.B.I.E.S. CLUB
Grant Medical Center, 111 S. Grant Ave., Columbus, 43215, 461-3737 or 461-3007

The Maternity Services Department has recently begun to offer a free membership to any woman who uses the services of a physician who is affiliated with Grant Medical Center. Club members receive prenatal and postpartum newsletters which provide helpful tips and information relating to various aspects of your pregnancy, special discounts and coupons offering savings on baby clothing, furniture, diaper services, photography, dinners and more. Information and discounts on parenting and wellness classes offered by the Elizabeth Blackwell Center at Grant Hospital are also included with membership. If you deliver your baby at Grant, you'll receive a special gift basket to take home which will be filled with samples and coupons for mom and baby. M-F 9-5.

COLUMBUS AUDOBON SOCIETY
1065 Kendale Rd. N., Columbus, 43220, 451-4591

Membership in this nature lovers group, includes a free monthly newsletter which provides information on bird sightings, new products of interest and happenings in the community. The many free and low cost society programs (most of which are open to members only) include nature hikes, birding trips, lectures, films and more. The society also sponsors the "Dial-A-Bird" hotline, 221-WREN, which provides taped information on bird sightings and society happenings. Annual membership fees are $20 for full time students, $21 for senior citizens, $23 for senior citizen and family members, $30 for individuals and $38 for families. Accepts checks.

COLUMBUS ROCK AND MINERAL SOCIETY
Hank Dowdy 486-7362 or Mary Lindner 486-6680

This group meets on the last Friday of every month at 7:30PM in the Trinity Elementary School at 1381 Ida Avenue. The monthly meeting features a discussion/slide program relating to geology, astronomy, natural history or gems and minerals. Plus, there are several free opportunities throughout the year to participate in rockhounding expeditions in Ohio and neighboring states , where you can collect fossils and gems. The club is a co-sponsor of the Gem and Mineral Show which takes place at Veteran's Memorial Auditorium each April. Family membership is $15 annually.

COLUMBUS ZOO
9990 Riverside Dr., Powell, 43065, 645-3550

Zoo membership entitles you to free admission to the Columbus Zoo and 85 other zoos and aquariums nationwide, free parking at the zoo, invitations to members only events, a free subscription to the newsletter, discounts at the gift shop, at classes and children's camp experiences. You will also be admitted for free to zoo special events such as many concerts, Easter egg hunts and the *Wildlight Wonderland.* Membership costs $45 for a family, $45 for grandparents and grandchildren or $35 for an individual membership. One time admission fees are $4 for adults, $3 for seniors and $2 for kids aged 2-11. Stroller rental is $3, wheelchair rental is $3.50. There is a Wendy's restaurant on the premises and ample picnic facilities as well. M-Sun 9-6. Also offers extended summer hours. Accepts checks and cash only.

EMBROIDERER'S GUILD, COLUMBUS AREA CHAPTER
C/O Joan Riegel, 3345 Kirkham Rd., Columbus, 43221, 451-5617

The local chapter of this national organization is involved in all aspects of the needle arts: embroidery, needlepoint, crewel, quilting and more. Meetings are held on the second Thursday of the month at 9:30AM in Dublin and include a discussion and/or a demonstration/workshop by local, regional and nationally recognized craftspersons and historians. Programs have included clothing embellishment, American needlework techniques, soft jewelry, achieving texture in needlepoint and many other interesting topics. Many of the programs are free, while others cost $10-$70. Most of their programs are not readily available elsewhere in Columbus and Central Ohio. Guild membership also permits you to borrow books at no cost from their extensive library. The guild also has several evening gatherings per month where specialty groups convene for informal "sew-ins" and to also work on community projects. This lively and enthusiastic group of women is a pleasure to be with. If you enjoy the needlearts, include this group in your life.

GOLDEN BUCKEYE CARD
466-3681

Seniors aged 60 and over, or any totally and permanently disabled individual aged 18 and over, can apply for this free discount card. It is valid throughout Ohio at about 35,000 merchants and businesses which offer 2-50% discounts on goods and services to card holders. Certain restrictions apply. M-F 9-5.

HOME VIDEO CLUB
C/O Upper Arlington Cultural Arts Commission, 3600 Tremont Rd., Columbus, 43221, 457-5080

This newly formed club was organized in the aftermath of the video workshop sponsored by the Arts Commission. The meeting days and times had not been finalized as of the time this book went to press. However, meetings will be held in Arlington and will include a sharing of techniques and ideas as well as the opportunity to hear presentations by prominent people in the community. Membership fees, if any, have not been established at the time of my contact with the group. Adults and teens are invited to become members.

LICKING COUNTY BICYCLE CLUB
C/O Lew Hullinger, 907 Granville Rd., Newark, 43055, 344-5683

If you enjoy social and recreational cycling, consider joining this group. Meetings are held once per month at the Holy Trinity Lutheran Church in Newark to discuss the ride schedule and special projects. Regular rides are held on Saturday mornings and Sunday afternoons year round, weather permitting. The group cycles 10-30 miles from Newark to sites such as the Black Hand Gorge and the Dawes Arboretum. Their annual event, the *Land Of Legend Tour*, is a 35- 100 mile cycling excursion. Membership is $7 per person annually. Accepts checks.

OHIO DESIGNER CRAFTSMEN
2164 Riverside Dr., Columbus, 43221, 486-7119

It is not necessary to be an artist to belong to this statewide guild of professional craftsmen, as they have many art supporters on their membership roster. The benefits include the opportunity to participate in a group health care plan which could save you up to 50% off the rate of a comparable non-group plan. Other benefits include a free subscription to their quarterly newsletter, free admission to *Winterfair*, the *Craftfair at Hathaway Brown* and other ODC sponsored fairs. The professional benefits include the opportunity to be juried as an exhibitor in the craft fairs mentioned, to participate in their juried marketing program and to enter artwork into their juried gallery exhibitions. The annual membership fee is $20. M-F 8-5, Sat 11-5. Accepts checks.

SELF KNOWLEDGE NETWORK
457-7642

Serious minded individuals who are interested in personal growth and self knowledge can become members of this nonprofit group. Meetings are held at 7:30PM on Thursdays, twice per month, at the Upper Arlington Municipal Building, 3600 Tremont Road. The program includes a video tape, discussion and/or an informal presentation on such topics as "Zen And Other Techniques For Self Development", "The Message Of Krishnamurthi", "Cosmic Consciousness Throughout History" and more. Meetings are open to the general public at no cost.

VOLUNTEER ADMINISTRATOR'S NETWORK
C/O CALLVAC Services, 370 S. 5 St., Columbus, 43215, 464-4747

Monthly programs are offered relating to volunteer recruitment and management as well as general administrative functions such as "Achieving Your Potential", "How To Write Good Newsletters", "Sensitivity To People Who Are Different" and other topics of interest. The annual membership fee is $15 and entitles you to receive a monthly newsletter and the opportunity to attend these free or low cost programs (usually for about $5). It is not necessary to be a volunteer coordinator to be a member as the program offerings are generally of broad interest to business professionals, especially those who work for non-profit organizations. M-F 8-5. Accepts checks.

ALSO SEE

AAA, Aardvark Video, American Youth Hostels, B. Dalton, Central City Comics, Clintonville Food Co-op, Columbus Folk Dancers, Columbus Museum Of Art, Columbus Polo Club, Executive Tour Golfer's Club, Golden Lifestyles, Riverside AdvantAge, Sears, White Parrot Pet Center, Worthington Arts Council and Wyandotte Lake.

CHARGES

CITIBANK VISA AND MASTERCARD
Account Fulfillment Center, POB 6105, Sioux Falls, South Dakota, 57117-9818

This company, the nation's largest issuer of Visa and Mastercards, has recently begun a policy which guarantees the lowest price to its cardholders on all purchases made with these charges. This *Price Protection Plan* allows customers to request a rebate for the price difference, within 60 days, if they find an item for less than they paid with their Citibank charge. There is a limit of $250 in rebates per item, and a printed advertisement of the competitor's item must be submitted. Art, antiques, air travel and entertainment tickets are not eligible for the rebates. You can earn free gifts by using your card, such as brand name electronics, housewares, clothing and more. Each time you use your card to purchase plane, ship, bus or train tickets, you will automatically be covered by a $100,000 common carrier travel accident insurance policy.

DISCOVER CARD
1-800-547-2683

There are a multitude of benefits which await you as a Discover Card customer. You can earn a cashback bonus of .25% to 1% based on the amount of your annual purchases. At the end of the year when you receive your cashback bonus check, you can deposit it into your *Discover Savers Account* and add additional funds to equal a $1000 deposit. Or you may open a new account and Discover Card will automatically double the value of your check, not to exceed a $25 payment. As another benefit of membership, *Value Finders* coupons are mailed periodically, which provide savings on products and services from selected Discover Card merchants. As a cardholder, you may also open a Discover Savings account or CD which pays interest rates higher than those available at banks. There is no annual fee to have a Discover Card. It is widely accepted throughout the United States. By joining the *Discover Card Travel Services Plan* for $34 annually, you will receive a variety of benefits. These include a 5% refund on airline, lodging, car rental or cruise reservations made on your card; guaranteed lowest published airfare on all airlines; 24 hour a day reservations; savings of up to 65% on last ,minute travel packages from a list compiled by the travel service; a free quarterly newsletter; custom travel planning which includes literature, members only discounted travel packages, cashback bonus (mentioned earlier), and coupons for savings at hotels, restaurants and more.

HENRI BENDEL
350 Columbus City Center Dr., Columbus, 43215, 228-4022

This upscale store offers their charge account customers invitations to free teas and special breakfasts, fashion shows and advance notice of sales which are open to the public. Some of the sales offer special times when charge card customers can shop before the general public is admitted. Often the programs designed especially for charge account customers, include a free bag of goodies such as product samples. So,me of their own branded merchandise is a particularly good value as compared to comparable quality designer merchandise. However, if you feel that their prices are still too high for your budget, wait until they have the end of season sales, which you would learn about as a charge card customer. By the way, the decorating and floor plan of this specialty store is definitely "a must see". Offers layaway. Gives refunds. M-F 10-9, Sat 10-7, Sun 12-5. Accepts checks, MC, Visa, AmExp, & Henri Bendel charges.

J.C. PENNEY'S
2724 Eastland Mall, Columbus, 43232, 861-0170
1721 Northland Mallway, Columbus, 43229, 267-1285
4311 Westland Mall, Columbus, 43228, 276-9011

Upon completion of a credit application, you will be entitled to a $5 gift certificate which must be redeemed in the store. Several times during the year, charge card holders will receive a coupon valid for 10-25% off your next purchase. The portrait studios provide an excellent price on a package of 29 color portraits of various sizes for only $19.95. There is a $2 sitting fee per person, and the package is available for all ages. Penney's features a high quality line of comforters, sheets and curtains under its private labels, Elizabeth Gray and Classic Traditions. Traditional, contemporary and country styles and patterns can be found in the most sought after fabrications and patterns. The quality is equivalent to that which you would find in upscale specialty and department stores, but a at a fraction of the cost. You can expect to save about 20-50% as compared to comparable products by other manufacturers. A 30 minute video, *Room To Room: Creating The Home Of Your Dreams,* is available for only $19.95, and is accompanied by a practical, 24 page decorating guide. Along with your purchase, which is shipped postage paid by Penney's, you will receive a $20 gift certificate which is valid when you purchase $10 or more of home furnishings such as those described above. Accepts checks, MC, Visa, AmExp.,and Penney's

JACOBSON'S
99 S. 3 St., Columbus City Center, Columbus, 43215, 221-2800

Charge account customers will receive invitations to free fashion shows, private previews of new merchandise and other special events. You will also receive their frequent gift and fashion catalogues. Gives refunds. M-, Tu, W, Sat 10-6; Th and F 10-9; Sun 12-5. Accepts checks, MC, Visa, AmExp, and Jacobson's charges.

LAZARUS
141 S. High St., Columbus, 43215, 463-2121
2667 S. Hamilton Rd., Columbus, 43232, 860-1594
1828 W. Henderson Rd., Columbus, 43220, 457-7670
4141 Refugee Rd., Columbus, 43232, 860-1573
3180 Kingsdale Ctr., Columbus, 43221, 459-6492
1649 Morse Rd., Columbus, 43229, 265-1383
3812 E. Broad St., Columbus, 43213, 236-0135
40 Westerville Sq., Westerville, 43081, 890-6322
4141 W. Broad St., Columbus 43228, 278-4893

Charge account customers will receive advance notice of sales that are open to the general public, which occasionally include premium times open to charge card customers only and/or the opportunity to receive additional savings. Charge account customers occasionally receive offers for free samples of cosmetics or perfumes. *Lazarus* also operates the *Y.E.S.* service which provides free shopping assistance by appointment. Gives refunds. The Final Countdown at the South High Street store, offers excellent savings in many departments. See description under the clothing category in this book. Offers layaways. M-F 10-9, Sat 10-6, Sun 12-5. Accepts checks, MC, Visa, and Lazarus charges.

MARSHALL FIELD'S
225 S. 3 St., Columbus, City Center, Columbus, 43215, 224-7234

This store offers 10-25% off sale items to charge account customers during their special *Field Days* mailings. Charge customers also receive advance notice of public sales. Field's offers a free shopping service to the general public, P.S. Field's, by appointment only. A trained sales consultant will shop with you to help you find what you need, and you will get personalized attention, complete with private dressing suites and complimentary refreshments. Or if you prefer, the consultant can set aside certain items which you can evaluate at the store.   You can use this service as your personal gift secretary. Staff members will phone you as special occasions draw near. They will even shop for you and mail out your purchase. This *P.S. Fields* service is available Monday through Friday 11AM-9PM and every other Saturday. Their direct phone line is 227-6352. Accepts checks, MC, Visa, and Marshall Field's charges.

ENTERTAINMENT

AARDVARK VIDEO
612 N. High St., Columbus, 43215, 461-6302

International cinema, art videos, experimental works, avant garde and collector items are available at this business which buys and sells new and used videos and rents new ones. The inventory of used videos also consists of those which have been previously viewed from the store's collection and can be purchased at a savings of about 50% off the "if new" prices. Used collector videos are priced according to market value and new videos are at full retail price. *Aardvark* is well known for its unusual selection not found elsewhere in the city. The business also offers a finders service. You can join their video club at a cost of $20 annually or $50 for a lifetime membership. This entitles you to a discount of about $1.75 off the usual rental rate of approximately $3.75 per video, so you'll only pay around $2. M-Sat 10-9, Sun 12-6. Accepts checks, MC, Visa, Am Exp & Discover.

ANHEUSER-BUSCH BREWERY
700 Schrock Rd., Columbus, 43229, 847-6270 or 847-6271

Free self guided factory tours provide an inside look into the processes used to create these fine beers. At the end of the tour, everyone will receive a free sample of Eagle Snack pretzels. Adults will also receive a free glass of beer. If you have a passion for souvenirs, the gift shop offers many items emblazoned with the Anheuser-Busch name at regular retail prices. M-F 9-4.

ACTOR'S SUMMER THEATER
444-6888

Watch free outdoor theatrical productions of Shakespearean and musical plays in German Village's Schiller Park. Performances are held Thursday-Sunday at 8PM from June-August. Bring a lawn chair or a blanket to sit on.

ARTICIPATION
139 W. Main St., Columbus, 43215, 645-7446

The City of Columbus, Recreation and Parks Department, offers an exciting 8 week series for adults on Saturdays from 6-9PM, and for kids on Fridays, from 4-6PM. The cost is $10 for the entire 8 week term and features a changing sampler of art programs including hands on workshops and excursions to visual and performing arts events and facilities throughout the city. The children's price includes transportation to events from a central site. The adults must carpool or provide their own transportation. Adult programs have included Ballet Met's Nutcracker at the Ohio Theater, CATCO's Thurber Carnival, a performance of the Columbus Symphony Orchestra, a calligraphy workshop and a trip to the Short North Gallery Hop. Children's programs have included a performance by a ventriloquist, a sketching trip to the North Market and the opportunity to see a Player's Youth Theater performance of A Secret Garden. Articipation is operated out of 5 recreation centers: Barnett, Schiller, Marion-Franklin, Westgate and Whetstone. Call to be put on their mailing list. This program has earned the distinction of being one of my personal favorites. Accepts checks.

BARBER MUSEUM
Canal Winchester, 43110, 833-9931

Free tours of probably the only museum of its kind in the United States, are available by appointment only. The attraction displays 6 barbershops from different decades and memorabilia dating back to 1790. You will find 600 razors in the collection, including an 8 foot one which was used as a promotional piece, 285 shaving mugs and the world's largest library on hair.

BASH ON THE BOULEVARD
Hyatt Regency Hotel, 350 N. High St., Columbus, 43215,
488-4321

The Hyatt Regency Hotel and WXMX radio have teamed up to offer a series of free, outdoor parties with food and entertainment on Friday evenings from 4-7PM. They will be held from mid June through late August. Food and drinks will be available for purchase and special promotions will be offered. Local and regional groups will perform.

BIG BEAR
Check the phone book to locate the more than 50 stores in Central Ohio

All area Big Bear and Harts stores offer savings of about $1-$2 off the ticket price to certain annual special events such as the Shriner's Circus, the Columbus Boat And RV Show, the Central Ohio Home And Garden Show, the Decorator's Show House and the Columbus Symphony's Picnic With The Pops. The stores also add on other special events throughout the year. Check at the customer service desk of your favorite store.

BLUE JACKET
POB 312, Xenia, 45385, (513) 376-4318

This epic outdoor drama about a white man adopted by Shawnee Indians, portrays how he became their chief 200 years ago. Performances are held Tuesday-Friday at a cost of $10, Saturday prices are $11. Children under 12 are admitted for $6 Monday through Saturday.

The best value, however, is on Sundays when all tickets are only $5. This is one of 3 similar outdoor dramas in Central Ohio, but is the only one to offer half price tickets for any of their performances. This family oriented production is held at 8PM from early June through Labor Day. The First Frontier sponsors these productions, and is located on Stringtown Road near Xenia.

CAPITAL UNIVERSITY
2199 E. Main St., Bexley, 43209, 236-6411 (music dept.), 236-6497 (theater dept)

Free faculty vocal and instrumental recitals are held every Wednesday at 7:30PM from September-April and feature such virtuosos as Michelle Horsefield. A variety of styles are represented. The *NOW Music Festival* is held annually in February and celebrates contemporary music with concerts by the composer-in-residence, students, faculty, prominent local musicians and other guest artists. Admission is $2 for adults and $1 for seniors and children. Four quality theatrical productions, some of which are family oriented, are held from October-April at a cost of $4 for general admission and $3 for seniors. Past productions have included "Once Upon A Mattress", "Monsters In My Spumoni" and "A Shayna Maidel", and have been aimed at adult and/or family audiences.

CINEMARK MOVIES 12
2570 Bethel Rd., Carriage Place Shpng. Ctr., Columbus,
43220, 538-0403

Ohio's largest discount movie theater opened in May, 1991, featuring a $1 general admission fee at all times. This second run theater, as it is called in the industry, also provides you with free admission on your birthday as long as you bring proof.

COLUMBUS ASTRONOMICAL SOCIETY
POB 16209, Columbus, 43216, 459-7742

The Perkins Observatory in Delaware is the site of free monthly programs which include a film, discussion on astronomy and the opportunity to view the night sky through a powerful telescope (weather permitting). The 2 hour weeknight programs are sponsored by the Columbus Astronomical Society, OSU and Ohio Wesleyan University. You may request up to six tickets by mail. Be sure to include a self addressed stamped envelope. The presentation is suitable for adults and children.

COLUMBUS MUSEUM OF ART
480 E. Broad St., Columbus, 43215, 221-6801

An annual membership at the museum costs $50 for a family, seniors or students. Benefits include members only previews; unlimited free admission to all special exhibitions; discounts on museum sponsored concerts, lectures and workshops for adults, teens and youths; 10% discount on purchases in the gift shop; discount subscriptions to Dialogue and other arts magazines; a subscription OT a members' newsletter; discounts to off site performances of Opera Columbus, Ballet Met and the Columbus Symphony. Reciprocal membership benefits are granted at the Dayton Art Institute, the Cleveland Museum of Art, the Cincinnati Museum of Art, the Contemporary Arts Center (Cincinnati) and the Akron Art Museum. Parent/child workshops are offered for children aged 3-5 with an adult companion and include gallery tours and creative hands-on activities. The fees are generally $4-$7 per class. A variety of workshops for youths of other ages is available at similar prices. Every Friday at 7:30PM, you can watch a film or several shorts for $3.50. Each month, the museum has a different theme for the movies which includes experimental, historic and non-traditional flicks. A brief discussion generally precedes the showing. Admission to the museum is free at all times, with the exception of the special exhibits, having about a $4.50 admission fee. The popular, Tuesdays At 1 program, presents free lectures on art history and other topics on a weekly basis. In the summer, the Meet Me In The Garden series presents quality weekly jazz performances. The cost is only $4 per concert or $20 for the series. Closed Monday. Tu-F 11-5, Sat 10-5, Sun 11-5. Accepts checks.

COLUMBUS POLO CLUB
Plays in Granville, 43023, 224-PONY (7669)

The Bryn Du field in the picturesque town of Granville, is the site of weekly polo matches from early June through late September. This exciting spectator sport can be enjoyed by young and old alike. Admission is $3 per person or $7 per carload. Children under the age of 12 are admitted for free. A season membership fee costs $50 and entitles an entire carload to free admission, discounts on Polo Club merchandise and special events, plus a complimentary program guide at each match. There are about 30 matches per season which are scheduled every Sunday at 1PM, with many Saturday matches and special events throughout the summer. Bring your tailgate picnic, refreshments, lawn chairs or blankets and some sun screen.

COLUMBUS SWIM CENTER
1160 Hunter Ave., Columbus, 43201, 645-3129

This indoor pool offers year round fun and exercise for a mere 25 cents admission. Free swimming lessons are offered for pre-schoolers through adults in all skill levels. An adult water exercise class is also offered. Outside groups and individuals may rent the pool during non-recreational hours simply by submitting a request to the pool manager at least 2 weeks in advance. The cost is $10 per hour, plus $7.50 per hour for each lifeguard needed. This is a fun and low cost way to have a private party. Ample free parking is available on premises. The pool is operated by the City of Columbus, Recreation and Parks Department which also operates 15 outdoor pools around the area, from May-September, at a similar admission fee. To find out about the other pools, call 645-3300. Sat & Sun 2:30-5:30, Tu 8PM-9:30PM, F 1-3:45 & 7-9:30PM, Th 11AM-2PM, W 1-3:45.

COMEDY CLUB
1213 E. Dublin Granville Rd., Columbus 43229, 431-0663

The club features performances by local, regional and nationally known comedians such as Sinbad, Paul Reiser, Tom Parks, George Miller and the Comedy Caravan. Ticket prices, regardless of the performer's reputation, are always $3-$7. Showtimes are 8:30PM Tuesday through Thursday. Friday and Saturday show times are at 8:30 and 10:45PM. On Tuesday, admission is $3, Wednesday and Thursday tickets are $5. Friday and Saturday seating is $7. You do not need to purchase any drinks once inside, but these, and light food items, are available if you so choose. The club, located within the Ramada Inn North, caters to the under 30 crowd. Don't miss the excellent improvization done by the Midwest Comedy Tool And Die, who regular appear here. Tu-Th 12-10PM, F and Sat 12-12. Accepts MC & Visa.

CONTEMPORARY AMERICAN THEATER COMPANY (CATCO)
512 N. Park St., Columbus, 43215, 461-0010

This unpretentious theater, with its faux finished exterior, reminds me of the off-Broadway theaters in New York. You can attend their preview night performances on the Wednesday prior to the official opening night, for half the regular ticket price of $9-$18. So you'll pay only $4.50-$9 per seat. On this night, the director has the opportunity to make any last minute changes before the official opening. Changes, if needed, are made after the performance, never during. This is not a dress rehearsal. Another savings opportunity is to purchase a subscription which consists of 8 coupons for $80, which are valid at any performance. This amounts to a savings of up to 40% off the individual ticket price. Persons who cannot afford to pay full ticket price, may purchase tickets on the day of the performance at whatever price they can afford to pay! There is a limit of 2 tickets per person. Inquire about their dinner plus theater packages at Aristotle's, Rigsby's and Schmidt's. You can save $3-$8 per meal through a pre-arrangement at the time your CATCO tickets are purchased. M-F 10-5. Accepts checks and cash only.

COVER TO COVER BOOKSTORE
3337 N. High St., Columbus 43202, 263-1624

An enormous selection of books for parents and children can be found here at regular retail prices. Sign up for their mailing list to learn about their many free events for kids including meet the author book readings, story times with seasonal and fun themes, performances and craft sessions. Gives exchanges. M, W and Th 10-8; Tu, F and Sat 10-6. Accepts checks, MC & Visa.

DELAWARE COUNTY CULTURAL ARTS CENTER
190 W. Winter St., Delaware, 43015, 1-369-2787

This new organization on the cultural horizon is not to be missed. Housed in an older building resembling a small castle, and perched high on a hill, it is a delight to visit as well as participate in their programs. In a brief period of time, this facility has managed to develop and implement a large and varied selection of programs and exhibitions. Rush over to your phone and sign up for their mailing list. Come on now..... Delaware is not far from Columbus, especially for those of you living in the North end. The arts center offers an extensive selection of visual, literary, performing and culinary art workshops, lectures and performances for the entire family in day, evening and weekend times. Programs are fairly priced and are consistent with others in the community. However, they also offer many free concerts, literary readings, book discussions and other special events. Don't miss browsing through their gift shop which features handmade arts and crafts, jewelry and gift items from artists across the state. While the prices reflect those typical of a gallery, the selection is unique. Proceeds from the gift shop are used to support the programs at the Delaware County Cultural Arts Center. The gift shop is open Monday through Saturday from 11-4. Provides exchanges only. Accepts checks.

DELAWARE COUNTY METRO PARKS
40 N. Sandusky St., suite 201, Delaware, 43015, 368-1805

The free, Nature Lovers Lecture Series is held year round and features a monthly presentation on such topics as bird watching, wildlife photography, geology and environmental toxicology. The programs are generally held at the Perkins Observatory on

Thursday evenings, but occasionally include daytime hikes to see impressive natural formations. Oddly enough, there aren't any Delaware County metro parks, but this organization is the driving force behind obtaining land for this purpose. Call anytime to inquire.

DELAWARE SQUARE MOVIES
1141 Columbus Pike, (Rte. 23 N) Delaware, 43015, 363-6634 recording), 363-6624 (management)

Central Ohio's best price for first run movies (those which have just been released) is available at this theater. Matinees are offered daily at a cost of $2 per person before 6PM. Evening prices are $4 for adults and $2 for kids aged 11 and under. Bargain night is Tuesday evening where all seats are only $2. This modern theater is only 15 minutes north of Worthington. Accepts cash only.

DENISON UNIVERSITY
Granville, 43023,

The music department, at 587-6220, offers free and low cost performances featuring faculty, students as well as regionally and nationally recognized artists. A variety of musical performances are featured including the Denison Jazz Ensemble, directed by Rick Brunetto. The theater department at 587-6231, features quality adult productions such as Poor Murderer, Miss Firecracker Contest and Antigone and Joe Egg. The fee is $5 for adults and $2 for students or seniors. The dance department at 587-6712, features 4 productions during the school year which feature students, faculty and the visiting artist. Ticket prices are $5 for adults and $2 for seniors and students. All programs are held from October-April,. Call each department to be added to their mailing list. Plan to spend some time in the quaint and peaceful city of Granville which features antique and gift shops. M-F 9-4. Accepts checks and cash only.

DOWNTOWN DANCE CLUB
YWCA, 65 S. 4 St., Columbus, 43215, 231-3760

This club has been in existence for 20 years offering instruction and dancing opportunities. You can learn the foxtrot, waltz or other ballroom dancing from 6:30-7:20PM every Sunday. It is followed by ballroom dancing and a little square dancing, from 7:30-10:30PM. The fee is $2 for the lessons (observers do not have to pay!) and an additional $2 to attend the dance. Refreshments are included with your admission fee. While the dances attract single adults aged 40-60, they are open to the general public, so couples are welcome. Approximately 100-150 people attend the dances and about 25 attend the lessons. Accepts cash only.

DREXEL THEATERS' PREMIER MOVIE CLUB
2254 E. Main St., Columbus, 43209, 231-9512
4250 N. High St., Columbus, 43214, 263-4416

For an annual fee of $40, you can become a member of this club which offers you a pair of tickets to a minimum of 8 movie previews and private screenings (in 1990 they offered 12) of major new releases at the Drexel and other area theaters. You'll also receive invitations to previews of the top alternative films shown at the Drexel and Drexel North Theaters. Passes to movies have included: Pretty Woman, Glory, Driving Miss Daisy and Mermaids!

Seating is on a first come, first served basis. Your membership also entitles you to $1 off the general admission price of tickets everytime you visit each of the two theaters. Other benefits include 2 for 1 coupons at West Coast Video Stores, reduced price admission to AMC and General Cinema movie theaters and a free month's trial membership at Aardvark Video, which will save you 50% off the price of rentals. M-F 9-5. Accepts checks.

ENTERTAINMENT 91/92/93 BOOK
4465 Professional Pkwy., Columbus, 43125, 836-7283

This annual publication contains discounts on hundreds of restaurants, theaters, sports, travel opportunities and services usually as "buy one, get one free" or a percentage off arrangement. There are also a few coupons which entitle you to 50% off a meal when dining alone. Some use restrictions may apply. You can purchase the book for $34.95 at all Lazarus stores, Sears, J.C. Penney's, Readmor Bookstores, Super X or Waldenbooks. Or you can save $5 by purchasing it through local nonprofit organizations. This coupon book has earned the distinction of being one of my personal favorites. Call to obtain a listing. M-F 8-5.

FAMILY CONCERTS ON THE GREEN
c/o Worthington Parks and Recreation Dept., 436-2743

Every Sunday evening from mid-May through mid-August, the free, outdoor music series offers a variety of family, musical concerts. The programs are held at 7PM on the Village Green, High Street and West Dublin-Granville Road. Bring a lawn chair or a blanket to sit on. In case of inclement weather, the concert will be cancelled. Performers have included local and regionally recognized groups such as Arnett Howard's Creole Funk Band, the Worthington Civic Band, the Sounds Of Swing, the Sweet Adelines and Rainbow Canyon. The concerts are open to the general public. Call between 9-5, Monday-Friday if you have any questions.

FIRST CONGREGATIONAL CHURCH
444 E. Broad St., Columbus, 43213, 228-1741

Throughout the Lenten season, from mid February through late March, the church offers a free series of lunchtime organ recitals on Tuesdays from 12:15-12:45PM. Guest performers have included such virtuosos as Stanley Osborn of Kenyon College and G. Dene Barnard. You may bring your lunch. Reservations are not needed. Other free organ concerts are held September through May intermittently on Sunday evenings. M-F 9-5.

FLICKERS CINEMA PUB AND FLICKERS EAST
5227 Bethel Center Mallway, Columbus, 43220, 457-0492
4501 Refugee Rd., Columbus, 43232, 861-6622

You will find great prices on movies and a buffet at these cinema pubs. Seven days a week, at 6:15PM, you can try their "all-you-can-eat" pizza, sub, soup and salad buffet with a movie for only $5.95 for adults or $4.95 for children aged 12 and under. Wednesday evenings after 6:30PM, admission to the movie alone is only 98 cents for all seats. Saturday and Sunday matinees are $1.50 for all seats. All other days and times, admission is $2 for adults , and $1.50 for children under 17 and seniors aged 60 and over. Beer and wine are available at the Bethel Road site, and just beer is available at the Refugee Road location. At all times, no one under 17 is admitted unless accompanied by a parent.

FRANKLIN COUNTY METRO PARKS
Battelle-Darby Creek, 1775 Darby Creek Dr., 43119, 891-0700
Blacklick Woods, 6975 E. Livingston Ave., Reynoldsburg,   43068, 891-0700
Blendon Woods, 4265 E. Dublin-Granville Rd., Westerville, 43081. 891-0700
Chestnut Ridge, Lancaster-Winchester Rd., 891-0700
Highbanks, 9466 N. High St., Worthington, 43235, 891-0700
Inniswood, 940 Hempstead Rd., Westerville 43081, 891-0700
Pickerington Ponds, Bowen and Wright Rd., Pickerington, 43147, 891-0700
Sharon Woods, 6911 Cleveland Ave., Columbus, 43231,891-0700
Slate Run Living Historical Farm, 9130 Marcy Rd., 43110, 833-1880
Slate Run, 1375 State Rt. 674 N., 891-0700
Spring Hollow, 1069 W. Main St., Westerville, 43081, 891-0700

Eleven area metro parks offer the opportunity to experience nature at its finest. Bicycling, hiking and jogging trails take you through scenic areas filled with animal observation sites, wildflowers and natural formations. Each park has its own personality and I recommend that you visit each one. The Metro Parks offer an extensive selection of year round programs for preschoolers through seniors including hikes, bird and animal watches, campfires, canoe trips, junior naturalist programs, salamander hunts, wildlife exhibitions, lectures and craft programs, most of which are free. Many Metro Parks have picnic areas and reservable shelters for family gatherings and special events. The *Lens And Leaves Camera Club* meets on the second Thursday of each month at the Blacklick Woods site, and presents a discussion on photography techniques relating to the outdoors or to nature. The meetings are free and open to the public. The beauty and diversity of the Metro Parks makes them among my personal favorites listed in this book. Call to be added to their mailing list, or stop by any public library to pick up one of their flyers. Parks are open 6:30AM-dusk year round.

FUNNY BONE
6312 Busch Blvd., Columbus, 43229, 431-1471

Presents local and regional comedy acts for $5-$8. However, prices to see nationally known comedians such as Emo Phillips, Elaine Booster and Judy Tenuta are about $18-$22. Showtimes are Monday-Thursday at 8:30PM and cost $6 per ticket. On Friday, admission is $7 and showtimes are at 8:30 and 10:45PM. Saturday seats costs $8 and showtimes are at 7:45, 10:00 and midnight. Sunday admission is $6 with showtime scheduled for 8:00PM. There is a 2 drink minimum (alcoholic or non-alcoholic) per person. Drinks start at $1.50. The Funny Bone is located in the Continent. Has a mailing list. M-Th 12-10PM, F and Sat 12-midnight. Accepts checks, MC, Visa & AmExp.

GAHANNA COMMUNITY THEATER
471-0438

Family oriented productions such as Mame, are presented by this local troupe of amateur and professional thespians. Two yearly performances, at Gahanna-Lincoln High School, include a musical in February and a 3 act play in October. Prices range from $3-$4.50 per seat. Call M-F 9AM-10PM.

GOLDEN AGE PASSPORT
c/o U.S. Fish And Wildlife Service, 6950-H Americana Pkwy.,Reynoldsburg, 43068, 469-6923

Free lifetime admission to all of the federally operated parks, recreation areas and monuments throughout the United States, which generally charge an admission fee, is available to seniors aged 62 and older. All companions travelling with the senior in a noncommercial vehicle, will be admitted for free as well. Seniors will also be entitled to a 50% discount on federal use fees which are charged for such things as parking, camping and boat launching. Proof of age is required to obtain the free membership card. Interested individuals must apply in person. M-F 8-3.

GRANDVIEW HEIGHTS PUBLIC LIBRARY
1685 W. 1 Ave., Columbus, 43212, 486-2954

As is the case with many community libraries, the one in Grandview Heights offers a multitude of mostly free lectures, performances, book readings, kids' programs, crafts workshops for all ages, films, storytimes and special events. In the past, they have had lectures on rare books, consumer law for the layman and managing your financial future. Workshops have included CPR and tee shirt painting. Their annual *Music In The Atrium* series is held from November-April and features free instrumental performances once a month, on Tuesday evenings. Three to five year olds and their caregivers can enjoy stories, creative dramatics, fingerplays, puppet shows and simple crafts on Thursdays at 7PM. A similar program is offered for 1 1/2-3 year olds on Tuesday mornings at 10:30AM and Wednesday evenings at 7PM. Their annual *Paper Airplane Contest*, for first-sixth graders, is held in the fall and features contests and instruction in creating the airplanes. The annual, *Ghosts Of Baker Street-Sherlock Holmes And More*, is held in January to celebrate the birthday of Sherlock Holmes. The free event features a reception, readings, in addition to information and facts about the author, Sir Arthur Conan Doyle. Their semi-annual book sale, usually held in October and February, provides you with the chance to purchase magazines for 50 cents and under as well as books for 25 cents to about $1. The free, *Music On The Lawn* program, is held on the second and fourth Tuesday at 7PM, from June-August. at the nearby Edison Kindergarten Annex. The rainsite is at the Grandview Heights High School. Prominent local groups such as Trilogy and Arnett Howard's Creole Funk Band, perform hour long concerts. Some programs require advance registration or tickets, even though they are free. Stop in the library to pick up their quarterly flyer of events. M-F 9-9, Sat 9-5.

GRANDVIEW THEATER
1247 Grandview Ave., Columbus, 43212, 486-6114 or 486-6120

Admission is only $1 on Tuesday evenings and $2 at all other times at this second run theater. A raffle is offered before each performance which provides you with the opportunity to win free admission. The theater features an annual Three Stooges Convention in mid October which presents these classic films, guest appearances, memorabilia, souvenirs and contests. Admission to this event is $5. M-F 7:15PM-11:30, Sat and Sun 5:15PM-11:30.

GRANVILLE RECREATION COMMISSION
Box 483, Granville, 43023, 587-1976

A free, summer outdoor concert series is held every other Sunday at 5:30PM on the lawn of Monomoy House, the residence of Denison University's president. The rainsite is Burke Recital Hall at Denison University. Concerts are held from May-August and feature a wide range of styles. Local as well as regionally known performers have included the OSU Alumni Band, the Hotfoot Quartet, the Windrich Quintessence Woodwinds, Seona McDowell and others. You'll enjoy visiting the quaint town of Granville, which is only 30 minutes from the east side of Columbus, so save time to browse through the downtown area and drive through the surrounding neighborhoods. M-F 9-5.

GRINS EASTSIDE COMEDY CONNECTION
2100 Brice Rd., Reynoldsburg, 43068, 863-4746

Local, regional and nationally touring comedians are featured at Columbus' newest comedy club. Ticket prices are $6-$7 for most shows, with prices to see top name entertainers at about $18-$25. Showtimes are Fridays at 9:00PM and Saturdays at 8:30 and 10:40PM. In addition to your admission fee, there is a 2 item minimum per person which could be purchased as drinks and/or food. F 12-10, Sat 12-12. Accepts MC & Visa.

HEADLINERS
1664 E. Dublin-Granville Rd., Columbus, 43229, 523-2004 or 523-2495

This 23,000 square foot night spot has been dubbed an "entertainment resort" by its owners, and I must agree. It features 7 bars, a sports and billiards room, a private area for VIP members, a jazz and blues room as well as a large dance floor. Sometimes there is a DJ and at other times you will find live music or even a comedian. Monday night is big band night. Thursday-Saturday are live comedy nights with 2 shows being featured each evening. Wednesday is Ladies Night in which women are admitted for free and can also purchase cocktails or any other beverages at the bar for only 75 cents apiece. The club has also scheduled some nationally known recording artists such as James Ingram, Dino and Donny Osmond as well as Styx. The decor features lots of glitter and glitz, marble floors and lots of brass. Keep your eyes on the large color coordinated paintings which intermittently become hidden behind large screens on which you can view rock videos. Headliners maintains a strict dress code and identification is checked at the door. The crowd is a mixture of 25-55 year olds. The cover charge is $3 week nights and $5 on week ends, regardless of the type of performance scheduled. Your admission fee permits you to enjoy any and all performances throughout the building. The large dinner buffet, which is included in your admission price, is served Wednesday-Friday from 6-8PM and offers a varied assortment of well prepared hot and cold dishes such as carved ham, marinated tortellini, cold seafood salad and more. It is best to arrive early for the buffet on Thursday and Friday as you could wait several minutes on line, once inside the club, before you reach the food. Drink prices are reduced during the happy hour. Call for information on their special promotions. M-Sat 5PM-2:30AM. Accepts MC, Visa & AmExp.

HOT SPOTS
Columbus City Center, Columbus, 43215, 1-800-627-4762

Offers free travel and recreational opportunities brochures for cities throughout the United States. Find out where to go to enjoy white water rafting, historic sites, beaches, golf resorts, camp grounds, bed and breakfasts and more. *Hot Spots* also has a number of free travel videos which can be viewed in the store only. This is not a travel agency and as a result, does not make any travel arrangements. M-Th 10-8, F and Sat 10-6, Sun 12-5.

I FIORI MUSICALI SERIES
C/O Pontifical College Josephinum, 7625 N. High St., Worthington, 43235, 885-5585

This annual performing arts series is offered from September to June and features monthly vocal, instrumental and theatrical programs, many of which are free or under $10 per seat. While days and times vary, the presentations are always in the evenings at the St. Tiribius Chapel, a fine example of neo-Gothic style architecture. Past programs have included organ music, the Cantari Singers of Columbus, the Lancaster Chorale, Touch Of Elegance flute and guitar duet as well as holiday music. M-F 9-5. Accepts checks, MC & Visa.

THE HYATT ON CAPITOL SQUARE
75 E. State St., Columbus, 43215, 228-1234

The former Rally In The Alley, has taken up a new home at the Hyatt on Capitol Square, where, on one Friday per month, the Affair On The Square (as it is now called) features free outdoor concerts. The events are held from early June through late August. at Darby's Cafe. Local and regionally known performing groups such as Beauty And The Beats as well as Arnett Howard's Creole Funk Band will perform from 5-8PM. The Affair is co-sponsored by WTVN Radio. Food and beverages will be available for purchase. On all other Fridays, during these months, the Hyatt features a similar after work gathering, but with a little less hoop-de-lah. Admission is free at all times.

KATZ AND DAWGS
440 Dublin Ave., Columbus, 43215, 621-1414

This nonprofit gallery is located within the Old Buggy Works and serves as a platform for fresh, exciting, provocative and usually non-commercial artwork. As an event oriented facility, Katz and Dawgs features free and low cost entertainment (usually $3 and under) such as performance art, poetry readings and musical performances intermittently throughout the year. Life drawing classes are held Mondays from 7-10PM at a cost of $3 for students and $5 for practicing artists. The classes do not offer instruction, but instead provide a drawing opportunity for individuals. The gallery may also be rented for private parties. Hours vary.

KIDS DISCOVER COLUMBUS
645-3300

Registration opens in early April for this highly recognized travelling day camp program for kids aged 6-11. Campers can board a special COTA bus at designated Columbus recreation centers and take off for a fun filled adventure. They will explore various sites and attractions around Columbus such as the Park Of Roses, factory tours, COSI and other interesting attractions. The fee is $25 per week and includes all site admission costs, bus fares, a tee shirt and a daily beverage. Children can attend one or more weeks. The program is sponsored by the Columbus Recreation and Parks Department. The camp is held from mid-June to mid-August. M-F 9-5. Accepts checks and money orders only.

KROGER
30 area stores, see telephone book for listings

All area Kroger supermarkets are the pick up sites for free Zoopons, in the fall of each year. These coupon booklets can save you up to $50 off food, train rides and gift shop purchases at the Columbus Zoo during the fall and the winter seasons. The Zoopons are available while supplies last. This supermarket chain also serves as the site to purchase discount tickets to a variety of major entertainment and special events in the Columbus area such as the Ice Capades, Sesame Street Live, the Archie Griffin Tennis Classic, the Parade of Homes, the New Car Auto Show and Wyandotte Lake. Savings are usually $1-$3 off the ticket price. All Kroger bakery departments offer a free sugar, chocolate chip or peanut butter cookie to children ages 12 and under at any time, when accompanied by a parent. Coupons are not required. The chain also offers double manufacturers cents off coupons up to a 50 cent face value. Seniors who have a Golden Buckeye Card, may pick up a free Kroger Golden Buckeye Tuesday Coupon Book (in the spring) which provides special weekly savings at the stores through July. Open 24 hours, 7 days per week.

LASER LIGHT SHOW
645-3300

Columbus is the only city in the country to offer a free laser light show nightly. Every evening from Memorial Day through Labor Day, the downtown Scioto riverfront features a spectacular neon-fiber optics display which dances and moves to oldies and contemporary rock, symphony and movie tunes. Lasers are projected onto several downtown buildings which line the riverfront, creating abstract, geometric, cartoon and other images. The free, 45 minute light show provides an exciting diversion for young and old alike. The best seating is on the West side of the Scioto River near Central High School. Bring a blanket or a lawn chair to sit on or try to find a seat at the adjacent Riverfront Amphitheater. Why not plan to come early and enjoy one of the free, Music In The Air concerts at 7:00PM along the river? (see this chapter for a description of Music In The Air). The light show is sponsored by the Columbus Recreation and Parks Department and area corporations.

LICKING COUNTY PLAYERS
OSU-Newark Theater, Founders Hall, Newark, 43055,
366-2133, 366-6793, 235-7522

Quality theatrical productions feature amateur and professional performers. Performances, some of which are family oriented, are usually held on Fridays and Saturdays. Past productions have included the Lion In Winter and Everybody Loves Opal. Ticket prices are $5 for general admission, $4 for students and $3 for seniors. Call M-F 10-4. Accepts checks and cash only.

LITHOPOLIS AREA FINE ARTS ASSN.
Wagnalls Memorial, 150 E. Columbus St. Lithopolis, 43146, 837-4765

Here's your chance to enjoy quality theatrical and musical performances with local, regional and nationally known artists utilizing a wide variety of styles. Individual tickets are usually $6-$10, or you can purchase a series subscription and save 20-30% over the single ticket price. Seniors can save almost 50% off the single ticket price at all times. Programs are held in the Wagnalls Memorial Auditorium, an extraordinary Tudor-Gothic building which also features libraries, artifacts and special collections. Lithopolis is about half an hour from downtown Columbus and is just south of Canal Winchester. M-F 8-5 (box office). Accepts checks, MC & Visa.

LITTLE THEATER OFF BROADWAY
3981 Broadway, Grove City, 43123, 875-3919

Seven quality productions such as comedies, musicals and dramas, are held annually featuring professional and non-professional performers. The 1991-92 season will feature Steel Magnolias, 1940's Radio Hour, The Bad Seed, The Little Shop Of Horrors, Barefoot In The Park and Cinderella. The plays, which are adult and family oriented, are held Thursday-Saturday at 8PM and Sundays at 7PM. Tickets for musicals are $6-$8 and non-musicals are $5-$7. Tickets for children, students and seniors are $2 off the general admission price. A subscription to the series will save you about 25% off the single ticket general admission fee.

MARTIN LUTHER KING CENTER FOR THE PERFORMING AND CULTURAL ARTS
867 Mt. Vernon Ave., Columbus, 43203, 252-5464

Performances, lectures, demonstrations and hands-on workshops, most dealing with topics relating to the African-American experience or featuring Black artists, are offered year round. Programs vary in price, but there are several free and low cost diversions which are offered throughout the year. The adjacent Garfield School, also affiliated with the MLK Center, features the Elijah Pierce Gallery which offers changing exhibits with a similar focus. Gallery admission is free. M-F 9-5.

MILO ARTISTS COLONY
617 E. 3 Ave., Columbus, 43201, 291-3702 or 421-2536

The former Milo public school has been converted to a residential artists' colony. Workshops, films and an open stage for performers and poets are offered to the community. The last Sunday of each month at 7:30PM, the Readers' Theater offers an uncensored, open mic to poets, performing artists and acoustic musicians. Admission and refreshments are free.

MUSIC IN THE AIR
645-3800 (24 hour taped hotline May-September),
645-7995 at other times of the year

This free, annual showcase of local, regional and nationally recognized performing artists features poetry readings, children's programs, special events and concerts several times per week from Memorial Day weekend through Labor Day. Programs are held at area parks throughout the city including Bicentennial Park, the Riverfront Amphitheater, Schiller Park, Westgate, Griggs Reservoir, the Statehouse Lawn and Sensenbrenner Park. The latter two are held during a weekday lunchtime, and the balance are held on weekends. The Magical, Musical, Mornings In The Park are held on Wednesdays at 11:30AM at Westgate Recreation Center and at the same time on Thursdays at both the Park of Roses Gazebo and the Livingston Park. Performances have included Kirk's Puppets, African storytelling, theatrical productions and more. Annual special events, which are held downtown along the riverfront include the 2 day Mcdonald's Gospelfest in mid June, musical entertainment on July 3 at the Red, White and Boom Celebration, the Jazz and

Ribfest in late July and a 3 day Labor Day Blues weekend. Music In The Air is a program of the City of Columbus, Recreation and Parks Department, but it also has many corporate sponsors. It has earned the distinction of being one of my personal favorites.

NICKLEBY'S BOOKSTORE CAFE
1425 Grandview Avenue, Columbus, 43212, 488-BOOK (2665)

This full service bookstore is one of the largest independent bookstores in Central Ohio. It offers seating throughout the store, including a cozy room with a fireplace and highback chairs, where you can leisurely browse through books and magazines. Their books are sold at cover price, but there is a bargain area where savings are up to 70%. Nickleby's has recently begun offering a *Befuddled Cat Book Cart* which features used books from the Columbus Metropolitan Library priced at $1.99 for hardbacks and 99 cents for paperbacks. Proceeds from these books are donated to the library. Special orders and book searches are available and free gift wrapping is offered. During the first 2 weeks in August each year, the store features their *Super Gold Mine Book Sale* in which savings are up to 80% off a select group of discontinued and overstocked books. The store features free live musical performances 6 times per week, with local and regional artists including Gary Metheny on the piano, Renaissance music, Marji Hazen's Parlour Band, new age music by Robert Baker sand more. There are many free discussions on such topics as holiday makeup, taxes, wine tasting, travel and massage; book discussions; poetry readings and author visits. Children's programs have included a Halloween party with face painting, storytelling and games. Call to be added to their mailing list to receive the free monthly newsletter. The store is open every day except Christmas, and it frequently presents free programs on holidays. The sit down cafe offers coffee, tea, expresso and capuccino which may be sipped as you browse through the store. Their tantalizing desserts and light foods such as smoked salmon and shrimp in brioche ($5.95), quiche Lorain with tomato chutney ($5.25), seafood lasagne ($6.25), cheesecakes and other delectables can only be eaten in the cafe area. There is a very warm, friendly atmosphere which abounds at Nickleby's. This has earned the distinction of being one of my personal favorites. Offers layaways. Gives senior discounts. M-Th 8AM-10PM, F and Sat 8AM-11:30PM, Sun 8AM-10PM. Accepts checks, MC & Visa.

OHIO HISTORICAL CENTER
Colonel Crawford Inn, 297-2684
Ohio Village, 297-2680
Ohio Historical Center, 297-2680

The Ohio Historical Society operates these facilities at 1985 Velma Avenue (Columbus, 43211) which offer free and low cost educational and entertaining programs, concerts, special events, performances, gallery talks, demonstrations and hands-on workshops. The Historical Center houses exhibits relating to Ohio's geological, archeological and historic past.. It offers a Family Sunday program once per month which generally coordinates with their gallery exhibit. Past programs have included a concert of nature and environmental songs, bird feeding in the bird sanctuary area and native American Indian films. Other programs have been a lecture on Lost Tribes And Flying Saucers, various performances, a winter Distinguished Lecturer Series ($2 admission) and more. Programs are generally free to about $6 per person. The Ohio Village provides the chance for you to experience life as it existed in Ohio in the mid 1800's through the observation of crafters demonstrating different skills, oral interpreters, workshops for young and old (tinsmithing, wood engraving, basketry), special period events (All Hallows Eve, Fourth Of July

Celebration) and performances. Many programs are free while others, except the workshops are about $5 and under. While the variety of workshops is extensive, I feel the prices are reasonable and about typical. However, you should be aware that many of these types of workshops are not available elsewhere in the area. They provide an excellent learning opportunity and should therefore be seriously considered as a interesting diversion for you and your family. Free summer weekend entertainment at the Ohio Village includes music, old time magic and medicine shows and interactive programs. Another summertime diversion is the Ohio Village Muffins, a costumed 19th century baseball team, who play there about twice per month. The Colonel Crawford Inn offers a delectable menu in an authentic old time atmosphere Delicious lunch and dinner meals are served at moderate prices. Holiday buffets as well as dinner/entertainment packages are very enjoyable and moderately priced. Parking at the Ohio Historical Center is $2 per carload, and admits you to the Colonel Crawford Inn and the Ohio Village as well. Program schedules can usually be found at area libraries. If you join the Ohio Historical Society at a cost of $32 annually for a family or $27 for students and seniors, your membership fee will be well worth the investment. You will receive discounts on workshops and other programs, a subscription to the newsletter which lists upcoming events, invitations to members only programs, gift shop discounts, free admission to over 50 state memorials and facilities, and a parking fee waiver at the Ohio Historical Society in Columbus. The Ohio Historical Center, Ohio Village and the Colonel Crawford Inn are among my personal favorites. M-F 9-5.

OHIO PASS PLUS PROGRAM
c/o Ohio Dept. of Travel and Tourism, 77 S. High St.,
Columbus, 43215, 1-800-282-5393 (1-800-BUCKEYE).

Simply call this number and request your free Ohio Pass Plus Getaway Card and the participating merchants' book. By presenting your card at any of the more than 500 hotels and motels, restaurants, attractions or shops in Ohio, you will be able to save 5-50% off the regular price. Open 7 Days per week, 24 hours per day for recorded assistance. A touchtone phone is needed. If you would like to speak with a counselor, call Monday-Friday 9-5.

OHIO STATE UNIVERSITY ARTS HOTLINE
292-ARTS (2787)

This taped hotline operates 24 hours a day, 7 days a week. It provides information on all of the events taking place at OSU which are open to the public including those at Mershon Auditorium, Weigel Hall, the Wexner Center and those offered through the dance, theater, photography, architecture and other departments. Many of the programs are free or low cost. You can also request to be on the mailing list of the College Of The Arts by writing them in care of the Office of Communications, 1871 N. High Street, Columbus, 43210.

OHIO STATE UNIVERSITY-COLLEGE OF HUMANITIES
186 University Hall, 230 N. Oval Mall, Columbus, 292-1882

Sponsors many free programs for the general public in day and evening times, throughout the week and on weekends. Previous programs have included literary readings, lectures on *Aristotle On Artifacts, Judaism And Law, Medieval Disputation, Race, Class And Gender In U.S. Society* and a play on AIDS. From 9:30-10:30AM on Saturdays during the fall and winter seasons, the *Saturday Scholar Series* presents free lectures such as *Excavation Of*

Greek Ruins Yields Link To Olympic Games, Feminist Looks At Hollywood Actresses, Politics Of Style and Renaissance Exotica And Erotica. A continental breakfast is served at no charge. The programs are held at the Fawcett Center. Phone 292-1882 for information on the *Saturday Scholar Series.* The Humanities department publishes a free calendar of events which you can obtain by calling this same phone number. Other departments within the College of Humanities which you might want to contact directly about free programs include the English Department (292-6065), the College of Law (292-0967), the Department of Philosophy (292-7914), the Black Studies Department (292-4459) and the Center For Women's Studies (292-1021). Most programs on held on campus and all are open to the general public. M-F 9-4.

OHIO STATE UNIVERSITY-DEPT. OF ARCHITECTURE
189 Brown Hall, 190 W. 17 Ave., Columbus, 43210, 292-5567

Offers a free lecture series in the autumn, winter and spring on such topics as geological architecture, European castles etc. There are 18 two hour programs offered each year at various campus sites, generally on Wednesday evenings. The programs are open to the public. Call to be added to their mailing list. M-F 9-5.

OHIO STATE UNIVERSITY-THEATER DEPARTMENT
292-2295

Presents a variety of quality programs from October through May at several campus theaters. Prices range from free to about $10 and have included such productions as an MFA Actors' Showcase, musicals, dramas, comedies and mysteries.

OHIO THEATER SUMMER MOVIE SERIES
55 E. State St., Columbus, 43215, 469-0939

A changing sampler of classic and old movies from the 1920's to the 1960's is shown annually in this much anticipated series. Showtimes are on Wednesdays at 1:30 and 7:30, Friday at 7:30, Saturdays and Sundays at 2:00 and 7:30. Past movies have included Hitchcock thrillers, Dr. Zhivago, Anatomy Of A Murderer and others. The series is held from July 5-August 31. General admission is $2.50 or $2 for seniors. Save about 25% by purchasing a strip of 10 tickets for only $18.50, by July 15. M-F 9-5. Accepts checks, MC & Visa.

OHIO WESLEYAN UNIVERSITY
Delaware, 43015,

Features free lectures in the fall, on world affairs and political issues as part of the *OWU National Colloquium Speakers Series.* Topics such as The Promise Of Democracy , are discussed by local, regional and nationally recognized individuals. Phone 368-3335 for details. The University also offers frequent free student/faculty vocal and instrumental performances from October-April each year. Intermittent performances by the Central Ohio Symphony Orchestra cost $5. Phone 368-3700 for information. A performing arts /lecture series is held on Friday evenings from September through April and features theatrical productions, discussions and musical performances by local, regional, national and internationally known artists. Single seat general admission is $6 for adults and $2 for students. A season series subscription for 10 events is $30 for general admission and $25 for seniors, which will save you about 50% off the single ticket price. For information, phone 368-3185. The Chapelaar Drama Center is the site of quality dance as well as theatrical performances from September through May at a cost of $4 for general admission and $3 for seniors and students. Phone 368-3845 for information. The Community Film Series is also held during this time and features about 10 old time, memorable films at a cost of $3 each. Phone 363-4914. Programs are open to the general public. M-F 9-4. Accepts checks and cash only.

OLIVER WENDELL HOLMES LECTURE SERIES
C/O Riverside Hospital, 3535 Olentangy River Rd., Columbus, 43214, 261-5003

Free lectures, slide presentations and demonstrations of general interest are held on the second Thursday of each month, year round. The programs are featured in the Susan B. Edwards Auditorium, from 12:15 to 1:00PM. In the past, presentations have included a *La Belle Pomme* cooking instructor giving a demonstration on holiday cooking, members of the *Grandparents Living Theater* in a performance, and a slide presentation on Norman Rockwell. The programs are open to the general public.. While you are there, plan to eat lunch or have a snack in the hospital's cafeteria, which offers an extensive selection of value priced foods that are delicious and healthy. Offerings include filet of sole, baked scrod, cubed steak with onions, teriyaki chicken, vegetable lasagne, vegetable salads, fruits and desserts. Expect to pay a few dollars to park your car unless you park several blocks away in a residential neighborhood.

OMNI HOTELS
1-800-843-6664

Members of the AARP (Association Of Retired Persons), receive a 50% discount off the regular room rate at any time, subject to availability. A 15% discount is also extended on meals purchased in the Omni restaurant Another option, which is. the Omni Select Guest Program, is available to the general public at no cost. Membership can be obtained by calling the above phone number. Participants in this program will be entitled to express check in, use of the private Omni Club floor, preferred reservation availability as well as discount coupons at attractions and businesses. Most of the Omni Hotels are on the East coast in New York, Boston, Charlotte, Charleston, Durham, Miami and Jacksonville in addition to Indianapolis, Cincinnati, Chicago, Dallas and Detroit. Rates vary, but are regularly about $69 per room with a queen sized bed for 1 night.

ORDINARY MYSTERIES
245 W. 5 Ave., Columbus, 43201, 421-2536 or 294-2000

On the second Thursday of each month, this curiosity shop features an open mic for area poets who are given 15 minutes in which to read their uncensored works. Some acoustic presentations are also included. Herbal tea and admission are free. The readings are coordinated by Charles Cicirella This interesting shop sells rocks, crystals, jewelry and unusual gift items at regular retail prices.

THE OTHER SIDE COFFEE HOUSE
C/O First Unitarian Universalist Church, 93 W. Weisheimer Rd., Columbus, 43214, 262-2730

Enjoy a coffee house with a variety of entertainment ranging from folk musician, Hank

Arbaugh, 60's revivalist, Bill Cohen, middle Eastern dancer, Shakira, and other local and national touring groups and individuals. The recurring themes in the performances are peace, hunger, homelessness and the like. Held the last Saturday of the month at 8PM, the program includes a main performance and a concert by the house band, Chaotic Good, a charismatic group with strong vocal skills. The open mic provides the opportunity for poets, musicians, vocalists and dancers to perform for 5 minutes each,. The informal atmosphere is warm and inviting. Admission is $3 plus a can of food. Seniors and children are welcome and are admitted for only $1.50. All proceeds benefit the Sanctuary Movement. Accepts checks. Call anytime.

OTTERBEIN COLLEGE
North Grove and College Ave., Westerville, 43081, 898-1508 and 898-1600

Presents quality theatrical productions year round at a cost of $7-$9 such as A Streetcar Named Desire. Free faculty and student vocal and instrumental performances are held from October through April on a frequent basis. A performing artist series is held monthly and features local and regionally known musicians in concert for about $5.

THE PATIO AT GIBBY'S
490 S. Front St., Columbus, 43215, 464-4297

This Brewery District restaurant/bar, features a large, outdoor patio where special weekly events are held mainly from late April to late October. Musical performances with top name local talent, bonfires, dance presentations and special events are featured. Some have free admission, while others can cost up to a $5 cover charge. You can follow the newspapers to find out about these special happenings, or call.

PEARLS OF WISDOM BOOKSTORE
3224 N. High St., Columbus, 43202, 262-0146

This full priced book store is a favorite of the New Age community. Sign up for their monthly newsletter which will describe new books, gifts, tapes, sales as well as their free, low cost and moderately priced classes, workshops, seminars and performances on ancient religions, tarot, psychic phenomenon, wellness and similar topics. Some recent free programs included a discussion on the biology of happiness by Steve Wilson and a Tibetan tea ceremony/discussion with Philip Sugden. The bookstore also has a video rental club which allows you to choose from over 300 titles not readily available elsewhere. Membership is $20 for the first year and drops by $5 per year. After your fourth year, membership is free. Videos rent for $2 the first day and $1 each additional day. Gives exchanges only. M-Sat 10-8. Accepts checks, MC & Visa.

PLAYER'S THEATER
77 S. High St., Columbus, 43215, 644-8425

Save about 20% (approximately $5) off tickets to Wednesday or Thursday preview night performances. Tickets on these nights will be $15-$20, but are usually $20-$25 at other times. During the preview nights, the director has the opportunity to make final changes to the play before opening night. If changes are necessary, they are made after the play is performed, not during the performance. In the past, Players Theater has performed dramas, comedies, mysteries and musicals such as Steel Magnolias, Misery, the Secret Garden and The Nerd. You can save about 25% off the single ticket price by purchasing a series subscription. Free monthly readings and discussions of area playwrights' works are held on Mondays at 7PM and are open to the public. M-F 10-4. Accepts checks, MC & Visa.

QUALITY INNS INTERNATIONAL
1-800-221-2222

Seniors aged 62 and older, can save 10% off their room rate at any time. A 30% savings is available to seniors if reservations are made 30 days in advance and a single night's deposit is given.

REALITY THEATER
736 N. Pearl St., Columbus, 43215, 294-7541

Columbus' experimental theater offers quality free and low cost performances (usually $2-$8). They have featured an MFA Actors Showcase, Metro General (a soap opera spoof), performances by works of winners of their playwrights' contest and other productions. Reality Theater is well noted for its large, sideways portrait of the Mona Lisa which is painted on the building's exterior. M-F 11-5. Accepts checks and cash

ROSEBRIAR SHAKESPEARE COMPANY
3923 N. High St., Columbus, 43214, 337-2423 or 645-3217

This newly formed theatrical group presents about 4 staged productions annually at the Whetstone Recreation Center, featuring the work of Shakespeare and other classical playwrights. Admission is free and reservations are required. Hours of operation vary.

SHORT NORTH CHAMBER MUSIC SERIES
291-5854

Seven annual concerts are held from fall to spring on Sunday afternoons at the Short North Tavern. The music includes a broad range of styles and has featured the Norton James Renzetti Trio (flute and harp), Terry Waldo (ragtime), Columbus Wind Octet and the Page Players (flute, violin, viola, cello). Performers are locally and regionally known. The series, sponsored by the Short North Performing Arts Association, was recently praised in Chamber Music, a national magazine. Their concerts have been broadcast on WCBE radio. Tickets are $8 apiece, $45 for the 7 concert series or $30 for 4 concerts. Obviously, the 7 concert subscription will save you the most money. Accepts checks.

SHORT NORTH SHOPS
464-0103, 461-6487, 461-9800 and 224-0366

On the first Saturday of every ,month, from 6-9PM, you can attend one of the most exciting events, the Gallery Hop. The businesses and galleries in the area bounded by North High Street from Goodale to Third and the adjoining streets, feature a giant opening reception for the new exhibitions. Entertainment is often found in the galleries and on the streets. Free munchies are also available in some of the galleries. Gallery Hop admission is always free. This is an exciting way to enjoy an evening as you walk through boutiques, exhibition spaces and galleries to find handwoven clothing, jewelry, antique furniture, pottery and a variety of other two and three dimensional media. The Short North has been likened to a mini Soho. The monthly *Taste The Arts* event, is generally less crowded than the *Gallery Hop*. It is featured on the last Thursday of each month, from 5-9PM, except in January, and offers the opportunity to browse and shop in the stores and galleries which offer free, delicious edibles from Rigsby's and other area eateries. Tu-Sat 11-5 . The stores are also open the first Saturday of the month from 6-9PM during the Gallery Hop.

SOUNDS OF SUMMER
C/O Westerville Parks And Recreation Dept., 890-8544

The Alum Creek Park Amphitheater on West Main Street in Westerville, is the site of a weekly series of free concerts from June through late August. The annual series is held on Sundays at 7PM and includes a wide range of styles by local and regionally known performers. Groups which have performed in the past have included the Greater Columbus Concert Band, the Delaware County Sweet Adelines,, the Bluegrass Hoppers, the DeVry State Band and the Columbus Pops. Concerts are suitable for families. Bring a lawn chair or a blanket to sit on. In case of rain, the concerts will be held in the Battelle Fine Arts Center of Otterbein College. To obtain more information, call M-F 9-5.

SNEAK PREVIEWS AT AREA FIRST RUN MOVIE THEATERS
see addresses below

All first run movie theaters feature a bargain matinee price before 6PM which can save you about $2 off the regular admission fee of about $5-$5.50. Another opportunity for savings exists in viewing preview movies which are screened at the theater before being officially released to the general public. Usually the movie theater will charge you their regular rate to see a first run movie and will allow you stay to "preview" another movie not yet released. It is like a two for one price. You need to follow the newspapers (read the fine print in the advertisements as the previews are not well publicized) or call the movie theaters and speak directly with someone in the box office. As this is usually a last minute decision, the theaters will generally know 3-6 days in advance. Also, area radio stations occasionally offer free movie passes at special community promotions such as new store openings and special events. Sometimes you can find out by calling your favorite station. At other times, you'll be surprised if you attend one of these community promotional events. I received free passes from a radio station to two new movies, at the time, Russia House and Mermaids at a new store opening for Hammond's Superstore on Morse Road. Sneak previews are a way in which film distributors can determine audience demographics which will assist in marketing efforts for the movies. Some theaters offering these special sneak previews include:

AMC Theaters: Eastland Plaza 6 (861-8585), Dublin Village 10 (889-0112), Westerville 6 (890-3344), Eastland Center 8(863-1539). Offers about 15 sneak previews per year at each theater. These are generally featured on Saturday evenings. Admission is $5.50 for adults, $4.50 for students and $3.50 for seniors. The theaters have recently begun a *Movie Watcher Club* which entitles you to free snacks during your first 4 visits to the theater. On the fifth visit, you will receive a pass valid for one free admission. Thereafter, you'll automatically be a lifetime member of the club, and will receive free posters, passes to sneak previews and other special opportunities. There is no charge to become a member of the club.
Loew's Continent 9: (846-6202). Usually one sneak preview per month is offered on a week night. Adult admission is $6, children under 12 and seniors admitted for $3.50
General Cinemas: Northland 8 (447-0066) and University City (263-5435). Sneak previews are offered about 6 times per year on varying days and times.

Cinemark Movies 12: (777-1010). Located in the Market at Mill Run, this theater offers about 4-6 sneak previews annually, often on a Thursday through Sunday evening. An unexpected surprise is that the theater will allow you a free pass to the theater on your birthday, just bring proof.

SOUNDS OF SUMMER
C/O Groveport Parks And Recreation Dept., 605 Cherry St.,
Groveport, 43125, 836-5301

This department offers a free summer concert series from June through September. The programs are typically held on the first Sunday of the month at 7PM. on the stage behind the Log House, near Wirt and College Roads. The type of music varies, but has included the Red Mud Ridge Band, the Sounds Of Swing and the Columbus Pops Concert Band. Bring a lawn chair or a blanket to sit on. Concerts are open to the public. M-F 9-5.

SPRINGFIELD ARTS FESTIVAL
C/O Springfield Arts Council, Box 745, Springfield, 45501, (513) 324-2712

In 1991, this annual performing arts festival celebrates its 25th year of quality, free programs. Annually, about 28 afternoons and evenings of performances from early June through mid July, include such groups as the Springfield Symphony Orchestra, the Springfield Concert Band, the Springfield Civic Theater, the Ohio Lyric Theater, the Ian Polster Orchestra, Phil Dirt And The Dozers, Johnny Lytle, the Letterman, the Platters, the Glen Miller Orchestra, the Irish Brigade and the National Shakespeare Company. Theatrical performances have included Sweet Charity, Oliver and the Man Of La Mancha. Each year, the schedule changes to include the brightest stars on the local, regional and national scene and features entertainment for the entire family. Events are held in the Veteran's Park Amphitheater off Cliff Park and Fountain Roads. Parking is also free. Call to be added to their mailing list.

STATE PARKS FAMILY FUN PACK
POB 282, Logan 43138, 1-800-762-9396

When you take your next family vacation, you can save hundreds of dollars on lodging, camping, shopping, food and entertainment in Hocking County by purchasing the Hocking County Coupon Book. The cost is $9.95, plus shipping and handling. Some of the businesses offering these savings include Old Man's Cave Chalet, Tecumseh, the Hocking Valley Central Scenic Railway, the Hocking Valley Canoe Livery, Top 'O The Caves Campgrounds etc. Coupons are valid during the year of purchase, and a new coupon book will be available annually. Sponsored by the State Parks Family Fun Pack and the Old Man's Cave Chalet. Call anytime. Accepts cashier's checks, money orders, MC & Visa.

STUDIO 35
3055 Indianola Ave., Columbus, 43202, 261-1581 or 262-7505

Admission is $2 at all times and provides you with the opportunity to see 2 movies. Pizza, beer and subs are available for purchase at typical take-out store prices.

SUNDAYS AT FIVE CONCERTS
Graves Recital Hall, 5798 Karl Rd., Columbus, 43229,847-4322

Local and nationally recognized performing artists present some of the world's finest music on the third Sunday of every month from September through June. The free concerts are held at 5PM and showcase a wide variety of styles. Guest performers have included Andre LaPlante (pianist), and Barbara Conrad (mezzo soprano of the N.Y. Metropolitan Opera). Call to be added to mailing list. M-Sat 10-9, Sun 12-5.

SUPER SAVER 8
5996 Westerville Rd., Westerville, 43081, 890-2624
5899 Scarborough Mallway, Columbus, 43232, 864-1064

If you like high tech decors, you'll love the fantastic star wars type tunnel with digital sound, and the magic light show which greet you prior to entering the movie. The ceilings in the lobbies are also filled with an unusual grouping of colorful lights, Astro Spiders (imported from Italy), which spin and shimmy as they create wild patterns on the walls. Young and old alike will enjoy the ambience. These movie theaters charge a $1.50 admission fee at all times, and feature second run movies. These theaters have earned the distinction of being among my personal favorites.

THIRD AVENUE PERFORMANCE SPACE
1066 N. High St., Columbus, 43201, 291-1333

Free and low cost performances for adults, children and families are offered on various days and times, year round. Past programs have included a children's clowning production, Susan Van Pelt Dance/Speak and Stuart Pimsler Dance Theater. Ticket prices are free to about $6. M-F 9-4. Accepts checks and cash only.

THURBER HOUSE
77 Jefferson Ave., Columbus, 43215, 464-1032

This former home of writer, James Thurber, offers guided tours of the building, followed by readings from the works of Thurber, at 2PM on the third Sunday of every month. The general admission fee is $2 or $1.50 for students and seniors. Operates the Thurber Country Bookstore which features quality works by small presses not typically found in area bookstores. Thurber House also features literary workshops and author readings as well as other special events. M-F 12-4, Sat 12-3, Sun 12-4. Accepts checks and cash only.

TRIUNE CONCERT SERIES
St. John's Evangelical Protestant Church, 59 E. Mound St., Columbus, 43215, 224-8634

Columbus' oldest church concert series was founded in 1966. It is featured annually on a Friday or Saturday evening in November, January, February and March. In the past, performances have included the Brass Band of Columbus,. Tom Battenberg's High Street Stompers, the Oberlin Baroque Ensemble, the Early Interval, Dennis James and the Columbus Symphony String Quartet. Admission is free. M-F 9-5.

UPPER ARLINGTON CULTURAL ARTS COMMISSION
C/O Municipal Services Ctr., 3600 Tremont Rd., Columbus, 43221, 457-8050

Free Music In The Park outdoor concerts are held at 7:30PM every Thursday at the above address, from early June through late August. The top local and regionally known talent is presented with all musical styles featured. Bring a lawn chair or a blanket to sit on at these family concerts. The rain site is indoors. The *Hausmusik Chamber Music Series* features 5 performances from June through December at a cost of $4 per concert or $16 for the series. The commission also sponsors changing exhibitions in its lobby at which admission is free. Free and low cost movies, lectures, workshops and other performances are offered year round. All programs are open to the public so call to be added to their mailing list. Their annual Labor Day Arts Festival presents some of the finest crafts and fine arts for sale by local, regional and nationally known artists.

WEATHERVANE PLAYHOUSE
100 Price Rd., POB 607, Newark, 43055, 366-4616

1991 marks this group's 23rd season of summer theater. Five quality productions are held from mid June through mid August, and have included musicals, comedies and mysteries for adults and families such as Nunsense, The Foreigner, the Bat and Kiss Me Kate. Center seating costs $10-$11 for adults and $8 for children aged 12 and under. Side seating costs $7-$8 per adult ticket and $5 for children. A series subscription for 5 performances costs only $79 and presents a saving of about 40% off the individual center seating ticket price. M-F 9-5. Accepts checks, MC & Visa.

WEXNER CENTER FOR THE ARTS
30 W. 15 Ave., Columbus, 43210, 292-2787

This highly recognized facility on the OSU campus, features regional, national and internationally acclaimed performances by the Paul Taylor Dance Company, the Juillard String Quartet, Eiko and Koma and others. Visiting artist book readings; restored, long unseen and controversial movies and videos; lectures and other special events are priced from $3 to about $20. Several other free programs are offered quarterly including guided tours of the exhibits, faculty recitals and more. Also has an *Occasional Sundays Series* of all types of performances costing about $5. Sign up to be added to their mailing list. M-F 9-5. Accepts checks and cash.

WOMEN'S MUSIC CLUB
POB 14722, Columbus, 43214, 224-4409

The club was founded in 1882 and boasts of being one of Ohio's oldest musical organizations. They present at least 4 free programs per year from September through May, including choral and instrumental music by its Symphony Orchestra and String Sinfonia. Programs are held at Weigel Hall Auditorium, 30 West 15 Avenue, and the Indianola Presbyterian Church.

WORTHINGTON ARTS COUNCIL
777 High St., Worthington, 43085, 431-0329

Well known for the quality of their performing arts series, you can be entertained by local, regional, national and internationally recognized artists such as Judy Collins and the Ballet

Folklorico. The ticket prices usually range from $6.75-$18.75, with many being $10 and under. Series subscriptions can save about 30% off the individual ticket prices. The Old Worthington Folklife Festival is an annual free event held on the first weekend in August. It is sponsored by the Arts Council and held on the Worthington Village Green at the corner of North High Street and East Dublin Granville Road. The festival features performances, demonstrations, traditional foods and vendors selling handcrafted wares. This delightful family oriented event is as educational as it is entertaining. M-F 9-5. Accepts checks , MC & Visa with a $2 service charge.

WORTHINGTON COMMUNITY THEATER
891-4313

Three major productions per year, in February, May and October , are presented by this theatrical group. Quality published plays such as Deathtrap, Cat On A Hot Tin Roof, Applause and others have graced the stage at the Kilbourne Auditorium, 50 East Dublin-Granville Road in Worthington. The actors and actresses include both amateur as well as professional status. While most of the productions are aimed at an adult audience, some are suitable for families. My husband and I enjoyed their recent production of Personals. Prices range from $4-$10 depending on the production, with a $1 discount offered to students and seniors. M-F 9-7. Accepts cash, MC & Visa.

WORTHY CITIZEN CARD
Worthington Board Of Education, 752 High St., Worthington, 43085, 431-6500

Seniors aged 60 and older can apply for this free card which entitles them to free admission to home athletic games, school orchestra and band concerts, as well as plays and musicals within the Worthington School District. Registration in the district's Extended Education Program is also free in classes which have available space. Or, seniors may choose to pay 50% of the class fee to guarantee a space in the class. The Extended Education Program includes classes in arts and crafts, cooking, gardening, business, personal growth and more. A Worthy Citizen Card is available to Worthington residents only. M-F 9-5.

WYANDOTTE LAKE
10101 Riverside Dr., Powell, 43065, 889-9283

Over 60 water rides, land amusement rides and entertainment make this a fun experience for the whole family at this theme park. You can ride the Sea Dragon roller coaster, the 11 water slides, the wave pool or the new Canoochie Creek Action River Ride. Young children will especially enjoy Kiddieland with its selection of water and land rides designed for their abilities and tastes. A family membership costs $139.95 or $39.95 for a single membership. If you purchase the membership between May1-July1 at area Kroger's, you can save $10 off the single membership rate. Kroger's also sells discounted daily passes to Wyandotte Lake for $9.50, regularly $11.95. Or you can enter the park any time after 4PM and pay a reduced rate of $6.95 per single admission ticket at the gate. Your membership allows you unlimited admission throughout the season which is Memorial Day through Labor Day. A picnic area is on premises but you must leave your extra food in a separate away away from the pools and rides. Members also have reciprocal privileges at Geauga

Lake Amusement Park in Aurora, Ohio and Darien Lake Amusement Park in Buffalo, New York. Wyandotte Lake also features special events throughout the season such as concerts and outdoor movies which are included in your admission fee. During the last week of August, their annual "Banana Bunch" discount promotion entitles you and 9 of your friends to admission for only $29 for the group. M-Th 10-7, F-Sun 10-9. Accepts checks and cash only.

ALSO SEE

AAA, Aardvark Video, American Youth Hostels, Ameritech Pages Plus, Berwick Plaza Lanes, Big Walnut Skate Club, Big Western Lanes, Columbus Charter Coach, Columbus Clippers, Columbus Cultural Arts Center, Columbus Dispatch, Columbus Square Bowling Palace, Columbus Zoo, Consumer Reports Travel Letter, Dawes Arboretum, Delaware County Metro Parks, Fiesta Lanes, Gahanna Lanes, Gold C Savings Spree, Harts, Henri Bendel, Hillcrest Bowling Lanes, Just For Feet, Laces Rolling Skating Center, Learning Guild, Licking County Bicycle Club, Little Professor Bookstore, the Lobby, Lucy's, Mr. Bill's Northern Lights, ODNR Division of Watercraft, ODNR Rent-A-Camp Program, OSU Department of Photography, OSU Office of Women's Services, R&R USA, Roller Chalet, Sawmill Lanes, Scarlett's At The Radisson, Skate America, Skate Town, Southwest Community Center Indoor Pool, Special Sales And Events Index, United Skates Of America, U.A. High School Natatorium, U.A. Library, Wines Inc.

FABRICS/LINENS/ WALL & WINDOW COVERINGS

FABRICS

BEXLEY FABRICS
2476 E. Main St., Columbus, 43209, 231-7272

Over 100 different lines of drapery and upholstery fabrics are available at savings of 20-60% off suggested retail prices. The first quality decorator goods are largely current stock from Waverly, Schumacher, Covington, Spectrum, Kauffman and others. A shop at home service is available. M-Sat 10-5. Accepts checks, MC & Visa.

BOONE FABRICS
6100 Huntley Rd., Columbus, 43229, 785-0121,

Save 25-70% off moderate to designer quality home decorating fabrics by Waverly, Robert Allan, P. Kauffman, Mastercraft and other popular brands. Over 1500 bolts of upholstery and drapery fabric are in stock at all times. Their extensive selection is certain to satisfy you. All sales are final. M-Sat 9:30-6. Accepts checks, MC & Visa.

DECOR FABRICS
1254 Morse Rd., Columbus, 43229, 436-4998

Over 100 different lines of drapery and upholstery fabrics are available at savings of 20-60% off suggested retail prices. The first quality decorator goods, are generally current stock from Waverly, Schumacher, Covington, Spectrum, Kaufman and other companies. M-Sat 10-4:30. Accepts checks, MC & Visa.

FABRIC AND DRAPERY MART
1037 Mediterranean Ave., Columbus, 43229, 888-5640

Over 50,000 yards of mill direct drapery, upholstery and multi-purpose fabric is in stock at all times. Savings are 25-50% off suggested retail prices. The store maintains an inhouse workroom with qualified seamstresses, which enables even custom orders to be priced at similar savings. Over 40 window treatments are on display. The store offers a free shop at home service. Return policy varies with some items are subject to a restocking charge. M-Th 10-7, F and Sat 10-6. Accepts checks, MC & Visa.

FABRIC FARMS
3590 Riverside Dr., Columbus, 43221, 451-9300

Sells Waverly, P. Kaufman, Covington and other decorator quality lines of garment, home decorating and upholstery fabrics at savings of 20-50% off manufacturer's suggested retail prices. The merchandise consists of past season, overstocks and some irregular goods. Frequent craft and home decorating classes are offered. Call to be added to their mailing list. Gives exchanges. M-F 10-9, Sat 10-6, Sun 1-5. Accepts checks, MC & Visa.

HANCOCK FABRICS
1987 Morse Rd., Columbus, 43229, 263-2031
4868 W. Broad St., Columbus, 43228, 878-8006
34 Westerville Sq., Westerville, 43081, 899-1320
1286 Brice Rd., Reynoldsburg, 43068, 755-4020
1920 W. Henderson Rd., Columbus, 43220, 451-0065
2138 N. Limestone St., Springfield, 45501, (513) 390-2703

Offers first quality sewing, upholstery, home decorating and bridal fabrics at savings of about 20-40% off regular retail prices. The stores have a special section where irregulars and misdyed fabrics are sold at $1.44 per yard, a savings of about 50-75% less than the "if perfect" price. Another section features other specials at $1.88 a yard with values to about $12.99 per yard. This full service business also features a "notion of the week" sale item which is reduced 30-50% off their regular price. Watch the newspapers for other frequent sales. Offers free and low cost sewing seminars several times during the year. Gives refunds. M-Sat 10-9, Sun 12-5. Accepts checks, MC & Visa.

JO-ANN FABRICS
6400 Tussing Rd., Consumer Sq. E., Reynoldsburg, 43068, 864-0076
455 Agler Rd., Gahanna, 43230, 471-1182
6653 Dublin Center Dr., Dublin Village Ctr., Dublin, 43017, 889-8865
101 Southland Mall, Columbus, 43207, 491-4955
1877 W. Henderson Rd., Columbus, 43220, 457-3897
4666 W. Broad St., Lincoln Village Plaza, Columbus, 43228, 870-6052
2270 Morse Rd., Columbus, 43229, 471-8394
581 S. State St., Westerville, 43081, 891-7357
2885 Olentangy River Rd., University City Shpng. Ctr., Columbus, 43202, 262-9052
924 E. Sandusky Ave., Bellefontaine, 43311, (513) 592-7438
1080 N. Bridge St., Chillicothe, 45601, 773-1607
21 Troy Rd., Delaware, 43015, 363-3464
1311 Delaware Ave., Marion, 43301, 389-2141
633 Southgate Shpng. Ctr., Newark, 43055, 522-4700

Save about 20-30% off comparable fabrics, lace, ribbons and other sewing notions and related needs at this national chain. A large selection of fabrics for home decorating, bridal wear and fashion apparel can be found. Their private label, Beechwood, includes craft and sewing products such as glues, fabric paints and other items at savings of 30-50% less than popular brands for similar quality. The stores also sell sewing machines and gifts at similar savings. Sign up for their mailing list to keep posted of their frequent sales. M-Sat 10-9, Sun 12-5. Accepts checks, MC & Visa.

MCGRAW'S SHOWCASE FABRICS
1 E. Main St., S. Vienna, 45369, (513) 568-4257

Following a fire in their Westside Columbus store, the business has decided not to reopen in Columbus. Instead, you may travel a half hour to the West to find their main store which offers an even larger selection. Upholstery fabrics, tools and supplies are priced at 20-60% less than suggested retail. The large inventory consists of remnants, mill ends, bolt ends and discontinued fabrics, all of which are first quality. Gives exchanges. M-Sat 10-6. Accepts checks, MC & Visa.

NANCY'S FABRICS
140 W. Olentangy St., Powell, 43065, 766-5660

Designer drapery, slipcover and upholstery fabrics are sold at savings of about 30-60% off regular retail prices. The inventory consists of first quality, short bolts, mill overstocks and inspected seconds. Custom made draperies and other window treatments, slipcovers and upholstered work can be done by the staff. However, you might want to consider taking one of the store's "how to" classes" which will teach you the methods of creating jabots, swags and shades, or even ways to design and paint a faux finish on your walls! The classes are actually demonstration sessions and cost about $15-$25. Major sales are held in March, June, September and in November at which time, savings are even greater. M-Sat 10-5, Sun 1-5. Accepts checks, MC & Visa.

ALSO SEE

Camp And Williams, Experienced Possessions, Frugal Fox Wallpaper Outlet, Liberty Street Interiors, Nettlecreek Inc., Northland Sewing Machine Center, Nu Look Factory Outlet

LINENS

Department and specialty stores typically offer *White Sales* in January and August. Savings are 30-50% off linens, towels, comforters, bedspreads and related items.

BEDSPREADS AND THINGS
6355 Sawmill Rd., Dublin, 43017, 766-0661

Quality comforters, blinds, curtains, bathroom accessories and linens are available at savings of about 10-30% off manufacturers' suggested retail prices. You'll find upscale, first quality, current merchandise by Fieldcrest, Croscill, Nettlecreek, Waverly, Burlington and Levolor. Gives refunds. M-F 10-8, Sat 10-6. Accepts checks, MC, Visa & Discover.

CARRINGTON'S
113 S. Ohio Ave., Wellston, 45692, 1-384-5656

A small selection of first quality buyouts and closeouts of towels, sheets, pillows, shower curtains and other textiles is offered at savings of 25-50% off regular retail prices. Such labels as West Point Pepperell, Springs Industries and Saturday Night can be found here. Gives refunds. M-Sat 9-5. Accepts checks, MC & Visa.

LESHNER OUTLET
1250 Central Ave., Hamilton, 45011, (513) 868-6700

This manufacturer of towels, tablecloths and placemats offers a discount of 30-70% off regular retail prices on first quality and irregular merchandise. Their products are typically found in K Mart, Meijer and Wal-Mart stores. Gives refunds. M-Sat 9:30-5:30. Accepts checks, MC, Visa & Discover.

LINENS AND WARES
5891 Scarborough Blvd., Columbus, 43232, 864-1665
771 S. 30 St., Indian Mound Mall, Heath, 43056, 522-3741
1635 River Valley Circle S., River Valley Mall, Lancaster, 43130, 654-4476

Sheets, linens, comforters, pillows, towels and an assortment of bathroom and kitchen items are found here at savings of 20-60% off regular retail prices. You will find such brands as Fieldcrest, Cannon, Wamsutta, Laura Ashley, Utica and others. Most of the merchandise is first quality. A few seconds in towels are clearly marked. On a recent visit, I purchased a designer comforter for $19.99, regularly $55. Gives refunds. M-Sat 10-9, Sun 12-5. Accepts checks, MC & Visa.

LINENS 'N THINGS
7623 New Market Center Way, New Market Mall, Columbus, 43235, 764-0311

Save 20-70% off the regular retail prices on towels, linens, tablecloths, placemats, area rugs, bedspreads, shower curtains and bath accessories as well as related items. The store carries such popular brands as Wamsutta, Cannon, Beacon Hill, Royal, Springmaid, Laura Ashley, Burlington and others. The inventory consists of first quality and irregulars. On a recent visit, I saw a 100% wool blanket for $39.99 regularly $80, a Burlington bedspread for $79.99 regularly $120 and other items. Gives refunds. M-Sat 10-9, Sun 12-6. Accepts checks, MC & Visa

THE LINEN STORE
817 Bethel Rd., Olentangy Plaza, Columbus, 43214, 451-4585
6791 Dublin Ctr. Dr., Dublin, 43017, 766-6766
990 Morse Rd., Columbus, 43229, 888-2238
Quality towels, sheets, tablecloths, bedspreads, bath and table top accessories, as well as curtains are available at savings of 20-50%. Brand names offered include Martex, Nettle Creek, Cannon, Wamsutta, Croscill and other upscale companies. The merchandise is mostly first quality with some irregulars and consists of discontinued, overstock and special purchases. Gives refunds. Accepts checks, MC, Visa & Discover.

NETTLECREEK, INC.
2200 Peacock Rd., Richmond, Indiana, 47374, (317) 966-2551

Decorator Nettlecreek bedspreads, pillows, fabrics and mini blinds are available at savings of 30-60% off regular retail prices. This manufacturer's outlet store sells first quality and irregular merchandise. It is well worth the trip, but expect to drive about 3 1/2 hours to get there. Nettlecreek is located off I-70 West at exit 149A. All sales are final. M-Sat 9-5:30, Sun 12-4. Accepts checks, MC & Visa.

ALSO SEE

Bazaar Home Fashions, Burlington Coat Factory, Lazarus Final Countdown, Marshall's, T.J.Maxx, Odd Lots, J.C. Penney Outlet, J.C. Penney Portfolio, J.C. Penney Department Store, Schottenstein's, Sears Outlet, Tuesday Morning and Uhlman's Clearance Center

WALL & WINDOW COVERINGS

AMERICA'S WALL AND WINDOW
3395 Dahlgreen Dr., Westerville, 43081, 442-0800

Mini blinds and verticals, in a variety of patterns and materials, are available here at savings of 55-65% off regular retail prices. The business carries Graber, American and Hunter Douglas brands, and has also begun to manufacture its own verticals at similar savings. Custom made valences, draperies and other fabric window treatments are about 25-50% less than those of comparable quality in other stores. This company was formerly located in a storefront on Bethel Road, but has recently moved to a warehouse in Westerville as a result of changing from a walk-in retail business to an exclusively shop at home service. M-Sat 10-10. Accepts checks, MC & Visa.

BALDAUF DO-IT CENTER
36 Troy Rd., Delaware, 43015, 1-363-3648
1001 S. Prospect St., Rt. 4, Marion, 43302, 1-387-0454

Save 30% off list price on popular brands of wallcoverings and borders. Anderson windows are discounted from the distributor's list price. Wood Mode brand of quality wood kitchen cabinets are offered at savings of 15-40% off manufacturer's suggested retail price. Wallcoverings refunded with receipt. Sat 10-6. Accepts MC & Visa.

BAZAAR HOME FASHIONS
5640 Columbus Sq., Columbus, 43231, 890-8441

An extensive selection of ready made curtains plus blinds, towels and comforters is available at savings of 20-70% off regular retail prices. You'll find upscale, first quality Nettlecreek, Springmaid, Stevens and other brands as closeout, overstock, discontinued and special purchase items. This is an excellent source for your home decorating needs. Gives refunds. M-Sat 10-9, Sun 12-6. Accepts checks, MC, Visa & Discover,

CAMP AND WILLIAMS
18 N. State St., Westerville, 43081, 898-7092

Upscale fabrics, blinds, wallcoverings, custom florals, carpeting and antiques are available at this interior design studio. Robert Allen, Waverly, Carol, Brunswig And Fils and other fabrics are discounted 15% on in-stock and special orders. The store features custom upholstering, curtains and draperies and custom pillows at about 15-30% less than in full price stores. Decorator pillows are part of their wholesale division which creates these unique home decor accents for department and specialty stores throughout the United States. Graber and Kirsch wood and vertical blinds are discounted 50%. Save 15-30% on in-stock and special order decorator wallpapers by Ralph Lauren, Blonder, Thibony, Kenny, Payne, Schumacher and other brands. Carpeting and custom florals are discounted 15%. The business offers a $35 per hour consultation fee to come to your home and help you make decorating selections. There is also an accessory shopping service. This unique service charges you 20% above the cost of an item, which the owners will purchase for you at a local discount store, if it is not available in their own store. According to the owner, you will still be saving money. Many of their clients are busy with other commitments and/or don't have the decorating finesse to shop for home accessories, so this service helps in many ways. As a special thank you for recommending a friend to *Camp and Williams*, the store generally offers you a coupon valid for a discount on your next purchase or sometimes even a free gift. Gives refunds. Tu-Th 10-5, Sat 10-3, M and F evening by appointment. Accepts checks, MC, Visa, AmExp and Discover.

FRUGAL FOX WALLPAPER OUTLET
634 W. Schrock Rd., Westerville, 43081, 898-6996
60 E. Powell Rd., Powell, 43065, 847-9511
1735 Brice Rd., Reynoldsburg, 43068, 755-9411
3706 Riverside Dr., Columbus, 43221, 459-1882

Instock wallcoverings are discounted 50% and more with prices starting at $1.99 per roll. Special order fabrics are 20-25% off and special order wallpapers are up to 50% off manufacturers' suggested retail prices. The inventory is all first quality and includes brands such as Waverly, C&A Wallcoverings, Warner, Blonder, Seabrook and others.

You'll find an enormous selection of contemporary, decorator quality merchandise. Has a free shop-at-home service. For $35, one of their interior designers can come to your home and help to plan your wallcovering purchase. Offers free wallpaper hanging clinics about 5-6 times per year. Restocking fee on returned special orders. Gives refunds on instock merchandise. M-Sat 10-6, Sun 12-5. (hours may vary from store to store). Accepts checks, MC, Visa & AmExp.

GRANDMA'S COUNTRY RUFFLES
6259 E. Main St., Columbus, 43213, 861-5904
771 S. 30 St., Indian Mound Mall, Heath, 43056, 522-4498
2885 E. Pike, Zanesville, 43701, 453-3585

The largest area selection of country style ruffled curtains is available at these stores, which feature over 2,000 pairs in stock. Curtains, lampshades, swags, bedspreads, shams, tiers, valences, chair pads and toss pillows are available in coordinating decorator colors. The merchandise is value priced and provides custom made quality from mass manufactured goods. If you enjoy ruffled curtains, you'll love Grandma's Country Ruffles. Gives refunds. M-Sun 10-6. Accepts checks, MC, Visa & Discover.

L.T. INTERIORS
890-5667

In home decorating services are available by appointment only. Custom window treatments such as pleated shades, verticals, wood and mini blinds by Hunter Douglas, Verisol and others are available at savings of at least 50% off manufacturer's suggested retail. Lafayette custom draperies, available in a choice of 3000 fabrics, are discounted 20%. Bedspreads by Norman's Of Salisbury are similarly discounted. Quality traditional and contemporary furniture is discounted 25%. Wallcoverings, in a variety of patterns, are about 20% off. This interior decorator charges a $35 consultation fee which is waived if you make a purchase. Accepts checks, MC & Visa

MAJESTIC PAINT OUTLET STORE
1665 Parsons Ave., Columbus, 43207, 444-4847

The *Back Room Warehouse* section offers quality wallpaper and borders by Mayfair, Vymura, Blonders and other brands at prices of $1-$6.99 per single roll. Window shades, blinds, painting tools, paints, stains, driveway sealants as well as varnishes are all discounted 50-75% off regular retail prices. The inventory consists of discontinued, closeouts as well as scratch and dent merchandise. The annual warehouse clearance sale is held for 5 days in mid April. Savings are up to 80% off during this sale. All sales are final. M-F 8AM-9PM, Sat 8AM-6PM, Sun 11-5. Accepts checks, MC, Visa & Discover.

MAJESTIC PAINT CENTERS
35 stores in Central Ohio. Check the phone book for listings.

Their "Frequent Applier Program" provides you with the opportunity to receive a $10 merchandise certificate which is valid in their stores after you have accumulated $200 in receipts. Simply mail the receipts in a specially marked envelope which you can obtain in any store. The businesses discount Kirsch and Personal Touch custom blinds, verticals and pleated shades by 60-70%. You can also save 10-30% off the regular retail price on art supplies, many of which are available in the store. Others will need to be mail ordered through their catalogue. You can sign up for the quarterly mailings in any store. You will find lap easels for $75.90, regularly $99.95, 4 piece sable watercolor brush sets for $47.90 regularly $69.90, watercolor paper postcards for $4.99 regularly $6.99. Carries Blonde, Schumacher, Waverly and other brands of contemporary and traditional quality wallpaper at about 20-50% discount. The savings on special order wallcoverings is about 20-30%. The stores offer a free rental of a video on how to hang wallpaper. The "Goof Proof Guarantee" allows you to exchange the wallpaper you purchased if it does not suit your taste once hung, or if you "goofed" in the hanging process. Inquire for details. In the spring and fall, the stores feature a series of free how-to clinics on such topics as faux finishes, sponge painting, easy decorating ideas, beginners' refinishing tips and wallpapering. The new Majestic line of custom order mini blinds, offers a savings of about 60-70% less than comparable quality products in full price stores and about 20-30% less than those in stores which discount mini blinds. The Majestic blinds are slightly lighter in weight, but wear well. There's 35 different colors from which to choose. Gives refunds. M-F 8AM-9PM, Sat 8-6, Sun 11-5. Accepts checks, MC, Visa & Discover.

PANEL TOWN AND MORE
1063 Dublin Rd., Columbus, 43215, 488-0334
4317 Linden Ave., Dayton, 45432, (513) 254-6127
4950 Springboro Rd., Dayton, 45432, (513) 294-4414
1050 N. Belmont, Springfield, 45503, (513) 323-0611

Over 30,000 rolls of first quality wallpaper are in stock from $1.99-$4.99 per single roll, and borders are priced at $4.99 each. You'll love the large selection of contemporary and traditional patterns. Hardwood floors, bathroom vanities, kitchen cabinets and countertops are discounted up to 20%. Save up to 65% on sheet vinyl flooring. Paneling starts at $2.99 per sheet. Full layout and design services are available. The stock consists of manufacturers' closeouts and discontinued goods. Brands offered include Armstrong Mannington, Domco, Congoleum, Bruce and Hartco. Gives exchanges. M-F 8-8, Sat 8-6. Accepts checks, MC & Visa.

VAUGHN PAINT AND WALLCOVERINGS
1392 S. High St., Columbus, 43207, 443-0002

Save 20-50% off manufacturer's suggested prices on popular brands of paints, varnishes, stains and wallcoverings. The inventory is first quality, overstocks and discontinued merchandise. Gives refunds. M-F 9-5:30, Sat 9-3:30. Accepts checks, MC & Visa.

WALLPAPER FACTORY CLOSEOUTS
3958 Broadway, Grove City, 43123, 871-4343

Over 15,000 rolls of wallpaper are in stock. The first quality merchandise is available by such brands as Borden and Walltex, and includes basic as well as novelty styles. Prices range from $2.75-$4.75 for a single roll, and $1 per yard for borders. Savings are about 50-80% off manufacturers' suggested retail prices. The store also stocks a small, but interesting selection of framed prints and lampshades. Gives exchanges. M-F 10-5:30, Sat 10-4. Accepts checks and cash only.

WALLPAPER 4-U
334 S. Hamilton Rd.(Hunters Ridge Mall), Gahanna, 43230, 475-2808

Save 30-50% off regular retail prices on first quality in stock and custom order wallpaper in such brands as Sanitas, York, Pfaltzgraff Collection, Eisenhart, York, Mayfair and Essex. There are hundreds of patterns to choose from starting at $1 for a single roll and $2 for borders. Free "how-to" wallpaper classes are offered four to five times per year. Occasionally you will find seconds here, but these are clearly marked. Provides layaways. Refunds within 30 days if unused. M & Th 9:30-8:30, T, W, F, & Sat 9:30-6. Accepts checks, MC & Visa.

WALLPAPER MADNESS
5470 Westerville Rd., Westerville, 43081, 890-1722

Over 40,000 rolls of first quality wallpapers and borders are in stock at savings of 30-65% off suggested retail prices. Special orders are also available at similar savings. The stock consists of first quality, seconds, closeouts and discontinued goods. The store features merchandise from Waverly, Imperial, Color Tree, Laura Ashley, Eisenhart, Louis Nicole, Color House, Milbrook and others. Coordinating fabrics are available at savings of 20-30% off manufacturers suggested retail prices. Children will love to play in the toy filled room while mom and dad shop. Provides layaways. Cash refunds within 30 days with receipt. No returns on special orders. M,Th, F 9:30-8:30, T, Wed, Sat., 9:30-6, Sun1:30-4. Accepts checks, MC, Visa & Discover.

WALLPAPER OUTLET
28 S. 3 Street, Newark, 43055, 345-4235
117 N. Main St. Mansfield, 44901, (419) 522-4646

Odd lots, overruns and discontinued wallcoverings are sold as first quality and seconds at a cost of $ 5.50-$9.50 per double roll. The prices are regularly up to about $20. Borders are available at a cost of $1.99-$5. On a recent visit, the wallpapers were simple patterns and florals in muted colors. Gives exchanges only. M-F 10-5:30, Sat 10-3. Accepts checks, MC & Visa.

WALLPAPERS TO GO
6464 Sawmill Rd., Columbus, 43235, 792-7776
4560 Morse Center Dr., Columbus, 43229, 431-0500
2561 S. Hamilton Rd., Columbus, 43232, 863-0415

Save 20-50% on first quality decorator wallpapers by Kingfisher, Mayfair, Cherry Hill, Legend and other popular brands. Offers coordinating paint, fabrics and window fashions at similar savings. The stores maintain a large selection of these upscale products. Free clinics are offered intermittently which provide instruction on how to hang wallpaper. Gives refunds. M-F 10-9, Sat 10-6, Sun 12-5. Accepts checks, MC & Visa.

ALSO SEE

Anderson's General Store, Berwick Corner Outlet, City Lighting, Color Tile, Fabric And Drapery Mart, Greystone Design, Harts, Nancy's Fabrics, J.C. Penney Furniture Warehouse Outlet, J.C. Penney Outlet, Schottenstein's,

FINE JEWELRY/LUGGAGE & PURSES/COSTUME JEWELRY & OTHER ACCESSORIES

FINE JEWELRY

ALLEN'S COIN SHOP
399 S. State St., Westerville, 43081, 882-3937

The coin shop offers savings of 50% on a large selection of pre-packaged stamps. Antique and pre-owned jewelry are displayed in cases in the coin store and include sterling silver charms for $2-$5, and an interesting selection of old stickpins for $4. The shop also has an extensive selection of stamps, coins and collectibles worth investigating. Gives refunds. M-F 9-7, Sat 9-5. Accepts checks, MC & Visa.

COLUMBUS GOLD AND DIAMOND EXCHANGE
2700 E. Dublin Granville Rd., Suite 510, Columbus, 43231, 891-3313

Top quality diamonds, gold chains and bracelets, as well as custom designed fine jewelry, are available at savings of about 50% less than comparable retail prices. The manager stressed that the store carries large sizes of diamonds not readily available in the area. Provides layaway. Gives refunds. Accepts Golden Buckeye Cards. M-F 10:30-5:30, Sat 11-3. Accepts checks, MC, Visa & Jewelry Express charges.

THE DIAMOND CELLAR
5025 Arlington Ctr. Blvd., Columbus, 43220, 457-0445 or 1-800-222-6642

The buyers travel around the globe to bring back quality diamonds which are priced far below market value. Some may be 20-30% larger than standard sized stones, but grade for grade, will cost you the same or less than their standard sized counterparts. The Diamond Cellar is unique in its field for offering independent grading of all of its diamonds, by an outside agency. The store offers a guarantee that you can't find a diamond of equal quality elsewhere for less money. Exclusive gold and gold/silver jewelry from New York designers, is sold here as the only Ohio representative for these lines. There are more certified gemologists in this store than in any other jewelry store in the city. Custom designs as well as all repairs and stone settings, are done on the premises. If you are seeking impeccable quality fine jewelry at excellent values, this 46 year old business is not to be missed. Gives refunds. M-F 9:30-8:30, Sat 9:30-5:30. Accepts checks, C, Visa, AmExp & Discover.

DIAMONDS, PEARLS AND JADE, INC.
1583 W. Lane Ave., Lane Ave. Shpng. Ctr., Columbus, 43221, 481-8444

This full service jewelry store offers direct import prices on an extensive collection of gold, blue baroque and black South Sea pearls, diamonds, cameos and other fine jewelry. Custom European style design service is available by Sophia Prinz, an internationally recognized designer. These designs are comparable in quality to that which can be found in the world's finest jewelry stores, at prices which are about 40% less. Mikimoto Pearls are also priced at similar savings. This business is able to offer such prices as a result of directly importing much of its merchandise, (the owner also serves as the broker) and overseeing its manufacture overseas. Provides layaway. Gives refunds. M-Sat 10-9, Sun 12-5. Accepts checks, MC, Visa, AmExp & Discover.

INTERNATIONAL DIAMOND AND GOLD COMPANY JEWELERS
1704 Morse Rd., Columbus, 43229, 431-2500
830 Bethel Rd., Columbus 43214, 459-4500
4401 Crossroads E. Center, Columbus, 43232, 861-7777

Save 20-30% off suggested retail prices on an extensive and unique selection of gold and diamond jewelry. This store also carries a large selection of wedding bands. It pays to have a goldsmith on premises as the store is able to eliminate the middleman needed for jewelry repairs. The prices on repairs are one of the best in town and include: prong repair $6, ladies' ring sizing $8-$10 and men's ring sizing $12. Savings on repairs are about 40-60% off the price at other jewelers. Offers 90 days same as cash financing to qualified purchasers. Provides layaway. Gives refunds. M-F 11-8, Sat 11-5:30. Bethel Road store is also open 12-5 on Sunday. Accepts checks, MC, Visa & Discover.

MONA'S JEWELRY OUTLET
7566 New Market Ctr. Way, Columbus, 43235, 761-2727
168 Southland Mall, Columbus, 43207, 491-0119
132 Westerville Mall, Westerville, 43081, 899-7275

Seiko watches, in addition to a full line of 14Karat gold jewelry, are discounted 30-60% off manufacturer's suggested retail prices. Provides layaway. Gives exchanges. M-Sat 10-8, Sun 12-6. Accepts checks, MC, Visa & AmExp.

RITCHEY'S
714 N. High St., Columbus, 43215, 294-2226

Fine jewelry repair and custom design services are available at savings of about 50% less than in traditional jewelry stores. There is also a collection of antique jewelry at similar savings. Funky and fashionable costume jewelry, as well as unique sculptural works, are offered at savings of about 20-40% at this jewelry and sculpture manufacturing studio. The business is open every day of the year except New Years, the Fourth of July, Thanksgiving and Christmas. The owner, Doug Ritchey, is a friendly and interesting fellow, who has been dubbed, "the emperor of the Short North". Provides layaways. Gives exchanges. M-W 1-6, Th and F 11-8, Sat 1-8, Sun 12-5. Accepts checks, MC, & Visa.

SPENCER'S GIFTS
1740 Northland Mallway, Columbus, 43229, 267-0201

Your favorite styles of 14 Karat gold, freshwater pearls or silver neck chains and earrings are available here at savings of 50-70% off regular retail prices. The gold consists largely of Italian imports, most of which are marked, "585", on the clasp. The store also features a unique selection of gifts at regular retail prices. Gives exchanges. M-Sat 10-9, Sun 12-5. Accepts checks, MC & Visa.

WAREHOUSE CLUB
4252 Groves Rd., Columbus, 43232, 863-6706 or 863-6682

Save 10-60% off nationally recognized name brands of watches, toys, baby strollers and accessories, furniture, hardware, bicycles, sports and exercise equipment, books, clothing for the family, lamps, fine jewelry, food and other items. Moderate to better priced merchandise is sold by Seiko, J.G. Hook, Field And Stream, Lord Jeff and other names you'll instantly recognize. Automotive supplies are similarly discounted. This business offers the lowest price in town on oil change, lube and filter at a cost of only $10.95. When you purchase tires here, you'll get a free road hazard warranty. This is a membership only club. Employees of certain major employers and members of certain clubs and groups are granted free membership which entitles them to an identification card and the opportunity to make purchases for 5% over the posted prices. A special membership card may be bought for $25 annually entitling you to pay posted prices. Seniors aged 55 and older can obtain a *Silver Savings Card.* entitling them to a $15 annual membership fee per year and the opportunity to pay posted prices as opposed to 5% above. This represents a savings of $10 off the membership fee. Gives refunds. M-F 9-9, Sat 9-7, Sun 11-6. Accepts checks, MC, Visa & Discover.

ALSO SEE

Baggerie, Berwick Corner Outlet, Central Ohio Gem-Mineral And Jewelry Show, Columbus Police Property Auction, Darby Sales, Drug Emporium, Extravaganza, Franklin County Sherriff's Department, Greater Columbus Antique Mall, Harts, International Gem And Jewelry Show, K Mart, Mared Consignments, Phar Mor, Revco, Schottenstein's, Service Merchandise, Springfield Show And Flea Market, Stratford Auction Center, T.J. Maxx, Topping Outlet Store, Uncle Sam's Pawn Shop and Value City Department Store

LUGGAGE & PURSES/COSTUME JEWELRY & OTHER ACCESSORIES

AFRICAN ART
3575 E. Livingston Ave., Livingston Ct. Flea Mkt.-Booth 72, Columbus, 43207

Handmade African jewelry , in addition to leather purses, is available at direct import prices. You'll find traditional ethnic styles incorporating seed beads, leather, cowrie shells, bone, horn, brass and copper in necklaces, bracelets and earrings. Prices range from about $3-$6 for jewelry and about $10-$35 for purses. All sales are final. F 12-6, Sat 10-6, Sun 1-6. Accepts checks and cash only.

AFRICAN ARTS-MAYORO N'DOYE
3575 E. Livingston Ave., Livingston Ct. Flea Mkt.-Booth 91, Columbus, 43227, 252-1828 (home)

A selection of authentic, imported African jewelry and small gift items is available through this vendor. Cowrie shells, leather, bone, seed beads, brass and copper are the components for the handmade earrings, bracelets and rings. Prices range from $3-$6. Mr. N'Doye also indicated that he sells his wares in front of the Society Bank on Broad and High Streets, from 10-5 on Monday, Tuesday, Thursday and part of Friday. He is open at the flea market on Fridays from 1-7, Saturdays from 11-6 and Sundays from 12-5. Accepts checks and cash only.

THE BAGGERIE
90 Worthington Sq. Mall, Worthington, 43085, 888-8511
101 Alex Bell Rd., Cross Pt. Ctr., Centerville, 45459, (513)435-5568
4810 Sawmill Rd., Columbus, 43235, 442-7767 (store called Excess Baggage)

Upscale and designer quality attaches, luggage, purses, pen sets and small gift items such as watches, unique calculators etc., are available at savings of 10-30% off suggested retail prices. Some merchandise is discounted up to 70%. The stock consists of mostly first quality goods including closeouts, discontinued merchandise, special purchases and some items especially made for this store. The owner is constantly searching for unique items for his businesses and you may be delightfully surprised at what he finds. On my recent visit, I stocked up on pocket calculators for $4 apiece, which were in a case that looked shockingly like a $100 bill! Gives refunds. M-Sat 10-9, Sun 12-5. Accepts checks, MC, Visa, AmExp & Discover.

DEAN'S DISCOUNT OUTLET
2430 W. Mound St., Columbus, 43204, 279-0219

Men's, women's, infants and children's sport, casual, dressy and novelty socks are priced at $1 a pair or 12 pairs for $7. Dungarees are priced at $8.99. Tee shirts are 3 for $10 and sweatshirts are $4-$6, both of which are generally found imprinted with a variety of designs. The store also carries other in-season wearables such as children's coats, adult and children's shorts, infant rompers and other changing items. On a recent visit, there was a selection of special purchase children's sweatshirts priced at 50 cents apiece! The store carries Russel, Bassett-Walker, Stedman, Bonjour and other brands in sizes infant to 5x, and some garments have had the manufacturers labels removed. Not every style is available in this size range. The inventory is first quality, overstocks, discontinued, past season and some misdyed/misprinted items. There are many bargains to be found in this small store! All sales are final. F and Sat only 10-5. Accepts checks and cash.

ILLUSIONS
400 N. High St., Columbus Convention Ctr., Columbus, 43215, 228-1316
1577 W. Lane Ave., Lane Ave. Shpng. Ctr., Columbus, 43221, 486-9116

These stores offer magnificent replicas of some of the world's finest jewelry, delicately handcrafted by master craftsmen, and layered with 14 karat gold. These fabulous fakes include cocktail rings, earrings and necklaces with cubic Zirconium in a multitude of colors. The settings are exactly what you would expect to find in gold and platinum jewelry. You can choose from dressy, business and casual styles ranging from $12-$250. These prices are 40-90% less than the gold and platinum originals from which they were copied. The jewelry, which comes with a lifetime warranty, has been purchased by such celebrities as Elizabeth Taylor, Joan Collins and Dolly Parton. Gives exchanges only. M-Sat 10-6, Sun 12-5.

JEWEL BOX
924 S. Yearling, Columbus, 43213, 239-9201

Traditional and high fashion jewelry is sold at 50-75% off suggested retail prices. The first quality merchandise consists of necklaces, rings (there's 70,000 in stock), pins and earrings. This small store has an inventory level which is hard to believe! Brand names can't be mentioned in print, but you'll instantly recognize them once you see the merchandise. All sales are final. Thurs-Sat 12-4. Accepts checks, MC & Visa.

SUZANNE'S SUEDE AND LEATHER
400 N. High St., Columbus Convention Ctr., Columbus, 43215, 221-1958

High fashion leather jackets and garments for men and women, luggage and purses are available here at savings of 20-30% off regular retail prices. Through the efforts of the knowledgeable buyer, he is able to select value wise items which are lower priced than those of other manufacturers, but still provide the quality you are seeking. There is also a large selection of clearance merchandise at 50% off their already low prices. The stock is all first quality upscale goods. The sales staff is friendly and eager to please. Gives exchanges only. Offers layaway. M-Sat 9-9, Sun 12-6. Accepts checks, MC, Visa, AmExp & Discover.

TOTES OUTLET
5300 Kings Mill Rd., Outlets Unltd, Mason, 45040, (513) 398-5615
10078 Kemper Rd., Loveland, 45140, (513) 583-2390

These Cincinnati area outlets offer savings of 40-70% off regular retail prices on the Totes brand of coats, hats, luggage, cosmetic bags, umbrellas, gloves and sunglasses. The merchandise consists of overstocks, discontinued styles and seconds. The businesses are located near Kings Island and The Beach, off I 71 South. Gives refunds. M-Sat 10-9, Sun 12-6. Accepts checks, MC, Visa & Discover.

TRAVEL SHOP
101 S. High St., Columbus, 43215, 224-4850
2994 E. Broad St., Columbus, 43209, 239-9126

Save on first quality luggage, attaches, wallets, travel gadgets and accessories as well as other small leather goods. The stores also stock many hard to find related items. The moderate to better quality merchandise is comparable to that found in other fine stores throughout the city. However, some of the brands are lesser known, while others you will instantly recognize. Savings apply to about half of the inventory. Gives exchanges.M-F 10-6, Sat 10-5. Accepts checks, MC & Visa.

ALSO SEE

Amos Indoor Flea Market, Amy Stoudt, Anne's Collection Outlet Store, Burlington Coat Factory, Benzle Porcelain Company, Byzantium, Deja Vu, Designer Shoe Warehouse, Dress Barn, Dress Barn Woman, Drug Emporium, Encore Shop, Extravaganza, $5 & $10 Apparel, $5-$10-$15-$20 Place, Golden Hobby Shop, Greater Columbus Antique Mall, Kids 'R Us, Lake Erie Factory Outlet Center, Liquidations Now, Madison's Grand Finale, Mared Consignments, Marshall's, T.J. Maxx, Office America, One More Time, Ritchey's, Sally Beauty Supply, Savings Zone, Schottenstein's, Tango's, Ten Below, Tuesday Morning, Uhlman's, Uncle Sam's Pawn Shop.

The *Bargain Hunting Zip Code Directory* fits into the glove compartment of your car and provides you with a geographic listing of the businesses in this book. See order form at the back of the index.

FLEA
MARKETS/AUCTIONS

FLEA MARKETS

Here's a few quick tips to help you through this experience: arrive early, bring a shopping bag or several, have plenty of singles and small change, look quickly and move on, wear comfortable shoes, bring a small magnifying glass to locate inscriptions, hallmarks and gold/silver markings.

AMOS INDOOR FLEA MARKET
3454 Cleveland Ave., Columbus, 43224, 262-0044

Take a shopping bag with you and be prepared to rummage through aisles of junk and hidden treasures: hair accessories, perfume samples, gold and silver jewelry, incense, antiques, seasonal fruits and vegetables, quality leather purses, bridal wear and more. Some merchandise is new while other items are used. Check your intended purchases carefully as most vendors will not accept returns. The food concession against the far right wall, sells hot dogs for only 25 cents. Vendors frequently change, and not all booths are open during regular posted hours. However, there are about 100 dealers under one roof. Admission is free and there is plenty of free parking. Check and charge acceptance varies with the vendor, but all accept cash. F-Sun 10-7.

CEASER'S CREEK FLEA MARKET
Wilmington, Ohio at the junction of I71 and S.R. 73,(513) 382-1669

Large, open air and indoor flea market features new and used crafts, clothes, housewares, jewelry, toys, tools, coins, produce, antiques and collectibles. About 300-400 vendors are set up selling their wares. The flea market is located about 1 hour and 15 minutes from Columbus. Open every Saturday and Sunday 9-5. Admission is 35 cents per person.

KINGMAN DRIVE-IN THEATER FLEA MARKET
Cheshire Rd., Delaware, 43015, 548-4202 or 548-4227

Bargains abound at this seasonal, outdoor flea market. From trash to treasure, you will find an assortment of new and used merchandise including antiques, collectibles, furniture, clothes, housewares, gifts, tools and who knows what.. Admission is 50 cents per carload and parking is free. The number of vendors varies each week but ranges from 50-150. All sales are final. Check acceptance varies among vendors, but all accept cash. Open Sundays from the first week of April to the last week of October, 7AM-2PM.

LIVINGSTON COURT INDOOR FLEA MARKET
3575 E. Livingston Ave., Columbus, 43227, 231-7726

Porcelain dolls, antiques, office supplies, Amish baked goods, books as well as miscellaneous new and used items, are available in this no frills atmosphere. Vendors frequently change and not all booths are open during the posted hours of operation. Hot dogs are available at the concession stand for only 25 cents apiece. There are over 100 vendors. Admission is free and there's plenty of free parking. All sales are final. F-Sun 10-7. Check and charge acceptance varies with each vendor, but all accept cash.

MANSFIELD FLEA MARKET
Richland Co. Fairgrounds, 237-3689

Mostly antiques and collectibles are sold on the last weekend of every month, except December, from 9-5. About 200-250 vendors are on hand to sell their wares. Take the Trimble Road exit off U.S. Route 30 to find the flea market. Check, MC & Visa acceptance varies with each vendor. All accept cash.

SOUTH DRIVE-IN THEATER FLEA MARKET
3050 S. High St., Columbus, 43207, 491-6771 or 491-2583

This seasonal, outdoor flea market features mostly used and some new merchandise from 125-200 vendors. You will find everything including toys, antiques, collectibles and what not. As with all flea markets, you have to dig through piles of merchandise to discover real "finds". Admission is 50 cents per carload and parking is free. All sales are final. W, Sat, Sun 7-2. Arrive early as many vendors close before 2. Open from the first week of April -endof October. Check acceptance varies among vendors but all accept cash.

SPRINGFIELD ANTIQUE SHOW AND FLEA MARKET
POB 2429, Springfield, 45501, (513) 325-0053

On the third weekend of every month, the Clark County Fairgrounds buzzes with excitement as 1000 vendors sell new and used merchandise including antiques and collectibles, tools, toys, furniture, food, jewelry and miscellaneous items. There's about 150,000 square feet of indoor space plus the outdoor spots, which allow this to be a year round bargain hunters' delight. The shows are held on Saturday and Sunday except for the extravaganza shows, where 2000-3000 vendors exhibit, which are held from Friday through Sunday. Admission is $2 per person to the extravaganzas and $1 to all other shows. All sales are final. Friday 5-8PM, Sat 8-5, Sun 9-4. Check and charge acceptance varies among vendors. However, all accept cash.

SUNBURY FLEA MARKET
Town Square, Sunbury, 43074, 965-2684

You can find an eclectic offering of new and used merchandise from 150-250 vendors, such as clothing. jewelry, antiques and collectibles, furniture and more. Admission varies from 50 cents to $1 depending on the flea market. Three major events are held on Memorial Day, the Fourth Of July and Labor Day each year. All sales are final. Check and charge acceptance varies with each vendor. 9-5.

URBANA FLEA MARKET
Champaign Co. Fairgrounds, (513) 653-6013 or (513) 653-6945

Usually held the first Saturday and Sunday of each month year round. You'll find antiques, collectibles and new and used items. There's about 200-300 vendors. Admission is free. The fairgrounds is located at Park Avenue, off U.S. Rte. 68. All sales are final. Check and credit card acceptance varies with each vendor. All accept cash.

WASHINGTON COURTHOUSE FLEA MARKET
Fayette Co. Fairgrounds, 278-2721

This show is open year round and features a sale once per month on a different weekend. The 3 day show features antiques, collectibles in addition to new and used merchandise. The June extravaganza show features about 500 vendors and other shows feature about 200 vendors. Admission is free. All sales are final. 8-4PM. Checks and credit card acceptance varies with each vendor. All accept cash.

AUCTIONS

Overbidding is the most frequent mistake people make at auctions. The fleeting obsession of being able to beat the competition -to win- overpowers the buyer so he bids more than he anticipated. A real success at an auction is a purchase which was made carefully and at the right price. Be sure to inspect the merchandise before the sale, set a bidding limit and stick to it. Drop out of the bidding if you are feeling uncomfortable. It is equally important to understand whether you are bidding on an individual item or a set of items called a "lot". Why not test the waters by initially going as a spectator to several auctions before actually participating? Check the back of the "help wanted" section of Sunday's Columbus Dispatch for a listing and description of area auctions. Many auctions do not maintain mailing lists and so you may only be able to find out about them by reading their ads in the newspapers or by calling them directly.

CITY OF COLUMBUS, POLICE DEPARTMENT
Impounding lot, 400 W. Whittier St., Columbus, 43215, 645-6400

Auto auctions are held intermittently, usually every six to eight weeks. The cars which are auctioned are those unclaimed cars which were recovered from thefts, as evidence in a crime or those impounded due to parking or traffic violations. The police department does not maintain a mailing list so call them to find out the date of the next auction or check the Sunday Columbus Dispatch's auction, listings. Payment must be made in cash only. All sales are final. M-F 9-4:30.

COLUMBUS POLICE PROPERTY AUCTION
1250 Fairwood Avenue, Columbus, 43206, 645-4736

Over 36,000 items are warehoused in this 50,000 square foot property room which were evidence in homicide cases, stolen or lost property. Five annual auctions feature new and used guns, bicycles, electronic equipment and more. They do not maintain a mailing list, so you will need to call periodically or follow the auction listings in the Sunday Columbus Dispatch at the back of the "help wanted" section. All sales are final and merchandise is sold "as is". M-F 9-5. Accepts checks only.

DEPARTMENT OF DEFENSE
DCSC Bldg. 14-1, 3990 E. Broad St., Columbus, 43213, 238-3244

Sales are held on the first Thursday of each month at 9AM, with inspections available on the Monday, Tuesday and Wednesday just prior from 8AM-3PM. The supply of items changes monthly subject to availability, but has included new and used items such as hardware, office furniture and equipment, clothing, vehicle equipment and components, fittings and specialities, engine accessories, aircraft components, transmission equipment, motors, televisions, sleeping bags, marine and support equipment. Once your bid is accepted, you have up to 5 days to remove your purchase. Call to be added to their mailing list. Savings are about 20-70% and more. All sales are final and merchandise is sold "as is". M-F 9-5. Accepts cash, certified check or company check

FRANKLIN COUNTY SHERIFF'S DEPARTMENT
370 S. Front St., property room, Columbus, 43215, 462-3316

Auction sales of confiscated new and used items are held about once a year whenever sufficient inventory has been accumulated. The date always changes. The stock varies widely and has included stereos, jewelry, hardware, automobiles and other items. A mailing list is not maintained so it is suggested that you call periodically, or check the auction listings at the back of the Sunday Columbus Dispatch's "help wanted" section. All sales are final, and merchandise is sold "as is". M-F 8:30-4. Check and charge acceptance varies.

KIEFER'S AUCTION GALLERY
4401 Lyman Dr., suite B, Mailing box 288, Hilliard, 43026, 771-4720

Find new and antique jewelry, antique furniture and other household items at this monthly auction . These are usually held on the fourth Sunday at the McCoy Center, Hilliard's old roller skating rink. Merchandise is sold "as is". All sales are final. M-F 9-5. Accepts checks and cash only.

OHIO AUTO AUCTION
3905 Jackson Pike, Grove City, 43123, 871-2771

All makes and models of repossessed cars, boats and motorcycles are offered for sale during specified times only: every Tuesday at 10:30AM and every Wednesday at 9:30 A.M. The latter is a bank sale. Vehicles are sold "as is" to the highest bidder, without expressed or implied warranties. I suggest that you bring along a copy of the current Consumer Reports or similar publication, to assist you in making an informed decision. You can inspect the offerings 2 to 3 days prior to the auction, at which time, you may sit in the car, turn on the ignition and look under the hood. The vehicles may not be driven. If you are handy or know enough about cars, this is a great way to save about 20-30% off the price at a used car dealer. I purchased my Toyota Camry here. At the time of the sale, the purchaser pays a $200 non-refundable deposit by cash or certified check, and the balance within 48 hours by the same method. M-F 9-5.

R&S AUCTION CENTER
810 S. Sunbury Rd., Westerville, 43081, 523-1810 or 431-0246

You can purchase gently and greatly used furniture, jewelry, collectibles and antiques at the Tuesday evening auctions which are held at 6:30PM. Payment is by cash or check with proper identification. All sales are final.

SMITTY'S AUCTION
1263 Parsons Ave., Columbus, 43206. 444-5001

Thursday evening auctions of antiques, collectibles, furniture and contents of homes are held at 6PM. Save about 20-40% less than you would pay in an antique or second hand furniture store. All sales are final, and merchandise is sold "as is".

STATE OF OHIO DEPT. OF ADMINSTRATIVE SERVICES
226 N. 5 St., Columbus, 43266-0564, 466-5052

State surplus merchandise such as vehicles, office furniture and equipment, computers, typewriters and miscellaneous items are sold about every 3 months at a Saturday auction. Occasionally, similar merchandise from the federal government is included in these sales. Payment is by cash on the day of purchase for all items except vehicles, which require 1/3 payment by cash on the day of sale and the balance by money order or bank check 3 days later. All merchandise is a final sale and is sold "as is". M-F 8-5.

STRATFORD AUCTION CENTER
2730 Stratford Rd., Delaware, 43015, 369-5085

Antiques and collectibles are auctioned on the first and third Fridays of the month at 5PM. This highly respected auction center specializes in quality Victorian pieces. Savings are about 30-40% less than in antique stores. All sales are final, and merchandise is sold "as is". Call M-F 9-5. Accepts checks and cash only.

WDLR RADIO
POB 448, Delaware, 43015, 363-1700, 548-5811

Delaware residents and those in the most northern sections of Franklin county, can tune in to 1550 AM every Saturday from 10AM-12 noon, to hear the Radio Discount Auction. Merchandise such as clothing, furniture, dried flowers, meals at restaurants and gift certificates are donated to the station by businesses in exchange for free on-air publicity. Listeners can't see the merchandise, but can place live bids on the air. Savings can amount to 30-75% off regular retail prices. WDLR also sponsors a television auction on the last Wednesday of the month at 7:30PM, which airs on TV 56 Delaware, a UHF station, to those within a 30 mile radius. Merchandise must be picked up at the donor's business which is in the Delaware area. All sales are final.. Accepts checks and cash.

FOOD

In this section, you'll find listings for supermarkets, general merchandise stores which carry food products, specialty food stores and bars which feature sizeable happy hour food buffets. There's also restaurants offering good values on certain days or at certain times during early bird or sunset specials.

Did you know that supermarkets and stores which sell health and beauty aids generally place their most costly items at eye level? This method is used because they know that consumers are likely to purchase these items on impulse. I suggest that you compare the various brands before you make a decision by looking high and low on those shelves .

ALDI
3831 E. Main St.., Columbus, 43213
633 Harrisburg Pike, Central Pt. Shpng. Ctr., Columbus, 43223
3350 Cleveland Ave., Columbus, 43224

Every day low prices at this full service grocery store, are about 30-70% lower than those found at other supermarkets. Their regular prices on Tyson chicken legs are 49 cents per pound, a 20 ounce package of Oven Fresh white bread is 25 cents, a 2 liter bottle of soda is 49 cents, a package of 8 burger or hot dog buns is 29 cents, canned tuna is 49 cents. The merchandise consists largely of products which have been made by nationally recognized companies, but do not bear their labels. Before you stock up on any one type of product, I suggest that you purchase one or two, test it out to see if you like it, then return to the store to make a larger purchase. The Aldi stores do not accept incoming phone calls. M-Th 9-7, F 9-8, Sat 9-6. Accepts cash and food stamps only. Does not accept checks.

ANTHONY THOMAS CANDY SHOPPES
1940 W. Henderson Rd., Columbus, 43220, 451-6389
2729 E. Main St., Bexley, 43209, 231-3556
4493 Refugee Rd., Columbus, 43232, 864-2970
80 N. Hamilton Rd., Gahanna, 43230, 475-9382
1941 W. 5 Ave., Columbus, 43212, 488-2531

2434 Stringtown Rd., Grove City, 43123, 875-1343
5665 Columbus, Square, Columbus, 43231, 890-3753
5157 W. Broad St., Columbus, 43228, 870-8899
400 N. High St., Columbus, 43215, 461-5341
7129 E. Main St., Reynoldsburg, 43068, 868-0394
5 Westerville Square, Westerville, 43081, 891-4890
5040 N. High St., Worthington, 43085, 436-2809
1160 W. Broad St., Columbus, 43222, 274-8405

Each of their stores has a selection of "sweet slips" which are factory goofs, at 50% off regular retail prices. The imperfection is usually a slightly underweight or misshapen piece of chocolate, which is just as fresh and tasty as their other products. The "sweet slips" are priced at $4.50 a pound, regularly $7-$9 a pound. All sales are final. M-Sat 9-9, Sun 11-5. Accepts checks, MC & Visa.

AUDDINO BAKERY
1490 Clara, Columbus, 43211, 294-2577

Fresh baked Italian bread, rolls, donuts, pies, cookies, croissants and sub buns are available at savings of 20-30% off retail. This wholesale bakery is passing the savings to you as a retail customer. M-Sat 6AM-5PM. Accepts cash only.

BASKIN ROBBINS
302 S. Hamilton Rd., Gahanna, 43230, 476-4331
1750 Brice Rd., Reynoldsburg, 43068, 866-0719
277 W. Bridge St., Dublin, 43017, 889-7425
1932 W. Henderson Rd., Columbus, 43220, 459-0260

Stop in to any of their stores and register your child for the Birthday Club. Kids aged 12 and under will receive a yearly coupon good for a free, deluxe junior scoop ice cream cone on their birthday. With 38 flavors to choose from, there's bound to be many to please your little one. M-Th. 11-9, F and Sat 11-10, Sun 11-9.

BEXLEY NATURAL FOODS CO-OP
508 N. Cassady, Columbus, 43209, 252-3951

This nonprofit business is the oldest natural foods storefront in Central Ohio. It features organic and natural foods such as whole grain cereals, herbs and spices and organically grown vegetables. Most of the stock is sugar, additive and dye free. A $5 annual fee enables you to become a member and to save about 20% off regular retail prices (15% above the wholesale cost price). As a member, you are obligated to volunteer 2-4 hours per month at the store. Nonmembers pay 25% over the posted store prices, which amounts to a savings of about 17% off regular retail prices. The co-op is operated by paid staff as well as volunteers. M-F 9-7, Sat 9-5. Accepts checks, MC & Visa.

BILL KNAPP'S
2199 Riverside Dr., Columbus, 43221, 488-1139
6851 N. High St., Worthington, 43085, 846-4030

This family oriented restaurant offers home cooked meals for $3-$7 such as baked fish, chicken, roast beef and more. The food comes with a choice of side dishes. Kids meals for ages 11 and under, cost $1.99-$4.99, and feature a varied menu of fish, chicken, burgers and more, accompanied by a side dish and dessert. On your birthday, you will be entitled to a percent off your meal equivalent to your age. If you are 50 years old, your meal will be 50% off. A complimentary chocolate birthday cake is also provided on your birthday. This special birthday promotion is available for adults as well as children. Sun - Sat 11-10. Accepts checks, MC, Visa & AmExp.

BLUE BIRD PIE THRIFT STORE
106 E. Moler St., Columbus 43207, 443-4808

Day old and surplus Archway cookies, Blue Bird Pies, cakes and lunchbox snacks as well as baked bread from a local grocery chain, are sold at savings of 40-60% off the regular retail price. The gaily decorated birthday sheet cakes sell for only $4.99. You can find similar birthday cakes in the bakeries of area supermarkets and specialty bakeries for $8-$12. M-F 9-5, Sat 9-4. Accepts cash and food stamps.

BROWNBERRY THRIFT STORE
1855 Northwest Blvd., Columbus 43212, 488-3189

This is the only Columbus thrift outlet for Entenmann's Bakery products and are offered for sale at $1.69 per box, regularly $2.29-$4.79. All natural Brownberry breads and rolls are 50% off retail. You will also find croutons and snack items, ideal for lunchboxes, at savings of 20-40% off retail. The merchandise consists largely of first quality overstocks. M-F 9-6, Sat 9-5. Accepts checks MC & Visa.

CAFE ON FIVE
Lazarus, 141 S. High St., Columbus, 43215, 463-2661

A mouthwatering selection of hot and cold items is served on the all-you-can-eat lunch buffet such as shrimp salad lemonnaise, marinated mushrooms, tarragon chicken salad, zucchini pasta salad, raisin slaw, crabmeat salad, marinated artichokes, assorted fresh fruits, green salad with toppings, chicken and walnut salad in addition to beef tetrazzini. The menu changes daily. Soup and assorted desserts are also included for one low price of $5.95 for adults and $3.95 for children aged 12 and under. On Sunday, there is a brunch buffet, which includes the types of food mentioned, in addition to some breakfast foods such as omelets, bacon and french toast. A pianist generally performs easy listening tunes during regular operating hours. The Front Street deli in Lazarus sells a cookbook, which is filled with recipes for many of the buffet foods. The cost is only $1.50. This restaurant has earned the distinction of being one of my personal favorites. M-F 11-2:30, Sat 11-3, Sun 12-3. Accepts MC, Visa & Lazarus charges.

CHARLIE ENDRE'S SALOON
4022 Broadway, Grove City, 43123, 875-1436

Their bargain buffet is offered every Thursday from 5:30-9PM and offers a changing menu with four entrees such as roast beef, lasagne, barbecue chicken and Seafood Newburg. There are vegetable specials including sauteed zucchini and squash, pasta salads, fruits and homemade desserts such as cherry strudel and brownies. If you arrive between 5:30-7PM, you will get the early bird price of $6.95 for adults. Between the hours of 7-9PM, the fee is $7.95. Children up to age 12, pay $3.95 for either seating. You'll enjoy the 1800's atmosphere of this cozy restaurant.

CHERYL'S COOKIES
2746 Eastland Mall, Columbus, 43232, 864-0206
6076 Busch Blvd., Columbus, 43229, 431-1676
3136 Kingsdale Ctr., Columbus, 43221, 457-7158
1677 W. Lane Ave., Columbus, 43221, 488-9157

During the last hour of business each day, you can purchase 10 cookies for $3.95, which is half the usual price. These delicious, homemade edibles include chocolate chip, macadamia nut, peanut butter chip and other melt-in-your-mouth goodies. M-Sat 10-9, Sun 12-5. Accepts checks, MC & Visa.

CHINA EXPRESS AT KROGERS
55 Schrock Rd., Westerville, 43081, 890-1410

The lunch special includes any one item in the case for $2.95, or any two items for $3.45. Portions are large, but the best value is with the two item meal. All entrees come with fried rice and lo mein. There's always about 6 different main dishes to choose from including broccoli and beef, Szechuan chicken in addition to sweet and sour pork. These authentic dishes are prepared by master Oriental chefs who would be happy to cook your meal with low or no salt/sugar upon request. Eat in or take out your purchase. Luncheon special is served from 11AM-3PM Monday through Saturday. Accepts MC & Visa.

CLINTONVILLE FOOD CO-OP
POB 02363, Columbus, 43202, 263-3444

This is Columbus' largest pre-order food co-op. It offers shampoo, fish, organic grains, spices, cocoa, fruits, vegetables, cheeses etc. The products offered are higher quality than those found in typical grocery stores and many of the products are not available through traditional retail outlets. Savings vary from 10-50% but average out to about 30% on your total order. The manager indicated that although prices on some items are higher than in traditional supermarkets, the value is still excellent due to the products' high quality. The prices are lower than those found in natural food stores, according to the manager. Co-op membership is $5 annually, and members are expected to share in the responsibilities which amount to about 2-4 hours per month. This nonprofit group is in the process of negotiating to open a retail business in the campus area in the fall of 1991. Prices will be a little higher in the store due to overhead expenses. The Clintonville Food Co-op sponsors an annual vegetarian coking contest which is open to the public. Optional meetings for members of the co-op are held 5-6 times per year and include slides, discussions and workshops on environmental topics. Accepts checks and cash. Call anytime.

CONFECTION PRODUCTS COMPANY, INC.
1459 E. Livingston Ave., Columbus 43205, 252-2104

Find gumballs, Good 'N Plenty and other candies at savings of about 25-40% less than you would pay through a vending machine. If you can use bulk packed (no individual wrapped products), large quantities of sweets, this wholesaler can supply your needs. The candies can be used for parties, school groups or individuals. M-F 9-5. Accepts cash only.

COOK'S PANTRY
3880 Lockbourne Rd., Columbus 43207, 491-9333

This local distributor, a manufacturer's outlet which is owned by the Sarah Lee Corporation, sells Jimmy Dean, Hillshire Farms, Kahn's and Sarah Lee products. Savings are 15-30% off regular retail prices on frozen pizzas, meats, seafood, vegetables, entrees and cheese. Some are packed in large quantities such as the five pound block of Borden cheese. Other foods are packed in smaller portions. The manager indicated that the business is currently searching for a separate site to house the cash and carry portion of the company. M-F 8:30-5. Accepts cash only.

CUB FOODS
5727 Emporium Square, Columbus, 43231, 899-0050
6500 Tussing Rd., Reynoldsburg, 43068, 863-0600
2757 Festival Lane, Dublin, 43017, 793-1495
3600 Soldano Blvd., Consumer Sq. W., Columbus, 43228, 279-8989

You can shop 24 hours a day, 7 days per week at this full service grocery store. Savings are 15-30% below regular grocery store prices. They feature a bakery where 2 extra large loaves of Italian bread are $1. Kids aged 12 and under, can obtain a free, "Kiddie Kookie Credit Card" which is good for 1 free cookie each time they visit the store. This same age group can also join the *Fruit of the month club*. The free membership card entitles the child to a free pre-determined fruit each month such as a tangelo, kiwi, mango, apple etc. The stores offer 40% off all brands of greeting cards, gift wrap and bows. The produce department has traditional and exotic fruits and vegetables. The fish section is well stocked and is also value priced. Leave your unwanted coupons and take those you need from the coupon exchange located at the main entrance. On Saturdays, Cub Foods is filled with at least 12 product marketers offering free samples of food, providing you with the opportunity to sample new products. Look for the T.P.R.'s (temporary price reductions) throughout the store. The presence of the green signs indicates an exceptional value. You will need to bag your own groceries at all of their stores except the one in Dublin. Accepts checks and cash only.

DELAWARE COFFEE AND TEA EXCHANGE
49 N. Sandusky St., Delaware, 43015, 1-363-9229

The teas and vinegars offered here are fairly priced. However, the best savings are to be found in purchases of their high yield coffee. One pound of coffee will make about 150 cups at the cost of $8, as compared to about $12 elsewhere for the same yield. Coffee beans are freshly roasted on the premises. This store features an extensive variety of products and is a delight to the senses. Cash refunds. M-W 9-6, Thurs.-Sat 9-8. Accepts cash, MC & Visa.

DENNY'S
2454 E. Dublin Granville Rd., Columbus, 43229, 891-0664
2550 S. Hamilton Rd., Columbus, 43232, 868-0323
23 Huber Village Blvd., Westerville, 43081, 882-5559
5979 E. Main St., Columbus, 43213, 864-8585
2209 S. Limestone, Springfield, 45501, (513) 324-3320

Adults or children can get any menu item for free on their birthday. The children's lunch/dinner menu for ages 10 and up, includes hot dogs, spaghetti, chicken sandwich, grilled cheese, brontaurus burger or a corn dog at a cost of only $2.20-$2.65. Some of these children's dishes come with fries. The kids' breakfast menu is $2.20-$2.40 and features pancakes, eggs, waffles and sausage combinations. The senior citizen menu, for ages 55 and over, includes halibut, roast turkey, chicken and other dinner items for $3.55-$4.60. The senior breakfast menu is $2.50-$3.50 and offers similar choices as those on the children's menu. These prices are all lower than those for adults or those on the general menu. Open 24 hours per day, 7 days per week. Accepts MC, Visa, Discover and cash.

DER DUTCHMAN AND DUTCH KITCHEN
445 S. Jefferson Ave., US Rte. 42 S., Plain City, 43064, 1-873-3414 (Der Dutchman)
8690 US Rte. 42 S., Plain City, 43064, 1-873-4518 (Dutch Kitchen)

You can enjoy the delectable home cooked meals of the Amish/Mennonite people in either of these restaurants. Both offer daily specials costing $4.20-$5.80 from 11AM-8PM Monday-Thursday and 11AM-9PM on Friday such as barbecue chicken, barbecue ribs or baked cod. Each comes with potatoes and a salad bar. All-you-can-eat family style meals, which are also offered, include 2 main dishes such as ham, roast beef and chicken, plus a salad bar, corn, mashed potatoes, bread, pie and a beverage. The all-you-can-eat meal ranges from $8.30-$8.85 per adult and is served for lunch or dinner during regular operating hours. Children's portions are $3.60-$4.20. For a special treat, you can enjoy your meal at Der Dutchman in the authentic atmosphere of the Amish buggy inside the restaurant. The buggy seats five people and is available on a first come, first serve basis. M-Th 6AM-8PM, F and Sat 6AM-9PM. Accepts MC, Visa and cash.

DI PAOLO FOOD DISTRIBUTORS
Cash And Carry Outlet, 3500 Indianola Ave., Columbus, 43214, 263-1247

This wholesale distributor sells imported Italian foods and confectionaries, canned and fresh fruits and vegetables, spices, frozen foods (fish, meat, vegetables,), specialty appliances, paper products and imported cheese. You'll even find many items not typically available in supermarkets. If you don't see what you want, ask for it, or ask to see their catalogue. The warehouse contains 4,000 square feet, most of which is not open to the public. On a recent visit, I stocked up on Perugina cakes and candies. Savings are 10-25% less than grocery store prices. Case prices offer slightly greater savings. Gives refunds. M-F 8-5, Sat 9-1. Accepts checks, MC & Visa.

DOLLY MADISON BAKERY THRIFT SHOP
3654 Cleveland Ave,.Columbus, 43224, 475-9640
2757 S. High St., Columbus, 43207, 491-2925

Sells surplus Butternut and Dolly Madison brands of bread, lunchbox snacks, rolls and donuts at savings up to 60% off grocery store prices. The merchandise consists of overstocks, first quality and some damaged cartons. Six loaves of bread cost $1.39, a 7 ounce pecan roll is $1.79, decorated birthday cakes the size of a half sheet cake, are $5.79. M-Sat 9-6. Sun 11-4. Accepts checks and cash only.

ELEPHANT BAR
995 E. Dublin-Granville Rd., Columbus, 43229, 846-4592

The complimentary happy hour buffet is offered Monday through Friday 4-7PM. The buffet always includes tortillas and salsa, a tray of vegetables and some snacks such as pretzels. Each day one or two different specials are added such as: pizza on Mondays, tacos on Tuesdays, barbecue beef and carved ham on Wednesdays, hot wings on Thursdays and submarine sandwiches on Fridays. Drinks during happy hour are about $1 off the regular prices. The DJ starts at 9:30PM and plays popular dance tunes. Seniors aged 60 and over can register for a free *Senior's Passport To Good Taste* card which entitles you to a 15% discount on your own meal in the restaurant (not the bar area). Anytime on Sunday and Monday, 2 children aged 12 and under, can eat for free when accompanied by an adult. They will be given a choice of several items from the kids' menu (regularly priced at $3.25) or may eat from the enormous Sunday brunch buffet. The buffet includes a large selection of breakfast and lunch foods such as freshly made waffles, pasta, prime rib, stir fry chicken, lasagne, made to order omelets, fresh fruits, sausage, croissants and a sundae bar. Soft drinks or fruit juices are also included. The cost is $10.95 for adults. Regular menu items are $4.95-$9.95. The early bird dinners are served daily from 4-7PM, and feature a savings of about $1-$5 off the regular menu prices of $8-$14. The entrees come with your choice of salad or soup, plus rice. There's no cover and no minimum to watch or participate. You'll enjoy the tastefully appointed jungle/safari decor. M-Sat 11AM-2AM, Sun 10AM-10PM. Accepts MC, Visa, AmExp & Discover.

ENGINE HOUSE NO. 5
121 Thurman Ave., Columbus, 43206, 443-4877

Seafood and American dinners are available at this 100 year old restaurant. You will be in for a special treat for your birthday. A complimentary oversized cupcake will be delivered to your table at the end of your meal, by a server who slides down a glistening brass fire pole. A dinner special, which changes daily, is priced at $10.75 and includes a selected menu item such as rainbow trout, stuffed cod, chicken primavera or prime rib, regularly $11-$20. The entree comes with a baked potato and a vegetable. Smaller portions, ideal for seniors, are available during the Sunset Special which is served from 4-6PM Monday-Saturday and 4-9PM on Sunday. The meal is accompanied by a baked potato and a vegetable. The prices range from $9-$13.50 which is about 20-30% less than their regular prices. Reservations are recommended. M-Th 4-10, F/Sat 4-11, Sun 4-9. Accepts checks, MC, Visa, AmExp & Discover.

FARM MARKETS OF OHIO
249-2430

Call to inquire about area farm markets or to request the free brochure which lists market locations, foods offered and the time of year available. The flyer includes those places where you can pick your own fruits and vegetables as well as those with retail operations. M-F 8:30-5.

FOURBAKERS
6614 Sawmill Rd., Columbus, 43235, 761-1333

The "Early Week Special" is offered Monday through Wednesday and features donuts, fritters, cinnamon rolls, bismarcks and twists for only 30 cents each, regularly 50 cents at other times. Stock up on their wide selection of delicious edibles. Although this business has other stores in Columbus,only the Sawmill Road site features this special. M-Sun 6AM-10PM. Accepts Checks and cash.

FRISCH'S BIG BOY
4775 W. Broad St., Columbus, 43228, 878-5337
3785 Indianola Ave., Columbus, 43214, 267-9245
4775 E. Main St., Columbus, 43213, 866-0940
831 N. Bridge St., Chillicothe, 45601, 775-3663
255 Lafayette St., London, 43140, 852-4515

The all-you-can-eat breakfast buffet is offered Monday-Friday from 7-11AM at a cost of $3.59 for adults, and Saturday and Sunday from 7AM-1PM at a cost of $4.55. Children aged 6-12, are charged $2.09 at all times and those aged 5 and under can eat for free. The buffet includes pancakes, french toast, scrambled eggs, hash browns and an assortment of fresh fruits and melons. Accepts cash only.

GEEM LOONG RESTAURANT
1773 W. 5 Ave., Columbus, 43212, 486-9651

Don't miss the $2.10 lunch specials which are offered from 11:30-2PM weekdays. There are usually 2 main dishes to choose from such as General Tso's Chicken, Beef And Vegetables, Rosey Chicken, Wor Sue Gai and Kung Pao Chicken. It is served with a scoop of white rice and tea. The portion is appropriate for a lunch time meal. Accepts cash only.

GOLD C SAVINGS SPREE
4465 Professional Pkwy., Groveport, 43125, 836-7325

This coupon book offers savings on entertainment and recreational activities, meals at fast food restaurants and savings at other retail businesses in the area. It contains cents off discounts and two for one coupons at about 300 establishments including movie theaters, roller skating rinks, video rental sites, Wyandotte Lake and more. The book, which will remind you of a mini "Entertainment 91", is sold through area schools as a fundraiser or available from the publisher by mail. Even if you already own the "Entertainment 91" book, this is a worthwhile investment for only $6. Many of the businesses in the Gold C book are not found in the Entertainment book. Accepts cash and checks. M-F 9-5.

GROCERY WAREHOUSE
3961 Hoover Rd., Grove City, 43123, 875-1331

Save 5-25% off regular grocery store prices at Big Bear's outlet store. The merchandise consists of overstocks, case lot packing as well as crushed or dented boxes. M-Sat 7AM-12 midnight, Sun 7AM-10PM. Accepts checks and cash only.

GROUND ROUND
12 S. James Rd., Columbus, 43213, 231-6219
5090 N. High St., Columbus, 43214, 885-4305
120 Phillipi Rd., Columbus, 43228, 279-0160
2690 E. Dublin Granville Rd., Columbus, 43231, 882-5850

On Thursdays, children aged 12 and under can pay what they weigh for a child's meal or can pay what the day's temperature is outside, at the rate of 1 penny per degree or per pound. The kids' meal, regularly $2.49, includes a choice of a burger, hot dog or grilled cheese, plus fries, fruit and a drink. Wednesdays and Fridays are all-you-can-eat fried flounder days. You pay only $4.69 and a bottomless flounder, french fries and cole slaw dinner is yours. Mondays-Fridays, their *Hot Spots* happy hour features free munchies such as hot hors d'eovres, fried zucchini, pizza, chicken wings etc. Drinks are regularly priced at $1.50-$3 during this time with no discounts. On your birthday, call ahead and the business will give you a free birthday cake with your meal in the dining room. There is no minimum number of people required in your dining group. The offer is valid for adults as well as kids. M-Sat 11-10, Sun 11-12. Accepts MC, Visa & AmExp.

HOULIHAN'S
6240 Busch Blvd., Columbus, 43229, 431-1852

Early Bird Dinners are served from 4-6PM, Sunday through Thursday and include an entree, dessert, beverage plus a choice of soup or salad for only $8.95. The list of thirteen entrees includes herbed chicken pasta, blackened chicken breast, rib eye steak, cajun shrimp, fajitas, barbecued baby backed ribs and more. If you were to order these at other times, you would expect to pay about $12-$16 for all components of the *Early Bird Dinner* on an a la carte basis. Accepts MC, Visa, AmExp. & Discover.

JP'S BBQ DRIVE-THRU
1077 Old Henderson Rd., Columbus, 43220, 261-RIBS

A former car wash has been converted into a drive through and dine in restaurant offering delicious meaty baby backed ribs. Daily specials offer a sampling from the mouthwatering menu. Monday is fill your face day where, for $5.95, you can have all-you-can-eat hot wings. Tuesday is buddy special night where you pay full price for a meal and your friend dines for 25% off his/her meal. Wednesday is family night: buy the ribs for $6.95 for a half slab or $11.95 for the whole slab and J.P.'s will give you a side dish for free (such as onion rings, au gratin potatoes or cole slaw), The fat daddy kid's menu for ages 6 and under, costs $2.25, and is available at all times. Kids can choose from a large frankfurter, fried shrimp, barbecue beef pork or chicken sandwich. Fries and a soft drink are included. M-F 11-9, Sat & Sun 3-9. Accepts MC, Visa & Discover.

JOLLY PIRATE DONUTS
3923 E. Broad St., Columbus, 43213, 231-7556
3260 W. Broad St., Columbus, 43204, 276-3136
5095 W. Broad St. Columbus, 43228, 878-0825
3554 Broadway, Grove City, 43123, 871-1070
1200 Harrisburg Pike, Columbus, 43223, 276-5749
5525 N. High St.,Columbus, 43214, 888-0021
4480 Kenny Rd., Columbus, 43220, 459-0812
1928 Lockbourne Rd., Columbus, 43207, 443-1966
6689 E. Main St., Reynoldsburg, 43068, 864-1085
2811 Morse Rd., Columbus, 43231, 471-0122
3718 Refugee Rd., Columbus, 43232, 236-5877
909 N. Memorial Dr., Lancaster, 43130, 654-7642
1643 E. Main St., Lancaster, 43130, 653-4920

On Tuesdays, you can save 80 cents off the regular price of $3.49 for a dozen donuts At all times, when you purchase a dozen donuts, the 13th donut will be free, as part of their baker's dozen special. The frequent purchaser plan provides you with a dozen donuts free after you have purchased 12 dozen. Ask for a free membership card, and be sure to have it stamped at any of their locations whenever you make a purchase. Open 24 hours, 7 days per week. Accepts checks and cash only..

KLOSTERMAN'S BAKING COMPANY
355 Lincoln Avenue, Rt. 22, Lancaster, 43130, 654-0963
508 W. Main St., Springfield, 45506, (513) 322-7658
2655 Courtright Rd., Columbus, 43232, 338-8111

Day old, surplus, package damaged and discontinued Klosterman's products are sold here at savings of 25-60% off regular retail prices. You'll find buns, rolls, snacks Italian bread, croissants, mini hamburger buns, and lunchbox treats. The manager said that her customers' favorite item is the bread priced at 3 loaves for $1.19 which is available at $1.39 each in the supermarkets. Discount to Golden Buckeye cardholders. M-F 9-6:30, Sat 9-5. Accepts cash and foodstamps.

KREMA PRODUCTS
1000 W. Goodale, Columbus, 43215, 299-4131

This factory outlet presents the full line of Krema products including nuts and peanut butter at regular retail prices. However, gift edibles in decorative tins, are priced at 10-15% below retail prices. Call ahead to ask when the store will be making the peanut butter. Young and old alike will enjoy looking through the big glass window in the outlet to watch the creamy stuff being made. Don't forget to pick up a free copy of the Peanut Butter Fact Sheet which offers facts and trivia on this delicious, healthy edible. All sales are final. M-F 9-5, Sat 10-2. Accepts checks, MC & Visa.

LA SCALA RESTAURANT
4199 W. Dublin-Granville Rd., Dublin, 43017, 889-9431

Every Sunday after 5:30 is "Pasta Night" at this popular Italian eatery. All regularly priced pasta dishes which are $7.95-$10.95 on the menu, such as spaghetti, ravioli and fettucini with seafood, are priced at only $5.95. You will also get a salad and an all natural Giobatti bread to accompany your meal. Monday through Friday evenings after 5:30, this restaurant features a choice of three different daily specials from their extensive menu at a cost of $5.95- $8.95. This is a savings of $2-$3 from their standard menu prices. Pasta specials come with a salad. Other specials such as baked cod or chicken parmigiana, come with a side dish and a salad. Monday through Friday from 11-3, you can feast on the all-you-can-eat lunch buffet for $5.95, which includes an assortment of hot and cold specialties. Dinner is served Monday through Thursday from 5-11PM, Friday and Saturday 5-12PM, and Sunday 5-9PM. Accepts MC, Visa & AmExp.

LITTLE CAESER'S
21 Central Ohio locations

Great prices and delicious pizza are what you will find here. At all times, you will get two pizzas for the price of one. For instance, for $13.49, 2 large single topping pizzas can be yours, or for $10.29, two medium single topping pizzas are available. Don't miss their crazy bread for $1.29 which includes a bag of freshly baked bread sticks topped with butter and Parmesan cheese. Little Caeser's is a frequent advertiser, so carefully watch the newspapers and the advertisements you receive in the mail. The stores generally advertise at the back of the *Sunday Dispatch's Teleview* television guide as well as other places. Each time you make a purchase, you will also get a coupon to use on your next order. The stores also offer many in store specials at additional savings. In a recent national survey conducted by *Restaurants And Institutions Magazine,* Little Caeser's was voted to be the best pizza value in America as compared to all other restaurant and pizza chains. Sun.-Th. 11-11, F and Sat 11AM-1AM. Accepts checks and cash only.

THE LOBBY
2390 S. Hamilton Rd., Columbus 43232, 863-0650

The complimentary happy hour buffet is offered Tuesday, Wednesday and Friday from 4-8PM and features a changing spread which includes several entrees such as lasagna, chicken wings and meatballs, a cold pasta salad and a vegetable or cheese tray. Drinks during happy hour are priced at about $1.25-$1.50 each, which is about half the usual price. Accepts MC, Visa & AmExp.

LUCY'S
175 Hutchinson Avenue, Columbus 43235, 885-3334

The complimentary happy hour spread is offered weekdays from 5-8PM and features a different theme each night. Mondays you can enjoy mini hotdogs, chicken wings and various condiments. Egg rolls and sweet and sour meatballs are featured during Tuesday's Oriental night. On Wednesday, you'll find mozzarella sticks and french bread pizza. Wednesday is also ladies night and drinks are only $1. Potato skins and chicken wings are offered on Thursdays. Fridays there's a much larger offering including carved roast beef, egg rolls, pizza, cheese sticks, nachos and more. Monday through Thursday, you may purchase five shrimp or three oysters for only $1 during happy hour. The DJ plays contemporary and rock tunes Monday through Saturday, beginning at 9PM. Lucy's is located in the Holiday Inn in Worthington. Be sure to get a glimpse of the hotel lobby which looks like a European street scene. Accepts MC, Visa & AmExp.

MCL CAFETERIAS
3160 Kingsdale Ctr., Columbus, 43221, 457-5786
2491 E. Dublin Granville Rd., Columbus, 43229, 882-4691
5240 E. Main St., Columbus, 43213, 861-6259
4500 Eastland Dr., Columbus, 43232, 866-7635

This family owned and operated Midwest chain prepares all of their foods from scratch-even the salad dressings. There is a large selection of tasty items on their Heartwise menu (a program sponsored in conjunction with Riverside Hospital's Heart Institute of Ohio) which is aimed at those having high blood pressure, elevated blood cholesterol level, obesity, diabetes or even health conscious persons. The balance of their menu is so extensive and delectable that there is something to please everyone's palate. There's carrot and raisin salad, fresh baked breads and muffins, carved prime rib of beef, stuffed flounder, baked cod and stuffed chicken breast. The desserts include pumpkin pie, coconut cream pie, cheesecake, strawberry pie, hot desserts and other delectables. Entrees are a la carte and range in price from $1.78-$3.50. The *Jack Benny Value Plate* offers a reduced size portion, ideal for seniors or anyone else. It includes an entree, 2 vegetables and bread and costs $2.50-$3.50. Kids' specials are $2.65. The Eastland Drive location has the nicest decor, both inside and out. This stately brick building features several carpeted rooms with mock fireplaces, faux fieldstone walls and decorator wallpaper. It is hard to believe that this is just a cafeteria. The staff is always friendly and courteous. M-Sun 11-8:30. Accepts cash only.

MARZETTI'S CONFECTION PRODUCTS
956 W. Broad St., Columbus 43222, 228-1535

Delicious popcorn and related products such as carmel corn and cheese corn, are available at savings of 40-50% off regular retail prices at this factory outlet. Near Christmas time, the store also stocks gift cans and other special items at similar savings. M-F 8-4. Accepts cash and checks only.

MEAT PACKERS OUTLET
317 S. 5 St., Columbus, 43215, 228-9074

If you don't mind purchasing cold cuts, bread, meat, cheese and other edibles close to their expiration date, then this is the place for you. A short shelf life plus volume buying and low markups, add up to savings of 10-50% off regular grocery store prices. You will find such popular brands as Oscar Meyer and others. You can also save about 20% on bottled cajun seasoning. Check the expiration date before paying. M-Sat 10-6. Accepts checks, cash and food stamps only.

MID EAST UNITED DAIRY INDUSTRY ASSOCIATION
3592 Corporate Dr., Columbus, 43231, 890-1800

Call to request a free copy of the recipe flyer which includes directions for a Chocolate Lovers Ice Cream Float, Raspberry-Chocolate Bombe, Toffee Crunch Float, Italian Ice Cream Cake and more. Also request their free flyer on homemade ice creams. M-F 9-4.

MR. BULKY'S
2713 Northland Plaza Drive, Columbus, 43231, 882-5839
New Market Mall, Columbus, 43235 (will open in fall 1991)

Candies, cookies, nuts, spices, pasta, rice and baking mixes are available here in bulk food bins and sold by weight. Decorative tins and containers, which can be filled with goodies, offer a unique gift giving opportunity. About half of the inventory is priced at about 10-30% lower than in a supermarket. However, the wide selection of hard to find items and sugar free candies, certainly makes this a store you won't want to miss. M-Sat 10-9:30, Sun 12-6. Accepts checks or cash only..

MY MAMA'S SWEET POTATO PIE COMPANY
1828 E. Hudson St., Columbus 43211, 476-8822

These delicious pies are available directly from this wholesale bakery. Baked pies are $5.20 each if you purchase less than 12, or $4.25 each if you purchase more than 12. Frozen pies are $4.95 each for less than 12, or $3.75 each if you purchase more than 12. The baked pies are typically sold at area supermarkets for about $6 each. M-Sat 12-8, Sun 12-4. Accepts cash only.

NICKLE'S BAKERY SURPLUS STORE
1255 Alum Creek Dr., Columbus, 43209, 253-6075
590 N. Hague, Columbus, 43204, 276-5477

Surplus baked goods such as breads, cakes, rolls, buns and lunch box snacks are sold at 30-50% off grocery store prices. All sales are final. M-F 6:30AM-7PM, Sat 7AM-6PM, Sun 10AM-4:30PM. Accepts cash only.

94TH AERO SQUADRON
5030 Sawyer Rd., Columbus, 43219, 237-9093

Monday through Friday from 4:30-7PM, you can enjoy the complimentary happy hour buffet which includes several items such as chicken wings, meatballs, fruits, vegetables and cheese. On Friday evenings, the buffet is expanded to also include a seafood bar with shrimp, crab legs or oysters. Drinks are $1 off their customary price during happy hour. Dancing begins at 7PM to current tunes which are played by the DJ. You'll enjoy the view of the Port Columbus runway. Accepts MC, Visa & AmExp.

THE NORTH MARKET
29 W. Spruce St., Columbus, 43215, 463-9664

The market is housed in a large Quonset hut, which is listed on the National Register of Historic Places. You'll find vendors selling an extensive selection of produce, meats, cheeses, spices, gourmet foods, poultry, flowers, freshly baked pastries and ethnic foods. One business sells baskets, beads, silver jewelry and ethnic arts and crafts. The prices at the North Market are often lower than you would find at area groceries and the food is very fresh. There's a few tables scattered throughout the market for those of you who would like to enjoy a light meal. The North Market features cooking demonstrations, entertainment and other special events intermittently throughout the year. Accepts checks and cash. Credit card acceptance varies among vendors. Tu, Th, F, Sat 7AM-5:30PM.

NORTHWEST NATURAL AND SPECIALTY FOODS
1636 Northwest Blvd., Columbus, 43212, 488-0607

Columbus' largest natural food store sells most of their stock at 15-20% less than you'll find elsewhere due to low markups. Solgar, Twin Lab, Nature's Plus and other brands are available. Greenhouse Ware (biodegradable products), cruelty free cosmetics (which were not tested on animals), body care lotions and conditioners, wheat and yeast free bread as well as salt and/or sugar free products can be found here. The store has also established quite a reputation as a gourmet food business selling such necessities as cooking vinegars and oils. There is a 5% additional discount on case purchases, and 10% off books and cassettes. Accepts Golden Buckeye Card. M-Sat 9-8. Accepts checks, MC & Visa.

OHIO PORK PRODUCER'S COUNCIL
135 Allview Rd., Westerville, 43081, 882-5887

Call to request free literature on pork preparation, recipes, facts and nutritional data.

OHIO POTATO GROWERS ASSOCIATION
4680 Indianola Ave., Columbus, 43214, 261-6834

Call to request a free copy of the pamphlet, *All About Potatoes* which provides nutritional information, how to buy and store potatoes, cooking tips and recipes. M-F 8:30-4.

OHIO SOYBEAN ASSOCIATION
249-2422

Call to request free brochures which provide delicious recipes using soybeans or soybean oil such as soybean chili, soybean bread and spinach stuffed mushrooms.

OHIO STEAK AND BARBECUE COMPANY
330 E. Naughten St., Columbus 43215, 221-3245

Most of the food in this wholesaler's stock is sold at about 20-30% below grocery store prices. You'll find Swift hams, Weber sausage, ribeye steaks, mozzarella cheese sticks, battered vegetable sticks, bacon, chicken and hot dogs. Bulk spices, usually in one pound tins, are priced about 50-70% less than the smaller quantities in supermarkets. The store's stock may be purchased in bulk or by the bag. Accepts Golden Buckeye cards. M-F 8-4:30, Sat 8:30-12 noon. Accepts checks

OLD COUNTRY BUFFET
2260 Morse Rd.,Columbus, 43229, 475-1191
3670 Soldano Blvd., Consumer Sq. W., Columbus, 43228, 279-6227
3834 E. Broad St., Town and Country Shpng. Ctr, Columbus, 43213, 231-0798

Great prices and tasty food await you at this all-you-can-eat buffet. Lunch costs $4.69 for adults, $4.29 for *Senior Club Card* members and 40 cents per year of age for children 10 and under. Dinner costs $6.29 for adults, $5.79 for *Senior Club Card* members and 45 cents per year of age for those 10 and under. The Sunday breakfast buffet costs $4.99 for adults, $4.59 for *Senior Club Card* members and 40 cents per year of age for those under age 10. Lunch and dinner menus include soup, about 7 entrees (baked fish, roast beef, teriyaki wings, baked chicken, meatloaf, lasagne etc), vegetables, salads, beverages and a dessert bar. The breakfast buffet features biscuits, french toast sticks, waffles, potatoes, scrambled eggs, sausage, bacon, carmel rolls, carved ham and other times. Seniors aged 60 and over can purchase a *Senior Club Card* for $1 annually, which entitles them to savings of 40-50 cents off the regular adult buffet price., The restaurants are open every day except Christmas. M-Sat 11-9, Sun 8AM-9PM. Accepts checks and cash only.

PEPPERCORN DUCK CLUB
350 North High St., Columbus, 43215, 463-1234

If you love salad bars, this one should be high on your list. Your taste buds will be pampered in the typical Hyatt manner. At the Market Stand, for only $8.50 for lunch or $13.95 for dinner, you will enjoy appetizers such as meat and seafood salads, pasta and vegetable salads. Chocolate lovers will not want to miss the Ultra Chocolatta Bar, served during lunch and dinner, at a cost of $5.95 a la carte or $2.95 with a meal. The desserts include chocolate cheesecake, chocolate strudels, chocolate mousse and other delicious goodies made on premises. This restaurant has earned the distinction of being one of my personal favorites. M-F 10-6, Sat and Sun 6-11PM. Accepts MC, Visa & AmExp.

PEPPERIDGE FARM OUTLET
1174 Kenny Center, Columbus, 43220, 457-4800

Save 10-50% off those delicious *Pepperidge Farm* cookies, breads, frozen foods, croutons and desserts. Most of the bread and rolls is 50% off the regular retail price. The merchandise in this factory outlet store consists of discontinued, overstocks, dented cans and low weight products. Some of the cookies are individually packaged for institutional use and are great to take on trips or to pack in your child's lunchbox. The store also sells a small selection of soups, cookies and other changing items from assorted companies. Gives exchanges with receipt. Accepts Golden Buckeye cards on Tuesday and Wednesday. M, T, F 9:30-6; W and Th 9:30-6:30 and Sat 9-5. Accepts checks.

PIZZA FIXINS
6261 Maple Canyon Dr., Columbus , 43229, 882-2418

You can purchase restaurant quality supplies to make your own pizza such as pre-baked crust, sauces, cheese, pepperoni and sausage. The savings are about 50% lower than you would pay for the same quality pizza in a pizzeria. You should also keep in mind that these brands are not available in supermarkets. You can save about 20-30% off the regular retail price on related cookware such as pizza pans and pizza cutters. Accepts Golden Buckeye cards. T and W 12-6, Th and F 12-8, Sat 10-6. Accepts checks and cash only.

PIZZA HUT
18 Columbus locations

Every Tuesday evening is kids' night after 5PM. When you order a medium ($8.88) or large ($12.88) pizza, two children aged 12 and under, will each get a free personal pan pizza, a free book of stickers and a free drink in a reusable, decorated Nickelodeon cup. Accepts checks and cash only.

PONDEROSA STEAK HOUSE
3875 S. High St., Columbus, 43207, 491-7552
837 S. Hamilton Rd., Columbus, 43213, 237-0767
2330 Morse Rd., Columbus, 43229, 475-2350
4720 Reed Rd., Columbus, 43220, 451-4265
355 Georgesville Rd., Columbus, 43228, 274-0213
11 Belle Avenue, Delaware, 43015, 1-369-6614
1671 E. Dublin-Granville Rd., Cols., 43229, 888-8229
2441 S. Hamilton Rd., Columbus, 43232, 861-7209
782 S. State St., Westerville, 43081, 890-1468
2370 Stringtown Rd., Grove City, 43123, 871-4181
6520 Tussing Rd., Reynoldsburg, 43068, 868-5540
828 Hebron Rd., Heath, 43056, 522-5265
1746 N. Memorial Dr., Lancaster, 43130, 654-3559
800 N. Bridge St., Chillicothe, 45601, 773-4460

This national chain offers budget priced steak and chicken meals accompanied by their Grand Buffet salad and sundae bar for $5-$8. Seniors aged 60 and over, can sign up to be a member of the *Golden Advantage Club* which provides a 20% discount on meals from 11AM-4:30PM Monday through Saturday and all day on Sunday. Kids' meals include a choice of a hot dog or a burger, fries plus all they can eat from the Grand Buffet. The kids meal is available during regular operating hours at a cost of 49 cents for those aged 5 and under, or $1.99 for those aged 6-10. M-Sun 11-9. Accepts MC, Visa & Discover.

PRESTIGE DINING CLUB
411 E. Town St., Columbus, 43215, 461-0555

Membership allows you to be able to buy one dinner and get one for free at over 100 participating Columbus restaurants such as Cockerell's, Mark Pi's, the Morgan House and Siam. Your $29.95 annual fee entitles you to receive a directory of restaurants and a membership card. M-F 9-6. Accepts checks, MC, Visa, AmExp & Discover.

RFS OUTLET STORE
1100 Morrison Ave., Gahanna, 43230, 863-3951

Satisfy your personal and party needs with restaurant quality edibles such as frozen seafood, french pastry, frozen hors d'oevres, canned goods and cheeses at savings of 15-20% off grocery store prices. Many items are available in large quantities. Non-food supplies include party trays, beer glasses and paper goods. The clearance area features savings of 30-60% on related products which are dented or close to expiration date. All sales are final. M-W 8-5:30, Th. and F 8-7, Sat 8-5. Accepts checks, MC & Visa.

R & R USA
6252 Busch Blvd., Columbus, 43229, 848-5011, 848-5020

For only $2 you can feast on the extensive and delicious happy hour buffet which includes several hot appetizers such as carved roast beef, tacos, pizza, meatballs, wings, plus pasta dishes, fruits, vegetables and several dessert offerings. The buffet is featured Monday through Friday from 5-8PM. Dancing to popular rock tunes begins at 8PM nightly. The high tech decor is tastefully done. Drink specials are offered during happy hour. M-Sat 5PM-2AM. Accepts MC, Visa & AmExp.

RAY JOHNSON'S
111 E. Main St., Columbus, 43215, 221-4203

Fish lovers line up to purchase the delectable, made to order fish specialties which are value priced. A red snapper sandwich is $2.75, filet of sole or cod is $2.25. The seafood salad is $3.50 and comes with lettuce and a variety of cold fish such as shrimp and crab. The spring rolls, which cost $1.50, are egg rolls filled with vegetables and lots of fresh seafood. While most of the fish is fried, it is surprisingly not greasy. If you are in a daring mood, why not try the turtle soup? The food portions are very generous. The owner, Ray Johnson, learned many of his culinary skills from Al Capone's former chef. You may call ahead to place your order if you wish. This business offers take out only, and has earned the distinction of being one of my personal favorites. Thank you, Elaine Goodman, for this delicious lead! M-F 9-6, Sat 9-4. Accepts cash and food stamps only.

RYAN'S FAMILY STEAK HOUSE
6075 E. Livingston Ave., Columbus, 43232, 866-1063
5550 Cleveland Ave., Columbus, 43231, 882-4886
E. Dublin Granville Rd. and Sawmill Rd. site to open in late 1991 (43235 zip)

This unpretentious family restaurant, offers the largest buffet/salad bar combination I have encountered in Columbus, about 50 linear feet. Hence, its name, *Megabar*. The cost is $4.99 for adults, $2.19 for kids aged 12 and under and free for kids under the age of 3. The main course area features salad with 20 different toppings, plus an assortment of dressings. The main courses have included a vegetable lasagne with cheese, broccoli, carrots and pasta; hot dogs, seafood salad, barbecue chicken, fried chicken and shredded barbecue beef. The side dishes include cole slaw, baked beans, carrot/raisin slaw and marinated potatoes. There are rolls and choices of 4 different soups including clam chowder and vegetable soup. The dessert bar is separated from the main bar, but is included in the price of your meal. You will find several flavors of soft serve ice cream and frozen yogurt with a variety of toppings. There are puddings, hot brownies and cookies. You can eat as much as you like because the Megabar meal entitles you to unlimited visits to the food. You can save even more money by going to Ryan's between 11AM-4PM Monday-Saturday and paying only $3.99 for the Megabar for adults. Another Megabar option is to purchase a petite sirloin steak with the bar for an additional 89 cents anytime after 4PM. The Monday evening Megabar is also a seafood buffet. Tuesday night is kids night and children under the age of ten can eat for free from a kid's menu, at the rate of 1 child for every paying adult. The restaurant also features other value priced foods including T-bone steak for $7.29 and Hawaiian Chicken for $4.99. The staff is exceptionally friendly and courteous. Sun.-Th 11AM-10PM, F and Sat 11AM-11PM. Accepts MC, Visa, & Discover.

SAM'S CLUB
3885 Morse Rd., Columbus, 43219, 471-9741
3760 Interchange Dr., Columbus, 43204, 278-9741
6300 Tussing Rd., Consumer Sq. E., Reynoldsburg, 43068, 864-2582

Businesses as well as consumers will find products of interest in this no frills environment. Quality name brand merchandise in stereos, toys, housewares, computers, office supplies, power tools, food, adult and children's clothing, books, hardware, health and beauty aids, furniture, fine jewelry, watches, appliances and sporting goods are available at savings of 10-40% off manufacturer's suggested retail prices. Tires and other automotive supplies are available at similar savings. Tires will be mounted and balanced for only $3.50 each, regularly $5-$10 each elsewhere. Offers a $3 per tire road hazard warranty. Offers moderate to better quality merchandise by nationally recognized brands. All card holders can participate in the *Sam's Travel Club* and save money on hotels, entertainment and car rentals. Inquire in the stores for details. Members may also participate in the Sam's/MCI long distance phone service at a special rate. This business, which is operated by Wal-Mart, was formerly called the Wholesale Club. Sam's Club is a members only operation. Large employers, AARP, AAA, health care providers and many other businesses have arranged for their employees to have memberships. Members will be issued an identification card which must be presented at the store's entrance as well as at the checkout. Members pay 5% above posted prices unless you purchase a special membership card for $25 annually, which will allow you to buy items at posted prices. Gives refunds. M-F 12-8:30, Sat 9:30-6, Sun 12-6. Accepts checks, Discover and cash.

SANTA FE SALOON AND EATERY
9300 Old Dublin Rd., Columbus, 43228, 793-8446

Their recession buster homemade daily specials range from $4.25-$5.25 and include: pot roast with vegetables, potatoes and gravy for $4.75, meatloaf with mashed potatoes, green beans and cole for $4.75, all-you-can-eat spaghetti with tossed salad and garlic bread for $4.50 and other specials. These are served Monday through Saturday from 11AM- 9PM. Accepts MC, Visa and AmExp.

SCARLET'S AT THE RADISSON HOTEL
1375 N. Cassady Ave., Columbus, 43219, 475-7551

The complimentary happy hour buffet is offered Monday through Friday from 4-8PM. Each night you will find a different entree, plus a fruit tray, cheese tray, a vegetable tray and snacks such as pretzels or potato chips.   The daily entrees include chili dogs on Mondays, a taco and nacho buffet on Tuesdays, a peel and eat shrimp bar on Wednesdays, and buffalo wings on Thursdays. Fridays you'll find the largest buffet, which features not one but five hot entrees such as quiche, meatballs, chicken wings, carved roast beef and a sandwich station. Many drinks are about 50 cents off during happy hour. A DJ plays contemporary and rock dance tunes beginning at 5PM. Accepts MC & Visa.

SCHMIDT'S SAUSAGE HOUSE
6800 Schrock Hill Ct., Columbus, 43229, 523-0900
1885 W. Henderson Rd., Columbus, 43220 459-7122
6336 E. Livingston Ave., Reynoldsburg, 43068, 868-0480
240 E. Kossuth, Columbus, 43206, 444-6808

The all-you-can-eat Great German Buffet is not to be missed. You'll find an array of Schmidt's specialties such as bratwurst, Bahama Mamas, German meatloaf, mild Bahamas, garlic knockers, beer beef stew as well as vegetables. The cost is $4.99 for lunch or $6.99 for dinner. Kids aged 12 and under can enjoy the buffet for only $1.99. The buffet is offered during lunchtime Monday through Friday and all day on Saturday and Sunday. Accepts MC & Visa.

SCHWEBEL'S BREAD OUTLET
4485 Reynolds Drive, Hilliard, 43026, 777-1556

Purchase Schwebel's products such as bread, buns, and rolls at savings of up to 50% off regular retail prices.   Other brands of edibles are offered such as Buckeye Biscuits, Hamburger Helper, Moon Pies and additional lunchbox snacks, Dolly Madison pastries and Grandma Shearer's potato chips at savings of 20-50% off regular retail prices.   The merchandise consists of surplus stock as well as day old products. Schwebel's products are certified Kosher. All sales are final. M-Sat 9-6. Accepts cash and food stamps only.

SHONEY'S
1030 Alum Creek Dr., Columbus, 43209, 252-1186
2045 Brice Rd., Reynoldsburg, 43068, 868-5300
6360 Frantz Rd., Dublin ,43017, 889-0512
4650 W. Broad St., Columbus, 43228, 878-4600
4865 Sinclair Rd., Columbus, 43229, 885-3161
1998 Stringtown Rd., Grove City, 43123, 875-8621
7475 Vantage Dr., Columbus, 43235, 888-6882
1337 River Valley Blvd., Lancaster, 43130, 687-0262

These restaurants feature an all-you-can-eat breakfast and fruit bar for $4.99 for adults on Saturdays, Sundays and holidays ($4.49 for seniors), and $3.89 Monday-Friday ($3.49 for seniors). Kids aged 12 and under can eat for $1.99 at all times. Kids aged 5 and under can eat for free with each adult breakfast and fruit bar purchased. The food is delicious and includes bacon, sausage, potatoes, muffins, buttermilk biscuits, Southern style grits, cold cereal, fruits, french toast sticks and more. Children aged 12 and under, can join the *Cub Club* which entitles them to a free kid's meal, plus dessert, on their birthday. Allow 60 days to process the application. Wednesday is family night with children aged 12 and under eating for free with each adult meal purchased, from 4PM to closing. The children can choose from several items on the kids' menu such as chicken, shrimp, spaghetti, fish and chips. The kids' menu items cost 99 cents-$1.99 and includes a drink and dessert. Adult menu items are reasonably priced from $4.29 to about $7.29 and include charbroiled chicken, Hawaiian chicken, steak and shrimp, lasagne and more. The restaurants also offer several light side calorie counter meals at 500 calories or less including baked fish and other options. There's free refills on purchases of large soft drinks. Senior citizen menu items, at reduced prices, are also available for those aged 60 and over. The restaurants feature a seafood bar on Fridays and Saturdays from 5PM-10PM at a cost of $8.99 for adults and $4.99 for children aged 12 and under. The offerings include baked fish, fried clams, shrimp scampi, corn on the cob, catfish, fried shrimp and vegetables. Children aged 12 and under will want to sign up for the birthday club, which provides a choice of a free dinner with dessert from the kids' menu on the child's birthday.

SON OF HEAVEN CAFETERIA
5186 E. Main St., Columbus, 43213, 755-4061

The owners have indicated that this is the only Chinese cafeteria in the United States. Over 50 different items are offered at a cost of 50 cents to $3.95 apiece, and the menu changes daily. The extensive list of food from their dinner menu is priced at about $2-$3 less than at other area restaurants. Son Of Heaven does not use MSG. The daily special is offered Monday through Friday from 4 to closing and includes a choice of 2 entrees. Rice, soup, egg roll and salad are included for $3.95. The luncheon special is served from 11AM-4PM and includes a choice of one entree. Rice, soup, egg roll and salad are included at a cost of $2.95. Another delicious option is the all-you-can-eat luncheon buffet offered Monday through Friday from 11-2 at a cost of $4.95. Several entrees such as sweet and sour chicken, lo mein, egg foo young, as well as beef and broccoli are included along with vegetable dishes, soup and assorted Chinese desserts. Offers senior discount. 15% discount for carryout. M-Sun 11-10. Accepts MC & Visa.

STAUF'S COFFEE ROASTERS
5793 Frantz Rd., Karric Sq. Shpng. Ctr., Dublin, 43017, 766-2000
1277 Grandview Ave., Columbus, 43212, 486-4861

Coffee is one of the world's oldest beverages. If you are a coffee aficionado, you'll love this store. It's brimming with coffee, espresso, cappuccino, cafe latte and other tastebud pleasers. The stores sell 60 different types and blends of high grade coffee beans which are freshly roasted on premises. The high yield beans are priced at about $6.50-$20 per pound and are about the lowest price in Columbus for this quality. The owner, Tom Griesemer, apprenticed for several years with a master roaster in California. This friendly and knowledgeable person is happy to answer all of your questions on how to brew good coffee, the best type for your coffee maker and other brain teasers. M-Sat 9-9. Accepts checks, MC & Visa.

SUPER THRIFT
3621 E. Livingston Ave., Columbus, 43227, 237-7100
350 S. Hamilton Rd., Gahanna, 43230, 337-2070

Most items in this grocery store are priced at 10-20% off regular supermarket prices. Some items are priced at higher savings. For example, a family pack of chicken is 39 cents per pound for drumsticks or thighs, boxed macaroni and cheese is 5 for $1. This is a full service grocery store. Money orders are only 59 cents each as compared to a $2 fee charged by most banks. Open 24 hours, 7 days per week. Accepts checks.

TAT-RISTORANTE DI FAMIGLIA
1210 S. James Rd., Columbus, 43227, 236-1392

Freshly made Northern Italian fare has been a hallmark of this family owned restaurant since 1935. For $13.95 per person, you can indulge in a 10 course meal which includes a glass of wine, Italian salad, homemade soup, Italian sausage, spaghetti, veal parmigiana, meatball, Sicilian bread, meat filled ravioli, ricotta cheese filled manicotti and a dessert of spumoni. Early bird specials are Tuesday-Saturday from 3:30-6PM and include a choice of several main dishes: spaghetti, eggplant parmigiana, veal parmigiana, tortellini, baked or fried fish or even fettucini alfredo for only $5.95. These come with a free appetizer and dessert. Prices are regularly $6.95-$9.95. Children under 10 can enjoy the kid's menu items for $2.95 which include chicken, spaghetti, perch or other items accompanied by a choice of 2 side dishes. Seniors will enjoy the *lighter side* menu offerings of smaller portions of selected menu items for $5.95-$6.25. Tu/Th 11AM-1AM, F/Sat 11AM-12 midnight, Sun 11AM-9PM. Accepts MC, Visa & AmExp.

TEDESCHI'S ITALIAN BAKERY
1210 W. 3 Ave., Columbus 43212, 294-3278

Fresh Italian bread, submarine buns, pizza crust and rolls are available to you at savings of 25% off retail. This wholesaler's products are typically sold in grocery stores and pizza shops. You can purchase large or small quantities. M-F 8-5, Sat 8-12 noon. Accepts checks. and cash only.

TERRACE RESTAURANT
1739 N. High St., OSU Ohio Union , 3rd floor, Columbus, 43210, 292-6396

The delicious all-you-can-eat lunch buffet is served from 11-1:15 Monday through Friday at a cost of $4.75. The bountiful display includes hot and cold foods such as salads, 3 different soups, pasta salads, roast beef, ham, turkey, pot roast, vegetables and more. Reservations are suggested. The restaurant is open to the general public year round, even when classes are not in session, with the exception of legal holidays. Accepts cash only.

TRIO FOODS
Family Wholesale Outlet, 185 Lex-Industrial Dr., Lexington, 44904, (419) 884-3038

This wholesale food distributor operates a cash and carry outlet where you can save 10-50% off frozen and pre-cooked foods, fresh meats (these need to be ordered a day in advance), snacks and canned goods. You'll find institutional and restaurant quality products, some of which are not available in your local grocery store, by such brands as Sunshine, Wyandotte, Delmonte, Pocahontas, Shasta and Icelandic. The manager indicated that the best values are on seafood and frozen vegetables. The stock is packaged in small quantities for the average consumer, or stock up on big quantities for your next party. All sales are final. M-F 9-6, Sat 8-1. Accepts checks and cash only.

TROPICAL FRUIT AND NUT FACTORY OUTLET
6580 Huntley Rd., Columbus, 43229, 431-7233

Save 20-70% off regular retail prices on a full line of dried fruits, spices, candy making supplies, nuts, tea, coffee, noodles and even popcorn at this factory outlet. The best savings are on large purchases, so consider sharing yours with a friend. Although, if you use a lot of a particular item, you can keep it for yourself as I do. Request a free copy of their extensive catalogue. Gives exchanges. M-F 9-5:30, Sat 9-5. Accepts checks and cash only.

TROPICS IN THE RAMADA INN
2100 Brice Rd., Reynoldsburg, 43068, 864-1280

The complimentary happy hour spread is offered on Thursdays and Fridays from 5-7PM. You'll find Italian foods such as pizza, meatballs, ravioli and cheeses on Thursdays. Fridays, the food consists of hush puppies, a vegetable tray, catfish, gumbo and fried clams. Beer as well as certain mixed drinks are priced at $1 during happy hour. A DJ plays contemporary and rock dance tunes from 7PM. Accepts MC & Visa.

VILLAGE CUPBOARD
666 High St., Worthington, 43085, 885-1370

Reasonable prices, generous portions and true home style American cooking, have endeared this restaurant to thousands of people. Even if you just want to indulge in dessert and a cup of coffee, you will adore the marvelous selection such as tapioca pudding, pumpkin strudel or carrot cake. Take a seat by the front window and compare the High Street ambience with that depicted on the handpainted wall mural which provides a glimpse of that area as it looked 100 years ago. M-F 7:30AM-2PM, Sat 8AM-2PM, Sun 8:30AM-1:30PM. Accepts cash only.

VISION VALUE CLUB
1451 W. 5 Ave., Columbus, 43212, 481-0201
3700 Fishinger Blvd., Hilliard, 43026, 771-6363
5700 Columbus Sq., Columbus, 43231, 882-5310
169 Graceland Blvd., Columbus, 43214, 888-5577
1775 Kingsdale Ctr., Columbus, 43221, 457-4751
1575 E. Dublin Granville Rd., Columbus, 43229, 888-0535
4665 Morse Ctr., Columbus, 43229, 885-0236
889 Bethel Rd., Columbus, 43214, 457-3635
2801 N. High St., Columbus, 43202, 268-0976
6674 Sawmill Rd., Columbus, 43235, 889-0308
2551 Schrock Rd., Columbus, 43229, 899-6244
4780 W. Broad St., Columbus, 43228, 878-5371
3606 Main St., Hilliard, 43026, 876-5217
1171 Hill St. N., Pickerington, 43147, 861-2311

Big Bear supermarket customers can accumulate points whenever they make a purchase at these selected stores. Points can be redeemed for valuable merchandise such as gold jewelry, small appliances, toys, bicycles, cameras, pet supplies and camcorders. Points are maintained on computer, so there is no need to save receipts. Fill out an application in the store and you will receive an identification card which needs to be inserted into a card reader at the checkout. You will be awarded points based on the total amount of your purchase, in addition to bonus points each time you buy certain brands or products such as Sarah Lee, Proctor and Gamble, Coca Cola and others. The club is in operation only at those Big Bear stores listed above. M-F 24 hours per day, Sat/Sun 7AM-midnight.

WINES, INC.
913 E. Dublin Granville Rd., Columbus, 43229, 846-5566

You will find an enormous selection of fine wines, beers and gourmet coffees, in addition to amateur wine,liqueur making and home brewing supplies. You can save 40-70% off the price of store bought products as compared to the make it yourself cost. Maturing time varies from several weeks to a couple of years depending on the type of beer or wine you produce. The shelf life also varies from 1-3 years. You can make the wines/liqueurs entirely from scratch using store bought or garden obtained fruits, or purchase concentrated juice as an option. It can cost you about $12-$20 to make a batch of beer which is equivalent to about 54 bottles. They also sell kits from $45-$55 which make great gifts. Why not sign up for one of their free or low cost (usually about $5) classes? Gives exchanges on flawed items. M-Sat 10-10, Sun 1-6. Accepts checks, MC, Visa, & AmExp.

WONDER HOSTESS THRIFT SHOP
609 Oakland Park Ave., Columbus, 43214, 263-8846
350 Johnstown Rd., Gahanna, 43230, 471-8586
1751 Brice Rd., Reynoldsburg, 43068, 861-1136
1866 Hard Rd., Worthington, 43235, 766-0447
5440 Westerville Rd., Westerville, 43081, 895-1069
225 N. Woodbridge, Chillicothe, 45601, 774-1646
1317 Hebron Rd., Heath, 43056, 522-3205

Surplus baked goods from Wonder bread and Hostess are available at savings up to 50% off regular retail prices. You'll find bread at 4 loaves for $1, donuts and other delicious edibles. Lunchbox snacks are available at similar savings and are priced at 5 for 99 cents at this factory outlet. Offers a frequent purchaser plan. M-Sat 9-6. Accepts checks, MC & Visa.

ALSO SEE

All For One, Anderson's General Store, Candlelight Outlet, Central Ohio Home And Garden Show, Columbus Dispatch, Consumer Information Center, Contemporary American Theater Company, Educable Channel 25, Entertainment 91 Book, Fishing, Flickers, Headliners, Home And Garden Line, Kaybee Toys And Hobby Shops, Lee Wards, Liquidations Now, 99 Cent Shops, Odd Lots, Ohio Pass Plus Program, Oliver Wendell Holmes Lecture Series, Only $1, Rousch Hardware, Schottenstein's, Springfield Antique Show And Flea Market, Warehouse Club, WDLR Radio, WOSU Channel 34 and World's Largest Bakesale

FURNITURE & BEDDING/GARDEN

FURNITURE & BEDDING

AARON SELLS FURNITURE
2975 Morse Rd., Columbus, 43231, 475-7437

This division of Aaron Rents Inc., the nation's largest furniture rental and sales company, sells previously rented home and office furniture at about 30-50% off the original price "if new". The business has depreciated the furniture so it can sell the traditional styled merchandise at rock bottom prices. All used furniture is guaranteed for one full year against structural defects. Gives refunds within 3 days of purchase. M-F 9-6, Sat 9-5. Accepts checks, MC, Visa, AmExp & Discover.

ANDERSON MANUFACTURING
5200 Winchester Pike, Columbus, 43110, 837-4358

Are you short on space in your home or apartment? This factory outlet manufactures wall bed/storage units in twin, double, queen and king sizes and can save you money off comparable products. The quality laminate exterior comes in an assortment of colors to suit your decor or you can order the units in wood at higher prices. You can select from in-stock styles or the business will help you design your own. A double sized laminate wall bed with cabinets and shelves on either side, will cost you about $1600. The manufacturing facility is located on the premises. The company has been in business since 1974 and had produced other items for government contracts. M-F 9-5 and by appointment. Accepts checks and cash only.

THE BED FACTORY
442 Harding Way W., Galion, 44833, 1-800-762-4993

Heirloom quality, solid brass headboards and beds are made in this factory for adults and children. They are sold for $89-$169 but compare to similar quality items which are sold in other stores for $200-$400. This business also imports many traditional, contemporary and novelty beds from Italy and France for adults and children and sells other American made products. You'll find top quality merchandise from Wesley Allen, Dresher, Taylor and other brands at savings of up to 50% off suggested retail prices. Mattresses are also available at similar savings. Send $1 for a fully illustrated color catalogue. The merchandise can be shipped to you if you choose. This business will be moving a few blocks away from its current location in the summer of 1991. Galion is about 20 miles west of Mansfield and about 1 hour's drive from Columbus. Gives exchanges. M-F 10-8, Sat 10-5. Accepts checks, MC, Visa & Discover.

BELAIR'S FINE FURNITURE
2600 Morse Rd., Columbus, 43231, 471-5682

This family owned business has been operating for over 20 years. Upscale and first quality bedding, furniture and accessories for the entire home, are available at savings of 20-30% off manufacturers' suggested list prices. The store sells Flex Steel, Jamestown Sterling, Lane and other brands. An enormous selection of Howard Miller grandfather clocks is also available at similar savings. 90 days same as cash financing is available to qualified buyers. Gives refunds. M-F 10-9, Sat 10-6, Sun 1-5. Accepts checks, MC & Visa.

BROWN-ROYAL FURNITURE COMPANY
80 E. Home St., Westerville, 43081, 882-2356

This family owned store has been in business for over 10 years and sells first quality furniture and bedding at savings of 25-40% below manufacturers' suggested retail prices. The furniture is available in a variety of styles to suit all tastes. Special orders are also available at similar savings. Delivery is free. M, W and Th 10-9, Tu, F and Sat 10-5. Accepts checks, MC & Visa.

BUSINESS,EQUIPMENT,ELECTRONICS
288 E. Long St., Columbus, 43215, 224-0144

40,000 square feet of new and used office furniture, accessories, desktop supplies and office machines are housed on 3 large floors of this building. Used items are sold at 50-75% off the "if new" price. New items which were purchased as manufacturers closeouts and overstocks, are similarly discounted. Current models of new office furniture and special orders are discounted 30-35%. There's chairs, desks, filing cabinets, bookcases, coat racks, end tables and a wide variety of other items, some of which could even be suited for your home. You'll also find a small selection of framed artwork such as photography, lithographs, etchings, prints, watercolors, oils as well as pen and ink works at about 75% off the "if new" prices. The artwork is found in varying quality levels. On a recent visit, I purchased 2 used solid walnut bookcases, which were 4 feet tall, for only $65 apiece. I also purchased a large framed lithograph of a boat scene, for only $28. This business also sells new office supplies, which can be ordered from their catalogue, at a savings of 20-40% off regular retail prices. All sales are final. M-F 8:30-5, Sat 9-12. Accepts checks and cash only.

CI BON INTERIORS
526 N. Cassingham Rd., Bexley, 43209, 253-6555

According to the owner, "This is the only high end design studio in the United States featuring low to medium furniture store prices. The values are so incredible, it allows you to move into a higher level of living. The store offers meaningful reductions from retail". Don't pass up the opportunity to visit Ci Bon. The 29 fully decorated rooms are brimming with tastefully appointed furniture, lamps, artwork and related accessories unlike any you have ever seen. The store offers personal, in home design assistance for a one time fee of $35. There is also a large catalog room where you can custom order from hundreds of manufacturers. In order to maintain their low prices, Ci Bon does not offer layaways, financing or delivery, but will provide you with names of movers upon request. The design studio also features a clearance room at the back of the business which offers greater savings on a small selection of discontinued merchandise. This design studio has earned the distinction of being one of my personal favorites. M & Th 1-9, Tu & F 1-7, Sat 10:30-5:30, Sun 12:30-5:30. Accepts checks, MC, Visa, & AmExp.

CONTINENTAL OFFICE FURNITURE WAREHOUSE OUTLET
2601 Silver Dr., Columbus, 43211, 262-5555

A large selection of top quality new and used office furniture is available at savings of 30-75% off regular retail prices. You'll find quality desks, chairs, files, tables and other items which are discontinued, overstocks and scratch 'n dent merchandise. All sales are final. M-F 8:30-5:30, Sat 10-3. Accepts checks, MC & Visa.

CORT FURNITURE RENTAL RESALE CENTER
48 70 Evanswood Dr., Columbus, 43229, 436-6440

New, discontinued and previously rented home and office furniture is available here at savings of 25-60% off. The furniture is sanitized prior to being sold to you. Lamps and accessories can be found at similar savings. Oak cocktail and end tables begin at $69, decorative lamps from $19 and sofas from $199. All sales are final. M-Th 9-7, F 9-5, Sat 10-5. Accepts checks, MC, & Visa.

DANIELLE FURNITURE GALLERY
627 High St., Worthington, 43085, 433-0448

Central Ohio's largest selection of quality leather furniture is available at savings up to 50% off regular retail prices. The buttery soft furniture is available in a variety of colors and unique styles to fit most any decor. M and Th 11-8; T, W, F 11-6, Sat 10-5; Sun 12-4. Accepts checks, MC & Visa.

DESK AND FILE
1019 Goodale Blvd., Columbus, 43215, 461-0845
1114 Dublin Rd., Columbus, 43215, 461-0845 (this location is called the Thomas Ruff Company)

A sizable selection of quality office furniture including chairs, desks, bookcases, filing cabinets and computer furniture is available in the back room at savings of 25-75%. A large portion of the inventory consists of liquidations from professionals who are retiring or upgrading their office furnishings, as well as manufacturer's overstocks and some trade-ins. On a recent visit, I purchased a solid oak 6 foot bookcase for $50 and a large walnut desk for $30. Desk and File is a division of Thomas W. Ruff and Company. Free delivery. M-F 8:30-5, Sat 9-5. Accepts checks, MC & Visa.

DINETTE GALLERY
2538 Morse Rd., Columbus, 43231, 476-5858

Volume buying enables this business to offer 30-50% off suggested retail prices on a large selection of in-stock and special order buffets, hutches, tables, chairs and barstools. This amounts to a savings of about $200-$600. The merchandise is sold as open stock, which means that you have the flexibility to mix and match pieces. The upscale inventory is by such brands as Douglas, Daystrom, Beechbrook and U.S. Furniture. It can be found in solid oak, laminates, veneers and glass, and includes first quality, first run merchandise. 90 days same as cash financing is available to qualified buyers. Gives exchanges. M-Sat 10-9, Sun 12-5. Accepts checks, MC & Visa.

EXPERIENCED POSSESSIONS
9226 Dublin Rd., Powell, 43065, 889-0454 (closer to Dublin than Powell)

Used consignment and new samples of home furnishings such as lamps, accessories, furniture, art, antiques, table and bed linens, china, crystal, rugs and silver are available at savings of 50% and more off "if new" or manufacturers' suggested retail prices. First quality roll end fabrics by Brunswig and Fils, Scalamandre and others in damasks, linens and silks are sold at $7 per yard, regularly $20-$150 per yard. The inventory is all better to designer quality and includes such brands as Drexel, Thomasville, Gorham, Kittinger, Wedgewood and others. All sales are final. M-Sat 10-6, Sun 12-4. Accepts checks, MC & Visa.

FAMOUS BRAND MATTRESS OUTLET
4741 E. Main St., Columbus, 43213, 575-0001

This sole Columbus distributor of the Chiro brand of premium quality bedding, offers a 50% discount off the manufacturer's suggested retail price on a variety of firmness and support options. Other brands such as Sealey are offered at minimal savings of about 10-15% off the manufacturer's suggested retail price. All mattresses come with full warranties through the manufacturers. Chiro brand merchandise is endorsed by the U.S. Chiropractic Association of America. The owner will allow you to exchange any mattress within 30 days of purchase if not satisfied. M-Sat 11-8, Sun 12-5. Accepts checks, MC & Visa.

FLYING EAGLE FURNITURE
5270 Cleveland Ave., Columbus, 43231, 891-9478

Quality oak desks, chairs, hutches, curio cabinets, dinettes and bookcases are available at savings of about 20-30% off comparable quality products in other stores. The entire inventory of contemporary and antique reproductions is well made and fairly priced. The business is able to save you money by factory direct purchasing and by using its own trucks to transport the furniture. Gives exchanges. M-Sat 10-6, Sunday 12-5. Accepts checks, MC & Visa.

FURNITURE LIQUIDATION CENTER
1810 N. Memorial Dr., Lancaster, 43130, 1-687-0031

Moderate to better quality lamps, bedding and furniture are sold at savings of 20-50%. "Our prices are low, our volume is great. That's how we operate" is the store's motto. This discounter sells Pioneer, People Lounger, Horizon, Basset, Standard Bedding, Medallion and other brands in traditional, early American and contemporary styles. Layaway, warranties and delivery are available at this family operation. M-Sat 10-6. Accepts checks, MC & Visa.

GLICK'S FURNITURE AND CARPET OUTLET
1800 E. 5 Ave., Columbus, 43219, 251-1408

Save up to 70% off furniture, carpet, bedding, lamps, dinette sets, living room and bedroom furniture and more. The inventory consists of special purchases, overstocks, discontinued and some new merchandise purchased exclusively for the store. Check out the *Rock Bottom Room* where items are marked down in a final reduction of 50-70% off "if new" prices. You will find odds 'n ends, reconditioned returns, "as is", floor samples, mismatched bedding and special order cancellations. M-F 10-9, Sat 10-6, Sun 12-6. Accepts MC, Visa & Discover.

GLOBE FURNITURE RENTALS
3659 E. Broad St., Columbus, 43213, 338-8666

Save 30-70% on previously rented furniture for your entire home. The moderate to better quality stock is in excellent condition, having been used in model homes and short term rentals. You'll find such brands as Lane, Brookwood, Douglas, National Office Furniture, Serta and others. There's cribs, beds in all sizes, living room, dining room, kitchen, bedroom and office furniture. Televisions, stereos and small appliances are also available. A 30 day warranty accompanies your purchase. If you sign up for their mailing list, you'll get invitations to their tent sales which are usually held twice per year in June and August, as well as 2 smaller garage sales in the spring and the fall. And, if you wear a tent to their tent sale (we're not kidding!), you'll get an extra 10% off your purchase. M 9-8, Tu, W, Th and F 9-6, Sat 10-5. Accepts checks, MC, Visa and Discover.

GREATER COLUMBUS ANTIQUE MALL
1045 S. High St., Columbus, 43206, 443-7858

Columbus' first antique mall was established in 1979 and presents 5 floors with over 75 dealers. 11,000 square feet of space features value priced antiques and collectibles including furniture, art, frames, gift items, lamps, costume and fine jewelry, architectural hardware as well as vintage clothing. The fun part about shopping in this mall, is that every inch of space has been utilized. You'll go in the attic, in closets and in rooms to search for unusual things. While the merchandise varies from kitsch to quality items, the smart shopper will take the time to look high and low to find the treasures. Don't be afraid to purchase a painting which needs to be rematted, or a chair which needs to be reupholstered. The extra expense can still amount to an excellent value for the piece. I have purchased many original paintings and etchings here in addition to fine and funky jewelry. Shop often as the inventory changes frequently. This store has earned the distinction of being one of my personal favorites. All sales are final. M-Sun 11-8. Accepts checks, MC & Visa.

GROLL'S FINE FURNITURE
149 N. Marion St., Waldo, 43356, 548-5700, 1-800-282-6745

A full line of furniture and bedding for the home at prices 25-40% below regular retail makes this store well worth the trip. It is only 35 minutes north of Worthington. In fact, about 60% of their business is from the Columbus area. You'll find quality brands such as Richardson Brothers, Bradington, Lane, Harden-Henkel-Harris, Century Designs, Jamestown Sterling, Hancock and Moore Leathers for every room of your home. Gifts, lamps, plaques as well as special orders, are similarly discounted. Thirteen buildings contain moderate to better quality traditional and colonial furniture. Their annual tent sale, a ten day event held in mid June, features greater savings on selected stock. Groll's operates a small warehouse outlet, a block away from their main store behind the church, which houses their cherry furniture. Savings at the outlet are 40% and more on discontinued and scratch 'n dent merchandise. M, W, and F 9-5:30; Tu, Th and Sat 9-9; Sun 12-5. Accepts checks, MC, Visa & Discover.

HOMEWAY FURNITURE
3278 Morse Rd., Columbus, 43231, 476-4919

Save up to 45% off the manufacturers' suggested retail prices on over 400 quality brands of furniture such as Hickory, Hooker, White, Stanley and Clover. Similar savings are available on lamps by Steiffle, Remington, Westwind and other brands. The showroom maintains some stock which is used as samples, but everything is special ordered from the North Carolina factories and shipped directly to your home. M-F 9-5 and Sat by appointment. Accepts checks, MC & Visa.

HOUSE OF BARGAINS
5200 Cleveland Ave., Columbus, 43231, 890-5235

Factory direct, first quality furniture, in addition to antiques and used merchandise, are available at savings of 25-30%. This one man business can afford to offer low prices because of low overhead and by directly purchasing and moving the furniture himself from the factories. The stock is displayed in about 15 different rooms. Delivery is $20 for 1 piece or a truckload. Gives refunds. M, Tu, F and Sat 12-7; Sun 12-5. Accepts checks, MC & Visa.

HOUSE OF FURNITURE
150 E. Granville St., New Albany, 43054, 855-7992
29 S. High St., Box 149, New Albany, 43054, 855-7545

Save about 30% off manufacturers' suggested retail prices on an extensive and unusual selection of quality dinettes, livingroom and bedroom furniture (for adults and kids) at both locations. The inventory features contemporary pieces, antique reproductions and some traditional furniture in addition to a limited selection of lamps and accessories. You'll find such brands as American Of Martinsville, Schweiger and Vaughan. The annual tent sale, held in late May through early June, offers hundreds of items at savings of up to 75% off suggested retail prices. This is well worth the trip especially if you have discriminating tastes as the stock is all top quality. Gives exchanges.

HOWARD BROOKS INTERIORS
7790 Olentangy River Rd., Worthington, 43235, 888-5353

Visit the newly expanded showroom of this upscale furniture and home accessories store which offers savings of 40% on leather furniture, 30% off wood and upholstered furniture and 20% off accessories and lamps. Similar discounts are available on special orders. The discounts represent savings from the manufacturers' suggested retail prices. You'll find such highly sought after brands as Hancock, Moore, Henredon, Tomlinson, Henrek and others. If you are seeking impeccable quality then this is the place to shop. Howard Brooks has been in business for over 50 years. Gives refunds. M-Sat 10-6. Accepts MC, Visa & Discover.

LAZARUS FINAL COUNTDOWN
141 S. High St., Columbus, 43215, 463-2121

With the recent closing of the Whittier Street furniture/small & major appliance/television warehouse, all of this inventory has been moved to the sixth floor Final Countdown. The stock on this floor also consists of carpet remnants as well as full and short rolls at savings of 45-80% off regular retail. There is a good variety of colors and textures from such brands as Karastan, Lees and Galaxy. The audio, video and electronics offerings include video recorders, cameras, typewriters and VCRs, some of which are overstocks. Savings are 30-60% off popular brands such as Mitsubishi and Sony. Giftware, linens and seasonal merchandise are offered at similar savings. A large selection of furniture includes plush leather sofas, dining room tables, end tables, hutches, entertainment centers and bedding. The Front Street special events center accommodates the clothing department of the Final Countdown. Men's, women's and children's wear usually from a previous season, have been collected from about twelve Lazarus stores in the region. You will find moderate to designer quality merchandise. The clothing and giftware at the Final Countdown is initially priced at least 50% off regular retail. The furniture, audio, video and electronics merchandise is initially priced at about 20-30% off. On the last Friday of each month, the inventory is reduced by 25% of the lowest price on the ticket. The longer the merchandise stays unsold, the more reductions will be made. Refunds within seven days. M-Th 10-9 F&Sat 10-6, Sun 12-5. Accepts checks, MC, Visa & Lazarus.

LIBERTY STREET INTERIORS
15 N. Liberty St., Powell, 43065, 433-7000

Quality furniture, art prints, accessories, lamps and fabrics are discounted 25% off regular retail prices for in stock and custom orders. Lines carried include Brunswig and Fils and Laura Ashley. Financing is available. Gives exchanges. M-F 10-4:30, Sun 1-5. Closed Saturday. Accepts checks and cash.

LIVING ROOM'S FURNITURE OUTLET (ALSO CALLED SOFA EXPRESS OUTLET)
4485 S. Hamilton Rd., Groveport, 43125, 836-4800
845 N. High St., Columbus, 43215, 836-4800

Sofas, loveseats, tables, recliners, leather and upholstered furniture, sleep sofas and more are sold at 20-50% off the low prices found in their other stores. The inventory consists of discontinued, overstocked, special purchase, customer cancellations, factory buyouts and "as is" merchandise. The High Street location has more giftware, lamps and artwork than the Hamilton Road site. Customer pickup or delivery (at an extra cost), must be made within 7 days of purchase. There's a 1 year limited warranty on all merchandise, except "as is". All sales are final. M-F 12-9, Sat 10-6, Sun 12-6. Accepts checks, MC & Visa.

MACK MATTRESS OUTLET
2582 Cleveland Ave., Columbus, 43211, 262-2088
7370 Sawmill Rd., Columbus, 43235, 793-1048
15 S. 3 St., Newark, 43055, 345-5923
2691 Independence Village Center, Columbus, 43068, 866-2817

Overstocks and factory seconds of Simmons, Sealy and Beautyrest mattresses and boxsprings are available at savings of 50% off the "if perfect" price. Minor cosmetic flaws or mismatched sets will not affect the wear. Hard to find sizes are also available. This Christ centered business also sells reconditioned, used mattresses which have been sterilized and bagged. These will cost you 60-90% less than the price of a comparable new mattress. Gives refunds. M-Sat 10-8, Sun 12-5. Accepts checks, MC & Visa.

MODEL HOME FURNITURE AND ACCESSORIES SALES

Check the classified ads section at the back of the Columbus Dispatch and the community newspapers to find out about these excellent opportunities. Builders typically furnish their model homes with rented or purchased furniture, accessories and window coverings. If it cannot be used in another model, the merchandise will be disposed of once the model home has been sold. You'll find moderate to designer quality furniture, lamps, gift items, pictures and related accessories which are virtually in new condition. Savings are 25%-60% off regular retail prices. Scan the newspapers regularly as these sales are held intermittently throughout the year by a variety of different builders and interior decorators.

NEW ANTIQUES
1662 E. Dublin Granville Rd., Columbus, 43229, 891-4066

Fine oak furniture in country and traditional styles, as well as reproductions, is offered here at savings of about 20-30% off comparable products elsewhere. While many items are value priced, some are at typical retail prices. Entertainment centers start at $158, bookcases from $53 and glass curios from $247. The business also sells bar stools, wine racks, magazine racks, bedroom furniture, dining room chairs, ice box end tables, hutches and other items, all for discriminating tastes. Some of the merchandise is manufactured in their own factory in Oklahoma., which helps to keep the prices low. Gives refunds. Call 1-800-468-3807 to obtain a free catalogue. M, W-Sat 10-6; Sun 12-5. Closed Tu. Accepts checks, MC & Visa.

J.C. PENNEY FURNITURE WAREHOUSE OUTLET
647 Harrisburg Pike (Central Point Shpg. Ctr.), Columbus, 43223, 274-8409

This clearance center features floor models, one of a kinds, discontinued as well as customer returned merchandise from area J.C. Penney stores. You will find bedding, chairs, sofas, entertainment units, odd tables, blinds, curtains and custom draperies, dining room sets as well as a limited amount of related accessories such as lamps and pictures. Savings are 30-60% off regular retail prices. Refunds within 3 days of purchase. No refunds on custom decorator window treatments. M-F 10-8:30, Sat 10-6, Sun 12-5. Accepts checks, MC, Visa, AmExp & J.C. Penney.

J.C. PENNEY PORTFOLIO
3776 E. Broad St., Columbus, 43213, 236-5333

"Is this really a J.C. Penney store, or have I accidentally stumbled into a White's or Glick's?" That is what you will ask yourself upon entering these tastefully stocked businesses. Popular furniture brands are discounted 15-30% off suggested manufacturer's list every day. Pictures, lamps and home decorating gift items are fairly priced, but not discounted. Returns accepted within 30 days if accompanied by receipt. M-F 10-9, Sat 10-6, Sun 12-5. Accepts checks, MC, Visa, AmExp & J.C. Penney.

THE PERFECT SEAT
442 Harding Way W., Galion, 44833, 1-800-762-4993

The owner says that if you can sit on it that it is bound to be in his store. You will find a large selection of patio, bar, upholstered, dining-room, kitchen and any other type of chair at savings of up to 50% off regular retail prices. This quality merchandise is priced at about $15-$300. It is made in the United States as well as imported from France and Italy. Low overhead helps to keep the prices down. This business will be moving a few blocks away in the summer of 1991. Galion is west of Mansfield and about 1 hour's drive from Columbus. Gives exchanges. M-F 10-8, Sat 10-5. Accepts checks, MC & Visa.

J. PETERS AND SON CUSTOM OAK FURNITURE
3681 Garden Ct., Grove City, 43123, 871-9663

Hand made furniture is available at savings up to 25% off the price of comparable quality merchandise in non-discount stores. You can choose from pre-built models on display in the showroom, handmade duplications from their catalogue or special custom requests. Although the store specializes in oak, you can choose from an assortment of other wood types. The store manufactures quality furniture for homes and businesses including tables and dining furniture, bookcases, entertainment centers, computer and office furniture in addition to bedroom furniture. Allow 10 days-2 weeks for custom work. Gives refunds or exchanges depending on the situation. M-F 11:30-8, Sat 10-6 and Sun 12-5. Accepts checks, MC & Visa.

PIECES OF OAK WAREHOUSE OUTLET STORE
6670 Busch Blvd., Columbus, 43229, 848-8400

Floor samples, close outs and "as is" merchandise are offered here at savings of 10-40% off the regular retail prices. The stock consists of dining room and kitchen tables, wall units, entertainment centers, curio cabinets and rocking chairs from their other Columbus stores. A limited amount of first quality, current stock is offered at regular retail prices. Accessories such as towel racks and lamps can also be found. Financing is available. No returns on "as is" merchandise. One week return on scratch or dent. M, T, Th and F 11-5, W 11-8, Sat 10-5. Accepts checks, MC & Visa.

PINE FACTORY
1677 W. Lane Ave., Lane Ave. Shpng. Ctr., Columbus, 43221, 488-9324
4196 Westland Mall, Columbus, 43228, 274-0080
2740 Eastland Mall, Columbus, 43232, 863-1609

These manufacturer owned and operated stores are the exclusive sources for you to purchase this furniture. Tables, bookcases, desks, bunk beds, dining room, den and living room furniture are available in southern yellow pine, which is semi-finished with a polyurethane sealer. Some furniture is a combination of wood and upholstery in a choice of about 30 different patterns ranging from southwest motifs to formal designs. The rustic looking pieces are sold at about 20-25% less than comparable quality products in other stores. The Pine Factory's motto is "Furniture for the time of your life". A variety of financing options are available including 90 days same as cash and a 5 month layaway without interest. In late May or early June, the annual warehouse sale features savings of 30-70% off scratch and dent and first quality customer returns or cancelled orders. M-Sat 10-9, Sun 12-5. Accepts checks, MC, Visa, Discover & Pine Factory charges.

ROSENFELD AND COMPANY LIQUIDATORS
399 E. Main St., Columbus, 43215, 221-9576

Used store fixtures, office equipment and office furniture are available at savings of 30-75%. The large inventory ranges from budget to top quality goods and is scattered through several buildings. If you don't see what you are looking for, ask for it. All sales final. M-F 9-5, Sat 10-3. Accepts checks, MC & Visa.

SCORZIELL MATTRESS COMPANY
3283 W. Broad St., Great Western Shpng. Ctr., Columbus, 43204, 278-2359
897 S. Hamilton Rd., Columbus, 43219, 338-0338
737 E. Hudson St., Columbus, 43211,262-1190

First quality electric beds, brass beds, waterbeds and mattresses are available at savings of 25-50% off manufacturer's suggested retail prices at this factory showroom. Odd size bedding can be made to order for campers. Offers a free bed frame and/or free old bedding removal with the purchase of a mattress set. Free delivery is provided within a 50 mile radius of Columbus on any matched set. Gives exchanges. M-F 10-9, Sat 10-6, Sun 12-5.

SOFA EXPRESS (ALSO CALLED THE LIVINGROOM'S SOFA EXPRESS
1460 Morse Rd., Columbus, 43229, 836-4800
2150 S. Hamilton Rd., Columbus, 43232, 836-4800
3592 W. Broad St., Consumer Sq. W., Columbus, 43228, 836-4800
913 Hebron Rd., Indian Mound Mall, Heath, 43056, 522-6633

Thousands of fabrics and styles of living room and family room upholstered furniture are available as custom orders within 35 days. The prices are about 20% less than those for comparable quality merchandise at other stores. Frequent sales provide additional opportunities for savings. The stores offer a free computer aided design service. They will make sure that your intended purchase will fit and will show you how your existing pieces can be used. Offers a "double the difference price guarantee" and a minimum 5 year spring and frame warranty. Special financing plans also available. (Also see the Livingroom's Furniture Outlet in this chapter which is the clearance center for these stores). M-F 12-9, Sat 10-9, Sun 12-6. Accepts checks, MC & Visa.

SUGARMAN LIQUIDATORS
971 W. Broad St., Columbus, 43222, 469-3444

Quality used office furniture, store fixtures, showcases, shelving, racks and more are sold at about 30-40% off "if new" or regular retail prices. The inventory consists of scratch and dents, special purchases and liquidations. All sales are final. M-F 8-5, Sat 8-12. Accepts checks, MC & Visa.

TAG SALES
E. Gwyn Gloss And Assoc., 486-1484
Katie and Dee, 268-7938 or 486-7876
Sue Ann Sales 237-1643 or 235-8348

These sales are conducted by professional sellers such as those above, who contract with a family or someone's estate, to sell all or part of the contents of their home. You'll walk through various rooms of a house or condominium to purchase artwork, furniture, computers, gifts, toys, clothes, antiques, housewares and more. These sales generally feature better quality merchandise than you would find at a garage sale, and often you can find decorator items. Arrive early as there are usually long lines to get into these tag sales. To locate tag sales, look in the classified ads section at the back of the newspapers. Also see "garage sales" in the housewares section of this book. All sales are final. Accepts checks. Charge acceptance varies.

TAYLOR WOODCRAFT
2783 Martin Road, Dublin, 43017, 764-9663

Quality kitchen, dining room and bedroom furniture is available in this manufacturer's factory outlet store at savings of about 20% off regular retail prices. The merchandise is first quality, but also includes some floor samples at special savings. You'll also find bar stools, computer furniture and shelving units. Financing is available. The Taylor Woodcraft products are sold at upscale department and specialty stores throughout the country. Provides layaways. Refunds within five days. M-F 10-9, Sat 10-7, Sun 12-5. Accepts checks, MC, Visa, AmExp & Discover.

TREN FURNITURE GALLERIES
965 Bethel Rd., Columbus, 43214, 459-0663
3275 Broadway, Grove City, 43123, 875-7457
6742 Cleveland Ave., Columbus, 43231, 898-9990
3794 Fishinger Blvd., Hilliard, 43026, 777-8757

Solid oak tables, chairs, bar stools, desks, curio cabinets, bookcases and entertainment centers are available at these stores. Savings are up to 33% less than comparable quality products at other businesses. The Broadway and Cleveland Avenue sites also sell mill ends, surplus and discontinued carpeting at similar savings. Gives refunds. M-Th 10-8, F 10-6, Sat 9-5. Accepts checks, MC & Visa.

VALUE CITY FURNITURE
1789 Morse Rd., Columbus, 43229, 431-1400
6067 E. Main St., Columbus, 43213, 866-8888
3385 S. Boulevard, Great Western Shpng. Ctr., Columbus, 43204, 276-5157

Casual and formal furniture by Lane, Roanoke and other brands is offered at savings of 20-70% off regular retail prices. While most of the furniture is budget quality, the store surprisingly stocks some moderate to better quality goods such as leather sofas. Due to the enormous buying power of this chain, the stores are able to purchase goods at substantial savings and pass the values on to you. The stock also consists of discontinued goods and closeouts. For example, a 5 piece rattan dinette with 4 chairs was $297 regularly $899, an ultra modern tubular steel framed bunk bed was $288 regularly $499 and a genuine leather chair and ottoman was $198 regularly $700 elsewhere. Gives exchanges. M-Sat 10-9, Sun 12-6. Accepts checks, MC, Visa & Discover.

WATERBEDS 'N STUFF WAREHOUSE OUTLET
3933 Brookham Dr., Grove City, 43123, 871-1171

About half of the inventory consists of scratch 'n dent waterbeds from their area stores at savings of about 20-40%. The balance of the stock is bedding and first quality waterbeds at their standard prices. All sales final on as is merchandise. M-F 9-5, Sat 10-4. Accepts checks, MC & Visa.

WHITE'S FINE FURNITURE WAREHOUSE STORE
5057 Freeway Dr., E., Columbus, 43229, 436-3300

Floor samples, cancelled special orders, discontinued items, factory buyouts, first quality and some slightly damaged furniture is available at savings of 30-60% off regular retail prices. Most of the merchandise is consolidated from their area stores which sell top of the line merchandise by Pennsylvania House, Thomasville, Broyhill and others. You'll find dining room sets, couches, chairs, bedroom furniture for the family, kitchen furniture as well as bedding. There is an extra charge for delivery. M-S 10-9, Sun 12-5:30. Accepts checks, MC, Visa & Discover.

ALSO SEE

Anderson's General Store, Aurora, Aurora Farms Factory Outlet, Builder's Square, Burlington Coat Factory, Ceaser Creek Flea Market, Children's Palace, City Lighting, Darby Sales, Decorator's Show House, Direct Imports, Garage Sales, Golden Hobby Shop, Just For Kids, Kids Quarters, L.T. Interiors, Lazarus Final Countdown, Mansfield Flea Market, Mostly Kids Stuff, My Cousins Closet, National Office Warehouse, Office America, J.C. Penney Furniture Warehouse Outlet, J.C. Penney Outlet, Sam's Club, Scioto Valley Hot Tubs And Spas, Service Merchandise, Smitty's Auction, Springfield Antique Show And Flea Market, Stork Exchange, Stratford Auction Center, Toys 'R Us, Urbana Flea Market, WDLR Radio, Warehouse Club, Washington C.H. Flea Market and Waterford Hall

GARDEN

THE ANDERSON'S GENERAL STORE
5800 Aleshire Rd., Columbus, 43232, 864-8800
7000 Bent Tree Blvd., Columbus, 43235, 766-9500

The bakery offers oversized, freshly baked delectables at value prices. You'll find pecan rolls, muffins and other specialities. The store offers excellent values in their seasonal garden center where the selection of perennials, annuals and shrubs is quite extensive. The year round horticulture section found indoors, also offers excellent values on a large selection of houseplants and trees. The savings on these garden items is about 20-30% less than in many other garden stores. Save 50% and more off the thousands of in stock wallpaper patterns and 30% off special orders. The businesses also feature an extensive selection of quality unfinished oak and other types of wooden furniture such as bookcases, desks, chairs, entertainment centers and microwave carts which are about 20-30% less than comparable quality products at other stores. The Anderson's is a general store which offers a full line of regular priced hardware, housewares, fishing supplies, home improvement supplies, fruits and vegetables as well as a small gourmet food and wine department. Gives refunds. M-Sat 8-9, Sun 10-6. Accepts checks, MC, Visa & Discover.

AURORA
4046 Knapp Dr., Grove City, 43123, 871-1367

Volume buying and low overhead enable this factory outlet store to offer savings of 20-65% off the manufacturer's suggested retail prices on wood stoves, gas grills, patio furniture, swimming pools, spas and ceiling fans. This specialty store offers a broad range of name brand products at discount store prices. The company prides itself on excellent customer service. Financing is available. M-F 10-8, Sat 10-6, Sun 12-5. Accepts checks, MC & Visa.

BACKSTROM
3332 Possum Run Rd., Mansfield 44903, (419) 756-3051

Nursery stock of shade trees, evergreens, flowering trees, flowering shrubs as well as ground covers are available at about 40-50% less than at other garden stores. Over 150,000 specimens are in stock for purchase at wholesale prices. Five foot tall pink flowering dogwoods are $36.95, 15" blue girl holly is $8.95, 24" Juniper is $14.95, 6 foot flowering cherry is $49.95, 15" rhododendrons are $5.95. If you bring a sketch and measurements of your yard, Backstrom's will provide a free landscape design service while you wait. The nursery, which grows all of its own stock, does not currently sell gardening tools or related supplies, but is planning to offer these in 1992 when it builds a garden center on the property. Adult gardening and landscaping workshops will be available at that time as well. All purchases are guaranteed for 1 year. M-Sat 8-8. Closed November through early March. Accepts checks, MC, Visa, AmExp & Discover.

CASHMAN
1748 U.S. Rt. 42 N., Delaware, 43015, 363-6073

Mulch, dog food, bird seed, rock salt, fertilizer and other lawn and garden products are offered at savings of 20-75% off regular retail prices. You will find such brands as Morton Salt, Buckeye Feeds and Dad's. This full service drive through business, sells individual bags at truckload prices. The store also has 2 large greenhouses, where plants and flowers are sold at similar savings. Cashman's holds the record of being the largest one store retailer of cyprus mulch in the nation. Gives exchanges. M-F 8-8, Sat and Sun 9-6. Accepts checks, MC & Visa.

COM-TIL
Columbus Compost Facility, 7000 State Rte. 104, Grove City, 43123, 645-3152

Com-Til is a rich compost and an excellent mulch, providing a constant organic feed for plants. It is available at the city's compost facility in a 40 pound bag for $3 including tax.

Area gardening stores sell it for $3.99 plus tax. Or, if you're real ambitious and want to buy it in bulk, you can load it into your truck unbagged. Another option is to bring bags or containers and fill them yourself. For these latter two options, you'll pay only 1 penny per pound! The compost facility staff will assist you in loading the Com-Til into your vehicle. M-Sat 7-3 year round. Accepts checks and cash only.

COLUMBUS STONE CENTER
1736 McKinley Ave., Columbus, 43222, 276-3585

Shop where the professionals shop! You can purchase patio brick pavers, landscaping wallstones, colored pebbles, marble chips and landscaping boulders at about 20-30% less than through a professional landscaping company. You'll be amazed at the varied selection. M-F 8-5, Sat 8-2. Accepts checks, MC & Visa.

DELAWARE SOIL AND WATER CONSERVATION DISTRICT
29 Grandview Ave., Delaware, 43015, 362-4011 ext 1921

Order low cost quality seedlings which are suitable for windbreaks, reforestation, CRP planting and wildlife food habitats. Tree packets cost $5-$18 and contain about 10-75 evergreens, hardwoods, blue spruce, wildlife fruit, wildlife flowers and/or black walnut seedlings. You may also purchase a ground cover packet consisting of wildflower seeds and native grasses for ornamental panting. Orders are accepted in March with pre-payment, and are available for pickup in April. M-F 9-5. Accepts checks and cash only.

GERMAN VILLAGE GARDEN CENTER
3265 Walcutt Rd., Hilliard, 43026, 771-0012

1,500 different species of plants and trees are available at this nursery, which, by the way, is not in German Village. Better quality and specimen quality horticulture is available. Annuals, perennials, shrubs, herbs, evergreens and waterplants, can be purchased at "direct from the grower prices". About 40% of the inventory is priced about 10-20% below the competition. M-Sat 8-5. From April through September, the store is also open Sundays from 9-4. Accepts checks, MC & Visa.

HOME AND GARDEN LINE
645-2020

This call in tape recorded library of over 300 messages, offers free home and garden tips. You can pick up a listing of tapes at any of the branches of the Columbus Metropolitan Library which co-sponsors this with the Franklin County Cooperative Extension Service. Topics include canning, freezing, drying and storing, jellies and preserves, picklemaking, fruitcrops, houseplants, insect pests, lawn care, ornamental plant care, vegetable gardening, winter holidays, stain and odor removal, home cleaning and repair, winter safety, food preparation, general nutrition, child development, parenting, recycling and litter prevention. M-Th 9-9, F-Sat 9-6. (Sun Sept.-May).

OHIO POTTERY WEST
1905 W. Main St., Rte. 40, Zanesville, 43701, 452-1858

Factory direct stoneware for your garden is available at savings of about 20-30% off regular retail prices. You'll find a large selection of fountains, religious figures, red clay flower pots, bird baths, large concrete baskets, animals and more. Take exit 152 off I-70. This business if about 1 hour from downtown Columbus. Gives exchanges. M-Sun 8-8 year round. Accepts checks, MC & Visa.

SCIOTO VALLEY HOT TUBS AND SPAS
4344 Lyman Dr., Hilliard, 43026, 876-7755

Save 20-50% off manufacturer's suggested retail prices on hot tubs, spas and outdoor furniture by such companies as Leisure Bay, U.S. Forming, Coleman Spas and Hotspring Spas. Special financing terms include 90 days same as cash or 6 months same as cash to qualified buyers. M-Sat 10-9, Sun 11-5

SPA AND HOT TUB OUTLET
4382 Indianola Ave., Columbus, 43229, 268-5761
6111 E. Main St., Columbus, 43213, 866-4666

Decks, gazebos, portable spas, pools, steam units and other similar items are available at savings of 10-50% off suggested retail prices. The inventory consists of first quality, liquidations and discontinued goods. Trade-ins are sold at 50-70% less than the new price. The manager said that he has customers coming from 6 states to purchase his products because the prices are so low. M-F 8:30-9, Sat 10-6, Sun 12-6. Accepts checks,MC, Visa & Discover.

SUN HOLIDAY POOLS
12981 E. Main St., Pataskala, 43062, 927-9686
2804 Johnstown Rd., Columbus, 43219, 471-1746

The strongest above ground pools in the United States are manufactured by this local company which also makes in-ground pools. A 30 year warranty is included. Savings are about 15-20% as compared to comparable (inground) and almost comparable (technically, there is no comparison because of their distinction) products. Installation costs are included in the price. April through September hours are M-Sat 8-8, Sun 11-5. September through April hours are M-Sat 10-6. Accepts checks, MC, Visa, Discover and Sun charges.

ALSO SEE

Ameritech Pages Plus, Aurora, Black And Decker, Columbus Coal And Lime Company, Dawes Arboretum, Educable Channel 25, Franklin County Cooperative Extension Service, Franklin County Soil And Water Conservation District, Frank's Nursery And Crafts, Robinson-Ransbottom Pottery, Rousch Hardware, Schottenstein's, Scioto Valley Hot Tubs And Spas, Service Merchandise, Spa and Hot Tub Outlet and Wines Inc.

GIFTS & HOUSEWARES/ DRIED FLOWERS

BERWICK CORNER OUTLET
2700 Winchester Pike, Columbus, 43232, 235-6222

Nationally recognized moderate to designer quality brands of cologne, shoes, small appliances, watches, crystal, computer games, office equipment, sporting goods, giftware, toys and apparel are offered at savings of 30-80% off manufacturers' suggested retail prices. The inventory comes from a variety of sources including nationally recognized upscale department stores. This no frills business is the site of some of the most chic and sought after merchandise. However, the stock changes so radically from shipment to shipment, that you'll never know what you will find. It is not unusual to see designer clothes strewn in boxes on the floor or hung with creases, on racks. You'll find a crystal vase, valued at $200, on a shelf next to a $2 candle. The store does not price all of its merchandise and often the pricing is confusing. When in doubt, ask. This is definitely the place to have your bargain hunting antennas fully extended. This store is absolutely not to be missed. Shop often as new shipments arrive daily. This store has earned the distinction of being one of my personal favorites. Store credits are issued for returns under $100. Refunds issued on returns over $100. M 3-8, W and F 10-4:30. Accepts checks, MC & Visa.

CANDLELITE OUTLET
POB 62423, Sharonville, 45262, (513) 733-0800

Candles, giftware and edibles are offered at savings of 20-60% off regular retail prices at this Lancaster Colony owned outlet. You'll find Indiana Glass, Marzetti, Mountain Top Pies, and other brands. The inventory consists of first quality, seconds and surplus goods. Gives refunds. M-F 9:30-8, Sat 9-6, Sun 12-6. Accepts checks, MC & Visa.

CANDLE SHOPPE
6144 Busch Blvd., Columbus, 43229, 888-1973

An enormous selection of unique, decorative candles can be found here at regular retail prices. Save 20% off all Baldwin brass candlesticks and other gift items, as well as 20% off all Colonial Candles Of Cape Cod. Gives refunds. M-Sat 10-9, Sun 11:30-5:30. Accepts checks, MC, Visa, AmExp & Discover.

CARGO EXPRESS
7690 New Market Center Way, New Market Mall, Columbus, 43235, 889-0260
6402 Tussing Rd., Consumer Sq. E., Reynoldsburg, 43068, 866-9631
1855 W. Henderson Rd., Arlington Sq. Shpng. Ctr., Columbus, 43220, 451-9004
Cleveland Ave. and Rt. 161 location to open in late 1991

Everything for the kitchen and dining room is here at savings of 15-50% off regular retail prices. You'll find kitchen gadgets, mugs, dish towels, flatware, fine china, bakeware, serving dishes, contemporary stemware, small appliances and other necessities and frivolities by such famous brands as Mikasa, Pfaltzgraf, Sasaki, Farberware, Cuisinart, Toscany, Mirro and Libbey. Gives refunds. M-Sat 10-9, Sun 12-5. Accepts checks, MC & Visa.

CRAZY ED'S GLASSWARE OUTLET
5290 Cleveland Avenue, Columbus, 43231, 890-7584

First quality, seconds, discontinued and overstock glassware by Libbey, J.G. Durand and Anchor Hocking are offered at savings of up to 50% off regular retail prices. Choose from simple or decorative patterns in glasses, vases and serving pieces. The store also sells greeting cards and paper/party supplies at savings of 50% off, in addition to budget and moderate quality gift items and planters. Gives refunds. M-Sat 10-6. Accepts checks, MC & Visa.

D.E.JONES
3531 Cleveland Ave.,Northern Lights Shpng. Ctr., Columbus, 43224, 261-9500
932 S. Hamilton Rd., Great Eastern Shpng. Ctr., Columbus, 43213, 861-9417
117 Graceland Blvd., Graceland Shpng. Ctr., Columbus, 43214, 888-9141
3781 S. High St., Great Southern Shpng. Ctr., Columbus, 43207, 497-9080
3287 Maple Ave., Zanesville, 43701, 454-9242

Among the budget quality housewares, comforters and children's clothing, you will find some moderate quality treasures such as Burlington hosiery, funky children's hair accessories, yarns and general merchandise. The store always stocks Fruit Of The Loom brand men's underwear and tube socks. Savings throughout the store are 30-50% off regular retail prices. The inventory changes frequently. Gives refunds. M-Sat 9:30-9, Sun 11-6. Accepts checks and cash only.

DARBY SALES
POB 96, Rte. 33 at Avery Rd., Dublin 43017, 889-8055

This mini department store sells early American contemporary and traditional furniture by Tell City, Nathan Hale, American Drew, Mobel, Fashion House, Flex Steel, Smith Brothers, O'Henry, Lane, Hooker and Bassett. You'll also find grandfather and tabletop clocks; gift pen sets; a small selection of gold and silver jewelry; watches by Pulsar, Jules Jurgensen, Citizen, Lorus and Timex; office equipment; leather attaches, portfolios and wallets; toys by Fisher-Price, Playskool and Century; children's wooden rockers; crystal by Mikasa, Rosemark and Colony; flatware and cutlery; Black and Decker and Stanley tools; camping equipment; sporting equipment such as baseball gloves, tennis rackets, golf clubs and bags, fishing rods and supplies; luggage; lamps; small appliances such as vacuum cleaners and mixers in addition to executive gifts. Savings are 20-50% off manufacturers' suggested retail prices on first quality, brand name merchandise. Special orders are available at similar savings. The annual spring sale features furniture savings of about 40-50% on a select group of merchandise. The prices are very reasonable because this store belongs to a buying group which makes volume purchases at low prices and passes on the savings to you. Gives exchanges only. M,W, F and Sat 9-5; Tu and Th 9-8. Accepts checks, MC, Visa & Discover.

DIRECT IMPORTS
2586 S. Hamilton Rd., Columbus, 43232, 866-3398
3575 E. Livingston Avenue, Livingston Ct. Flea Market, Columbus, 43227, 866-3398

Furniture, giftware and leather purses are available at savings of 20-50% off comparable retail prices. This direct importer of merchandise from China and Taiwan features a wide variety of styles in budget to moderate quality. Gives exchanges. M-Sat 11:30-8:30,closed W, Sun 1-6 (Hamilton Rd location). F-Sun 12-6 at Livingston Ave. Accepts checks, MC, Visa & Discover.

THE DOLL HOUSE
109 N. High St., Gahanna, 43230, 471-8484

This shop specializes in a large selection of Victorian, Country French and country dolls, crafts, gifts and collectibles at prices which are about 10-20% less than comparable retail prices or manufacturer's suggested retail prices. Dressed bears can be found as little girls, country boys, sophisticated ladies in fur stoles as well as outrageous gals in feathers and jewels. Bears can also be custom dressed for weddings or other special occasions. The most outstanding feature of this business, is its selection of collectible porcelain dolls which include Delton, Seymour Mann, Dynasty and Dolls By Pauline brands. These are priced at $32-$110. Handmade modern collectible dolls can be special ordered as well. The store also offers custom wedding flowers and accessories in addition to window swags at similar savings. Since many of the craft items are handmade by the owner and a few select local craftspersons, the middle man is eliminated and prices are kept to a minimum. Inventory changes frequently, with many unique one-of-a-kind gifts and collectibles available. The shopping experience takes place in the relaxed and friendly atmosphere of an older home converted to a doll's house. The store has earned the distinction of being one of my personal favorites. Gives exchanges. Tu-Sat 11-6. Accepts checks, MC & Visa.

EKCO OUTLET STORE
359 State St., Massillon, 44648, 1-(216) 832-5026

Seconds of bakeware, cookware and kitchen tools at savings of 40-70% off regular retail "if perfect" prices, can be found at this manufacturer's outlet store. Ekco as well as other popular brands are available. Gives exchanges. Tu and Th 10:30-2. Accepts checks, MC & Visa.

FAMILY DOLLAR
3409 Cleveland Ave., Columbus, 43224, 263-5040
645 Harrisburg Pike, Columbus, 43223, 274-3302
3777 S. High St., Columbus, 43207, 491-1596
570 E. Livingston Avenue, Columbus, 43215, 461-8224
1861 Parsons Ave., Columbus, 43207, 443-2009
180 Sunrise Ctr. Rd., Zanesville, 43701, 454-4111

Budget quality housewares, toys and clothes fill these stores. The knowledgeable and persistent shopper should return often as these businesses also feature buyouts of first quality overstocks and irregulars of moderate to better quality apparel and accessories. On my recent visit, the menswear department featured current season Hobie, Ocean Pacific, Graffiti and Surfstreet clothes for adults and children at savings of 50-70% off regular retail prices. Many of the manufacturers' garment labels had been removed. However, a careful examination of the merchandise could often disclose a manufacturer's name on a paper hang tag, a label which was not entirely removed or a logo imprinted on the front of the garment. During another visit, I stumbled upon a fantastic buyout of exclusive fashion earrings by Paolo Gucci (formerly with THE Gucci Company in New York). The earrings originally sold for $20-$35 in upscale department stores and boutiques, but were priced at only $5! At the back of the display cards for the Paolo Gucci earrings, there was this comment: "Paolo Gucci is no longer associated with Gucci America". Here is another fine example of a store which you should not bypass just because the quality of its stock may not usually be up to your standards. Gives refunds. M-Sat 10-9, Sun 12-5. Accepts checks and cash only.

FOREVER GREEN FOLIAGE COMPANY
7850 Olentangy River Rd., W. Worthington, 43235, 885-7455

Silk and fabric flowers are sold at 30-50% discount in the warehouse outlet at the rear of their store, for those who want to create their own arrangements. The front of the business features uniquely designed floral arrangements at regular retail prices. Classes in floral arranging for varying skill levels, are offered 4 times per year and cost $25-$35 for about 2 sessions. Gives exchanges. Tu-Sat 10-6. Accepts checks, MC & Visa.

FOSTORIA FACTORY OUTLET
1009 Lebanon St., Monroe, 45050, 1-(513) 339-9632
2311 S. Gate Pkwy., Cambridge, 43725, 1-439-3600

This manufacturer's outlet store sells closeouts as well as first and second quality merchandise at savings of 50-75% off regular retail and "if perfect" prices. You will find stemware, giftware, tableware and dinnerware items. Gives refunds. M-Sun 9-5. Open every day of the year except New Year's Day, Thanksgiving Day and Christmas. Accepts checks, MC & Visa.

GARAGE SALES

You'll find listings for these in the back of the community newspapers and in the back of the "help wanted" section of *Sunday's Columbus Dispatch*. Neighborhood sales provide you with the opportunity to shop at many sales in a limited area, thereby saving you time and gas. As many garage sales are not listed in the newspapers, sellers rely on drive-by traffic to see signs which they have posted by the roadside. Don't overlook the nonadvertised sales! An advantage of early arrival at any garage sale is that you will have the first pick at the merchandise. On the other hand, arrival towards the end of the sale often places you in a position to pay much less than the asking price because the seller is often more motivated to sell the remaining items than she would have been at the beginning of the sale. You'll find new and used merchandise including clothes, toys, hardware, housewares, furniture, arts and crafts and who knows what. Savings are 30-95%. Also refer to "Tag Sales" in the furniture section and "Salesmen's Sample Sales" in the clothing section. All sales are final. Accepts checks and cash only.

GOLDEN HOBBY SHOP
630 S. 3 St., Columbus, 43206, 645-8329

The art and handicrafts of seniors are showcased in this store which is housed in an old school. Many rooms are filled with paintings, darling clothes for Cabbage Patch and other dolls, toys, lawn accessories, gift items, dollhouses, birdfeeders, afghans, quilts and wearable art. While a large portion is bazaar type crafts, the knowledgeable shopper will spot the true quality items such as the paper and ceramic jewelry priced at $4-$8, crochet lace collars $6-$8, rag jackets $44, and stained glass jewelry boxes for $22. Of particular interest, is the handmade solid oak furniture on the first floor which includes a microwave cart for $139, a chest, desk and more. The shop is operated by the City of Columbus, Recreation And Parks Department which only takes a 10% commission on the sales to cover administrative costs. As a result, the prices are kept to a minimum and savings are 20-70% less than comparable quality items in art galleries and other retail stores. The shop also features free quilting classes for adults of all ages and craft demonstrations every weekend. All sales are final. M-Sat 10-5, Sun 1-5. Accepts checks and cash only.

HARTSTONE POTTERY
1719 Dearborn Rd., Zanesville, 43701, 452-9000

Save about 50% on discontinued and seconds in nationally recognized pottery at this factory outlet. You'll find hand decorated stoneware, dinnerware, serving pieces, microwave cook and bakeware, lamps as well as cookie and shortbread molds. Most of the flaws are hardly noticeable. The outlet also features a special patriot's room which is filled with patterns in stars, stripes and flags, many of which, have coordinating glassware. Zanesville is known as the pottery capital of the world. Gives exchanges only. M-S 9-4:00. Accepts checks, MC & Visa.

KITCHEN COLLECTION
621 N. Memorial Dr., Lancaster, 43130, 1-687-1750
5300 Kings Island Dr., Outlets Ltd. Mall, Mason, 45040, (513) 398-1031

First quality, seconds and factory serviced/reconditioned small appliances can be found at savings of 40-70% off regular retail prices. You will find Wearever cookery, Proctor Silex appliances, Anchor Hocking glassware, Bissell appliances, plus kitchen gadgets. Gives refunds. M-Sat 10-9, Sun 12-6. Accepts checks, MC & Visa.

KITCHEN PLACE
7675 New Market Center Way, New Market Mall, Columbus, 43235, 764-0318
771 S. 30 St., Indian Mound Mall, Heath 43056, 522-4672 (this store is called Lechter's)

This one stop kitchen source offers discounts of 20-40% off manufacturer's suggested retail prices on glassware, bakeware, shelf organizers, kitchen gadgets and even picture frames. You'll find such brands as Libbey, Ekco, Rubbermaid, Mikasa and Pyrex. The Kitchen Place has 400 stores throughout the United States. Gives refunds. M-Sat 10-9, Sun 12-6. Accepts checks, MC, Visa, AmExp & Discover.

LAKE ERIE FACTORY OUTLET CENTER
11001 Rte. 250 N., Milan, 44846, 1-800-344-5221

Here's your chance to buy direct at factory prices of 20-70% off regular retail, at Ohio's largest outlet center. There's 50 factory stores here including Farberware, Mikasa, Harve Benard, Bass Shoes, Jonathan Logan, Nilani, Leather Loft, Ribbon Outlet, Ruff Hewn, Wallet Works, American Tourister, Hanes, Toy Liquidators, Prestige Fragrances, Aileen, Swank, Van Heusen, Corning Revere, Hilda Of Iceland and other favorites. Call or write for information on special sales usually held once per month, where greater savings are available. Return policy varies with each store. M-Sat 10-9, Sun 10-6. Accepts checks, MC & Visa.

LANCASTER COLONY
1102 Bellefontaine St., Wapakoneta, 45895, (419)738-9540

You'll find Fostoria crystal and Indiana Glass brands of dishes, glasses, bowls and serving pieces. There are first quality, seconds and discontinued items at savings of 20-25% off regular retail prices. Gives refunds. M-Sat 9-6, Sun 12-5. Accepts checks, MC & Visa.

LESLIE CHARLES COLLECTIONS
711 N. Columbus, St., Lancaster, 43130, 687-1121

Ceramic pie dishes, needlework, stationery, designer baskets and other household items are sold at 30-60% off the regular retail price. The inventory consists of discontinued, one of a kind and slightly defective merchandise. *Leslie Charles* is an Ohio based manufacturer. All sales are final. M-F 10-5, Sat 10-1. Accepts checks and cash only.

LIBBEY GLASS FACTORY OUTLET
1205 Buckeye St., Toledo, 43611, (419) 727-2374

This is their only factory outlet in Ohio. You'll find more than 1500 unique glassware products such as dishes, serving platters, candle votives, punch bowls and glasses at savings of up to 50% off regular retail prices. The store also carries L.E. Smith glass items at savings of 10-30% off. Gives refunds. M-Sat 9:30-5:30. Accepts checks, MC & Visa.

LIQUIDATIONS NOW
1547 Lockbourne Rd., Columbus, 43207, 444-5333

Closeouts and buyouts of discontinued, odd lots, bankrupt, salvage and overstock merchandise are available at savings of 25-75% off regular retail prices. First quality and some irregular items (such as slightly misprinted garments which won't effect their durability) are found here. Household items, food, tools, fashion earrings at $1-$2 and moderate quality clothes can be found. Toys offered include such sought after brands as Playskool, Mattel and Parker Brothers. On my recent visit, I purchased a funky child's tie-dyed tee shirt for $2.69 regularly $12, Chicken Of The Sea salmon for $1.29 per can regularly $2.59, 4 cans of Contadina tomato paste for $1 regularly 49 cents each and gourmet Colosso brand waffle cones for 99 cents per box of 6 regularly $2. Some of the brands of clothing which were at the store during my visit included Wrangler, Pandora, Bijou, Beaches, Outrageous and Monte Carlo. Gives refunds. M-F 11-8, Sat 10-8. Accepts checks and cash only.

MY COUSIN'S CLOSET
16-18 E. College Ave., Westerville, 43081, 899-6110

Nestled among the quaint shops in uptown Westerville, you will find this consignment shop for giftware and home decorating items. Furniture, artwork, vases, baskets, bath accessories, silver serving pieces, area rugs, dried flowers and other gently used items are available at savings of 25-50% off "if new" prices. This business is equally rewarding for the shopper as it is for the consignor. This is a great place to dispose of your quality household items which you no longer need. All sales are final. M,Tu, Th-Sat 10-5; W 10-8, Sun 1-5. Accepts checks, and cash only.

99 CENT SHOPS
5695 Emporium Sq., Columbus Sq. Shpng. Ctr., Columbus, 43231, 890-9999
E. Broad St., Town and Country Shpng. Ctr., Columbus, 43213, 239-9997
3791 S. High St., Great Southern Shpng. Ctr., Columbus, 43207, 497-9999
3497 Cleveland Ave., Northern Lights Shpng. Ctr., Columbus, 43224, 878-9500
4766 W. Broad St., Lincoln Village Shpng. Ctr., Columbus, 43228, 878-9500
7730 Sawmill Rd., Old Sawmill Sq., Dublin, 43017, 798-1909
4714 Cemetery Rd., Hilliard, 43026, 771-9099

Closeouts, discontinued and liquidation merchandise is sold at 99 cents each or several items for 99 cents. You'll find hardware, housewares, toys, gift items, lunchbox snacks and other foods, health and beauty aids, hair accessories, tools, automotive supplies and who knows what. The ever changing inventory is budget to moderate quality and will satisfy every member of your family. On a recent visit, I purchased a Wizard Of Oz quartz watch for my daughter, a coffee mug and Chinese handmade straw jewelry boxes. Savings are up to 90% off regular retail prices. Most of the inventory is first quality. This store is a great source for stocking stuffers, party favors and every day needs. Gives refunds. M-Sat 10-9, Sun 12-6. Accepts checks, MC & Visa.

ONLY $1
711 S. 30 St., Indian Mound Mall, Heath, 43056, 522-4774
1244 Park Ave. W., Mansfield, 44901, (419) 529-6648
1635 River Valley Circle, Lancaster, 43130, 653-0342

Closeouts, discontinued and liquidation merchandise is sold at only $1 each or several items for $1. You'll find tee shirts, toys, housewares, gift items, health and beauty aids, hair accessories, tools, automotive supplies, lunchbox snacks and other foods, in a constantly changing inventory. The first quality merchandise is budget to moderate quality and can satisfy the whole family. This is a great spot for party favors, every day needs as well as stocking stuffers. Gives refunds. M-Sat 9-9. Sun 9-5. Accepts checks, MC & Visa.

REGAL WARE FACTORY OUTLET
156 W. Liberty, Wooster, 44691, 1-(216) 264-4009

This manufacturer's outlet store offers closeouts as well as first and second quality cookware such as pans, gourmet skillets, microwave ware, popcorn poppers, toasters, can openers and food processors. Savings are up to 50% off retail prices. You can take a free guided tour of their factory which creates aluminum pans. Tours are offered from 9AM-3PM Monday through Friday at 770 Spruce Street in Wooster. Gives exchanges. M-Sat 9:30-5. Accepts checks, MC & Visa.

RESTAURANT SUPPLY WAREHOUSE
599 S. Front St., Columbus, 43215, 228-6531

Gourmet cooks and the general public will delight in the enormous selection of large bowls and pots, china, knives, gadgets, serving trays, stemware, onion soup bowls, kitchen chairs, janitorial supplies, even bar stools on display at savings of 20-40% off regular retail prices. If you don't see what you want, ask for it. Undoubtedly, the staff can order it for you at similar savings. Gives exchanges. M-F 8-5, Sat 8-12. Accepts checks, MC & Visa.

ROBINSON-RANSBOTTOM POTTERY COMPANY
Box 7, Roseville, 43777, 1-697-7355

You can take a free, self guided tour through the factory to observe the various steps in the pottery making process. The Pot Shop Outlet store is adjacent to the factory. Here you will find bird baths, ornamental garden statuary, cookware, mixing bowls and more at savings of 20-50% off regular retail prices. First quality and seconds are available. All sales final. M-F 8:30-2:30. Accepts checks, MC & Visa.

SERVICE MERCHANDISE
2300 S. Hamilton Rd., Columbus, 43232, 868-0789
2680 Sawmill Place Plaza, Columbus, 43235, 792-5353
2727 Northland Plaza Dr., Columbus, 43231, 794-3434
4300 W. Broad St., Columbus, 43228, 275-3011

Save 10-30% off manufacturers' suggested retail prices on diamond and gold jewelry; watches by Casio, Armitron, Pulsar and Seiko; gift items such as crystal, silver plated serving pieces, and jewelry boxes; housewares by Farberware, Oneida and Pfaltzgraf such as pots, flatware, and dishes; small appliances by Eureka, Black and Decker and Kitchen Aid such as microwaves, waffle irons and blenders; sports equipment such as exercise machines and bicycles; children's toys, cribs and carriages; stereos, televisions, radios and keyboards; cameras, computers, bathroom accessories, small furniture and even lamps. Gives refunds. M-Sat 10-9, Sun 12-5. Accepts checks, MC, Visa & Discover.

TILES OF COLUMBUS
1217 Goodale Blvd., Columbus, 43212, 469-9121

A unique selection of decorator imported tiles and garden statuary is available at regular retail prices. However, the store maintains a small selection of closeout tiles, priced at 25 cents to $2 each, which make excellent, decorative trivets. Closeout tiles are final sale. M,Tu, Th, F 9-5; W 9-8; Sat 9-2. Accepts checks, MC & Visa.

TUESDAY MORNING
6819 Flags Ctr. Dr., Westerville, 43081, 895-1444
1349 W. Lane Ave., Columbus, 43221, 487-1301
6524 Riverside Dr., Village Sq. Shpng. Ctr., Dublin, 43017, 791-0060

Save 50-80% on first quality famous maker closeouts and discontinued items many of which are available in limited quantities. You can find giftware, china, seasonal items, crystal, luggage, toys, collectibles, linens, clocks, fashion jewelry and toddler sized clothing. This nationwide chain operates 150 stores throughout the United States and is only open during certain times of the year. The 1991 dates are February 14-March 17, April 25-June 16, August 15-September 22 and October 24-December 29. On my last visit I saw Silvestri collector porcelain dolls for $59 regularly $200, a Toscany crystal pitcher for $30 regularly $60, Royal Worcester Spode cake plates for $29.99 regularly $65, goose down pillows $39.99 regularly $80-$160 and Karastan oriental rugs for $200 regularly $400. Also operates businesses in Dayton. Tuesday Morning stores are among my personal favorites. Gives refunds. M, Tu, W, F, Sat 9:30-6, Th 9:30-9, Sun 12-6. Accepts checks, MC, Visa & Discover.

WATERFORD HALL
5911 Karric Sq. Dr., Dublin, 43017, 889-5141

Save about 20-40% off top quality home furnishings by Baldwin Brass, Frederick Cooper, Royal Doulton, Gorham, Steiff, Lenox China, Lladro, Herend, Pickard China (a company which makes place settings for embassies), Sedgefield lamps, Wedgewood and others. You'll find furniture, original artwork by internationally recognized artists, lamps, flatware, collectibles and other decorative items. Special orders are similarly discounted. Although this store sells Waterford Crystal, it is not discounted. Allows merchandise out on approval. M-Th 10-8, F/Sat 10-6. Accepts checks, MC & Visa.

WHOLE-TAIL
4161 Kelnor Place, Grove City, 43123, 871-8245

This wholesaler of seasonal holiday supplies in addition to silk and dried flowers, has opened up an outlet store where you can save 20-80% off regular retail prices. He features some very exotic and unusual florals not readily available in this area. During the Christmas season, I noted a 9 foot scotch pine garland for only $8.63 which would have cost about $33 elsewhere. The wholesale and retail businesses are under one roof. Gives exchanges only. M, Tu, Th 10-5, W 10-8, F and Sat 10-4. Accepts checks, MC & Visa.

ALSO SEE

All For One, Aurora Farms Factory Outlets, Baggerie, Camp And Williams, Cargo Express, Ci Bon, Decorators Show House, Drug Emporium, Drug World, Experienced Possessions, Extravaganza, Grand Finale, Greater Columbus Antique Mall, Groll's Fine Furniture, Hartstone Pottery, Jo-Ann Fabrics, Kitchen Collection, Lake Erie Factory Outlet, Lancaster Colony, Lazarus Final Countdown, Libby Glass Factory Outlet Store, Liberty Street Interiors, MPW, Marshall's, Middleton Doll Factory

Outlet, 99 Cent Shops, Odd Lots, Office America, Only $1, PM Gallery, Paul's Marine, J.C. Penney Outlet, J.C. Penney Portfolio, Pizza Fixin's, Ritchey's, Rousch Hardware, Salesmen's Sample Sales, Sam's Club, Schottenstein's, Sears Outlet, Service Merchandise, Sofa Express Outlet, Star Beacon, T.J. Maxx, Tag Sales, Uhlman's Clearance Center and Value City Department Stores

Do you want to learn about new bargain sources? Then subscribe to the quarterly *Bargain Hunting In Columbus Newsletter*. See order form at the back of this book.

HEALTH & BEAUTY/ EYEGLASSES

Did you know that supermarkets and stores which sell health and beauty aids generally place their most costly items at eye level? This method is used because they know that consumers are likely to purchase these items on impulse. I suggest that you look high and low on those shelves and compare the various brands before deciding on what you want to purchase.

<u>ALL FOR ONE</u>
2707 Northland Plaza Dr., Columbus, 43231, 899-7766
2835-2837 Festival Lane, Festival At Sawmill, Dublin, 43017, 798-0388
1739 Hill Rd. N., Pickerington, 43147, 759-4466
1779 Kingsdale Shpng. Ctr., Tremont Rd., 43221, 451-0017

Everything in this store is priced at only $1. You'll be amazed at the variety and quality of merchandise which can be purchased for this one low price. The store sells toys, housewares, gifts, jewelry, infant bottles and teething rings, cosmetics, hardware, stationery, gift items, health and beauty aids, snacks and who knows what. On my recent visit, I saw Chippendale underwear (regularly $3.50), Bain De Soleil tanning lotion (regularly $6), Max Factor makeup (regularly $4.50), Keebler cookies (regularly $2.50), decorative Neiman Marcus empty candy tins (valued at about $6), Snoopy hair clips (regularly $3) and many other wonderful items, Most of the merchandise is moderate to better quality. Savings are 50-90% below regular retail prices. All For One is operated by Consolidated Stores, the parent company of *Odd Lots.* Yet the display and type of merchandise is different.

The Store provides appealing merchandising techniques. The stock is so neatly maintained that you imagine the sales staff spends lots of time keeping it in order. This new chain has established its stores in upscale shopping centers as a way of reaching a different sort of clientele than its Odd Lots cousin. Don't overlook the Odd Lots description elsewhere in this book. All In One has earned the distinction of being one of my personal favorites. Gives exchanges. M-Sat 10-9, Sun 10-6. Accepts checks, MC & Visa

BARBER SCHOOL
6322 E. Livingston Ave., Reynoldsburg, 43068, 868-0668

This branch of the Ohio State School of Cosmetology, offers haircuts for $1.50-$3.95, perms for $15-$35, coloring for $20 and facials for $2-$2.50. Services are provided by students under the supervision of licensed individuals. No appointments are needed. Fridays and Saturdays are the busiest times, so if you don't want to wait long, try coming Tuesday through Thursday. Tu and W 11-7:30, Th and F 8-4:30, Sat 8-4. Accepts checks and cash only.

CENTRAL OHIO DIABETES ASSOCIATION
1803 W. 5 Ave., Columbus, 43212, 486-7124

Free blood tests for diabetes detection are available at various sites within the community, sponsored by this organization. Call for details. M-F 9-5.

COLUMBUS FREE CLINIC
1043 E. Weber Rd., Columbus, 43211, 268-7531

Every Thursday from 6:30-8:30PM, this clinic provides free simple health care checks for low income individuals. Shots will not be given. Call Dr. Howlison's office to schedule an appointment. M-F 9-5.

COLUMBUS WHOLESALE BARBER AND BEAUTY SUPPLY
962 N. High St., Columbus, 43215, 299-4000 or 299-2332

Shop where the professionals shop at this wholesale supplier of beauty and barbershop supplies and save 10-25% off comparable quality items. You'll find hair, skin, nail and scalp products including many hard to find items such as razor straps and professional shaving brushes. Colognes as well as bulk and large size products, are also available. Many of the brands cannot be purchased in regular health and beauty aid stores Some items such as bleaches, color tints and perm supplies can only be sold to licensed cosmetologists. This store has been in business for over 50 years and is the only full service barber and beauty supply house in Central Ohio. Many of the customers are institutions, hospitals as well as country clubs. All sales are final. M-F 8-5, Sat 8-12. Accepts MC, Visa and Cash.

DRUG EMPORIUM
5737 Columbus, Sq. Shpng. Ctr., Columbus, 43231, 890-3805
260 Graceland Blvd., Columbus, 43214, 888-6386
240 N. Wilson Rd., Great Western Shpng. Ctr., Columbus, 43204, 274-7711
789 Hebron Rd., Heath, 43056, 522-1767
4630 Tussing Rd., Consumer Sq. E. Shpng. Ctr., Reynoldsburg, 43068, 864-8972
3790 E. Broad St., Town and Country Shpng. Ctr., Columbus, 43213, 238-6661

2652 Bethel Rd., Carriage Pl. Shpng. Ctr., Columbus, 43220, 459-2040
5160 E. Main St., Columbus, 43213, 863-9722

This full service pharmacy and health and beauty aids store discounts all of its stock 10-50%. Designer fragrances are available at savings of up to 50% off manufacturers' suggested retail prices. You will find Anne Klein II, Oscar, Lagerfeld, Grey Flannel, Halston and other brands. Gold filled Cross pens and pencils are 30% off suggested retail prices and come with an unconditional lifetime mechanical guarantee from the manufacturer. American Greetings' Forget-Me-Not brand of candles, greetings, gift wrap and related items are sold at 40% off list price. In the film processing department, pay only 99 cents extra and you can get a second set of 3" standard film prints from your initial order at every day low prices. The Bethel Road, Graceland and East Dublin-Granville Road sites sell 14 Karat gold necklaces, earrings and bracelets at 40-50% off regular retail prices. These same 3 locations sell men's and ladies dress and casual Seiko brand watches for 30% off manufacturer's suggested retail prices.Save 30% off Timex watches. Save 50% off men's and ladies leather wallets by Amity. Russell Stover candy is discounted 10%, there's 50% off non-prescription reading glasses, 30% off Ray Bans sunglasses and 50% off other sunglass brands. Swarovski Austrian crystal pendants, small animals and figurines are discounted 30%. The stores offer a free computerized, self serve blood pressure check in the pharmacy section. Save 30-60% on quality name brands of replacement contact lenses by Bausch & Lomb, Sola-Barnes Hind, Wesley-Jessen, Cibavision, Coopervision and Acuvue Disposable. Simply bring in your prescription and your contacts will be available within 48 hours. No appointments are needed. The stores also stock a small, but interesting selection of contemporary silk type flowers at savings of 30%. Gives refunds. M-Sat 10-9, Sun 12-5. Accepts checks, MC & Visa.

DRUG WORLD
4850 E. Main St., Columbus, 43213, 864-6116
2572 S. Hamilton Rd., Columbus, 43232, 864-2371
2441 E. Dublin-Granville Rd., Columbus, 43229, 891-1527
4936 W. Broad St., Columbus, 43228, 878-7651
2800 N. High St., Columbus, 43214, 267-5607
3377 Cleveland Ave., Northern Lights Shpng. Ctr., Columbus, 43224, 267-6917

A full line of health and beauty aids is available at savings of about 10-60% off manufacturers' suggested retail prices. Photo processing, housewares, snacks and food items, office and school supplies are available at similar savings. Save 20% on L'eggs brand pantyhose, and 50% off Heatwaves sunglasses by Casablanca. Discounts about 50% on co-pays for the following prescription plans: Paid Prescriptions, Ohio Blue Cross, PCS, Medimet, and M.P.A. Save about 20-40% on soft contact lenses and eyeglasses at the optical centers, located at the North High, South Hamilton Road and West Broad Street locations. Brands offered include Bausch and Lomb, Ciba, Barnes-Hinds, Charmant, Logo, Neostyle, Silhouette and others. Timex watches are discounted 25% and all greeting cards are discounted 40%. Another excellent buy is on a wide variety of large bottles of spices at 89 cents each. Offers 2 prints for the price of 1 when developing film. Gives refunds. M-Sat 10-9, Sun 12-5. Accepts checks, MC, Visa, AMExp & Discover.

EYEGLASS FACTORY
2100 Morse Rd., Morse Center, Columbus, 43229, 848-7775
4636 W. Broad St., Columbus, 43228, 870-2121
893 S. Hamilton Rd., Columbus, 43213, 236-2400

You can buy one pair of eyeglasses or contacts and get one pair free at prices starting as low as $99.95. This 50 store national chain, based in Ferndale Michigan, sells manufacturers' overstocks and discontinued styles in such brands as Swank, Benelton, St. Moritz and Gazelle. M-F 10-6, Tu 10-8, Sat 9-5. Accepts checks, MC & Visa.

FACTORY OPTICAL OUTLET
6510 Huntley Rd., Columbus, 43229, 846-4037

Save about 30% on quality eyeglasses. Lenses are manufactured on premises which helps to keep the prices low. Bring your prescription here to be filled and choose from a large selection of classic and contemporary frames. M-Sat 10-6. Accepts checks, MC & Visa.

FIESTA HAIR AND TANNING SALONS
26 locations in Central Ohio

This hair care chain of 235 Midwest stores features low cost services such as $7.99 for an adult haircut, $5.49-$9.49 for a shampoo and set. A hair cut for kids aged 10 and under is $7.49. No appointments are necessary. You will be served on a first come basis. Fiesta uses popular haircare products by Nexus, Redken and Paul Mitchell. Gives a senior discount. M-F 8-8, Sat 8-6, Sun 10-6. Accepts cash only.

FIRST CHOICE HAIRCUTTERS
1516 Bethel Rd., Columbus, 43220, 457-1016
2716 Bethel Rd., Columbus, 43220, 459-3711
5109 E. Main St., Columbus, 43213, 866-9932
2254 S. Hamilton Rd., Columbus, 43232, 863-5548
5608 Cleveland Ave., Columbus, 43231, 882-4283
6038 Huntley Rd., Columbus, 43229, 847-9610
109 Westerville Plaza, Westerville, 43081, 882-6558

Haircare services are reasonably priced here. You can expect to pay $7.95 for a haircut and a fluff dry, $7 for a kid's cut for ages 9 and under, $40 for a perm-cut-style, or $10.95 for a shampoo-cut-fluff dry., This national chain of 80 stores is headquartered in Canada. They will honor all competitors' coupons. Appointments are not needed except when a chemical process such as a perm or a frosting is to be done. M-F 9-8:30, Sat 9-6. Most stores open Sun 11-5. Accepts checks, MC & Visa.

GOLDEN LIFESTYLES
C/O Mt. Carmel Health, 793 W. State St., Columbus, 43222, 225-1288
C/O Mt. Carmel Health, 6001 E. Broad St, Columbus, 43213, 225-1288

Seniors aged 60 and over, can obtain a free membership in the Golden Lifestyles Club. Benefits include a quarterly newsletter with health and community services information, a customized travel and tour program, discounts on valet parking at the hospital, gift shop discounts, 15% prescription discounts at their Eastside pharmacy and other amenities.

HARTS
4640 E. Main St., Columbus, 43213, 866-7011
1501 E. Dublin-Granville Rd., Columbus, 43229, 888-9550
3690 Fishinger Blvd., Hilliard, 43026, 771-6404
2081 State Rt. 23 N., Delaware, 43015, 363-1131

2020 Stringtown Rd., Grove City, 43123, 871-9400
1690 E. Main St., Route 22 E., Lancaster, 43130, 654-9770
680 Harrisburg Pike, Central Pt. Shpng. Ctr., Columbus, 43223, 221-1744
4600 W. Broad St., Lincoln Village Shpng. Ctr., Columbus, 43228, 878-9037
6310 E. Livingston Ave., Reynoldsburg, 43068, 864-2450
1680 N. 21 St., Heath, 43056 , 366-1395
475 Western Ave., Chillicothe, 45601, 773-5240

Save 25% off manufacturers' suggested retail prices on Clarion, Maybelline, Coty, Aziza, Cover Girl, Revlon, Wet 'N Wild and L'oreal brands of cosmetics.   Bonneau brand sunglasses, regularly $8-$16, are priced at 25% discount. L'eggs pantyhose is 20% off. In the photo processing department, you can purchase an extra set of prints for 99 cents if requested at the time you place your order. Borden wallcoverings are offered at a 25% discount. Harts also discounts Timex watches by 25%, and Seiko watches (regularly $110-$165) are discounted 50-60%. All area Harts and Big Bear stores offer savings of about $1-$2 off the ticket price to certain annual special events in the community such as the Shriners Circus, the Columbus Boat and RV Show, the Columbus Sports and Travel Show, the Central Ohio Home and Garden Show, the Decorators' Show House and the Columbus Symphony's Picnic With The Pops. The stores also add on other special events discount tickets throughout the year. Gives refunds. M-Sat 10-9, Sun 11-5. Accepts checks, MC, Visa & Discover.

HEALTH LINE
645-2020

This call-in tape recorded information library, will provide you with free physical and mental health information.   Topics include alcoholism, arthritis, birth control, cancer, dental health, diabetes, drug abuse, digestive disorders, eye care, hearing, heart problems, schizophrenia, pregnancy, respiratory ailments, skin disorders, smoking, women's health concerns, parenting and children's health issues.   It is sponsored by the Columbus Metropolitan Library. M-Th 9-9, F and Sat 9-6, (Sun 1-5 Sept-May only).

KENNETH'S DESIGN GROUP
5151 Reed Rd., Columbus, 43220, 457-6111

You can be a model and earn a free haircut. No experience is necessary. This prominent hairstyling chain, offers the opportunity for their apprentice stylists (those still perfecting their skills but who have studied at a trade school) to demonstrate their expertise to management towards the achievement of a full fledged "hair stylist" designation. The apprentices will cut wedged, layered or bobbed styles for women and teens with some input from you. It is important that you are flexible to allow the apprentice to demonstrate the skills requested by her supervisor. All hair types and lengths are acceptable. These apprentice cutting sessions are held on Mondays at 8PM. Call and leave your name. You will be contacted when a model is needed. Open M-Sat 9-8, Sun 9-6.

LENS CRAFTERS
1492 Morse Rd., Columbus, 43229, 846-4006
4427 Crossroads E. Shpng. Ctr., Columbus, 43232, 863-0199
771 S. 30 St., Indian Mound Mall, Heath, 43056, 522-3867
1635 River Valley Circle, River Valley Mall, Lancaster, 43130, 654-9734

Custom lenses are usually available in an hour as they are manufactured on premises. In avoiding the middleman, this business can pass the savings on to you at about 5-25% or about $10-$50 on a complete pair of glasses, as compared to comparable products at full price businesses. Lens Crafters also makes some of the frames themselves, while purchasing others. The stores also offers price incentives on the purchase of a second pair of glasses. M-Sat 9-8. Accepts checks, MC & Visa.

LORI'S SALON
4958 N. High St., Columbus, 43214, 885-6330

This salon will give you a perm and a haircut for $17.98; a perm, haircut and blowdry for $19.98, using the Jerri Rhedding "One And Only Perm" solution. Their frequent coupons in the Clintonville and Westerville newspapers indicate that you can get a curly perm or a body wave for only $9.99 (with coupon). However, Chuck, the owner, indicated that readers of this book only need to mention that price to get it without the coupon! A haircut or a finish cut is recommended, but not required, and can add another $7-$11 to the cost, which still is a great price. M-F 8-8, Sat 7:30-6. Accepts checks, MC & Visa.

MEIJER
6175 Sawmill Rd., Dublin, 43017, 766-4494
2675 Brice Rd., Reynoldsburg, 43068, 755-4112
775 Georgesville Rd., Columbus, 43228, 274-6708
5555 Cleveland Ave., Columbus, 43231, 899-6400
1155 N. 21 St., Newark, 43055, 366-7935

This full service grocery and general merchandise business offers savings throughout the store. Save 50% off the Forget-Me-Not brand of greeting cards and invitations, 20-40% off Speidel and Timex watches and 20-60% off the list price on a select group of Nintendo cartridges. During the first week of April, the stores feature a giant annual sporting goods sale in which luggage as well as fishing tackle, bicycles, camping equipment and other products, are reduced 30-50%. The video rental department features over 3000 titles including children's, personal growth and crafts videos. The cost per day is 49 cents per title or 3 for $1. New releases cost $1.49 each per day. Nintendo games are also available at a rental of 99 cents per night. The 24 hour drop box makes it convenient to return your rentals at any time. The pharmacy department offers free self-serve digital weight assessment equipment and computerized blood pressure analysis during regular operating hours. The stores also offer a 50% co-payment on most prescription plans. Membership in the senior citizen's 60+10 plan is free for those aged 60 and over, and provides a 10% discount off the price of prescriptions. The large selection of health and beauty aids are discounted and/or value priced. Popular brands of basic and designer perfumes cost about 10-30% less than manufacturers' suggested retail prices. Pick up free seafood recipes in the fresh fish department. You'll learn general tips on fish preparation plus delectable recipes such as Scallops Orientale and salmon with watercress and chive butter. Meijer will give you a 5 cent credit for each brown grocery bag you bring in which is used to bag your purchases, regardless of what store it is from. The book department features a 25% discount on New York Times best sellers and 10% off all paperbacks and magazines. Pick up a free, preferred customer discount card in the shoe repair department, which will provide you with a 10% discount on all shoe repairs. If you are shopping with a young child, be sure to give him/her a ride on the mechanical horse in the outer lobby of the stores. This fun experience will only cost you 1 penny! The special *Kids Week* celebration is held in January and August and features games, samples, special events, reduced prices on toys, special promotions, costumed characters and other interesting diversions. Participation is free. Gives refunds. Open 24 hours per day, 7 days per week. Accepts checks, MC &Visa.

OHIO STATE SCHOOL OF COSMETOLOGY
6320 E. Livingston Ave., Reynoldsburg, 43068, 868-1601
3717 S. High St., Columbus, 43207, 491-0492
4390 Karl Rd., Columbus, 43224, 263-1861
5970 Westerville Rd., Westerville, 43081, 890-3535

Beginning and advanced level students, under instructor supervision, provide hair and nail care services at savings of about 20-50% lower than at typical full price salons. Your cost depends on the skill level of the stylist. A haircut by a beginner is $4.95, or $6.25 by an advanced student. A beginner perm is $15-$25, or $20-$30 if done by an advanced student. Appointments are suggested. W and F 9-6, Th. 9-9, Sat 8-4:30. Accepts checks and cash only.

NATIONWIDE BEAUTY ACADEMY
5757 Karl Rd., Columbus, 43229, 888-0790
3120 Olentangy River Rd., Columbus, 43202, 261-7588
898 S. Hamilton Rd., Columbus, 43213, 864-1544
88 N. Wilson Rd., Columbus, 43204, 275-0153

Hair and nail care is provided by students under instructor supervision., Savings are about 30-50% lower than standard salon prices. A haircut is $3.75, perm and a haircut is $25, haircoloring or frosting is $18.50-$21.50, facial massage is $3.50 and a manicure is $2.25-$3. Appointments are suggested although walk-ins are welcome. M-F 8:30-9, Sat 8-4. Accepts checks, MC & Visa.

PHAR-MOR
2304 S. Hamilton Rd., Columbus, 43232, 864-2007
4131 W. Broad Plaza, Columbus, 43228, 275-4040
2605 Northland Plaza Dr., Columbus, 43231, 794-1722
6630 Dublin Ctr. Dr., Dublin Village Ctr., Dublin, 43017, 889-6411
1188 Park Ave. W., Mansfield, 44906, (419) 529-3501

Phar Mor operates 242 stores in 27 states. They offer savings of 10-60% on a full line of health and beauty aids and lesser discounts on snacks, soda, salad dressings, other food items, books and magazines, school supplies and toys. The stores offer double manufacturers' coupons savings every day, up to and including a 50 cent face value. Prescriptions are filled with lots of extra opportunities for savings..There is a free co-pay, up to $3, on prescriptions covered by most insurance companies. On co-pays over $3, you pay the difference. Phar Mor will add $2 to the value of a competitor's prescription coupon if redeemed here. If you had purchased a prescription from Phar Mor and filled it at another pharmacy for less at a later date, Phar Mor will triple the difference in price and refund it to you. However, certain restrictions apply. The pharmacy area can also save you about 65% when you have your contact lens prescription filled. Pick up copies of the free booklets on treating allergies, generic drugs, keeping poisons away from children and other important topics. The pharmacy department also offers free, self serve blood pressure testing. You can rent Nintendo and videos at a cost of 49 cents each or 3 for $1.25 for a 2 day rental period. The one time video club membership fee is $2 for a lifetime. As a club member, you will receive a $10 store gift certificate for every 100 videos you rent. There's no receipts to accumulate as their computers keep track for you even if you rented at several different stores. In this Phrequent Video Renter Program, there is no limit on how many gift certificates you can earn. Family members with one or multiple cards may combine tallies to receive gift certificates. You might want to consider purchasing a *Video Value Certificate Book* for $14.99. You will receive 50 video rental coupons that would save you $6.20 off the cost of individual rentals or $3.80 off the 3 for $1.25 price. These rentals will also count towards your accumulation of 100 videos to earn the gift certificate. Their stock of decorative calendars arrives in November and is generally sold at 50-60% off while supplies last. In other stores, you usually have to wait until February before the calendars are reduced. Watches by Lorus, Casio, Seiko and Timex are discounted 30-60% off manufacturers' suggested retail prices. Savings of 50% are available on all brands of greeting cards, gift wraps, bows and party invitations. The Hamilton Road site has the largest selection of office products of their local stores. The extensive assortment includes file cabinets, envelopes, pens and a full line of products at savings of 20-50%. Call 1-800-522-5444 from 8AM-9PM to order a free office supplies catalogue. Gives refunds. M-Sat 10-9:30, Sun 10-6. Accepts checks and cash only.

REVCO
1520 Bethel Rd., Columbus, 43220, 459-9521
5680 Columbus Sq., Columbus, 43231, 890-0870
34 N. High St., Columbus, 43215, 224-4261
564 E. Livingston Ave., Columbus, 43215, 464-2480
5965 E. Main St., Columbus, 43213, 861-5880
4657 Morse Center, Columbus, 43229, 885-9349
777 Neil Ave., Columbus, 43215, 224-9275
1618 Neil Ave., Columbus, 43201, 421-1323
6502 Riverside Dr., Dublin, 43017, 764-8028
435 Agler Rd., Gahanna, 43230, 475-2014
3677 E. Broad St., Columbus, 43213, 235-8605
926 N. High St., Worthington, 43085, 888-6366

Your free membership in their *Baby Bunch V.I.P. Club* entitles you to 10% off baby prescriptions, baby vitamins and *Revco* brand baby related products. You can enroll at a *Revco* store of your choice and your discount card will be valid at each of their locations. Seniors aged 62 and over, can join the *Senior Shoppers V.I.P. Club* at no cost. Members will receive 10% off all merchandise on Wednesdays and 10% off all prescriptions and *Revco* brand products every day. *Revco* discounts Timex watches by 25% off the manufacturer's suggested retail price. *Revco* brand health and beauty aids are generally about 20-40% cheaper than comparable quality products by famous brands. The Neil Avenue location offers a savings of about 35-65% on contact lens replacements in most popular brands. Eye examinations are not offered, so you will need to provide a prescription from your doctor. Gives refunds. M-Sat 10-9, Sun 12-5. Accepts checks, MC & Visa.

RIVERSIDE ADVANTAGE SENIOR HEALTH ASSN.
3535 Olentangy River Rd., Columbus, 43214, 261-5858

Annual membership in this senior citizens' group costs $20 for an individual or $35 for a couple. Benefits include low prices on prescriptions at 40 neighborhood pharmacies; discounts on eyeglasses, contact lenses and similar products at over 20 opticians' offices;

free blood pressure, and other preventative screenings through Riverside Hospital's Gerontology Services; free hearing tests and reduced prices on hearing aids at Riverside's Hearing Services;   discounts on medical equipment such as wheelchairs and canes; discounts on classes offered through the Elizabeth Blackwell Center at Riverside Hospital and other hospital sponsored wellness programs; a bi-monthly newsletter; recreational activities and day trips; discounts at area businesses and more. M-F 9-5. Accepts checks and cash only.

RIVERSIDE HOSPITAL HEALTH EDUCATION LIBRARY
3535 Olentangy River Rd., Columbus, 43214, 261-5230

Houses an extensive collection of information on more than 300 health topics. There are free informational pamphlets, more than 1,200 books, 100 video tapes, many health magazines, audio cassette tapes and an in-house educational television channel. Video and audio cassettes may be used in the library or checked out for 3 days at no cost. Books and journals may not be checked out, but a photocopier and reading room are available. The librarian is always on hand to assist you if needed. The library is located in the *Donald Vincent Medical Library* on the main floor and is open to the general public. M-F 8AM-8:30PM, Sat 8-4:30.

ST. ANN'S HOSPITAL
500 S. Cleveland Ave., Westerville, 43081, 898-4095

Several free community health programs are offered each month which address such topics as living with arthritis, parenting in the 90's, sports nutrition/ injury prevention and other health topics of general interest. The programs are held weekdays in day and evening times. The programs are open to the general public. Call to be added to their mailing list.

SALLY BEAUTY SUPPLY
4544 Indianola Ave., Columbus, 43214, 263-5905
3350 Cleveland Ave., Columbus, 43224, 267-4200
3728 E. Broad St., Columbus, 43213, 231-2898
3481 Great Western Blvd., Columbus, 43204, 274-8040
4400 Crossroads Center, Columbus, 43232, 863-3622
3719 S. High St., Columbus, 43207, 491-9667
1645 N. Memorial Dr., Lancaster, 43130, 653-7719
959 Hebron Rd., Heath, 43056, 522-8256
562 Lexington-Springmill Rd., Mansfield, 44901, (419) 529-5515
1013 Bechtel Ave., Springfield, 45502, (513) 322-9185

This national chain of 500 shops sells hair and nail care products, cosmetics and even decorative hair accessories. Many of these salon quality products are not available through regular retail outlets, but you will recognize some of the popular brands. Savings are 20-40% less then comparable quality products in other stores. If you like to have artistic or funky looking nails, try purchasing a nail art kit. Rhinestones or decorative designs can be easily applied at prices ranging from $3-$8 per kit. By doing it yourself, or having a friend help you, you can save 50-70% off the price of having this done at a beauty salon. The kits, in addition to other merchandise in the store, make great gifts or unusual stocking stuffers at Christmas. Pick up a free copy of their monthly special values flyer which provides coupons for additional savings. Gives refunds. M-Sat 9-6, Sun 12-5. Accepts checks, MC, Visa, AmExp & Discover.

STATE DISCOUNT
1782 N. High St., Columbus, 43201, 421-7555
1876 N. High St., Columbus, 43201, 299-2367

Health and beauty aids, CDs, OSU sweatshirts, vitamins and other similar products are sold at 10-50% off suggested retail prices. The merchandise is all first quality. Gives refunds. M-F 9-9, Sat 10-6, Sun 12-5. Accepts checks, MC & Visa.

TRI-VILLAGE OPTICIANS
1442 W. 5 Ave., Columbus, 43212, 486-4871

Manufacturers closeouts and discontinued designer eyeglass frames by such brands as Oscar de la Renta, Joan Collins and Diane von Furstenberg, are sold here at savings of about 50-80% off suggested retail prices. Most of the frames are in the $25-$40 range but typically sell for $85-$250. Save an additional 20% on your second pair of glasses. Bring your prescription to be filled here, as examinations are not offered. Tu-F 10-6, Sat 10-2. Accepts checks, MC & Visa.

T'S DISCOUNT BEAUTY SUPPLY
3575 E. Livingston Ave., Columbus, 43227, 236-0758
973 Mt. Vernon Ave., Columbus, 43203, 252-0500
2157 E. 5 Ave., Columbus, 43219, 258-2434

Popular brand name hair and beauty care products are available at savings of 20-30% off suggested retail prices. Cosmetologists and those in training, are offered additional discounts. Some of the brands featured include TCB, Carefree, Leisure Curl, Hawaiian Silky and others. The products are basically aimed at the ethnic customer. The 5th avenue location is open Monday to Saturday 10-7:30. Mt. Vernon Avenue is open Thursday to Saturday from 10-6. Livingston Avenue is open Friday through Sunday from 12-7. Gives exchanges. Accepts checks and cash only.

TEMA PERFUMES
82K Worthington Square Mall, Worthington, 43085, 888-0854

A large selection of popular, designer and hard to find brand name fragrances are available at savings of 10-50% off department store prices. You'll find men's and women's eau de toilette, perfume and after-shave in Obsession, Gucci, Boss, Armani, Aramis, Georgio, 273, Secret Of Venice, Rive Gauche, Anne Klein, Red, Eternity, Picasso, Boucheron, Caleche, Molinard, Monogram and other brands. If you purchase several items at one time, you'll be entitled to extra savings. This direct importer sells both wholesale and retail. Stop by *Tema Perfumes* and you'll see why some of the best things in life come in small packages. All sales are final. M-Sat 10-9, Sun 12-5. Accepts checks, MC & Visa.

UNIVERSITY HOSPITAL, MOBILE MAMMOGRAPHY UNIT
293-4455

This travelling health care service will provide a mammogram for only $60 which is about 35-50% less than the fee charged by private physicians and clinics. The procedure takes about 10-15 minutes. This service is accredited by the American College of Radiology. A physician referral is needed. Call to find out about the locations which constantly change. M-F 9-5. Accepts checks and cash.

ALSO SEE

All For One, Ameritech Pages Plus, Ask-A-Nurse, Aurora Farms Factory Outlets, Blockbuster Video, Cancer Call, Columbus Health Department, Columbus Speech And Hearing Center, Dial-A-Dietician, Drug Emporium, Drug World, Health And Harmony Fair, Marshall's, Northwest Natural and Specialty Foods, Odd lots, Ohio Affiliate/National Society To Prevent Blindness, Only $1, Outlets Limited Mall, Phar Mor, Riverside Methodist Hospital Foundation, Sam's Club, Schottenstein's, Star Beacon, Vision USA Program

HOME IMPROVEMENT LIGHTING/FLOORING

HOME IMPROVEMENT

BUILDER'S SQUARE
1881 Channingway Ctr. Dr., Columbus, 43232, 864-9702
5850 Columbus, Sq. Shpng. Ctr., Columbus, 43231, 891-3450

A full line of hardware and home improvement supplies is a available at about 10-25% less than suggested retail prices. Carpet and linoleum remnants, in addition to a small but varied selection of quality desks, chairs, bar stools, computer tables, bookcases and end tables, are value priced. Throughout the year, the stores offer free do-it-yourself classes on wallpapering, ceramic tile installation and other home improvement topics. Call the store or follow the newspapers to find out when the next class will be held. There's low prices on quality floor, hanging and table lamps, plus a large selection of ceiling fans, by such quality brands as Thomas, Hunter, Cheyenne and QualityMark. On a recent visit, I saw a 5 tiered swizzle stick chandelier with brass accents for $269 and a solid brass outdoor lamp for only $54. The stores also stock a large selection of replacement lamp globes. They will beat any competitor's advertised price by 10% on identical items, limited to in-stock merchandise only. Check the stores for details. Gives refunds. M-Sat 7:30AM-9PM, Sun 9-6. Accepts checks, MC, Visa, AmExp, Discover & Builder's Square charges.

COLUMBUS COAL AND LIME COMPANY
1150 Sullivant Ave., Columbus, 43223, 224-9241

Offers free brick patio classes once a month, from April through September. The classes are usually held on a Saturday, from 9-11AM. The store stocks a large selection of bricks for purchase which are good values. No purchase is necessary to attend the classes. Gives exchanges. M-F 7-5, Sat 8-12 noon. Accepts checks, MC & Visa.

COLUMBUS PAINT DISTRIBUTORS
588 W. Schrock Rd., Westerville, 43081, 523-1030

Save 50-60% off custom order blinds by Levolor, Bali, Kirsch and Graeber. In-stock and special order wall coverings are discounted 30-80%. Choose from such popular brands as Waverly, Imperial and Schumacher. The first quality wallpaper consists of current and discontinued patterns. If you have questions about installing wallpaper which you have purchased from the store, call their wallpaper hotline at 523-1031 during regular business hours. New home buyers can stop in the store to pick up a VIP card which will entitle them to a savings of 20-30% off regular retail prices on paint purchases and 25% off supplies. Discounts do not apply to sale items or those already discounted. A free, in-home decorating service is also available. Gives refunds on unopened merchandise. M-F 7:30AM-8PM, Sat 8-5. Accepts checks, MC, Visa & Discover.

DISCOUNT FENCE SUPPLIES
2763 Winchester Pike, Berwick Plaza Shpng. Ctr., Columbus, 43232, 236-1902

All types of wire, chain and wood fencing are available from this manufacturer at 10-40% off regular retail and comparable retail prices. This business also wholesales their products to other fence companies in the city, but you'll pay more if not purchased here. Delivery and installation services available. M-F 8-4:30. Accepts checks, MC & Visa.

GREYSTONE DESIGN
1246 Hill Rd. N., Pickerington, 43147, 759-7117

Save 50% off Starmark cabinetry, 30-40% off custom draperies, 20-30% off wall coverings, up to $4 per yard on carpeting, up to 25% on whirlpool baths, 50-60% on mini blinds, 35% on pleated shades and up to 50% off vertical blinds. The savings are based on manufacturers' suggested retail prices on these first quality products. M-Sat 10-7, Accepts checks, MC & Visa.

KINGWOOD LUMBER COMPANY
900 W. 3 Ave., Columbus, 43212, 294-3723

Check out the bargain barn at the back of the store, where savings are up to 75% off on seconds, returns and odd sizes of doors, lumber and formica counter tops. All sales are final. M-F 7-5, Sat 7012 noon. Accepts checks, MC & Visa.

KITCHEN DISTRIBUTING
32 E. Warren St., Columbus, 43215, 297-7791

Quality wood and laminate kitchen and bath cabinets by Homecrest Cabinetry and Cardell, are available at savings of 50% off the manufacturer's list price from this distributor. Installation is extra. M-F 9-5, Sat 9-2, and evenings by appointment.

MIDWEST CLOSETS
948 Freeway Dr. N., Bldg. 10, Columbus, 43229, 848-4400

This designer and manufacturer of adjustable custom closets offers factory direct prices to the public. You can save about 20% off the price of comparable products offered in department stores, although this manufacturer only sells customer direct. These high quality products range from about $250 to several thousands of dollars, and are designed for discriminating tastes. M-F 9-5, Sat 9-12. Accepts checks, MC & Visa.

ROUSCH HARDWARE
609 S. State St., Westerville, 43081, 882-3623
373 W. Bridge St., Dublin, 43017, 764-8900

Friendly and courteous salespeople can assist you in finding everything from nuts and bolts to birdhouses and giftware. The merchandise is often 10-20% lower than in traditional full price hardware stores, due to lower markups and special purchases. Watch the newspapers for sales and special values. Excellent purchases can be obtained on their Value Of The Month items which feature products at savings of 40-50% off regular retail prices. These can range from tools to housewares. Both stores offer a free bag of popcorn, no purchase required. The freshly popped kernels are served from 8AM-9PM on Saturdays, and 10-5 on Sundays throughout the year. The Dublin store also offers the popcorn on Fridays from 8AM-9PM. The stores have earned the distinction of being among my personal favorites. Gives refunds. M-Sat 8AM-9PM, Sun 10-5. Accepts checks, MC & Visa.

SPARTAN TOOL SUPPLY
1505 Alum Creek Dr., Columbus, 43207, 443-7607

Automotive, personal, industrial power and hand tools are offered at savings of 15-60% off suggested retail prices. There are over 10,000 different items in stock from 70 different companies. The merchandise consists of overstocks, liquidations and direct purchases of brands by AEG, Milwaukee, Black and Decker, Ingersoll-Rand, Bosch and Chicago Pneumatic. Gives exchanges only. M-F 7:30AM-6PM, Sat 8:30AM-2PM. Accepts checks, MC, Visa & Discover.

STOUT SALES
6320 E. Main St., Reynoldsburg, 43068, 866-4933

Over 20 styles of kitchen and bath cabinets are available from one of the largest wholesale cabinet distributors in Ohio. You'll find raised panel, cathedral and flat panel doors, Eurostyle laminates as well as solid wood, at savings of 40-50% below the manufacturer's suggested retail price. This business also has custom countertops, whirlpool tubs and wood flooring at similar savings. The *Handyman's Room* contains discontinued, scratch and dent and slightly discolored items at 50-80% off regular retail prices. M, Tu, Th and F 8-5; W 8-8; Sat 9-1. Accepts checks, MC & Visa.

URBAN HOMESTEADING PROGRAM
C/O City of Columbus, Dept. of Human Services, 645-7336 or 645-8534

If you are willing to invest time, energy and money to rehabilitate a deteriorating home, you can enter this lottery in which winners pay only $1 to purchase a house. The program reduces the number of vacant eyesores in the community while providing individuals and families with the opportunity to purchase a residence. Many houses are located within inner city neighborhoods. In order to be eligible, applicants must be at least 18 years old, be a U.S. citizen or registered alien, not own another residential property and be able to repair or pay for repairs and improvements to the property. The total housing expenses must not exceed 28% off the applicant's gross monthly income. Once the lottery has been won, the person must move in within a year, bring the house up to code within 3 years, and must live in the home for at least 5 years. In 1992, the guidelines may be altered to be less stringent. Homesteaders may be eligible for low interest rehabilitation loans through the City of Columbus. Lotteries are held about twice per year and depend on property availability and federal funding. Call to be added to their mailing list.

ALSO SEE

Amos Indoor Flea Market, Black And Decker USA, Chores Program, Columbus Stone Center, Consumer Information Center, Darby Sales, Department Of Defense, Extravaganza, Franklin County Home Weatherization Service, Franklin County Sheriff's Department, Franklin County Soil And Water Conservation District, Garage Sales, General Merchandise Sales, Greater Columbus Antique Mall, Liquidations Now, Majestic Paint Outlet, Majestic Paint Stores, Mendelson's Electronics, 99 Cent Shops, Odd Lots, Only $1, Panel Town And More, Parson's Floor And Cabinet Warehouse, Residential Rehabilitation Assistance Program, Sam's Club, Schottenstein's, Self Help Program, Service Merchandise, Vaughn Paint And Wallcoverings and Warehouse Club

LIGHTING

CITY LIGHTING
790 Bethel Rd., Columbus, 43214, 451-1220

Over 400 floor, table and hanging lamps made from brass, porcelain and blown glass, are available at savings of 30-70% off the manufacturers' suggested list price. Lamp tables are discounted 20-60%. There is a select group of lamps available at a "buy one, get one free" special at all times. Distinctive cocktail and end tables, made from quality woods and wood veneers, are offered at savings of 30-40% off. Graber and Superior brands of blinds are discounted 10-50%. Special orders are sold at greater savings because the business does not have to inventory these. This small store has a large, diverse inventory of quality merchandise worth investigating. Gives refunds. M-F 12-8, Sat 10-6, Sun 12-5. Accepts checks, MC, Visa & Discover.

CLASSIC LIGHTING COMPANY
6011 Columbus Pike (Rte. 23), Delaware, 43015, 548-5689

Save 40-60% off manufacturers' list prices on lamps and fans for the entire home. The top grade, first quality merchandise includes such brands as Quoizel and Wilshire. Gives exchanges. M, W and F 10-6, Tu and Th 10-8, Sat 10-4. Accepts checks, MC, Visa & Discover.

DAN'S FAN CITY
1170 Kenny Ctr., Columbus, 43220, 459-1146
4537 E. Main St., Columbus, 43213, 235-0801

Ceiling fans are availableat savings of 20-60% off manufacturers' list prices.   You can expect to pay approximately $29-$165 for comparable fans which retail for $70-$230. This company, which operates over 100 stores, manufactures the Gold Coast brand, which is sold directly through their stores.   They also carry such brands as Emerson and Hunter. Store warranties vary from 5 years to a lifetime on parts and labor.   Gives exchanges.   M-F 10-9, Sat 10-7.   Accepts checks, MC & Visa.

ELGEE LIGHTING
1030 W. 3 Ave., Columbus, 43212, 294-6261
6530 Riverside Dr., Dublin, 43017, 766-0551
440 S. Hamilton Rd., Columbus, 43213, 866-0123
1070 W. 3 Ave., Columbus, 43212, 294-6261

Quality lighting consisting of discontinued merchandise and first quality floor, table and ceiling lamps, is available at savings of 25-50% off manufacturers' suggested retail prices. Special orders and electrical supplies are available at similar savings.   You'll find brass, stained glass, novelty as well as crystal lighting.   Mark your calendars for their annual, *Off The Wall, Ceiling, Floor And Table Lamp Sale* in mid December, where you can save 40% off in-stock items at their 1070 West 3rd Avenue and Riverside Drive lighting centers. The other two sites sell only electrical supplies.   Returns are handled on an individual basis.   Hours vary per store.   Accepts checks, MC, Visa & Discover.

HOME LIGHTING
6055 Cleveland Ave., Columbus, 43231, 794-0777

Lamps, mirrors, track lights, ceiling fans and chandeliers, from more than 200 manufacturers, are sold at 20-50% off regular retail prices.   Mark your calendar for their annual, four day post Christmas sale at the end of December, when savings are 50% off the manufacturers' list price on every light in the store.   Gives exchanges.   M,F and Sat 10-6, Tu,W and Th 10-9, Sun 12-5.   Accepts checks, MC, Visa & Discover.

STAINED GLASS DESIGNS
890-5156 (Jan), 889-7640 (Erin)

Beautiful stained glass lamps, window panels, mirrors, jewelry boxes and specialty items are available from two talented artists, Jan Maloney and Erin Strausbaugh.   They frequently exhibit at area craft shows and will also do custom work.   Their original designs such as carrousel horses, wizards and florals, are eyecatching accents to any home decor. You will be delighted by the prompt, courteous service and the quality of their craftsmanship.   While a specific percentage of savings cannot be quoted, you will find excellent values.   By appointment only.   Accepts checks, MC & Visa.

ALSO SEE

Belair's Fine Furniture, Builder's Square, Ci Bon, Cort Furniture Rental And Clearance Center, Experienced Possessions, Extravaganza, Furniture Liquidations

Center, Glick's Outlet, Greater Columbus Antique Mall, Groll's Fine Furniture, Homeway Furniture, Liberty Street Interiors, Model Home Furniture and Accessories Sale, J.C. Penney Furniture Warehouse Outlet, J.C. Penney Portfolio, Schottenstein's, Service Merchandise , Sofa Express Outlet and Waterford Hall

FLOORING

A JACK FLOORING OUTLET
877 E. 11 Ave., Columbus, 43211, 299-5445

Countertops, ceramic tiles as well as vinyl and wood flooring are available at savings of about 10-20% at this wholesale distributor. M-F 7:30-4:30. Accepts checks and cash only.

BUDGET CARPET WAREHOUSE
4356 Indianola Ave., Columbus, 43214, 262-0765

Buyouts and short rolls of carpeting, vinyl and hardwood flooring are available at savings of about 25% off regular retail prices. Padding and carpet supplies can be purchased for those who wish to install the flooring themselves. Delivery, installation and binding are available. M-Th 10-5, F and Sat 10-3. Accepts checks, MC& Visa.

CARPET JUNKYARD
318 S. Glenwood Ave., Columbus, 43223, 469-9402

Full rolls, mill seconds, short rolls, irregulars, remnants, discontinued styles, used, new and scraps are found at this business. Savings are 40-50% off regular retail prices. All sales are final. M-Sat 10-6. Accepts checks, MC & Visa.

COLOR TILE
2367 S. Hamilton Rd., Columbus, 43232, 888-0270
2524 Morse Rd., Columbus, 43231, 475-5150
4152 W. Broad St., Columbus, 43228, 276-0128
3710 S. High St., Columbus, 43207, 491-0436
789 Hebron Rd., Heath, 43056, 522-8551

This national chain sells floor, countertop and wall tiles in ceramic, wood and marble in addition to linoleum and carpeting by such brands as Armstrong, Tarkett, and Weardated. You can enjoy a 25% discount for life on all products bought in the store for the maintenance of your purchase. In-stock and special order wallcoverings are discounted 20-50%. Blinds are discounted 30-50%. Open a charge account and you will receive a free gift valued at up to $10, such as your choice of a vinyl floor cleaner, grout tile cleaner or a carpet cleaning solution. The stores feature free rentals of how-to videos on flooring installation and wallpaper hanging. A small, refundable deposit is required. The Color Tile Goof Proof Guarantee offers a full replacement of materials to correct a problem which you may have caused during installation of wall or floor coverings. The Color Tile Ultimate Guarantee is an unusual opportunity to save on your carpeting purchases for life. Once you buy carpeting in any of their stores from the Color Carpet Emerald or Diamond Collections, if you are ever (as in FOREVER) dissatisfied with the quality, performance or even color of carpeting, you will be entitled to a credit of up to 50% of your original purchase price towards the purchase of new carpeting. This guarantee also applies to any changes in your room's color scheme and decor. Even if you move and leave the carpet behind, Color Tile will give you a credit towards your next carpeting purchase. The percentage varies from 10-50% depending on how long you own the carpeting. M-F 8AM-9PM, Sat 8-5, Sun 11-5. Accepts checks, MC Visa, AmExp & Discover.

DALTON MILLS CARPET OUTLET
1320 S.R. 37 W., Delaware, 43015, 1-369-6455

Carpet and vinyl flooring for commercial and residential use is available at this family owned business. All of the merchandise is first quality with brands such as Salem, Galaxy, Congoleum, Tarkett and others. M-F 9-5:30, Sat 10-3. Accepts checks, MC & Visa.

DESIGN MATERIALS OF OHIO
43 W. Vine St., Columbus, 43215, 224-8453

Shop where the contractors shop! This direct importer of high quality marble and ceramic tiles sells Mexican Tile, Jasba Mosaics, Crossville, IAC Laufen and other brands at savings of 40-60% off regular retail prices. You will find handpainted tiles, unusual designs as well as basic tiles. A selection of hardwood flooring is available at similar savings. A free decorating service is also available. If you will be installing the tiles or flooring yourself, you can borrow their tools, videos and how-to manuals at no cost. Occasionally, the business offers free seminars. If you are redecorating or building a new home and want to make a strong decorating statement, this is the place to shop. Save some time so you can stop at the North Market and the Columbus Convention Center, both of which are within two blocks. M-F 7:30-4:30, Sat 9-1, and by appointment. Accepts checks, MC & Visa.

DIAL ONE, MARCS CARPET SERVICE
1223 1/2 Cleveland Ave., Columbus, 43201, 299-2168

First quality carpeting mill remnants, special purchases, short rolls, overstocks, irregulars and some special order seconds, are available at savings of 30-35% off typical retail prices. Please note that these seconds are "off color" being a different color than the manufacturers' sample, which will not affect its wearability. Vinyl flooring and tiles are available at savings of 20-25% off regular retail prices. Popular brands such as Armstrong, Tarkett, Salem, Cabincraft, Congoleum and Mannington are available. M-F 9-5, Sat 9-12. Accepts checks, MC & Visa.

DIRECT CARPET MILLS OUTLET
4029 Morse Rd., Columbus, 43219, 471-1269
5181 N. High St., Columbus, 43214, 848-6560
401 S. Hamilton Rd., Columbus, 43213, 235-0800

Volume buying enables these locally owned stores to buy flooring directly from the mill, thereby avoiding the middleman. The values are passed on to you so you can save 20-30% off regular retail prices. The store carries first quality Monsanto, Stainmaster, Anso and other carpet brands and also sells wood flooring and tiles. Financing available. M-Th 10-8, F 10-5, Sat 10-8, Sun 12-6. Accepts checks, Mc, Visa & Discover.

DURATILE TILES AND DISTRIBUTING
3100 Cleveland Ave., Columbus, 43224, 261-0602

Approximately one half of the inventory is discounted 5-30% and includes first quality, overstocks, remnants and seconds in countertops, vinyl flooring and ceramic wall coverings. Brands offered include Kentile, Sunglow, Tarkett, Roppe and Cambridge. This family owned and operated business has been in existence since 1946. M-F 8-6, Sat 11-3. Accepts checks, MC & Visa.

FLOOR COVERINGS INTERNATIONAL
5270 Linworth Rd., Worthington, 43235, 538-9100

Unique shop at home carpet service saves you at least 20% off quality carpeting and padding. The distinctive carpet showroom on wheels, features a complete line of first quality, name brand carpeting from DuPont Stainmaster, Monsanto, and others. A definite plus to this service is the fact that you can match carpeting to your decor in its natural surroundings. The business is part of a franchise which buys mill direct and avoids the middle man's markup. The lack of overhead costs as a result of not having a storefront, also contributes to this business's ability to keep its prices low. A variety of financing plans are available as is quality installation. M-Sat 9-9. Accepts checks, MC & Visa.

MR. B'S ADD- A- BUCK FLOOR STORE
4121 E. Main St., Columbus, 43213, 231-0040

Low overhead allows this flooring business to save you about 20% off manufacturers' list prices on a full line of carpet, vinyl flooring and ceramic tiles. Some of the quality brands represented include World Carpet, Armstrong and Mannington. M-Th 1-7, F 1-5:30, Sat 10-2. Accepts checks, MC & Visa.

OHIO REMCON ,INC.
888 W. Goodale, Columbus, 43215, 224-0489

Residential and commercial carpet, tile, linoleum, ceramic and parquet flooring are available at savings of 25% off regular retail from this wholesale builder's carpet source. Now in its 20th year, this business stocks merchandise from 20 different mills including Philadelphia, Cabincraft, Armstrong-Salem, Mohawk Horizon, Galaxy and others. M-F 9-5, Sat 9-1. Accepts checks, MC & Visa.

PARSONS FLOOR & CABINET COMPANY WAREHOUSE OUTLET
1641 Harmon Avenue, Columbus, 43223, 445-7181

You can shop where the builders shop at great savings. You will find discontinued, closeout and roll ends of carpet, countertops, surplus wood cabinets and more, some of which are manufactured on premises. Savings are 30-35% off regular retail prices. Don't miss the huge spring and fall clearances from March through May and September through October, where savings are up to 70% off regular retail prices. Checkout the bargain bin of surplus, salvage and scratch and dent products by Armstrong, Tarkett and Congoleum flooring as well as cabinets and countertops at savings of 50-70% off regular retail prices. Flooring installation is extra. Parsons was proud to have their cabinets displayed in the 1991 Parade of Homes. M and Th 8:30-8, Tu, W and F 8:30-5:30, Sat 9-5. Accepts checks, MC & Visa.

POOR OLD PEDDLERS CARPET BARN
6960 Refugee Rd., Canal Winchester, 43110, 837-8594

Save 40-60% off first quality carpet by Salem, World, Shaw Industries and Horizon. Oriental rugs, remnants as well as commercial and residential carpeting are available in a wide range of colors and patterns. The prices are low because the store has personal connections to a Dalton, Georgia carpet mill. M-Sat 9-6, Sun by appointment. Accepts checks, MC & Visa.

R.A.P. FLOORING DISTRIBUTORS
2544 Billingsley Rd., Columbus, 43235, 761-3766

Purchase carpet and area rugs at savings of 20-40% below wholesale prices at this wholesale distributor. The first quality goods include closeouts and overruns, of plushes, textures and berbers by Stainmaster, Anso 5, Ultron, Wear Dated and others. Imported area rugs from Mainland China and Bangladesh include Orientals, dhurries and other types. Carpeting is available for home, office or commercial use. The store has an annual spring sample sale of one of a kind merchandise and discontinued styles at greater savings. The business if locally owned and operated by Rebecca Ann Palmer. Open by appointment only. Accepts checks and cash only.

RAINBOW FLOORS-THE REMNANT ROOM
5571 Westerville Rd., Westerville, 43081, 882-2430

Rolls and remnants of vinyl flooring and carpets are available at savings of 20-60%.off regular retail prices. This store carries such brands as Armstrong, Cabincraft, Mannington, Cornett, Galaxy and Salem. The inventory consists of first quality, remnants, mill ends and overstocks. 90 days same as cash financing is available to qualified buyers. M-Th 10-7, F 10-5, Sat 10-4. Accepts checks, MC, Visa & Discover

RITE RUG CARPET OUTLET
45 Great Southern Blvd., Columbus, 43207, 261-6060

This site houses the clearance outlet for the area Rite Rug showrooms and also sells full price merchandise. You'll find bargains on area rugs including Orientals, remnants, discontinued and special purchases in carpeting at savings of 30-50% off their regular low prices. Gives exchanges. M-Sat 10-9, Sun 12-5. Accepts checks, MC & Visa.

ALSO SEE

Builder's Square, Camp And Williams, Glick's Outlet, Greystone Design, Lazarus Final Countdown, McSwain Carpet Showdown, Panel Town And More, Stout Sales and Tren Furniture Galleries

MUSICAL INSTRUMENTS/ RECORDS, TAPES & CDs

MUSICAL INSTRUMENTS

ARTS MIDWEST JAZZ LETTER
528 Hennepin Ave., Suite 310, Minneapolis, Minnesota, 55403
A free, bi-monthly jazz letter is available upon written request. It contains stories on topics which affect the development and continuation of jazz in the Midwest, in addition to reviews of recordings by regional artists and highlights of individual achievements. The jazz calendar provides a listing of jazz happenings in clubs, lectures and city jazz hotlines within the Midwest.

DURTHALER
1967 Lockbourne Rd., Columbus, 43207, 443-6867

The largest selection of pre-owned organs in Central Ohio is available at this business at savings of 30-50% off "if new" prices. Similar savings are available on pre-owned pianos and player pianos. M-Sat 10-6. Accepts checks, MC & Visa.

KAWAI PIANO AND ORGAN CENTER
4944 N. High St., Columbus, 43214, 888-5444

An extensive selection of all types of pianos and organs, as well as new buyouts of bankrupt stock, manufacturers closeouts, other special purchases and trade-ins are available at savings of 20-40%. You'll find synthesizers, modules, monitors, digital pianos and other items. Some of the stock is not discounted. Gives exchanges. M-F 10-8, Sat 10-6, Sun 12-5. Accepts checks, MC & Visa.

MORSE ROAD MUSIC
2749 Morse Rd., Columbus, 43231, 475-6589

This family owned store has been in business for over 37 years. It is currently housed in a small garage, but don't be discouraged by its unpretentious appearance. The store sells used wind, percussion, brass and string instruments at about 50% off the cost of new instruments. They repair all instruments on premises, thereby avoiding the middleman, and saving you about 25-40%. The store also does not have a minimum charge on repairs, unlike most music stores. A complete clarinet overhaul would cost $90 here, but could be about $120 elsewhere. According to the owner, the business is responsible for repairing about 80% of the instruments used by the City of Columbus Public Schools. The store also repairs government band instruments form across the United States. You can also purchase supplies such as reeds, for about 20-40% lower than elsewhere. Gives exchanges. M-Th 12-9, F 12-6, Sat 9-4:30. Accepts checks and cash only.

UNCLE SAM'S PAWN SHOP
225 E. Main St., Columbus, 43215, 221-3711

An extensive selection of used and antique fine jewelry, watches, cameras, stereos, televisions, musical instruments, luggage, guns, Nintendo and Sega games as well as radios can be found at savings of about 20-40% off "if new" prices. You'll find such sought after brands as Pentax, Minolta, Seiko, Sony, Louis Vuitton and others. Much of the jewelry did not appear to have as much of a savings as the other items in the store, but you'll find some very unusual pieces not found in typical jewelry stores. Be sure to browse through all of their rooms. Offers 30 day warranties on mechanical items and cameras. All other sales are final. M-Sat 9-5:30. Accepts checks, MC & Visa.

USED PIANO WAREHOUSE
480 D East Wilson Bridge Rd., Worthington, 43085, 888-3441

A huge selection of quality new and used pianos is available. The used instruments are reconditioned before being sold and are priced at about 50% less than a comparable new piano. Provides a 3 year warranty on parts and a 1 year warranty on labor. Provides layaway. M-Th 12-8, F 10-4, Sat 10-2. Accepts checks, MC & Visa.

RECORDS/TAPES AND CDs

CAMELOT
6313 Sawmill Rd., Dublin Sawmill Ctr., Dublin, 43017,792-3503
2355 S. Hamilton Rd., East Pt. Ctr., Columbus, 43232,575-2955
2753 Northland Plaza Dr., Columbus, 43231, 794-0992
4091 W. Broad St., Columbus, 43228, 274-6558

Camelot is another business which offers a frequent purchaser plan. Your free *Repeat Performance Card* will be punched in $10 increments whenever you make a purchase. Depending on the number of punches you accumulate, you can redeem your card for a particular gift or cash such as a stereo, a tee shirt, Laser Disc player and more. Some gifts may be obtained in the store, while others will be mailed to your home. Certain rules and restrictions apply.   100% satisfaction guarantee allows exchanges on opened record/cassette and CD packages and refunds on unopened packages. M-Th 10-9, F and Sat 10-10, Sun 10-6. Accepts checks, MC, Visa & Discover.

PAT'S RECORDS, CDs AND TAPES
31 N. Sandusky St., Delaware, 43015, 1-363-3198

A full line of CDs, records and cassettes by major recording artists, is sold at about $2-$4 lower than most other stores, according to the owner. Special orders are available at similar savings. The store is a TicketMaster outlet and also stocks a full line of Marvel and DC comics at regular retail prices. Gives exchanges. M-F 10-8, Sat 10-6, Sun 12-5. Accepts checks, MC, Visa & Discover.

RECORD AND TAPE OUTLET
791 Bethel Rd.,Olentangy Plaza, Columbus, 43214, 451-5174
1502 Alum Creek Dr., Columbus, 43209, 252-1098
4366 Indianola Ave., Columbus, 43214, 262-0400
4345 E. Broad St., Columbus, 43213, 231-0900
2174 W. 4 St., Mansfield, 44906, (419) 747-3355

Low overhead and big volume enable these stores to offer 20-30% savings off manufacturer's suggested list prices on records and tapes from major artists and labels. The stores carry a full range of current music types including a small selection of children's music. Special orders are available at similar savings. Gives exchanges only. Accepts checks, MC & Visa.

SINGING DOG
1630 N. High St., Columbus, 43201, 299-1490

Buy or sell used records, cassettes and compact discs at this store. Purchases are at a savings of 20-50% off the new price. Cassettes and records sell for 99 cents-$4.99 each and CDs sell for $4.99-$9.99. You'll find an assortment of contemporary music including jazz, rock, soul and folk. Gives refunds. M-Sat 11-9, Sun 12-7. Accepts checks, MC & Visa.

USED KIDS RECORDS
1992 N. High St., Columbus, 43201, 294-3833

A large selection of used records, CDs and cassettes are sold here at 50 cents and up which is a savings of 50-90% off the "if new" price. New merchandise is also discounted about 30-50%. From the Stooges to George Jones, you'll find it here. The stock changes frequently. The store's name is actually a misnomer; it does not sell children's records. All sales are final. M-Sat 10-8, Sun 12-6. Accepts checks, MC & Visa.

WAVES (FORMERLY NATIONAL RECORD MART)

1661 W. Lane Ave., Columbus, 43221, 488-4430
2597 S. Hamilton Rd., Columbus, 43232, 861-4440
109 Westerville Mall, Westerville, 43081, 891-6149

Each month, you'll find several records, cassettes and CDs which are being sold through a no risk music guarantee as a way for the record companies to promote unknown and new recording artists. You will be entitled to a money back guarantee on any used/opened merchandise on the current month's list if you are not satisfied for any reason. This is a wonderful way to sample new music and have return privileges if it doesn't suit your taste. M-Sat 10-9, Sun 12-5. Accepts checks, MC, Visa, AmExp & Discover.

ALSO SEE

Book Warehouse, Extravaganza, Half Price Book Store, Hausfrau Haven, Outreach Christian Books And Records, Record Convention and Worthington Public Library

OFFICE SUPPLIES & EQUIPMENT/ STATIONERY

OFFICE SUPPLIES & EQUIPMENT

ARVEY PAPER AND SUPPLIES
431 E. Livingston Ave., Columbus, 43215, 221-0153

Volume buying for 50 stores in the U.S., allows this business to make purchases at far below typical wholesale prices. This translates into savings of 5-70% off list price on a full line of office, school and graphic arts supplies. The store also sells papers in all weights and colors at savings of about 20-30% off typical retail prices. Gives refunds. M-F 8-5:30, Sat 9-1. Accepts checks, MC & Visa.

DUBLIN BUSINESS SERVICES
63 Corbins Mill Dr., Dublin, 43017, 766-2400

The best price in town for 8 1/2" x 11" color copies is at this business. A Canon Laser copier is used to print quality copies at only $1 apiece with no minimum order required. As the copies are usually $2-$2.50 each at other printing stores in town, you are saving at least 50% . M-Sat 10-5. Accepts checks, MC & Visa

NATIONAL OFFICE WAREHOUSE
500 W. Broad St., Columbus, 43215, 228-2233
637 E. Dublin Granville Rd., Columbus, 43229, 888-4177

A full line of office supplies is available at savings of 15-60% off regular retail prices. A large area at the back of the West Broad Street location, offers factory seconds, floor models and trade-ins of office furniture at savings of about 30-70%. Gives refunds on office supplies. Hours vary between stores. Accepts checks, MC & Visa.

OFFICE AMERICA
5685 Emporium Square, Columbus Sq. Shopping Ctr., Columbus, 43231, 794-9977
6635 Dublin Center Dr., Dublin Village Ctr., Dublin, 43017, 793-1950
2736 Brice Rd., Reynoldsburg, 43068, 863-6633

Save 10-70% off their full line of nationally recognized brands of office supplies in addition to desks, chairs, computers, typewriters, personal stationery, filing cabinets, answering machines, telephones, luggage, small appliances for office use, leather briefcases and related merchandise. Gift items such as decorative frames and pen sets, are similarly discounted, as are art and drafting supplies for adults and children. Business related books are discounted 25% off the cover price. There is no cost to sign up for their mailing list to become an *Edge Card* member. Members pay posted prices and nonmembers pay 5% above posted prices. Each month, about 30-40 items are specially priced at 10-30% below the store's usual discounted price. This extra savings is not available to the general public. Also, as an *Edge Card* member, you will receive about 4 mailings during the year which describe the company's products, sale items as well as a special coupon section for extra in-store savings available to *Edge Card* members only. The stores offer a variety of printing, copying and binding services at low, low prices. Photocopies on 8 1/2" x 11" white paper are 3 cents regardless of the quantity. Faxes cost $1.95 per page to send and 95 cents per page to receive. Gives refunds. M-F 8AM-9PM, Sat 9-6, Sun 12-5. Accepts checks, MC, Visa & Discover.

PEERLESS OFFICE SUPPLY
3465 Refugee Rd., Columbus, 43232, 239-9009

Business and commercial accounts can save 20-70% off regular retail prices on a full line of office supplies. Orders must be placed over the phone or by Fax and will be filled within 24 hours. Offers free delivery for orders over $20. M-F 9-5. Accepts checks, MC & Visa.

STAPLES
2800A S. Hamilton Rd., Columbus, 43232, 575-2801
1664 Dublin-Granville Rd., Columbus, 43229, 890-6619
4505 Kenny Rd., Columbus, 43220, 442-5554 or 442-5585

This full service store features an extensive selection of office supplies, office furniture and equipment, related books, lighting, luggage and portfolios. at savings of 30-70%. You'll also find similar savings on a limited selection of art supplies for adults and kids as well as gold jewelry. Membership is free and is open to the general public. Non-members pay 5% above the posted prices. The stores also feature in-house business centers which offer value pricing on photocopying, binding, fax transmission and receipt ($3 for the first page and $1 for each additional) and other printing related needs. The stores also feature an extended service program option will allows you to purchase an extra warranty for office equipment.Gives refunds. M-F 7AM-9PM, Sat 9-6, Sun 12-6. Accepts checks, MC, Visa & Staples charges.

TORONTO BUSINESS EQUIPMENT
1159 W. Broad St., Columbus, 43222, 272-5500

New IBM, Hewlett Packard, Casio and Royal typewriters, computers and calculators are discounted about 25%, and come with full manufacturer's warranties. Used items are sold at about 75% less than if they were new. The warranty will be in effect for 30 days. Toronto Business Equipment has been in business for over 30 years. Return policy varies with the item purchased. M-F 8-5. Accepts checks, MC & Visa.

ALSO SEE

Aaron Sells Furniture, Business Equipment Electronics, Columbus Metropolitan Library, Columbus Police Property Auction, Computer Success, Continental Office Furniture Warehouse Outlet, Cort Furniture Rental Resale Center, Darby Sales, Department of Defense, Desk And File, Drug World, Globe Furniture Rental, Hyperstore, Mendelson's Electronics, Odd Lots, Paper Factory, Phar Mor, Pine Factory, Rosenfeld Liquidators, Sam's Club and Sugarman Liquidators

STATIONERY

K.G. MARXX PAPER PARTY OUTLETS
1466 Bethel Rd., Columbus, 43220, 451-1806
3662 Karl Rd., Columbus, 43224, 262-6520
882 S. Hamilton Rd., Columbus, 43213, 863-2324
4205 Shoppers La., Westland Mall, Columbus, 43228, 276-8200
2611 Northland Plaza Dr., Columbus, 43231, 794-0444
6661 Dublin Village Ctr. Dr., Dublin, 43017, 793-1803

An extensive selection of paper and party goods is available at typical retail prices. However, you can save about 20-25% on case lot purchases for your next party. Save 25% at all times, on a complete line of custom wedding and special occasion invitations. Gives refunds. Accepts checks, MC & Visa.

PAPER FACTORY
Madison Commons Factory Direct Mall, W. Jefferson. Scheduled to open April 1992.

An extensive selection of gift wrap and bows, table coverings, party supplies and table decorations, stationery and some paper office supplies are available at savings of 30-60% off regular retail prices. You'll also find some children's coloring/activity books, puzzles and games at similar savings. This business is an outlet for the Drawing Board. The stock consists of first quality, seconds, irregulars and past season merchandise. You'll remember this business from its former location in Columbus' at the New Market Mall. Gives refunds. M-Sat 10-9, Sun 12-5. Accepts checks, MC & Visa.

TULLER PRINTING AND GRAPHICS
5828 Sawmill Rd., Dublin, 43017, 889-5959

Save 20% off an extensive line of custom order invitations and special occasion cards from several companies. Note pads in assorted sizes and paper stocks are priced at 20 cents each as a result of being remainders from custom printing jobs. .M-F 8-5.

WHITE'S DISTRIBUTING
1530 S. High St., Columbus, 43207, 444-3716

Paper party goods, supplies, seasonal and holiday decorations as well as inexpensive children's and adults' novelty items are available at savings of 10-50%, depending on the quantity you purchase. Consider this source when planning a party, carnival or fundraiser. Gives refunds. M-Sat 9-4. Accepts checks and cash only.

ALSO SEE

All For One, Arvey Paper, Crazy Ed's Glassware Outlet, Cub Foods, Drug Emporium, Meijer's, Odd Lots, 99 Cent Shops, Phar Mor,and Yankee Trader

---

The *Bargain Hunting Zip Code Directory* fits into the glove compartment of your car and provides you with a geographic listing of the businesses in this book.   See order form at the back of the index.

PETS

THE BARKING LOT
1872 Tamarack Circle S., Columbus, 43229, 431-2090

Here you will find top of the line premium pet foods and supplies which are not available in grocery stores. Brands offered include Four Paws, Iams, Doskocil and others at savings of 10-40% off in-stock and special order merchandise. Gives refunds. M-F 10-7, Sat 10-6, Sun 12-5. Accepts checks, MC & Visa.

CAPITAL AREA HUMANE SOCIETY
2770 Groveport Rd., Columbus, 43207, 497-2181

Kittens, cats, hamsters, mice, dogs, puppies and gerbils are available for adoption at this animal shelter. The fee is $69.99 for dogs/puppies and $54.99 for cats/kittens. First shots, excluding rabies, are included in the cost for dogs and cats. The animal's first worming, spaying/neutering and license are included where applicable. This shelter is a nonprofit organization. W 11-7, Th-Sun 12-5. Accepts checks, MC & Visa. Dogs and cats from the Humane Society are also available at similar prices at Animal Fair, a privately owned pet shop at 811 Bethel Road in the Olentangy Plaza Shopping Center. The store can be contacted at 459-0516.

CAT WELFARE
736 Wetmore Rd., Columbus, 43224, 268-6096

This shelter houses about 200 cats of all breeds (mixed and pure bred), sizes and ages. Your $30 fee includes the cost of spaying or neutering, the animal's first shots, worming and if appropriate, a rabies shot. Inquire about their low cost spay and neutering clinic for cats which were not purchased through this organization. M-Sun 10-3:30. Accepts checks and cash only.

CRITTER COUNTRY
2744 Festival Lane, Dublin, 43017, 766-2473

If you have squirrels, raccoons or other animals in your attic, you can rent a trap for $5 per day, up to a maximum of 7 days, for $35. Thereafter, you own the trap. By catching the critters on your own, as compared to spending $125-$250 through an animal control company, your savings will be substantial. However, you will have to set the trap and transport the animal to the country somewhere, so it won't return to its nest. This low cost, humane way of capturing the intruders, is an excellent way to rid your nest of their nest. The store also stocks a large variety of wild bird feeders, seeds, books, nature gifts and related items at regular retail prices. Backyard habitat planning services are also available. Gives exchanges. M-F 10-6, Sat 12-5. Accepts checks, MC & Visa.

DELAWARE COUNTY HUMANE SOCIETY
4920 State Rte. 37 E., Delaware, 43015, 548-7387

Many pets are available for adoption from this animal shelter. You'll find pedigrees as well as mixed breeds. Puppies or full grown dogs cost $45, kittens or full grown cats are $35. The fee includes spaying/neutering, the animal's first shots and worming. A low cost spaying/neutering clinic for animals which were not obtained at this shelter, is available at a cost of $30 for cats and $35 for dogs. All sales are final. M-F 9-4, Sat 1-4. Accepts checks and cash only.

GERMAN VILLAGE AQUARIUM
188 E. Whittier St., Columbus, 43206, 445-6000

This little German Village shop has a full line of fresh and saltwater fish and accessories at savings of 25-30%. M-Sat 11-7, Sun 12-6. Accepts checks and cash only.

JACK'S AQUARIUM AND PETS
6641 Dublin Ctr. Dr., Dublin, 43017, 764-8770
2631 Northland Plaza Dr., Columbus, 43231, 794-0184
6404 Tussing Rd., Consumer Sq. E., Reynoldsburg, 43068, 863-0290
3634 Soldano Blvd., Consumer Sq. W., Columbus, 43228, 278-2255

By joining the *Fish Of The Month Club* for a $1 annual fee, you will be entitled to 1 free fish per month from a choice of several, savings on purchases of additional fish from this pre-selected group, as well as a $5 credit toward the purchase of fish or live plants. Certain rules apply towards earning this credit. Check the store for details. *Jack's* prices are about 15-20% lower than in full price stores, on their entire inventory of fresh and saltwater fish, tanks and supplies, and about 10% lower on their cat and dog food. The frequent purchaser plan, called the *Baker's Dozen Club,* allows you to get your 13th bag of dog or cat food free. Ask for details. Fish are guaranteed for 24 hours with full replacement. Within 6 days of purchase, fish will be replaced for half the selling price. Gives refunds. M-Sat 10-9, Sun 12-5. Accepts checks, MC & Visa.

PET ADOPTION SERVICE
POB 06212, Columbus, 43206, 444-0076

This privately owned referral service matches up families who, for a variety of reasons, need to find a new home for their pets, with people who want to adopt a pet. Most of the animals who need homes are pedigree or mixed breed dogs, in addition to cats, and occasionally birds and rabbits. Among the many reasons people can no longer keep their pets and ultimately turn to this service are: allergies, divorce, a move to a retirement community, a new baby in the home, job related situations or a death in the family. A one time, $5 charge is assessed to enter your pet into the adoption program. This is less than the cost of running an ad in your local newspaper. The adopting family/individual is charged a $15-$30 fee when they adopt a cat or a $25-$50 fee to adopt a dog. Fees may vary depending on special circumstances. Adoptive families are not always met by the referral service. A new opportunity has been developed which is a foster care program where, for $100 per month, a temporary home is found for your pet. This is ideal when planning a trip and enables the animal to be in a more personal environment than a kennel.. Kennel fees are about $300 per month. Shorter foster care times can also be arranged. While most of the adoptions have taken place within Franklin county, the *Pet Adoption Service* has recently begun to assist people throughout Ohio.

PET BUTLER
235-0104

I was told by the owner, that this is the only service in Franklin county which will come to your home to remove animal droppings in your yard. At a cost of only $5 per visit, this is an inexpensive way to clean up the yard and provide yourself with the time for more enjoyable pursuits. If your yard has not been cleared in a long time, there is likely to be a slightly higher fee for the initial visit. You can sign up for as many visits as you like. as there's no minimum number of visits required. Call anytime for an appointment.

PET FOOD SUPERMARKET
2899 Morse Rd., Columbus, 43231, 475-3333
705 Ann St., Columbus, 43206, 443-4685
5875 Chantry Dr., Columbus, 43232, 575-2222

This full service pet food and supplies company sells premium brands at savings of 10-30%, most of which are not readily available in grocery store chains. Pet food, animal sweaters, bird feeders, bird seed, pet toys, cages, books, aquariums and supplies line the shelves. You'll find products by IAMS, Bil Jac, Mighty Dog, Kal Kan, Cat's Pride, Purina and other companies. Bring your pets and let them browse through the store, sample the products and choose their favorites. Gives refunds. M-F 9-9, Sat 10-6, Sun 12-5. Accepts checks, MC, Visa & AmExp.

PETLAND
2568 S. Hamilton Rd., Columbus, 43232, 866-6661
129 Westerville Mall, Westerville, 43081, 882-1001
Graceland Blvd., Columbus, 43214, 848-6206
4626 W. Broad St., Columbus, 43228, 878-2583
4729 Reed Rd., Columbus, 43220, 451-0658
Town And Country Shpng. Ctr., Columbus, 43213, 235-2205

Every 3 months, the stores offer a buy 1 fish, get 1 free sale. The annual *Cabin Fever Sale* is held in February and features 30% off most pet accessories in the store which includes supplies for dogs, cats, fish, birds, snakes and even rats. Adjacent to the Hamilton Rd. store is *Vet 1*, also owned by *Petland*, which features a free first visit with a veterinarian who will check your pet. Subsequent visits are $18 and do not include the cost of shots or other needed services. Membership in *Club Pet* is $10 annually and provides you with a 10% discount on all *Petland* brand products, 10% off all fresh or saltwater fish, savings of up to 50% on select *Club Pet* fish specials every 2 weeks, 10% off all self service bid seeds, free bird wing clipping, a free subscription to a pet magazine published several times per year and other specials. The stores will match any competitor's price on advertised pet accessories, supplies or food. M-Sat 10-9, Sun 11-6. Accepts MC, Visa & Discover.

WHITE PARROT PET CENTER
1914 Brice Rd., Reynoldsburg, 43068, 868-8320

For only $4 per year, you an join the fish club and enjoy such benefits as 10% off any non-sale pets and supplies every Saturday and 20% off fish food once per month. Additional benefits include your choice of one fish per month for 50% off the selling price or a free staff selected fish once per month. You may enjoy any or all of these benefits at your option. M-Sat 10-9, Sun 12-6. Accepts checks, MC & Visa.

ALSO SEE

Ameritech Pages Plus, Consumer Information Center and Franklin County Soil And Water Conservation District,

Do you want to learn about new bargain sources? Then subscribe to the quarterly *Bargain Hunting In Columbus Newsletter*. See order form at the back of this book.

SENIORS/FREQUENT PURCHASER PROGRAMS/ BIRTHDAY FREEBIES & VALUES

SENIORS: see index listings of

American Youth Hostels, Bearly Worn Clothes For Kids, Capital University, Charlie Endre's Saloon, China Express At Kroger's, Chores Program, Columbia Gas Of Ohio, Columbus Police Crime Prevention Unit, Columbus Square Bowling Palace, Denny's, ESP Fashions, Elephant Bar And Restaurant, Executive Tour Golfer's Club, Fiesta Hair And Tanning Salons, Fishing, Franklin County Metro Parks, Gahanna Lanes, Golden Age Passport, Golden Buckeye Card, Golden Lifestyles, Licking County Bicycle Club, Licking County Players, Little Theater Off Broadway, MCL Cafeterias, Nationwide Beauty Academy, Ohio Department of Aging, Olde Country Buffet, Omni Hotels, OSU Program 60, Other Side Coffee House, Pet Adoption Service, Ponderosa Steak House, Presidential Greetings Office, Quality Inns, Revco, Riverside AdvantAge, Sears, Senior Free Audit, Senior Mediation Service, Shoney's, Sneak Previews At Area First Run Theaters, Southwest Community Center Indoor Pool,.m Summer Tech, Super thrift, Thurber House, Uhlman's, Upper Arlington Older Adults Educational Network, VQ Originals, Warehouse Club and Worthy Citizen Card

FREQUENT PURCHASER PROGRAMS

Many stores or businesses offer a frequent customer card in which every time you make a purchase of a particular item or a certain dollar amount, a card is punched to record the transaction. You keep the card with you and present it when making your purchase. After you have reached a pre-determined amount, you are entitled to a bonus of some sort: a free menu item, a gift certificate in the store, cash etc. Another similar method which some stores have is that you save your receipts and when a certain dollar amount is accumulated, you will be entitled to one of the items mentioned above. See the alphabetical index at the back of this book under frequent purchaser cards, for a listing of those businesses which offer this opportunity.

see index listings for:

Another Glance, Camelot Music, Children's Palace, Crafts 'N Things, Electronics Boutique, Famous Footwear, Jack's Aquarium And Pets, Jolly Pirate Donuts, Just For Feet, Majestic Paint Store, Petland, Phar Mor, Readmor Bookstores and Wonder Hostess

BIRTHDAY FREEBIES & VALUES:

see index listings for:

Baskin Robbins, Bill Knapp's, Borders, Cinemark Movies 12, Denny's, Engine House No. 5, Ground Round, Ohio Department of Aging, Presidential Greetings Office, Sears Portrait Studio, Shoney's and WTTE Channel 28 Kids Club

---

The *Bargain Hunting Zip Code Directory* fits into the glove compartment of your car and provides you with a geographic listing of the businesses in this book. See order form at the back of the index.

SERVICES

AMERITECH PAGES PLUS, TOUCH 4 SERVICE
899-8000

The front section of the white pages of your phone book lists 125 hotlines which can provide you with a free, tape recorded ,message on topics including news and finance, weather reports in 24 U.S. cities, horoscopes, lottery, adult and children's entertainment, sports information, soap opera updates, travel tips, pet care, gardening, automotive and health tips. The hotlines are updated periodically to provide you with current information. You will need a touch tone phone to access the hotlines. 24 hours a day, 7 days a week.

ANGIE'S TAILOR
5244 Cleveland Ave., Columbus, 43231, 523-1665

Expert alterations are available at prices which are about 15-25% less than those at other businesses. The fees include $5 to hem slacks or skirts (regularly about $6.50 elsewhere), $10 to cuff a jacket sleeve (usually $12.50-$16 elsewhere) and $6 to replace a zipper (usually $8-$9 elsewhere). The business specializes in alterations and custom designing of formal and bridal wear. A made to order bridal gown will cost about $350. Leather alterations are also available at similar savings. W-F 12:30-7, Sat 10-7, Sun 12-5. Accepts checks and cash only.

ASK-A-NURSE PROGRAM
293-5678

The OSU Hospitals sponsor this free, 24 hour a day phone line, general health service, which is staffed by registered nurses. About 90,000 callers per year receive information on thousands of symptoms and 180 ailments. The medical information is accessed through a computer and is combined with the RN's knowledge to assist callers. The service cannot make a diagnosis.

ATTORNEY GENERAL'S OFFICE
Consumer Protection Division, 30 E. Broad St., Columbus, 43266-0410,
1-800-282-0515

This state agency enforces Ohio's consumer protection laws which were designed to protect the public from deceptive or unfair business practices. If you feel you have been victimized, call this office and you will be sent a complaint form to complete. In most instances, this agency will be able to assist you in resolving the problem by investigating your complaint and contacting the company or person you dealt with directly. You should expect a response within 30 days. The agency does not provide legal advice and will not act as your attorney. Services are provided free of charge without regard to income. M-F 9-5.

BETTER BUSINESS BUREAU OF CENTRAL OHIO
527 S. High St., Columbus, 43215, 221-6336

This local affiliate of a national consumer advocacy and awareness group, handles consumer complaints against area businesses. Call to request a complaint form. They also provide you with free single copies of consumer information booklets on such topics as buying a home computer, mail order profit mirages, buying tires, charitable giving, long distance phone services, tips on travel packages and more. The BBB also provides free mediation and /or arbitration of consumer/business disputes. M-F 8:30-4.

CANCER CALL
Riverside Hospital Regional Cancer Institute, 3535 Olentangy River Rd.,Columbus, 43214, 261-4321 or 1-800-752-9119

This free, confidential phone line provides you with the information you need to help prevent many types of cancer. You can learn about early diagnosis and the latest treatment options from one-on-one phone contact with a trained staff member.M-F 8-5.

CENTRAL OHIO LUNG ASSOCIATION
4627 Executive Dr., Columbus, 43228, 457-4570

If you would like to quit smoking, purchase a self help kit for $5 from this organization, which includes a day to day plan for quitting. Accepts checks and cash only. M-F 9-5.

CHORES PROGRAM
City of Columbus, Human Services Department, 50 W. Gay St., Columbus, 43215, 645-7440

Free home repair service is available for homeowners who are permanently disabled or persons aged sixty and over. Applicants must reside in designated inner city areas of Columbus. Those accepted to the program will receive assistance with minor home repairs that might otherwise force them from their homes. M-F 8-5

COLUMBIA GAS OF OHIO
939 W. Goodale Blvd., Columbus, 43272, 460-2263

Seniors aged 62 and older are eligible to receive more than a dozen free services designed to save you time, energy and money from the *Service For A Lifetime* program. The options guarantees that your service will not be disconnected in the winter months if you are late in your payments. Other "Service For A Lifetime" options are available. M-F 8-5.

COLUMBUS CANCER CLINIC
65 Ceramic Dr., Columbus, 43214, 263-5006

Low cost cancer screenings are available at various sites in the community through this clinic, in day and evening hours to suit your personal schedule. The screenings are conducted by a physician and include a thorough physical, risk assessment and a brief education session. The cost is $10, but no one will be denied a screening if they are unable to pay. Appointments are needed. M-F 9-5.

COLUMBUS CHARTER COACH
876-0302

Free shuttle buses can transport you from German Village through the north end of downtown and back. The scarlet and grey vehicles, emblazoned with the words, "Free Shuttle Bus", run every 15 minutes. They stop at each COTA bus stop along the following routes: (heading south) Ohio Center at North High and Nationwide Boulevard, 3rd street to Whittier Street and South High Streets. (heading north) South High Street and Whittier, Front Street to Ohio Center. The buses run Monday through Friday from 10AM-2PM.

COLUMBUS HEALTH DEPARTMENT
181 Washington Blvd., Columbus, 43215, 645-2437

Free, anonymous Aids and pregnancy testing, in addition to free education and counseling sessions are offered to residents of the City of Columbus. The clinic is open from 8-3:30 Monday, Tuesday, Wednesday and Friday, and 9-3:30 on Thursdays. By appointment only

COLUMBUS HOUSING LAW PROJECT
1066 N. High St., Columbus, 43201, 291-5076 and 221-2255

The "Landlord/Tenant Advice Only Clinic" operates at 11 A.M. on Wednesdays and 10:30 A.M. on Fridays at the Third Avenue Community Church, 1066 N. High St. It is imperative that you arrive when they open as the lawyers will leave shortly thereafter if no one appears for their assistance. This free service is sponsored by the Columbus Housing Law Project.

COLUMBUS POLICE CRIME PREVENTION UNIT
120 W. Gay St., Columbus, 43215, 645-4610

If you are concerned about security, members of this crime prevention unit can send a police officer to your home or business to provide an assessment. They will also suggest ways in which shoplifting and robberies can be discouraged and how you can better secure a building. To be eligible for this free service, you must live in or have a business in the City of Columbus, not within an incorporated area. M-F 8-5.

COLUMBUS SMALL BUSINESS DEVELOPMENT CENTER
C/O Columbus Chamber of Commerce, 37 N. High St., Columbus, 43215, 221-1321

Sponsored by the Columbus Chamber of Commerce, this free service provides technical

COLUMBUS SMALL BUSINESS DEVELOPMENT CENTER
C/O Columbus Chamber of Commerce, 37 N. High St., Columbus, 43215, 221-1321

Sponsored by the Columbus Chamber of Commerce, this free service provides technical assistance to small businesses and prospective small businesses. They have a network of over 160 volunteers who are business leaders willing to assist you in determining venture capital strategies , evaluating cash flow problems, developing accounting and record-keeping systems and more. You do not have to be a chamber member to participate. Call to request a packet of information. Several forms will need to be completed and mailed before your counseling session can be scheduled. M-F 8-4:30.

COLUMBUS SPEECH AND HEARING CENTER
4110 N. High St., Columbus, 43214, 263-5151

Licensed audiologists will perform a free, 10 minute hearing evaluation on Wednesdays from 1-5PM. No appointment is needed.

COMMUNITY MEDIATION SERVICE OF CENTRAL OHIO
80 Jefferson Ave., Columbus, 43215, 228-7191

Free mediation assistance is provided to help resolve disputes involving neighborhoods (noise, pets etc.), families, businesses (consumer/merchant disputes of faulty merchandise or service), employees/employers, school disputes (involving teachers, staff, students, parents) landlords/tenants etc. This service is available to the entire community without regard to income including private citizens, businesses and community organizations The service helps to resolve disputes before they reach a level of seriousness requiring the use of courts, police or attorneys. It can help you to improve valuable personal or professional relationships while helping you to participate in creating your own solutions to problems. However, this service does not handle disputes involving serious violence or those needing legal assistance such as filing a lawsuit, criminal defenses, wills etc. This service has earned the distinction of being one of my personal favorites. Appointments are available from 6-10PM Monday-Friday and from 10-2PM on Saturday. Call M-Th 9-6 or F 10-6.

COUPON CLEARING HOUSE
145 S. Lexington-Springmill Rd., Mansfield, 44906, (419) 529-4425

If you want to save money at the grocery store but dislike having to cut out coupons, contact Cathy McWherter. There is no membership fee to become a customer of the Coupon Clearing House. For every dollar you send in, you'll get $5 worth of coupons. And, if you shop at a grocery store which provides double the value of manufacturers coupons, you'll save even more! You can request coupons for the specific brands or types of products you are interested in. Kathy does not offer coupons for cigarettes, but can supply coupons on most any type of supermarket product. She'll return your order promptly. Be sure to include a self addressed stamped envelope. Even if you can't use this service, Kathy is always interested in receiving your neatly cut, unwanted coupons. Those with no expiration date are preferred, although any which will expire at least 2 months away are accepted. Kathy has a progressive, degenerative muscular disease. Her determination and positive attitude are truly inspirational.

CONSUMER CREDIT COUNSELING SERVICE OF CENTRAL OHIO

697 E. Broad St., Columbus, 43215, 464-2227
399 E. Church St., Marion, 43302, 464-2227
35 S. Paint St., Chillicothe, 45601, 464-2227
1 Marion Ave., Mansfield, 44903, (419) 526-2770
121 W. Mulberry St., Lancaster, 43130, 464-2227
40 N. Sandusky St., suite 203, Delaware, 43015, 464-2227

This free service will advise you on ways in which you can repay your creditors and avoid filing for bankruptcy. In most cases, your credit rating will not be affected. After a repayment plan has been established, you will be protected from collection efforts by your creditors. The Columbus phone number handles the scheduling for all of the branches except the one in Mansfield. M-F 9-5.

DEBTORS ANONYMOUS

488-4130

If your spending habits have become uncontrollable, this free self help group, which uses an approach similar to the "twelve steps", may be able to assist you. Meetings are held every Wednesday from 7:30-8:30 P.M. in the Allen Lounge of the Worthington United Methodist Church., 600 N. High St. A new daytime meeting has been added which meets on Fridays at 12 noon at the Central Presbyterian Church, 132 S. 3 St., downtown.

DIAL-A-DIETICIAN

221-9142

Have you ever wondered how much fiber is the recommended amount to have in your daily diet? Or how much chocolate your child should be allowed to eat daily? Free nutritional advice, on a broad range of topics, is available from this hotline sponsored by the Columbus Dietetic Association. You may call 24 hours a day, 7 days a week and leave a message. A registered dietician will return your call within 48 hours.

FRANKLIN COUNTY COOPERATIVE EXTENSION SERVICE

1945 Frebis Ave., Columbus, 43206, 443-6200

There is a wealth of free and low cost assistance available through this agency. If you enjoy gardening, sign up to receive the free monthly newsletter, Extension Garden News. It lists planting and pruning tips, horticultural happenings around town, plus special features such as plants and shrubs which will give good fall foliage color. The Expanded Food And Nutrition Program (EFNEP) is free to low income families with young children, who want to learn to improve the quality of their life. Participants are taught basic nutrition concepts, food buying skills, proper food management of available resources etc. You can receive a free subscription to the Home Living Newsletter, which provides helpful tips on cooking, cleaning and home maintenance. This agency also operates 2 hotlines, at 443-6419, which can provide you with instant information. The Horticulture Hotline is open from 8AM-12 noon Monday through Friday and can answer your questions about growing fruits and vegetables, lawn and garden care, the use of pesticides, holiday plant care etc. The Home Economics Hotline operates from 12:30-4 Monday through Friday and can answer your questions relating to stain removal, cooking, food poisoning, selecting toys for your child, balancing work and family and more. Free and low cost pamphlets are available by mail on a variety of related topics. This organization sponsors many workshops and seminars in the community on such subjects as how to start and operate a bed and breakfast, a homemaker's mini college (craft workshops, gardening, parenting, nutrition and other topics) a perennial plant seminar and others. The workshops cost about $3-$15, but there are also several which are free. M-F 9-5

FRANKLIN COUNTY ENGINEER'S OFFICE
970 Dublin Rd., Columbus, 43215, 462-3030

Provides free maps of Franklin county listing streets, highways, shopping centers, golf courses and heliports. Maps, which are revised every 2 years, must be picked up at their office. M-F 9-5.

FRANKLIN COUNTY HOME WEATHERIZATION SERVICE
C/O Mid Ohio Regional Planning Commission, 285 E. Main St., Columbus, 43215, 228-1825

MORPC provides free attic insulation, storm windows, caulking and weather stripping to eligible low income residents of Franklin county who live outside the city of Columbus. Service is provided about 60 days after your request is received. Longer delays might exist if your request is made during the peak winter season. M-F 8-5.

FRANKLIN COUNTY SOIL AND WATER CONSERVATION OFFICE
1945 Frebis Ave., Columbus, 43206, 443-9416 or 443-2440

You can obtain a free soil survey with maps that identify, by location, the characteristics for all soils within Franklin county. Free soil suitability interpretations are provided upon request. This information can be used to determine subsurface and surface drainage conditions which are necessary in evaluating waste disposal options and possible flooding concerns. People interested in building a "home in the country", are urged to consult with this free service to avoid any unnecessary problems. Their annual spring fish sale provides you with the opportunity to purchase bass, blue gill, catfish and amur for pond stocking. The cost ranges from 25 cents each to 60 cents each for all but the white amur which costs $10 apiece. Orders should be placed in March and will be available for pickup in April. The Tree And Shrub Packet Program provides landowners with the chance to purchase a variety of trees and shrubs seedlings which are suited for wildlife habitat improvement, windbreak establishment, living hedges or screens or reforestation. There's no restrictions on where they may be planted. Austrian Pine, Colorado Blue Spruce, White Dogwood, Forsythia, Hardy Pecan, Black Walnut, Sycamore and other types are available at a cost of $8-$12 for 5-25 seedlings. Orders are placed in March for April pickup. M-F 8-4.

JOHN KALMBAUGH INSURANCE
190 S. State St., Westerville, 43081, 890-7222

This independent insurance agent represents such well established companies as Safeco, Great American, Erie and Reliance for home or car coverage. He carries Erie, Safeco, Occidental, Golden Rule and Jefferson National Life Insurance lines as well as commercial, business, disability and health coverage. In comparing his prices with other agents', I have found this agency's to be about 20-30% lower. M-F 8-5.

NATIONAL RELOCATION SERVICES
New Homes Planning Center, 7243 Sawmill Rd., Suite 205, Dublin , 43017, 889-0306
If you are interested in building a home in the Columbus area, this one stop source can provide you with a wealth of free information on the area's leading builders. This business features hundreds of floor plans, photos of new homes, tips on how to hold the costs down, financing tips, information on builders' spec homes, tips on how to select a builder, assistance in developing plans as well as neighborhood information.   Visits are by appointment only. You will save time and gas by finding everything under one roof.

OHIO AFFILIATE/NATIONAL SOCIETY TO PREVENT BLINDNESS
1500 W. 3 Ave., Columbus, 43212, 464-2020

The society offers free glaucoma screenings every Thursday from 9:30-12 year round. No appointment is necessary. Glaucoma is one of the leading causes of irreversible blindness. It progresses without pain or symptoms in its early stages, but early detection can prevent further vision loss. The office is open M-F 9-5 to answer your questions.

OHIO DEPARTMENT OF AGING
Communications Dept., 50 W. Broad St., Columbus, 43266-0501, 466-3253

Senior citizens aged 100 and over, can receive a free certificate of congratulations on their birthday, which is signed by the Governor and the director of the Ohio Department of Aging. This treasured keepsake has a bright gold seal affixed to it and is the state's way of spreading birthday cheer on these landmark occasions. You can order the certificate over the phone or by mail. Allow 3-5 weeks for delivery.M-F 9-5.

OHIO TUITION TRUST AUTHORITY
589-6882 or 752-9200

College tuition costs are growing at nearly twice the cost of living index. The Guaranteed Tuition Program allows you to prepay college tuition at the current rate per credit hour when your child attends any of the 35 public universities, community colleges or technical colleges in Ohio. The program was created in 1989 as a way for you to buy tomorrow's education at today's prices. The current cost is $35.50 per tuition credit. If your child decides to attend a private or out of state college, there is a refund policy which is available, details of which, can be obtained from OTTA. M-F 9-5.

POSTAL ANSWER LINE
469-0305

Use your touchtone phone to hear your choice of over 75 different informative tapes relating to such postal topics as sending valuables through the mail, mail forwarding, mail hold when vacationing, international mail, unsolicited merchandise, removing your name from mailing lists, mail order fraud, mail security, stamp collecting, stamps by mail, express mail and more. You can call the hotline, then press code 328 and you'll hear a menu listing tapes and their code numbers.

PRESIDENTIAL GREETINGS OFFICE
White House, Washington, D.C.20500

The White House will send a free personal letter to any senior aged 75 and older to congratulate him/her on their birthday. Simply put your request in writing. Allow 6-8 weeks for delivery.

RAPE EDUCATION AND PREVENTION PROGRAM
408 Ohio Union, 1739 N. High St., Columbus, 43210, 292-0479

Free classes in personal safety and assault protection techniques are offered year round to the general public at the OSU campus and other sites in the community. There are no physical requirements to be met. The classes are also targeted to specific groups such as Black women and people with disabilities at various times throughout the year. M-F 9-5.

RESIDENTIAL REHABILITATION ASSISTANCE PROGRAM
City of Columbus, Department of Human Services, 50 W. Gay St., Columbus, Ohio 43215, 645-8550

Technical advice and financial assistance, in the form of low interest or deferred payment loans, are available to homeowners who are interested in rehabilitating single to four family dwellings located in certain designated inner city areas. Property will be evaluated by housing code inspectors to identify unsafe conditions and necessary repairs. M-F 8-5.

RIDESHARE
Mid Ohio Regional Planning Commission,(MORPC) 285 E.
Main St., Columbus, 43215, 1-800-875-POOL or 1-800-VAN-RIDE

The MORPC offers a free commuter assistance program which utilizes a computer based system to match you up with someone who lives and works near you, for the purpose of carpooling. The intake occurs by phone. Simply call 1-800-875-POOL and a representative will assist you. Within a few days, you will be sent a list of commuters who are interested in carpooling. A similar program, VanOhio, has a nominal fee and serves those who live 25 miles or more from work. You would meet a MORPC van at a central site and would be driven to your place of business or a convenient drop off spot. Phone 1-800-VAN-RIDE. Commuters using either of these pools, can average about a $25 per month savings over using their own car to commute to work. M-F 8-5.

SCORE (SERVICE CORPS OF RETIRED EXECUTIVES)
85 Marconi Blvd., Columbus, 43215, 469-2357

If you are a potential small business owner, or currently operating a business, you can obtain free professional advice from this organization. A face-to-face meeting will provide you with answers to many of your questions from volunteers who are retired business executives. About 4 low cost business seminars are offered monthly on such topics as government contracts, record keeping, credit and collections, marketing etc. The classes are from 4-7 hours long and cost $10-$20. Pre-register so you can save $5 off the ticket price at the door. Classes are held at the Fawcett Center. Call to be added to their mailing list. M-F 9-5. Accepts checks and cash only.

SELF HELP PROGRAM
Columbus Department of Human Services, 50 W. Gay St., Columbus, 43215, 645-7440

Painting equipment and basic tools for landscaping and general home repair, are available on a free loan basis to inner city residents. Homeowners, tenants with the homeowner's permission and nonprofit organizations are eligible to apply. Income is not a factor. The program's mobile tool vans and paint trucks operate throughout the service area from 8-5. Ask for the Division of Neighborhood Services if you call.

SENIOR MEDIATION SERVICES
645-7250

Do you need assistance resolving a dispute between neighbor, family member, business or landlord? Trained mediators will provide free assistance to seniors by identifying ways to resolve the issue and assisting with the negotiation of a settlement. Both parties must be present. No problem is too big or too small to be handled by this office. The service does not decide who is right or wrong, does not take sides and does not tell you how to resolve your dispute. The process is less time consuming than the traditional legal process. You can take other actions if not satisfied. The mediation remains private. The service is sponsored by the Ohio Commission on Dispute Resolution And Conflict Management and the City Of Columbus, Recreation And Parks Department's Central Ohio Area Agency On Aging. Appointments are suggested. M-F 9-5.

SIX ON YOUR SIDE
C/O WSYX T.V., 1261 Dublin Rd., Columbus, 43215, 821-9799

Call the hotline number above and you will be sent a form to fill out on which you will describe the consumer related problem you are experiencing. Channel six will investigate the problem and try to resolve it for you. Very often, a business will respond quite readily to resolve the issue as they are afraid of televised publicity about the problem. "Six On Your Side" airs a featured problem/resolution weekly, but attempts to resolve all requests they receive. M-F 9-5

SKILLSBANK AT CALLVAC SERVICES
370 S. 5 St., Columbus, 43215, 464-4747

If you would like to become a volunteer, contact the Skillsbank at CALLVAC, which is a computerized system that matches your interests and skills to the volunteer needs of more than 100 nonprofit organizations in Franklin county. Volunteering can help you advance a cause, improve services provided in your community, add a dimension of meaning to your life, help you avoid boredom and loneliness, help you to acquire new skills or refresh old ones, as well as help you make career, college and vocational decisions. The latter two are very helpful for personal growth and can assist you when listing experience on a job resume. Volunteer opportunities can be tailored to suit your personal schedule. Volunteerism is a no or low cost way to learn, grow, share and enjoy. M-F 8-5.

STARR CLEANERS
246 Lincoln Circle, Gahanna, 43230, 475-5006

Prices here are 20-30% lower than comparable dry cleaning prices at other businesses. They will honor all other competitors' coupons. Save 20% off these already low prices by prepaying your dry cleaning order. As an example of their prices, shirts can be laundered here for 88 cents which would cost you $1.30-$1.50 elsewhere. M-F 7 A.M.-8:30 P.M., Sat 7 A.M.- 7:30 P.M.

SUBURBAN NEWS PUBLICATIONS
919 Old W. Henderson Rd., Columbus, 43220, 451-4422 or 861-2400

"For Sale" ads which have been published in the classified section and prepaid, will be repeated for free, if needed, up to two times. The types of ads which qualify for this offer include: miscellaneous for sale, boats/marine, recreational vehicles and cars, trucks and motorcycles. Changes or deletions may not be made to the ads, which must run on consecutive weeks with no skips. This offer is only available to individuals, and not to groups or businesses. The SNP publishes 21 papers in the Columbus area. If you purchase a garage sale classified ad, which is not included in this special repeat offer, you will be entitled to one free garage sale lawn sign Accepts checks, MC & Visa. M-F 9-5.

SWAN CLEANERS
42 area locations. Check the phone book.

You can have your American flag dry cleaned for free, year round, at any branch. No coupon is needed.

THIS WEEK NEWSPAPERS
841-0444

When you advertise your garage sale in the classified section of any This Week edition, you will be sent a free garage sale kit which includes sale signs, colorful balloons and color coded price stickers. If you have ever tried to design your own sign, you know how taxing it can be on your patience. The This Week newspapers feature 16 different papers covering Franklin and the adjacent counties. M-F 8-5. Accepts checks, MC & Visa.

WHY USA
246 Lincoln Circle, Gahanna, 43230, 337-0990
2043 Stringtown Rd., Grove City, 43123, 875-0990
3780 Fishinger Blvd., Hilliard, 43026, 777-0990
1141 Hill Rd. N., Pickerington, 43147, 575-0990
6797 N. High St., Worthington, 43085, 431-0990
2527 Schrock Rd., Westerville, 43081, 899-4900

Why pay 6 or 7% commission on the sale of your home? You can save hundreds to thousands of dollars through this new service in the Columbus market. Several independently owned and operated franchises in town offer you a $990 initial listing fee, plus a commission of 3 1/2- 4 1/2 %. Full representation, including newspaper advertising, market evaluation, contract preparation and the other typical realtor assistance is included. Why USA also offers another cost savings measure in which the homeowner's name and phone number can be listed on their "for sale" sign. You can conduct your own open house if your choose, and if you find your own buyer, the commission (not the listing fee) will be waived. M-F 10-8, Sat 10-6, Sun 12-5.

ALSO SEE

Cat Welfare, Consumer Reports Auto Price Service, Entertainment '91 Book, Lazarus, Marshall Field's, Nu Look Factory Outlet, OSU Office of Women's Services, Ritchey's, Pet Adoption Service, Pet Butler and Vacu-Medic Plus

SHOES/SPORTS

SHOES

Each manufacturer cuts their clothes and shoes differently. So don't be stubborn about trying on something which is several sizes smaller or larger than you usually wear. Carry a tracing of family members' feet with you, so that when you stumble upon an unexpected bargain in shoes, you'll know instantly if it will fit. When my children were younger, this was an excellent way of buying them shoes when they weren't with me. I admit, I received more than my share of giggles and stares from sales people. But I was the one who benefitted in the long run because I was prepared.

J.J. BERGIN/J.L. TAYLOR
(716) 688-9364 or (901) 755-6059

If you have discriminating taste in shoes then run, don't walk to these special sales offered 3 times a year at changing sites throughout Columbus. You'll find Andrew Geller, Sesto Meucci, Anne Klein, VanEli, Mr. Seymour, Sacha London, Perry Ellis, Margaret J, Enzo, Proxy, Petra, Naturalizer, Nickels, Jasmin, Bandolino, Air Step, deLiso and other brands of women's dress and casual shoes. Boots and sandals are sold seasonally. Sizes range from 4-12. The merchandise is all first quality and includes overstocks and credit cancellations. You'll find supple suedes and leathers, painted snakeskins and other high fashion materials. These brands of shoes are typically sold at Saks 5th Avenue and other upscale department and specialty stores throughout the United States. Quality boutique purses are also available and include casual and dressy styles in leather, snakes, suedes and novelty combinations. The savings throughout the sale are 40-80% off regular retail prices which are typically $40-$180. A limited amount of clothing is available at a savings of 50% off manufacturer's suggested retail prices. On my recent visit, I saw Nike jogging suits, but opted to purchase a pair of beaded sneakers for only $30, regularly $90 elsewhere. The 3 day sales are usually Friday through Sunday and are held in May or June, August or September and December or January. Sales are also held in Dayton and are tentatively planned for Cleveland, Cincinnati, Akron and Toledo. Admission is free. Call to be added to their mailing list. All sales are final. Accepts checks, MC & Visa.

BROOKS SHOE FACTORY OUTLET
45 E. Canal, Nelsonville, 45764, 753-3130

The "Rocky" brand of men's and women's boots and shoes is manufactured in this factory. Find seconds and overstocks of Brooks merchandise at savings of 30-50% off retail, plus first quality athletic shoes from other companies at savings of 20% off retail. Stop by this outlet on your way to the Hocking Hills State Park and Old Man's Cave. Gives exchanges only. M-Sat 9-7, Sun 11:30-5:30. Accepts checks, MC, Visa & Discover.

CAPEZIO FOOTWEAR
771 S. 30 St., Indian Mound Mall, Heath, 43056, 522-5612
1635 River Valley Cir., Lancaster, 43130, 687-6318

Save 20-40% off first quality men's, women's and children's dress, sport and casual shoes. You'll find such brands as Calvin Klein Sport, Capezio, Dexter, Eastland, Nunn Bush, Rockport, Cobblers and Arpegio in traditional and contemporary styles. Capezio Footwear is owned by the U.S. Shoe Corporation and operates businesses in the Burlington Coat Factory Warehouse stores as well as independently. Gives refunds. M-Sat 10-9, Sun 12-5. Accepts checks, MC & Visa.

DESIGNER SHOE WAREHOUSE
3901 W. Dublin-Granville Rd., Dublin, 43017, 791-1115

Nationally recognized brands of moderate to designer quality women's shoes and purses are sold at 30-70% off regular retail prices. The first quality merchandise, which sells for up to $170 in other stores, includes closeouts, overstocks and discontinued casual, career and dressy styles for discriminating tastes. You'll find traditional and the ultimate in chic contemporary styles in all widths for sizes 5-11. Brand names can't be mentioned in print, but you'll instantly recognize them once inside the store. Designer Shoe Warehouse has 20,000 pairs of shoes in stock and offers the most unusual selection of quality women's shoes in Central Ohio. It has earned the distinction of being one of my personal favorites. Gives refunds. M, Th, F, Sat 10-9; Sun 12-5. Closed Tu and W for restocking. Accepts checks, MC, Visa, AmExp & Discover.

EL-BEE SHOE OUTLETS
113 Graceland Blvd., Columbus, 43214, 885-8332
124 N. Wilson Rd., Great Western Shpng. Ctr., Columbus, 43204, 272-0257
2871 Olentangy River Rd., Columbus, 43202, 261-8125
1841 W. Henderson Rd., Columbus, 43220, 457-8720
7616 New Market Center Way, Columbus, 43235, 764-2469
3750 E. Broad St., Town and Country Shpng. Ctr., Columbus, 43213, 231-3901
2711 Northland Plaza Dr., Columbus, 43231, 891-4774
5803 Scarborough Mallway, Columbus, 43232, 868-5661
52 Westerville Sq., Westerville, 43081, 882-4809
760 Hebron Rd, Heath, 43056, 522-4949
3287 Maple Rd., Zanesville, 443701, 452-4259

208 Chillicothe Mall, Chillicothe, 45601, 773-3844
1475 Marion-Waldo Rd., Marion, 43301, 389-1121
1315 Delaware Ave., Marion, 43301, 389-1121

First quality current and prior season footwear for men and women is available at savings of 15-40%. The moderate to better quality merchandise includes traditional and contemporary styling in regular, narrow and wide widths by Calico, Joyce, Leslie Fay, Pappagallo, Hush Puppies, Bass, Nunn Bush and others. A small selection of women's purses is also available at similar savings. The New Market, Northland and Westerville sites also offer kids' dressy and casual shoes at similar savings. Gives refunds. M-Sat 10-9, Sun., 12-5. Accepts checks, MC, Visa & Elder-Beerman charges.

FAMOUS FOOTWEAR
4121 W. Broad St., Columbus. 43228, 274-0855
859 Bethel Road, Olentangy Plaza, Columbus, 43214, 451-1115
2703 Northland Plaza Dr., Columbus, 43231, 794-2102
4408 Crossroads East Center, Columbus, 43232, 866-9857
7663 New Market Center Way, Columbus, 43235, 766-6323
3764 E. Broad St., Town and Country, Shpng. Ctr., Columbus, 43213, 231-0722
5840 Scarborough Mallway, Columbus 43232, 866-9830

Each store carries over 20,000 pairs of first quality national name brands for men, women and children such as Nike, Keds, Eastland, Nunn Bush, Cherokee, Bellini, Mushrooms, Reebok and more. Choose from dressy, casual or sport styles, including soccer shoes, at savings of 10-50% off regular retail prices. Purses are also offered at similar savings. Famous Footwear has recently begun a frequent purchaser program in which $300 in shoe, sneaker and accessories purchases will qualify you to receive a $25 store gift certificate. Simply save your receipts and return them to the store in one of their frequent purchaser envelopes. Gives refunds. M-Sat 10-9, Sun 12-5. Accepts checks, MC & Visa.

JUST FOR FEET
3165 Dublin Center Dr., Dublin, 43017, 792-FOOT (3668)

The world's largest athletic shoe store has a frequent purchaser program where, after you have purchased 12 pairs of sneakers, your 13th pair is free, based on the average purchase price of your 12 pairs. There is no need to bother saving the receipts as it is all computerized. Watch the newspapers for their frequent "second pair half price" sales. Adidas, New Balance, Diadora, Rockport, Reebok, L.A. Gear, Etonic and other brands of athletic shoes are offered, in addition to clothing such as warm ups, tee shirts, socks, sport bags and accessories. Even if you don't need any sneakers, you won't want to miss this multi level, high tech store which is equipped with an arcade, food concession as well as a basketball court. Street shoes are not allowed on this mini court, but kids, and even adults, will enjoy shooting a few baskets. The second level has a running track, which may be used to test your intended purchase or just for fun. No purchase is required. Don't miss the clearance area at the front of the store, which offers a large selection of closeout, discontinued and special purchase athletic shoes for the family, at savings of 30-70% off regular retail prices. Merchandise throughout the store is available for men, women and children. Gives exchanges only. M-Sat 10-9, Sun 12-6. Accepts checks, MC, Visa, AMExp & Discover.

KARI SHOES
84 N. High St., Columbus, 43215, 365-9032

Better women's shoes are discounted 20-40% off the regular retail prices. The *Back Room Outlet,* located at the rear of the store, features savings of 50-80% off the original price. The inventory consists of overstocks, discontinued and closeout merchandise in narrow, regular and wide widths, sizes 5-11. You'll find such popular brands as Liz Claiborne, Jazz, Nickels, Naturalizer, Bandolino and others. Clearance merchandise is a final sale. Gives refunds on other shoes. M-F 10-6. Accepts checks, MC, Visa & AmExp.

SHOE SENSATION
7640 New Market Center Way, Columbus, 43235, 764-0130
5766 Scarborough Mallway, Columbus, 43232, 868-0095

Save 20-50% off regular retail prices on men's women's and children's dress and casual shoes by Zodiac, Calico, Rockport, Fanfare, Evan Picone, Dexter, Nina, Bass, Eastland, Nike, Reebok, French Schriner, Bally and more. Coordinating purses are offered at similar savings. Narrow, regular and wide widths are available. Gives refunds. M-Sat 10-9, Sun, 12-6. Accepts checks, MC, Visa & Discover.

SHOE WORKS
3819 E. Broad St., Columbus, 43213, 237-6603
5620 Cleveland Ave,.Columbus, 43231, 882-3456
803 Bethel Rd., Columbus, 43214, 457-1927
6456 Tussing Rd., Reynoldsburg, 43068, 863-0247
5937 E. Main St., Columbus, 43213, 863-1928
881 N. Bridge St., Chillicothe, 45601,
1469 Marion-Waldo Rd., Marion, 43301, 389-4710

Find casual and dressy women's shoes and boots by Cherokee, Bon Vivant, Predictions, Paalos and other popular brands in regular, narrow and wide widths, sizes 5-12. Women's shoes are priced at $19.98 and under. This store also sells men;'s boots as well as casual and dressy shoes by Stacy Adams, Brassboot, L.A. Gear, Etonic and more. Savings on their first quality merchandise, which is largely private ;label, are up to 50% off regular retail prices. Provides layaway. Gives refunds. M-Sat 10-9:30, Sun 12-6. Accepts checks, MC, Visa, AmExp & Discover.

SNEAKER ALLEY
3150 Southwest Blvd.,Grove City, 43123, 871-1443

This specialty store can save you 20-60% off brand name sneakers for the entire family. You'll find Pony, Keds, Saucony, L.A. Gear, Vision Street Wear, Kanga Roos, Nike, Converse, Airwalk and Mitre brands. The stock consists of current merchandise at savings of 20-25% as well as closeouts of discontinued styles at savings of up to 60% off regular retail prices. This store is also one of the few in the area to carry skateboarding shoes, also at similar savings. Baseball and soccer cleats are also available. *Columbus Monthly* recently named the store as one of the best places to buy athletic shoes in the city. Gives exchanges only. M-Sat 10-8, Sun 12-5. Accepts checks, MC, Visa & Discover.

SPORTS AFOOT

3733 E. Broad St., Columbus, 43213, 231-1138

6091 McNaughten Center, Columbus, 43232, 863-0327

1156 Kenny Center, Columbus, 43220, 451-3549

2569 S. Hamilton Rd.,Eastland Plaza, Columbus, 43232, 861-7427

Formerly called, Second Sole Athletic Footwear, this chain of individually owned discounters offer savings of 5-10% on the most sought after brands of athletic shoes and clothes such as Reebok,Adidas, Nike and others. Adult shoe sizes are up to 14, and the stores also stock infants and children's footwear. Gives refunds. M-F 10-9, Sat 10-6, Sun 12-5. Accepts checks, MC & Visa.

U.S. SHOE FACTORY OUTLET STORE

U.S. Rte. 52, S. 2 St., Ripley, 45167, (513) 392-4630

First quality overstocks of women's better shoes, sold under the Easy Spirit, Pappagallo, Capezio, Cobbies and Joyce brands, are available at savings of 50-70% off regular retail prices. This outlet, which is located adjacent to the factory, sells all widths in sizes 4-12. Located off U.S. route 62 South, on the Kentucky border, about 45 minutes from Cincinnati. Gives exchanges. M-Sat 10-6, Sun 1-6. Accepts checks, MC & Visa.

ZZ BOOTS

2264 S. Hamilton Rd., Columbus, 43232, 863-3320

Thousands of men's, women's and some children's boots are available at savings of 20-40% off manufacturers' suggested retail prices. You'll find rare and exotic leathers, studded, sequined and handpainted boots, calf, knee high and thigh highs in hunting, traditional, biker and contemporary styles. The first quality merchandise is available in all of the popular brands such as Tony Lama, Zodiac, Acme, Dan Post, J. Chisholm, Nocona and Laredo. The store also sells men's and women's leather coats and jackets at similar savings. Gives exchanges. M-F 10-9:30, Sat 10-6. Accepts checks, MC, Visa and Discover.

ALSO SEE

Anne's Collection Outlet Store, Burlington Coat Factory Warehouse, Extravaganza, General Merchandise Sales, Kids Quarters, Lake Erie Factory Outlet, Mared Consignments, Marshall's, T.J. Maxx, Outlets Limited Mall, J.C. Penney Outlet, Schottenstein's, Sears Outlet, Shapely Outlet Center, Uhlman's Clearance Center, Value City Department Stores

SPORTS

AMERICAN LUNG ASSOCIATION OF MID OHIO

1700 Arlingate Lane, Columbus, 43228, 279-1700

If you like golf, purchase a *Golf Privilege Card* for $30 from this nonprofit group. The card will permit you one round of golf during the current season, at 35 courses in Central Ohio such as Mohican Hills, Oxbow, L.C. Boles Memorial, Hickory, Grove Briar and others. The usual price to play a round of golf is $12-$15, so if you used all of the coupons in the book, you would save about $400. Proceeds from this annual fundraiser will be used to help support an asthma camp for children, lung health education and pulmonary research. A portion of your purchase price may be tax deductible, so check with your accountant. M-F 8:30-4:30. Accepts.checks.

AMERICAN YOUTH HOSTELS
POB 14384, Columbus, 43214, 447-1006

The name of this organization is actually a misnomer as membership is open to all ages. Over 5,000 inexpensive overnight accommodations are available throughout the United States and the world to members of this organization. These include lodging in a lighthouse in California, a tree house in Georgia, a rustic farmhouse in Ohio, a battleship in Massachusetts and other sites such as YMCA's. Membership is open to young and old alike at a cost of $10-$35 annually depending on the age of the individuals and type of membership. Workshops are available at low cost to members including canoeing, sailing, bicycle maintenance, back packing, mountain climbing and leadership skills. Low cost, outdoor equipment rentals as well as adventure trips are also available to members.

AMERICA'S FITNESS WAREHOUSE
5794 Columbus Sq., Columbus, 43231, 891-3633
2763 Martin Rd., Festival At Sawmill Shpng. Ctr., Dublin, 43017, 792-6668

Save 10-20% on top quality exercise equipment such as that found in Nautilus and workout facilities. Brands offered include Tinturri, Image, Body Guard and others. Gives exchanges. M-Sat 10-7, Sun 12-5. Accepts checks, MC & Visa.

BIG WALNUT SKATE CLUB
345 McGill St., Sunbury, 43074, 965-3022 or 965-1365

This indoor roller skating rink offers several special rates. Family skate is Sunday from 1:30-4PM and Tuesday from 7-9:30PM, where a family of 5 can skate for only $4. Kids' Funskate, for ages 12 and under (with or without a parent), is Saturday from 10AM-12 noon at a cost of $1.50 per person. During this time, the rink also includes lots of fun games which are used to teach basic skating skills. The regular admission price is $4 on Friday and Saturday from 7:30PM-midnight during the open skate. Skate rental is $1.

BIKE NASHBAR OUTLET
4733 Reed Rd., Columbus, 43220, 442-0202

Closeouts, overstocks and discontinued first quality goods are available at savings of 15-30% off their regular retail prices at this national catalogue outlet. During intermittent sales, savings are up to 60% off. You'll find everything for the cycling enthusiast including clothes, helmets, bicycle accessories and more. Bicycle repairs are priced about 10-15% lower than in other stores. Gives exchanges. M-F 10-8, Sat 9-5. Accepts checks, MC & Visa.

BERWICK PLAZA LANES
2817 Winchester Pike, Columbus, 43232, 237-9008

All you can bowl specials are offered Fridays and Saturdays from 10PM-1AM at a cost of $8 per person , and midnight to 3AM at a cost of $15 per lane.   Another special is weekdays from 11AM-6PM where you can bowl for $1.50 per game, regularly $2.

CITY OF COLUMBUS SPORTS DEPARTMENT
C/O Columbus Recreation and Parks Dept.,

Free adult volleyball and basketball clinics are offered at the Berliner and Anheuser Busch Athletic Complexes. Phone 645-3366. Free golf clinics are offered for high school clinics in the fall at the Walnut Hills Golf Course at 6001 East Livingston Avenue. Phone 645-3300 for information. The department also offers a variety of other free and low cost sports instructional classes and activities through their community recreation centers and senior centers. Call 645-3300 for details.

BIG WESTERN LANES
500 Georgesville Rd., Columbus, 43228, 274-1169

All you can bowl specials are Sundays from 9Am-noon and Monday through Friday from 12 noon to 3PM. The cost is $3.50 per person and $1 for shoe rental. The single game price is usually $1.50 per person.

COLUMBUS CLIPPERS
1155 W. Mound St., Columbus, 43223, 462-5250

Save $5 off the price of general admission to the Clippers games when you order a book of 5 tickets for only $10. The tickets are valid for any scheduled season contest with the Clippers, but are not valid for exhibition or play-off games or concerts. Individual reserved seating along the third base line is $3.50. General admission is $3 for adults and $1 for children aged 12 and under. Certain games have themes, special appearances by costumed characters, giveaways such as pennants or autographed baseballs, low cost food such as "dime a dog" night" or even fireworks, several times during the season. Admission to these games is $4 for all seats. Games are held from April through August. The Clippers also feature a series of post game concerts where for one low price of $4-$8 per seat, you can enjoy the game and a performance with top name entertainment such as Frankie Valli and the Four Seasons, REO Speedwagon, Gary Puckett And The Union Gap, Al Denson, Lee Greenwood and others. M-F 9-5. Accepts checks, MC & Visa.

COLUMBUS SQUARE BOWLING PALACE
5707 Forest Hills Blvd., Columbus, 43231, 895-1122

Special "all you can bowl" rates are offered Monday through Friday from 12AM-3AM and 12 non to 3PM, as well as Sundays from 9AM-noon or 9PM to midnight. The rate is $4.50 per person, plus $1.25 for shoe rental. Seniors aged 55 and over, may bowl at anytime for $1.40 per game. The regular game rate is $2.25. Open M-Sun 24 hours a day.

DUNHAM'S SPORTING GOODS
45 Graceland Blvd., Graceland Shpng. Ctr., Columbus, 43214, 848-3100
260 N. Wilson Rd., Columbus, 43204, 274-9200

Save 10-15% below suggested retail prices on name brand sports and casual wear for adults and children, by Nike, Adidas, Reebok and other manufacturers. Shorts, sweats, athletic shoes, jogging suits as well as camping and fishing equipment is offered at these savings. They carry a limited amount of "big man" sizes. Dunham's has two large sales during the year. In mid March, additional savings are available during the "spring sport/fishing sale". In August, the "back to school sale" offers further savings off the already low prices. Gives refunds. M-Sat 10-9, Sun 12-5. Accepts checks, MC & Visa.

EXECUTIVE TOUR GOLFER'S CLUB
1429 King Ave., Columbus, 43212, 1-800-686-5555

Save over $2000 (if you use every coupon in the book) on golf games, accessories and travel at courses, driving/practice ranges, miniature golf, private instruction , golf travel arrangements as well as purchases at golf pro shops. Membership costs $19.95 annually, plus $1.65 to ship the coupon book. During 1991, the plan includes a free round of 18 hole golf when you rent a cart or 50% off the green fees without a cart rental. In 1992, the plan will change to include free green fees with a cart rental or 25% off green fees without a cart rental. The participating courses are currently in Columbus and Central Ohio and include such favorites as the Bent Tree Golf Club, the Shamrock Golf Club and Turnbury. Miniature golf courses include Fantasy Golf, Putt Putt and Westerville Golf Center. In 1992, the owner of this club hopes to expand the offerings to include additional courses in other parts of the state. There's 100 coupons in the 1991 edition which include 2-5 passes at each course. The coupons are transferrable to friends or relatives. About 70% of the coupons are valid weekdays before 4PM. Others are valid on weekends after 1PM. Call anytime. Accepts MC, Visa & checks.

FIESTA LANES
1291 W. Lane Ave., Columbus, 43221, 488-3003

Bowling specials are Sundays from 9AM-12 noon at a cost of $5 per lane, or 8:30PM-11:30PM at a cost of $8 per lane. The regular price is $1.90 per person per game after 5PM daily, or $1.50 per person per game before 5PM. Shoe rental is $1 at all times.

THE FINISH LINE
7633 New Market Center Way, Columbus, 43235, 764-2425
6420 Tussing Rd., Consumer Sq. E., Reynoldsburg, 43068, 863-0421
3658 Soldano Blvd., Consumer Sq. W., Columbus, 43228, 351-0902
771 S. 30 St., Indian Mound Mall, Heath, 43056, 522-5943
1475 Columbus Lancaster Rd.,River Valley Mall, Lancaster, 43130, 653-8874
2715 Northland Plaza Dr., Columbus, 43231, 274-0774

Nationally recognized athletic wear by Champion, Umbro, Ocean Pacifac, Adidas, Nike, Converse and other brands, is available at savings of about 15-20% below retail. The first quality merchandise includes athletic shoes, sweat shirts, swimwear, nylon jackets and tennis wear, most of which are available in sizes for men, women and children. The stores pride themselves on excellent customer service and a knowledgeable sales staff. Gives refunds. M-Sat 10-9, Sun 12-5. Accepts checks, MC, Visa & Discover.

FISHING

Fishing is an enjoyable activity for all ages. In addition to being a low cost form of enjoyment, you can catch food for your next meal. Free fishing licenses are available to seniors aged 66 and over, holders of veteran license plates, permanently disabled veterans, former prisoners of war and physically limited people who require someone to assist them while fishing. Youths under age 16, members of the U.S. Armed Forces on annual leave and individuals providing assistance to a fisherman with a disability (when both are using the same fishing line), are exempt from purchasing a license. A license is not required when fishing in a private pond or on a body of water which they or their parents own. In all other instances, a fishing license is required at a cost of $12 annually for residents of Ohio, and $19 for non-residents. Free fishing licenses to the groups mentioned above, as well as licenses to be purchased, can be obtained by contacting the Ohio Department Of Natural Resources at 836-2304. Licenses may also be purchased at area sporting goods stores. The ODNR offers free publications of interest to sportsmen including "Ohio Public Hunting And Fishing Areas" and "When And Where To Fish", Call the aforementioned phone number. A toll free hotline, 1-800-282-0546, has been established by the state of Ohio, department of health, which can provide you with free information on contaminants found in fish in Ohio. The hotline operates Monday-Friday, from 9-5.

GAHANNA LANES
215 W. Johnstown Rd., Gahanna, 43230, 471-1111

Bowling specials are Monday through Friday from 12noon-5PM for $1.25 per game per person. Flat rate unlimited bowling is Friday from 11:30PM-2AM for $5 per person, Saturdays from 11PM-2AM for $4.50 per person and Sundays from 9AM-noon at a cost of $4.50 per person. Games are regularly $2 per person. Shoe rental is $1 at all times. Accepts Golden Buckeye Cards for regular bowling rates.

HACKER'S HELPER
630 W. Schrock Rd., Westerville, 43081, 899-6969
6720 Riverside Dr., Dublin, 43017, 793-0660

Everything for the golfer is under one roof here at savings of 20-50% off suggested retail prices. You will find golf bags by Professional, Hogan, Spaulding and Hot-Z, golf shoes by Foot Joy, Etonic, Reebok and Nike, as well as clothes and accessories. Junior clubs for 5-14 year olds are also available. All of the merchandise is first quality, current season and year. Golf club regripping is $3-$5 per club. Gives refunds. M-Sat 10-9, Sun 10-5. Accepts checks, MC & Visa.

HANDY BIKES CORPORATION
1055 W. Fifth Ave., Columbus, 43212, 299-0550

Mopeds and bicycles for adults and children are sold at savings of about 25% off regular retail prices through this distributor. The first quality merchandise includes such brands as Puch, Hercules, Columbia, Quentin and Victoria. Parts and service are offered at prices which are about 10-15% lower than in retail stores. Gives exchanges. M-Sat 9-6. Accepts checks, MC & Visa.

HILLCREST BOWLING LANES
3440 W. Broad St., Columbus, 43204, 274-7555

Bowling specials are Monday-Friday from 9AM-5PM, Thursdays from 9PM-11:30PM and Fridays from 12 midnight-2AM. The cost for unlimited bowling at these times is $4 per person. At all other times, bowling is 75 cents per game. Shoe rental is $1 for adults and 75 cents for kids at all times.

KEGLER 'N CUE
3800 Sullivant Ave., Columbus, 43228, 276-5616

New and used bumper pool, foosball and pool tables are available. However, the used items, which are all reconditioned, are sold at 40-50% lower than you would expect to pay for a comparable new item. As the inventory level of used merchandise tends to vary, it is best to call ahead to see what stock is on hand. M-F 11-7:30, Sat 11-6. Accepts checks, MC & Visa.

KIDS DISCOVER FITNESS
Driving Pk. Recreation Ctr. 1100 Rhoads Ave., Columbus, 43206, 645-3328
Linden Recreation Ctr., 1254 Briarwood Ave., Columbus, 43211, 645-3067
Marion-Franklin Recreation Ctr., 2801 Lockbourne Rd., Columbus, 43207, 645-3160
Thompson Recreation Ctr., 1189 Dennison Ave.,Columbus, 43201, 645-3082
Westgate Recreation Ctr., 455 S. Westgate Ave., Columbus, 43204, 645-3264

This exciting program is sponsored by the City of Columbus, Recreation and Parks Department, and is offered during the summer time, as well as during the spring and Christmas school breaks. Youths aged 6-12 can enjoy a variety of fitness related programs in addition to off site trips. The program is ideal for working parents as it is offered from 7AM-6PM on specified weekdays. The cost to attend the 6 full day Christmas break program was only $18, which comes to a mere $3 per day. The summer fee is $15 weekly or $105 for the entire 7 week term. Register early as the program fills up quickly. Accepts checks and cash.

LACES ROLLER SKATING CENTER OF COLUMBUS
3663 E. Main St., Columbus, 43213, 237-3736

Skating specials are offered on Sundays from 6:30-9PM at a cost of $8 for a family of 5 or $2.75 for a single admission. The admission price is usually $3-$5 at all other times.

MR.BILL'S NORTHERN LIGHTS
3525 Cleveland Ave., Columbus, 43224, 267-0321

Bowling specials are Sunday evenings from 8:30-11PM at a cost of $12 per lane. The price is usually $1.95 per game per person. Shoe rental is $1 at all times.

NEWARK GOLF COMPANY FACTORY OUTLET
99 S. Pine St., Newark, 43055, 1-800-222-5639

Sells golf clubs, balls, clothing, golf bags and shoes by such popular brands as Ram, PGA Tour, Brunswick, Miller, Nike, Etonic, Dunlop and others. Golf bags are priced at $35-$99, shoes start at $43, and 12-15 golf ball packs start at $15. Savings on this first quality merchandise for adults and kids is 40-60% off regular retail prices. The store offers free custom fitting of golf equipment utilizing their practice rooms and swing computers. Gives refunds. M-W 8-6, Th 8-8, F 8-6, Sat 9-6. Accepts checks, MC & Visa.

O.D.N.R. DIVISION OF WATERCRAFT
Fountain Sq., Bldg. C-2, Columbus, 43224, 265-6480

A free home study course, *Ohio Boating Basics-A Small Craft Primer*, is available from the Ohio Department of Natural Resources. Successful completion will earn you an Ohio Boating Basics Certificate, and possibly enable you to be eligible for a 5-20% discount on your boat insurance. Low cost boating and watercraft safety courses are also offered throughout Central Ohio. Call for details. M-F 9-5.

O.D.N.R. RENT-A-CAMP-PROGRAM
Fountain Sq., Bldg. C-3, Columbus, 43224, 265-7000

Twenty-three Ohio State parks are available as Rent-A-Camp sites through the Ohio Department of Natural Resources' popular seasonal program. For only $17 per night, an entire family can enjoy a fully equipped campsite with a 10x12 foot lodge type tent erected on a wooden platform, a picnic table, 12 foot square dining fly shelter, 2 cots, 2 foam sleeping pads, 60 quart cooler, a propane stove, camplight, fire extinguisher, broom and a dustpan. Rentals must be made after March 1, for the May 1-September 30 season. A $10 deposit must accompany your registration. Call between 8-5 M-F.

PAUL'S MARINE-THE DOCK SHOPPE
2300 E. Dublin-Granville Rd., Columbus, 43229, 899-1616

A large selection of boat accessories are available at savings of 15-25% off regular retail prices. Nautical inspired gifts such as jewelry and clothes, are sold at full retail prices. Gives refunds. M-Sat 10-8, Sun12-5. Accepts checks, MC & Visa.

PLAY IT AGAIN SPORTS
7420 Sawmill Rd., Columbus, 43235, 791-9344
1153 Columbus Pike, Rt. 23, Delaware, 43015, 363-2664

Save about 50% off regular retail prices, if new, on gently used sports equipment for baseball, softball, hockey, football, scuba diving, golf, weight lifting, tennis, camping, roller skating, water-skiing, wind surfing, fishing, soccer, lacrosse and more. This franchised operation sells such brands as McGregor, Spaulding, Wilson, Cooper and Rawlings. A limited amount of never used merchandise is sold at about 10-20% off retail. The inventory is a combination of consigned and purchased merchandise .for adults and children. Accepts trade-ins. Gives refunds. M-Th 10:30-9, F and Sat 10:30-7, Sun 12-5. Accepts checks, MC & Visa.

PRO GOLF DISCOUNT
2009 E. Dublin Granville Rd., Columbus 43229, 436-8714
5871 Sawmill Rd., Dublin, 43017, 792-3553
1359 Brice Rd., Reynoldsburg, 43068, 864-0110
3712 Riverside Dr., Columbus, 43221, 459-4111

Several hundred of these franchised stores can be found throughout the U.S. in which savings are about 20% off the price of first quality, current merchandise. You'll find clubs, balls, bags, shoes and clothes for the golf enthusiast. Offers low markups on a full selection of nationally recognized brands such as Ping, Hogan, Powerbilt, Wilson, PGA Tour and others. Offers layaway. Gives refunds. M-F 10-8, Sat 10-6, Sun 11-4. Accepts checks, MC & Visa

ROLLER CHALET
50 Charring Cross Dr., Westerville, 43081, 891-5100

The lowest prices for skating can be found on Saturdays and Sundays from 1-3PM. Admission to this open skate is $3.50 and skate rental is free. At other times, admission is $4-5.

SAWMILL LANES
4825 Sawmill Rd., Columbus, 43235, 889-0880

All you can bowl specials are Monday-Friday from 3-5PM for $3.99 per person, Fridays from 11PM-2AM for $10 per lane(up to 5 people), Saturdays from midnight-2:30AM for $5 per person(rock and bowl with DJ). Another special is offered Thursday and Friday from 12 noon-5PM at a cost of $1.25 per person per game. During the summer months, prices are dropped about 25% per game at all times and on Tuesdays, children aged 17 and under can bowl for free from 12-2PM. The shoes are free for children during this two hour time in the summer. During the Christmas school break, Sawmill Lanes has a special promotion for ages 17 and under, which includes 3 games of bowling, shoes, a hot dog and a soda for only $4.95 per person.

SKATE AMERICA
4357 Broadway, Grove City, 43123, 875-3181

Family roller skating specials are offered on Saturdays from 7:30-11:30PM at a rate of $11 for a family of 4, and Sundays from 1-5 at a cost of $9 for a family of 4. Skate rental is $1..Admission is usually $3-$4 at other times.

SKATE TOWN
7227 E. Main St., Reynoldsburg, 43068,866-5165

Roller skating specials are Saturday and Sunday from 1:30-4:30PM for $2 per person plus a $1 skate rental, and Sunday from 6-9PM for $1 per person plus a 50 cent skate rental. The admission fee is regularly $3 at other times. *Skate Town* is closed during the summer months.

SOUTHWEST COMMUNITY CENTER INDOOR POOL
3500 First Ave.,Grove City, 43123, 875-1880

This large indoor pool has been recently renovated. The annual membership fee is $50 per year per person, plus $25 for each additional family member. Seniors aged 55 and over, pay $30 per year. Another option is to pay $1 per person per visit instead of the annual fee. As of the time this book went to press, the pool had not confirmed its year round operating hours. It is open to the entire community and you do not have to reside in Grove City.

SPECIAL-TEE GOLF-TENNIS-RACQUETBALL

1870 W. Henderson Rd., Columbus, 43220, 457-3238
868 S. Hamilton Rd.,Columbus, 43213, 868-0794
1668 E. Dublin Granville Rd., Columbus, 43229,891-4653

Top quality brands of golf, tennis and racquetball clothing, shoes and equipment are sold at savings of 20-30% off manufacturer's suggested retail prices. The merchandise is first quality, current and past season goods, as well as some used merchandise. Brands offered include Ping, Hogan, Spaulding, Etonic and others. Adult and children sizes are available. This family owned business operates 16 stores in Ohio. Gives refunds. M-Sat 10-9, Sun 11-5:30. Accepts checks, MC, Visa, AmExp & Discover.

SPORTS SALES

1750 Idlewild Dr., Columbus, 43232, 268-7463

Custom imprinted and embroidered shirts, jackets and shorts for teams or clubs are available at savings of about 20% according to the owner. From design to conception, *Sports Sales* can emblazon anything made out of fabric for adults and children. This business also has a "no minimum order", unlike most custom businesses. All sales final. M-F 9-6. Accepts checks, MC & Visa.

SUPREME GOLF SALES, INC.

6421 Busch Blvd., Columbus, 43229, 888-8815
2256 S. Hamilton Rd., Columbus, 43232, 868-0754

All price ranges of first quality golf clothes and related accessories are discounted by about 25% off suggested retail prices. Merchandise is available for children as well as adults. Gives refunds. M-F 10-8, Sat 10-6, Sun 10-4. Accepts checks, MC & Visa.

UNITED SKATES OF AMERICA

4900 Evanswood Dr., Columbus, 43229, 846-5626
3362 Refugee Rd., Columbus, 43232, 239-7201

Roller skating specials are held on Saturdays from 10AM-12 noon for children aged 12 and under, at a cost of $2.75. On Wednesdays from 4-6PM, the open skate admission is 50 cents per person. On Fridays from 4:30-7PM, the open skate is $3. Regular admission prices are $3.25 at all other times. Skate rental is $1.50.

UPPER ARLINGTON HIGH SCHOOL NATATORIUM

1950 Ridgeview Rd., Columbus, 43221, 487-5213

Open swim time is from 2-4PM every Sunday during the school year. The fee is $1 per person. Lifeguards are on hand at all times at this large indoor pool. You do not need to be a resident of Upper Arlington to use the facility. Showers and lockers are also available. M-F 9-4 for inquiries.

WESTERVILLE BICYCLE CLUB

POB 356, Westerville, 43081, 882-CYCL

This fun and healthy leisure activity of bicycling can be enjoyed with this club. you don't have to be a member to ride with the group, which travels 25-100 miles depending on the trip. Rides are featured on Wednesdays in the spring, summer and fall, and on weekends year round. All skill levels and ages are welcome. Monthly meetings are held in the winter and include discussions and/or slide programs of interest.

ALSO SEE

Ameritech Pages Plus, Agler Davidson Annual Sale, Beulah Park Jockey Club, Children's Palace, Columbus Police Property Auction, Columbus Polo Club, Columbus Swim Center, Darby Sales, Deja Vu, Department of Defense, Famous Footwear, Franklin County Metro Parks, General Merchandise Sales, Golden Age Passport, Just For Feet, Kite Festival, Koval Knives, Licking County Bicycle Club, Meijer, J.C. Penney Outlet, Sam's Club, Sears Outlet, Schottenstein's, Scioto Downs, Service Merchandise, Toys 'R Us, Uncle Sam's Pawn Shop and Warehouse Club

SPECIAL EVENTS & SPECIAL SALES

In this section, you'll find special sales which don't have a year round walk-in location as well as special events lasting for one or several days. Other special events can be found in the entertainment chapter. Follow the newspapers or call the sponsoring organization for the exact dates of these sales and events. The listings in this chapter offer quality, low cost entertainment options and/or the opportunity to purchase artwork and other items at excellent prices. Refer to the description of the Ohio Arts Council in the arts and crafts chapter for pertinent information about arts festivals. Don't overlook attending some of the smaller shows and even church bazaars. Sometimes the prices will be lower than in the larger shows. Often, an artist who is just creating art as a hobby may not be prepared for the rigid entry requirements of some of the bigger arts festivals. However, it does not necessarily mean that their work is inferior. Also, artists have more overhead at larger, more prominent arts fairs and so their prices may be higher as a result, but not always. Remember that holidays are a popular time for stores to run large sales-President's Day, Memorial Day and the like. I have tried to list as many of the special events and special sales as possible, but due to space limitations, I have not been able to include all of them. For this reason as well, those which are listed only include brief descriptions. Follow the newspapers to learn of others. Consider subscribing to the *Bargain Hunting In Columbus Newsletter* to stay posted of other special sales, events and other shopping options not included in this book. See the end of the book for the order form. Programs are held in Columbus unless otherwise noted.

JANUARY

ACORN WAREHOUSE SALE
4 day event where end of season better women's apparel is reduced 40-60% and merchandise for the upcoming season is on sale for 40% off. The inventory is consolidated from 40 stores. Sale sites vary. Free. 764-8868

AGLER DAVIDSON ANNUAL 40% OFF SALE
Once a year in early January, the entire inventory is reduced 40% off their selling price for 1 day only at their 5 Columbus area stores. You'll find sporting goods, athletic apparel and footwear for the family. 457-1711.

J.J. BERGIN SHOE SALES
see description in shoes chapter

CIA'S ANNUAL CLEARANCE SALE
This popular bridal shop reduces selected wedding gowns, veils and special occasion dresses on the third weekend of January, where savings are 40-80%. On a year round basis, the store has a large selection of discontinued gowns and veils which are reduced 40-50%. 2149 W. Dublin-Granville Rd.., 885-4541.

COLUMBUS CHAPTER, OHIO SOCIETY OF C.P.A.'S
535 Metro Pl. S. Dublin, 43017, 764-2727 (Pat Moore)

A free, annual tax seminar is offered by the Taxation Committee of this local organization in late December or mid January at a site in the community. Local certified public accountants are on hand to discuss changes in the tax laws, how to decide if you should file jointly with a spouse or as an individual, child care credit and more. A question and answer session follows. Registration is required. M-F 8-5.

FABRIC FARMS ANNUAL WINTER SALE
20-50% savings throughout the store off their already discounted prices on quality home decorating and garment fabrics. 3590 Riverside Dr., 451-9300

GHOSTS OF BAKER STREET
see Grandview Library description

HOCKING HILLS WINTER HIKE
A 3 or 6 mile walk at your own pace along Ohio's most scenic trail with interpretive stops, food for purchase and return busing. Late January. Free. Hocking Hills State Park in Logan. 385-6841.

HUNTINGTON ICE SCAPES
Outdoor ice sculpting competition and exhibition on the Statehouse lawn to benefit the Open Shelter. 2 day event. Free. 461-0407.

ICE CAPADES
World renowned ice skaters in a spectacular family oriented show on ice. Opening night tickets are half price (you'll pay about $4-$6) and benefit a local charity. Held at the Columbus Convention Center late January to early February. 221-9191.

JUNK-A-MANIA
Large indoor garage sale, flea market and antique sale of all types of new and used items. Usually held at Veteran's Memorial Auditorium. 3 day event. $1.25 admission. 1-800-869-6881 or 221-4341

MARTIN LUTHER KING JR. CELEBRATION
Annual celebration featuring a march through downtown, performance by nationally recognized group and lectures. Held on the third Monday in January. Free, but ticket is required. 645-7410.

MEIJER'S KID'S WEEK
see Meijer's description elsewhere in this book

NOWHERE MUSIC FEST
2 day event held at a different Campus bar each year, in which underground bands have the opportunity to perform alternative, folk and other types of music. $3. 294-4006.

PERCUSSION DAY
Local, regional and nationally recognized jazz musicians present concerts, workshops and lectures. Co-sponsored by Coyle Music and held at OSU's Weigel Hall. Free. 885-2729 or 292-8050

ROCK AND ROLL EXPO
One day children's and teen's event featuring local and nationally recognized performing artists, products for sale, community service booths, fashion show and other fun diversions. $2. Usually at the Columbus Convention Center. 221-6700 or 221-9191.

SIDEWALK SALES
January is a popular month for shopping malls to have these indoor sales where savings are 30-80%.

TALBOTT'S FAMOUS SEMI-ANNUAL SALE
See June description

VISION USA PROGRAM
The Ohio Optometric Association offers an annual program for low income families during Save Your Vision Week, the first week of March. Participating optometrists will provide free exams for working Ohioans who do not have health insurance to cover the eyecare. Potential candidates may enroll from January 15-31 only by calling 1-800-766-4466. Qualified applicants are then matched with a volunteer optometrist in their community. This free service includes an eye exam and free glasses, if necessary.

WHITE SALES
January and August are popular times for department and specialty stores to feature their white sales (special sales on linens, towels, bedspreads and similar items). Savings can be 30-50% off and sometimes even higher.

WOODWORKING WORLD
Demonstrations, exhibitions and sales of machinery, tools, woods and supplies for the woodworker. Many lectures by nationally recognized experts are also included in your $6 admission fee. 3 day event usually at Veterans Memorial Auditorium. 1-800-521-7623 or (603) 536-3768.

FEBRUARY

AMERICAN MUSIC FESTIVAL
5 days of free lectures and low cost concerts (about $6) on early and contemporary American music with local, regional and nationally acclaimed performing artists. Sponsored by OSU School Of Music. 292-2354.

BARGAIN DAYS
4 day event at Weiss' Department Store featuring savings of 50-80% on better women's apparel by Leslie Fay and other brands. Downtown Marysville. (513) 642-3888.

CENTRAL OHIO HOME AND GARDEN SHOW
Lots of demonstrations on American and ethnic cooking, cake decorating, food preparation and more. See and learn about new products and purchase items at special show prices. Discount tickets available at Big Bear stores. 8 day event in late February through early March at the Ohio State Fairgrounds. $5. 644-3247.

CHOCOLATE FANTASY FAIR
Enjoy free samples of candy, pastries and ice cream by local and national companies and chocolatiers at this 1 day event. Continuous entertainment, demonstrations and specialty boutiques. Benefits Central Ohio Lung Association. Columbus Convention Center. $5 adults, $2 children. 457-4570 or 1-800-592-8563.

COLUMBUS SPORTS, VACATION AND TRAVEL SHOW
9 day event featuring over 200 displays on travel, resorts, campgrounds, sports, motor homes and more. Free fishing clinics, rockclimbing demonstrations, seminars and kids activities. Offers many show specials. Ohio State Fairgrounds. Pickup discount tickets at Kroger and sporting goods stores. $5 adults, children under 13, free. 481-7534.

DOWNTOWN DELAWARE WINTER DAYS
Stores on route 23 and routes 36/37 in Delaware, feature huge clearances of crafts, hardware, shoes, sports equipment, furniture, stationery, records, fine jewelry, books and clothes at savings of 30-80%. Free. 369-6221.

GRANDVIEW LIBRARY BOOK SALE
see library description in the chapter on entertainment

INTERNATIONAL GEM AND JEWELRY SHOW
3 day sales and exhibition event featuring loose gems and semi-precious stones, 14 karat and gemstone jewelry, costume jewelry and gift items. Held at Veteran's Memorial Auditorium. $5. 221-4341.

MCSWAIN CARPET SHOWDOWN

Leading mills show latest styles, hottest colors and best prices with over 1,800 selections. Dublin,Worthington and Eastland stores. 431-0555 or 864-0255.

NOW MUSIC FESTIVAL

see Capital University description in the chapter on entertainment

OHIO WINTER SKI CARNIVAL

Watch serious and comical ski racing including the bikini race. $2. Snow Trails Ski Resort, Mansfield. (419) 522-7393

RECORD CONVENTION

1 day event where you can buy, sell or trade new, used and collectible albums. Veteran's Memorial Auditorium. Free. 261-1585.

UNITED BLACK WORLD WEEK CELEBRATION

Ohio State University celebration in observance of Black history month includes soul food luncheons, lectures, videos, children's activities, Igbajo Ball and other festivities. Most programs are free. 292-6584.

WEEK OF PRAYER FOR CHRISTIAN UNITY

Week long celebration culminates in major performances by church choirs, liturgical dancers and bands at a local church. Sponsored by the Metropolitan Area Church Board. Free. 461-7103.

MARCH

ARCHEOLOGY DAY

Held in March or April featuring hands on demonstrations of methods, slide shows of expeditions and excavations. Free. Suitable for adults and children. Held on the West campus of OSU in Pressey Hall. Optional lunch available for $4.50. 292-6446 or 292-2721

BELLEPOINTE SEMI-ANNUAL SALE

Manufacturer's warehouse sale of first quality better women's sportswear, skirts, sweaters and knit tops. Current season and upcoming season's merchandise is available at savings of 60-75% off regular retail prices. Week-end sale features daily reductions and bargain tables. This company manufactures for Pappagallo, Lord and Taylor, the Acorn and other upscale boutiques and department stores nationwide. Sale site varies. Free. 792-5309.

COLUMBUS SPRING SWAP

Car past swap/sale at the Ohio State Fairgrounds. Adults $3, kids 12 and under, free. 644-3247.

DECORATORS' SHOW HOUSE

Different Columbus area home each year is tastefully decorated by some of the top interior designers in the area providing you with valuable decorating ideas. You can also shop at the adjacent tag sale featuring new decorators' scratch and dent pieces and donated new and used giftware and home furnishings. Tag sale savings are 30-60% off store prices. At the end of the Show House, the items used in its decoration are sold at about 30-60% off regular retail prices. Benefits Columbus Museum Of Art. Month long event from late April to late May. $6 admission. 888-2917.

EXTRAVAGANZA
Buy furniture, fine jewelry, toys, audio/stereo systems, clothes, gifts, hardware, luggage and leather goods, tools, books, shoes, spas, musical instruments and more. Savings are 20-80%. Dates are March 12-15, 1992 and March 11-14, 1993. Ohio State Fairgrounds. Free show admission, but $3 site parking fee. 644-3247 or (517) 332-3053.

GENTRY ANNUAL WAREHOUSE SALE
See Gentry description in the chapter on clothes

NEW HOUSE SEMINAR
Displays of house plans by area builders and discussions relating to building a new home. Order free tickets by mail or pick them up at the Columbus Dispatch. 461-5204.

PUBLICK TIMES IN THE COLONIES
110 costumed artists sell early American theme crafts. Ohio State Fairgrounds. $3. 644-3247 or (216) 835-1765

ST. PATRICK'S DAY FESTIVITIES
Free downtown parade followed by evening concert ($5-$8). Sponsored by the Shamrock Club of Columbus. 491-4449

SHRINE CIRCUS
Clowns, animal acts, acrobatics and more will delight young and old alike. 8 day event held in late March through early April. Ohio State Fairgrounds. Adults $4-$7, children under 12 $2-$3.50. Pick up discount tickets at Big Bear supermarkets. 475-0058 or 644-3247.

VISION USA PROGRAM
see January description

APRIL

ACORN WAREHOUSE SALE
4 day sale of first quality, previous season women's apparel, consolidated from 41 stores, at savings of 60-70% off regular retail prices. There's also a selection of special purchase current season clothes at 40% off . Sale site varies. 451-4909.

CENTRAL OHIO, GEM, MINERAL AND FOSSIL SHOW
2 day event featuring educational exhibits, lectures, sales, demonstrations, silent auctions, free gem identification and children's activities. Sponsored by the Columbus Rock and Mineral Society and the Licking County Rock and Mineral Club. Held at Veteran's

Memorial Auditorium. $4 adult admission, $1 for children aged 6-16, under six admitted free. 221-4341.

COLUMBUS BOOKFAIR
1 day event at the Aladdin Temple Shrine featuring 35 dealers in rare, used and collectible books, prints and other paper items. $2. 263-2903.

GOLDEN HOBBY SHOW
1991 marked the 43rd year for this event which showcases the artistic talent of seniors. Art demonstrations, continuous performances, lectures and an exhibition, highlight this family event. Held at the Martin Janis Senior Center. Free. 644-7492.

INDOOR BEACH PARTY
Complete with sand and palm trees, this re-created beach atmosphere features surfing and bikini contests, dancing, a surfside lounge, video surf simulator, entertainment and special guest appearances. Food and drinks available for purchase. $5 admission. 221-6700.

KITE FESTIVAL
Held on the third Saturday of April, this event features kite flying for all ages, kitemaking competitions, children's kitemaking classes, stunt kite demonstrations, vendors and kite flying lessons. Free admission to all programs. Held at the Park of Roses. 645-7464.

OSU FRIENDS OF THE LIBRARY BOOK SALE
2 day event features great bargains on books and magazines, most priced at $1 and under. Held at the OSU Main Library. 292-3387.

OSU JAZZ FESTIVAL
1 day event featuring local, regional and nationally known performers. Free. Held at Weigel Hall Auditorium. 292-2787.

VOICES FROM THE SQUARE
A series of free, dramatic/musical/historical vignettes based on actual events in the history of Columbus and Ohio, performed against the backdrop of Capitol Square's architecture. Lunchtime performances are held outdoors on the McKinley Stage with the Riffe Center lobby as the rain site. Month long program from mid April through mid May. Call to be added to their mailing list. Contact Doreen Uhas Sauer. 365-6681.

WALKER'S APRIL FOOL'S SALE
1991 marked the 38th year for this annual sale of men's famous maker and designer labelled suits, sportcoats, casual and dress slacks, shirts, neckwear, hose, shoes and sweaters. The first quality, upscale merchandise is on sale for 40-50% off their regular prices at the Tremont Avenue site only. 486-0281.

MAY

ARCADE ART AFFAIR
2 day juried show and sale of fine art and crafts by 45 artists at the Licking County Art Gallery, Newark. Free. 369-8031.

J.J. BERGIN
see shoes chapter

BOARD SAILING REGATTA
Midwest wind surfers race at Alum Creek State Park near Delaware. 1 day event is free to observers. 890-1546.

DELAWARE ARTS FESTIVAL
Large juried show and sale of fine arts and crafts on the streets of downtown Delaware. Live entertainment. Free. 363-2695.

FEAST OF THE FLOWERING MOON
Theme event featuring native American pow-wow, mountainmen rendezvous, historical re-enactments and arts and crafts for sale. Free. Held at Yoctangee Park in Chillicothe. 775-4100.

FUN FAIR
2 day children's event featuring games, face painting, performances and other free activities. Columbus Metropolitan Library, 96 S. Grant Avenue. 645-2770.

GASLIGHT REVUE
Vocal and dance performances by employees of Columbus Gas. 1991 was the 50th year for this event, which is held at Veteran's Memorial Auditorium. Free. 460-2000.

GERMAN VILLAGE VALUABLES DAY
1 day community wide yard sale at many homes throughout the Village. Pickup a free map at the German Village Society Office, 624 S. 3 St. 221-8888.

HERB AND CRAFT FESTIVAL
Sale of live medicinal and cooking herb plants, baked goods and craft items in Gahanna. 1 day event. Free. 471-4219.

HOME BUYERS SEMINAR
Free lectures on topics of interest to potential home buyers. Co-sponsored by the Columbus Dispatch and the Columbus Board of Realtors. Site varies for 1 night event. 461-5204.

INTERNATIONAL FAIR
2 day festival of dancing, foods, costumes and entertainment by Central Ohio ethnic groups. Held on the square in Sunbury. Free. 965-3901.

MEDIEVAL AND RENAISSANCE FESTIVAL
Step into living history during this unusual event featuring musical and other performances, jousting, human chess game, period crafts for sale and other activities in this re-created medieval fair. 1 day outdoors event at OSU. Free. 292-2324.

OHIO CAMERA COLLECTORS SOCIETY SHOW AND SALE
2 day event over Memorial Day weekend, featuring collectible and used cameras and equipment. Some new items are offered. $3 admission. 885-3224.

R.A.P. ANNUAL SPRING SAMPLE SALE
see description in flooring chapter

RECORD CONVENTION
1 day event featuring albums and 45's bought, sold and traded. Held at Veteran's Memorial Auditorium. Free. 261-1585.

VOICES FROM THE SQUARE
see April description

WHITE ELEPHANT SALE
1991 was the 27th year for this 2 day garage sale which offers new and used merchandise such as clothing, sporting goods, toys, housewares, live plants etc. Held at Veteran's Memorial Auditorium to benefit the Columbus Cancer Clinic. Free. 235-5184.

JUNE

J.J. BERGIN
see shoes chapter

COLUMBUS ARTS FESTIVAL STREET FAIR
Features over 300 artists from across the United States, selling their work, continuous entertainment on several stages, children's activities, demonstrations, food concessions by local chefs and fine restaurants. One of the top 25 arts festivals in the country. Don't miss this event. 3 day festival on downtown riverfront. Free. 224-2606.

COUNTRY CRAFT SHOW
2 day show featuring 130 artists selling their work plus family entertainment. $1 admission to show at Rolling Acres Farm and Stable in Delaware. Also has pony and hay rides at a nominal fee. 369-9962.

HERB DAYS
Gahanna is known as the herb capital of Ohio. Festival features continuous entertainment for adults and kids, herb sales, herb cooking demonstrations, midway and arts and crafts booths. Free 3 day event. 475-0404.

POWELL DAYS
95 artists and antique/collectible dealers sell wares on the street. Entertainment is also featured. Free. 841-0990.

ROSE FESTIVAL
The peak of the rose season features a celebration with entertainment, arts and crafts, plant sales and the opportunity to see and smell 9,000 roses in the largest municipal rose garden in the U.S. 3 day event at the Park of Roses. Free. 645-3300

ROUSCH HARDWARE SIDEWALK SALE
see description in hardware chapter

SENIOR SALUTE AND SENIORAMA
The Palace Theater is the site of an expo featuring booths with businesses that serve the needs of seniors and a free concert by the Columbus Symphony for seniors only. Free 1 day event, but you must pickup tickets in advance. 224-3291.

SUNFEST
Patterned after a Florida Reggae festival, this 2 day event in late June, features continuous entertainment, boat displays, sail boat clinics, regatta, surfing clinics, free rollerblade rentals, fishing clinics, petting zoo, kite making clinics, kite flying demonstrations and volleyball tournaments. Free. Held at the Hoover Reservoir in Westerville. 794-1222 or 890-8542.

TALBOTT'S SEMI-ANNUAL SALE
see January write-up

TUESDAYS AT TRINITY
Summer music series throughout the month at the Gloria Dei Worship Center of the Trinity Lutheran Seminary in Bexley. Features popular, classical and contemporary vocal and instrumental performances. Free. 235-4136.

YELLOW SPRINGS STREET FAIR
Arts and crafts fair and flea market features new and used merchandise, entertainment and food concessions in this quaint town. 45 minutes from Dublin. Free. (513) 767-2686.

JULY

ANNE'S COLLECTION WAREHOUSE SALE
see December description

DOODAH PARADE
This satire parade is held on the Fourth Of July through the Short North streets and includes spoofs on political and social institutions and people. It is followed by entertainment on North High Street. Free. 299-4008.

JAZZ AND RIB FEST

Ribs prepared by local restaurants, rib tasting contests, continuous jazz performances by local groups, plus headliners such as Chick Corea Band. Held in conjunction with the riverfront Jazz Festival. 3 day event held on the last weekend of July along the downtown riverfront. Free. 221-1321 or 645-3300.

KIDS EXPO

Features appearances by costumed characters, continuous entertainment, exhibitor booths, samples of products. Held the last weekend in July at the Columbus Convention Center. Sponsored by WTTE 28 Kids Club. Free. 895-2800.

KINKO'S ANNIVERSARY SALE

Semi-annual sale on 8 1/2 x 11 " autofed copies for 2 1/2 cents apiece and Canon laser color copies for 99 cents apiece. No minimum and no limit. Available at all area Kinkos for a week in mid July.

KROGER SENIOR EXPO

2 day event presents exhibitor booths with information on a wide variety of products and services of interest to seniors, product samples, health screenings and seminars. Local, regional and nationally recognized entertainment, such as the Guy Lombardo Orchestra, will perform throughout the expo. Free admission to Golden Buckeye cardholders. $2 for all others. Held at the Columbus Convention Center. 221-6700.

LANCASTER FESTIVAL

In mid July, this 11 day music, art, theater and dance festival highlights some of the most noted regional, national and internationally acclaimed artists. Over 50 public performances and exhibitions are held in various Lancaster sites and include programs for adults, families and children, many of which are free. Ben Vereen, Tony Randall, Christopher Reeve, Roberta Flack, the Chicago Brass Quintet have appeared as guest artists. Call to be added to their mailing list. Held at various sites in Lancaster. 687-4808 or 653-8251.

OHIO DESIGNER CRAFTSMEN MIDSUMMER FAIR

Displays and sales of wearable art jewelry, fiber, ceramics, glass, enamel and graphic artworks by 170 of the most talented craftsmen in the region and nation. Craft demonstrations and entertainment are also featured. This is sponsored by the same organization which puts on Winterfair. 3 day event at the Wellington School in Upper Arlington. Free. 486-7119.

RED, WHITE AND BOOM

On July 3, there's entertainment from noon to midnight with prominent local, regional and nationally recognized performers. A children's entertainment area, parade at 7PM and fireworks highlight this event. Held on the downtown riverfront. Free. 645-3300.

SCIOTO SUPERFEST

Features homemade and comical raft races, water ski shows, celebrity paddleboat race, power boat races, boat show, children's activities and musical entertainment. 2 day event along the downtown riverfront. Co-sponsored by the Columbus Recreation and Parks Department. Free. 645-3325.

SIDEWALK SALES
July is a popular time for malls and strip shopping centers to have sidewalk sales where savings are 30-80% off regular retail prices. Lane Avenue Shopping Center, Arlington Square, New Market mall and other shopping spots typically have these sales during the second week of July. Watch the newspapers.

WESTERVILLE MUSIC AND ART FESTIVAL
Held on the second weekend in July on the Otterbein College campus. Features over 160 fine art and crafts artists exhibiting and selling their works, demonstrations, continuous entertainment and a children's activity area. Free. 882-8917.

AUGUST

ARTS AND CRAFTS FESTIVALE
Enjoy the picturesque setting of a European street at the Continent as you browse amongst 75 booths where arts and crafts are being sold. 2 day event with strolling entertainment. Free. 846-0418. (Continent sidewalk sale is the third weekend)

BACKYARDS BY CANDLELIGHT TOUR
Tour 10 private German Village gardens. 2 day event. $5. 221-8888.

J.J. BERGIN
see shoes chapter

DUBLIN IRISH FESTIVAL AND COLUMBUS FEIS
Showcases traditional Irish arts and culture through vocal, musical and dance entertainment, demonstrations and other activities. 2 day event at the Dublin High School and Coffman Park. $4 adults, kids under 18 admitted for free. 792-7666.or 1-800-544-4940.

FESTIVAL OF AMERICAN CULTURE
Fashion shows, exhibits, performances, lectures, recreated environments and multi-media presentations. 1991 festival will focus on the decade of the 1950's. 1992 festival focuses on the decade of the 1960's. Don't miss this free 2 day event at the Columbus Cultural Arts Center which is operated by the Columbus Recreation and Parks Department. 645-7047.

GREEK FESTIVAL
The Greek Orthodox Church, 555 North High Street, is the site of a 3 day celebration of Greek culture over the Labor Day weekend. Entertainment, demonstrations, arts and crafts, dancing, and food concessions. Adults $2.50 for 3 days, seniors $2 for 3 days, kids under 12 are free.

HEALTH AND HARMONY FAIR
Sales booths, demonstrations and workshops on earth consciousness, holistic products and services, spiritual awareness, healing modalities, healthy foods, crystals and more. Held in mid August at the Murphy Archeological site in Newark. $3 for adults and $1 for kids. 587-3361

MEIJER'S KIDS WEEK
see Meijer's description in the health and beauty chapter

NICKLEBY'S SUMMER GOLD MINE BOOK SALE
Save up to 80% off the cover price on a large selection of overstocked and discontinued books at this bookstore cafe during the first 2 weeks in August. Check this store's listing in the chapter under entertainment for additional information on their year round opportunities. 488-2665

OHIO STATE FAIR
Commercial, agricultural and international exhibits and vendors, midway rides, entertainment on several stages and in all musical styles, demonstrations, celebrity appearances are all included in your $6 admission fee for adults or $4 for ages 3-4, seniors $2. Admission to the opening night is only $3 as some exhibitors will not be open. Nationally recognized entertainment (such as Bob Hope, Wayne Newton, the Statler Brothers) will perform in the new 12,000 seat Celeste Center at an additional fee of $3. Parking is $3. 644-3247.

ONE MORE TIME ANNUAL SIDEWALK SALE
see description in the chapter on clothes

SALT FORK ARTS AND CRAFTS FESTIVAL
Over 200 artists and craftspeople from across the country exhibit and sell their work. There's demonstrations, classes and continuous entertainment. Worth the drive to Cambridge's City Park for this 2 day event, which is 2 hours from Columbus. Free. 432-2022

WHITE SALES
White sales are typically held in August and January and provide the opportunity for you to purchase linens, blankets, bedspreads, towels and similar items at substantial savings. The department and specialty stores typically offer 30-60% savings on many items in their inventory.

WORTHINGTON FOLKLIFE CELEBRATION
see Worthington Arts Council description in the entertainment chapter.

SEPTEMBER

ACORN WAREHOUSE SALE
see January description

ARTISTS-IN-SCHOOLS PREVIEW NIGHT
The Greater Columbus Arts Council's program holds an annual showcase of over 125 professional artists which includes displays, demonstrations and ongoing sample performances in music, theater, dance, video and multi-arts. While the event provides facilities/organizations which present performances, the opportunity to evaluate the artists before contracting with them, The general public is welcome to attend and will find this quite enjoyable. Held at the Galbreath Pavilion of the Ohio Theater. Free. 224-2606.

J.J. BERGIN
see shoes chapter

CREATE -A-CRAFT SPECTACULAR
Discover the latest in fashion, craft and home decorating ideas through demonstrations, vendors booths and free instructional classes. Coupons, door prizes, and show specials make this a very interesting place to shop and learn. 3 day show held on the last weekend of September. $5 general admission, $4 seniors. 644-3247.

DUBLIN FESTIVAL OF THE ARTS
Over 125 artists exhibit and sell their works, entertainment, food concessions and kid's activities are also featured. Sponsored b the Dublin Women's Club on the second Sunday in September in historic Dublin. Free. 766-585.

FAMOUS SPORTSWEAR 2 DAY SALE
see description on page 50

FIELD PUBLICATIONS/WEEKLY READER SALE
Over 150,000 children's and teens books in all subjects are sold during this 2 day warehouse sale. The regular cover price is about $4-$5, but the books are sold here at 2 for $1. A limited selection of desk accessories and small appliances are also available at savings. Costumed characters and entertainment make this a family event. The warehouse is on the west side of Columbus on Dividend Drive. The sale is usually held on the last weekend of September. Free admission. 771-0006.

GAHANNA FLEA MARKET
Held on the third Sunday in September, this event features over 300 booths of new and used merchandise in addition to antiques and collectibles. Held on Mill Street in Old Gahanna. $1 admission. 471-1657.

GREEK FESTIVAL
see August description

GROVE CITY ARTS IN THE ALLEY
100 artists sell their work, entertainment and kids activities are included. Free 2 day event. 871-9049.

HOT TIMES IN OLD TOWN EAST
Community arts festival and streetfair featuring music, exhibits, entertainment and kids activities. 2 day event is held along Parsons Avenue. Free. 221-4411.

KIDSPEAK KIDSFEST
Children's festival with entertainment on 5 stages, costumed characters, rides, parade, puppet shows, fireworks, contests, vendor booths, games and more. 1 day event is held on the downtown riverfront. Sponsored buy the Columbus Recreation and Parks Department. Free. 645-3380.

MIAMISBURG STARVING ARTISTS SHOW
Over 235 artists/craftsmen sell their work priced at $25 and under. Held at Library Park in Miamisburg, about 1 1/2 hours from Columbus. This is well worth the trip. Arrive early. (513) 859-5626 or write to the show at: POB 144, Miamisburg, Ohio, 45342.

NORTHWEST ARTS AND CRAFTS FAIR

Over 65 artists sell their work at this 1 day event on the first weekend of September. Held at the Bethel Center Shopping Center. Free. 451-2908 or 442-1957.

OKTOBERFEST

Celebration of German culture with music, dancing, amusement rides, arts and crafts, adult and children's activities and food vendors. 3 day event is held in the downtown area. Admission is $4 for adults, $3 for seniors, $2 for ages 6-16. If you enter any day between 11-3, you'll only pay $2. 464-4705.

OLD WORTHINGTON MARKET DAY

1 day event featuring arts and crafts sales, demonstrations, old fashioned games, continuous entertainment, a farmer's market and a flea market. Held on High Street in old Worthington. Free. 888-3040.

POWELL VILLAGE ANTIQUE AND FLEA MARKET

2 day event last weekend in September. See May listing.

UPPER ARLINGTON LABOR DAY ARTS FESTIVAL

see Upper Arlington Cultural Arts Commission listing in the entertainment chapter

WORLD'S LARGEST BAKE SALE

Over 100 non-profit organizations will sell home baked foods and bazaar type crafts. Held at the Ohio State Fairgrounds on the third Saturday in September. Free admission. 523-0000.

YANKEE PEDDLER ARTS AND CRAFTS FESTIVAL

330 artists sell their work over 3 weekends in a pioneer festival setting. There's new artists each weekend. Continuous entertainment offered. Held at Clay's Park Resort in Canal Fulton. Admission is $1.50 to the first show and $5.50 or $7 to the second and third shows respectively. Well worth the trip and the price of admission. (216) 239-2554

OCTOBER

BARGAIN BOX

Giant garage sale of new and used household items, furniture, clothing, antiques and collectibles, toys and sporting goods donated by merchants and families. Held on the first weekend of October to benefit the Junior League. This is Central Ohio's largest garage sale. 2 day event held at Veteran's Memorial Auditorium. Free. 464-2717.

CIRCLEVILLE PUMPKIN SHOW

Pumpkins and pumpkins products are on display and for sale, parades, contests, food concessions and arts and crafts are also featured. Held over 4 days, the third weekend in October in downtown Circleville. Free. 474-4224 or 474-7000.

COLUMBUS CHIPPERS EXPO
Exhibit and sale of handcarved wooden artwork by talented artisans from the Midwest. 2 day event held at Veteran's Memorial Auditorium. $2 adults, $1.50 for children. 267-6242.

COLUMBUS USA WEEKEND
Arts festival, midway with rides, family games, local/regional/nationally recognized entertainment, fireworks and a parade. 3 day event held the first weekend in October along the downtown riverfront. Free. 481-7534.

GAMBIER FOLK FESTIVAL
Concerts, workshops, crafts and demonstrations focus on Ohio's rich cultural heritage. 3 day event, the last weekend in October at Kenyon College in Gambier. Free. 427-2875.

GIANT COLUMBUS FANTASTIC CAMERA SHOW AND COMPUTER SWAP
60 dealers buy, sell and trade new and used cameras and computer equipment and related items, computer programs, photographs, stereo cards and books. Free appraisals of old photographic items. 1 day event at the Aladdin Temple. $4. 475-2609.

INTERNATIONAL GEM AND JEWELRY SHOW
3 day event. See February description.

SECRET SANTA HOLIDAY HOUSE CRAFT SHOW
70 artists exhibit and sell their works at the Wellington School in Upper Arlington. $2. 487-2499.

SERVICE MERCHANDISE $1 MILLION DOLLAR GOLD SALE
see store listing in book

TRICK OR TREAT STREET
Kids dress in costume and go trick or treating at this indoor mall to receive surprises from the merchants. Followed by headliner children's entertainment such as the Teenage Mutant Ninja Turtles. Held on the weekend before Halloween at the Columbus Convention Center. $3 advance sale tickets only. 221-9191.

YELLOW SPRINGS STREET FAIR
see June listing

NOVEMBER

EDDIE BAUER WAREHOUSE SALE
Over $8 million in overstocked and discontinued items from their national catalogue and 180 stores is available at savings of 50-60% (higher discounts towards the end of the sale). You'll find linens, towels, specialty foods, luggage, travel accessories, men's and women's apparel/outerware/shoes. This month long sale is held at their Westside Columbus warehouse. 777-0794 or 771-2900.

BELLEPOINTE SEMI-ANNUAL WAREHOUSE SALE
see March description

COLUMBUS ARTS AND CRAFTS FAIR
Over 150 artists sell quality, handmade works in all media. 2 day event held in late November at the Aladdin Temple. $2 admission. 486-4991 or 268-4554.

COLUMBUS INTERNATIONAL FESTIVAL
Food, music, dancing and vendors representing the rich ethnic culture found in Ohio are featured in this 2 day spectacular event at Veteran's Memorial Auditorium. 228-4010.

COLUMBUS RECORD CONVENTION
Columbus' original record convention offers new and used records, cassettes and sheet music for sale or trade. Held on the first Saturday in November at Veterans Memorial Auditorium. $2.50 admission. 261-1585.

COLUMBUS WINTERFAIR
Contemporary crafts by 350 of the nation's finest artisans are on sale at this Ohio Designer Craftsmen sponsored event. Features some entertainment as well. Spectacular artisan showcase for discriminating tastes, held on the last Thursday in November through the first Sunday in December at the Ohio State Fairgrounds. This is one of my personal favorites. $4 adult admission, children 12 and under admitted for free. 486-7119.

FESTIVAL OF THE TREES
Spectacular display of over 100 professionally decorated holiday trees and wreaths, children's activities, handmade gingerbread houses by area chefs, arts and crafts for sale and non-stop entertainment. Trees are auctioned in a private patron preview party before the event officially opens to the public. Held on the Wednesday through Sunday of Thanksgiving at the Columbus Convention Center. Also open Thanksgiving day. Don't miss this event regardless of what is your religious belief..$5 adult admission, $3 for kids. 221-6700 or 436-2691.

HOLIDAY MARKETPLACE
Toys, jewelry, art and clothes by African-American artists and vendors are available for purchase. Held on the third Saturday of November at the Martin Luther King Center For The Performing And Cultural Arts. Free . 252-5464.

RAZZLE DAZZLE RALLY
Award winning program which teaches children about the dangers of drugs in a fun filled festival atmosphere. Special guest appearances and entertainment are included. Held on the first Saturday in November at Veteran's Memorial Auditorium. Co-sponsored by the Columbus Recreation and Parks Department. Free. 645-3300.

SECRET SANTA HOLIDAY PARADE
Marching bands, giant helium character balloons, Santa and floats are featured in Ohio's largest parade. Held on the third Sunday of November in downtown Columbus. Free. 766-0037.

TWIG BAZAAR
5 acres of handcrafted items, antiques, homemade baked goods, toys and gifts are featured at the world's largest one day bazaar. Benefits Children's Hospital. Held on the second Sunday in November at the Ohio State Fairgrounds. Free. 644-3247.

DECEMBER

ANNE'S COLLECTION SEMI-ANNUAL WAREHOUSE SALE
see July description

J.J. BERGIN
see shoes chapter for description

COLUMBUS WINTERFAIR
see November description

HILLIARD HOLLYFEST
82 arts and crafts booths, continuous entertainment, Santaland, and display of professionally designed wreaths are featured in this 3 day holiday event. Held on the first weekend of December at the Hilliard High School. $2 admission. 876-7666.

HOLIDAY CHOIRFEST
Hundreds of senior citizens in Franklin county choruses perform holiday and popular tunes at the Martin Janis Senior Center. Free. 644-7492.

OHIO PERIODICAL DISTRIBUTORS
Warehouse sale of hardcover and paperback books for adults and kids at savings of 50-90%. Usually held on first weekend of December. Free. 777 West Goodale Blvd. 224-4901.

WHITE LIGHTS OF CHRISTMAS
Tour of the downtown holiday lights aboard gaily decorated COTA busses. Tours leave from the COTA terminal at Columbus City Center from the first Monday in December to a few days before Christmas. Monday through Saturday 5:45-9:30PM. Free. 275-5800.

TOYS

CHILDREN'S PALACE
4300 W. Broad St., Columbus, 43228, 272-5388
2261 S. Hamilton Rd., Columbus, 43232, 861-8090
2296 Morse Rd., Columbus, 43229, 475-3232

A full line of children's toys, games, school supplies, bicycles, sporting equipment, cribs and other furniture, carriages and car seats, by all nationally recognized brands, are available at a savings of about 10-15% less than manufacturers' suggested retail prices. The stores feature a large clearance section of toys where savings are up to 50% on discontinued, seasonal, scratch and dent or items with damaged cartons. Other clearance items, reduced 20-30%, are scattered throughout the stores and are marked with red or green stickers. The stores have a frequent purchaser plan, The Diaper Club, which will provide you with a $5 gift certificate after you have purchased 12 packages of diapers. Your club membership card, which is free, must be stamped each time you make a purchase. Gives refunds. M-Sat 10-9, Sun 12-5. Accepts checks, MC, Visa, AmExp & Discover.

DROWSY DRAGON
34 Maplewood Avenue, Columbus, 43213, 231-8534

A large selection of unusual chess games can be found at fair prices. The store specializes in role playing games, board games, lead and pewter miniatures and historical games. Offers a 10% discount on TSI products. The far corner of the store has a sizeable offering of similar types of used games at least 40% off the new price. Gives exchanges only. M and W 11-6, Tu and Th 11-9, F and Sun 10-3. Accepts checks, MC & Visa.

KAYBEE TOYS AND HOBBY SHOPS
1719 Northland Mallway, Columbus, 43229, 267-8120
2715 Eastland Mall, Columbus 43232, 863-6800
4337 Westland Mall, Columbus, 43228, 272-8254
157 Columbus City Center Dr., Columbus, 43215, 221-9258
264 Southland Mall, Marion, 43301, 389-6266
1635 River Valley S., Lancaster, 43130, 687-0313

Half of the inventory consists of first quality prior season and discontinued toys which are available at savings of about 20-60%. You will find all of the highly sought after brands such as Fisher-Price, Playskool, Coleco, Buddy-L and others. Nintendo games are also available at similar savings. A selection of unusual and fun candies is available near the checkout. Gives refunds. M-Sat 10-9, Sun 12-5. Accepts checks, MC, Visa & Discover.

MIDDLETON DOLL FACTORY OUTLET
268 Front St., Marietta, 45750, 374-3655
1301 Washington Blvd., Belpre, 45714, 423-1481

The delightful, handmade Middleton Dolls are available as seconds for 40% off the regular retail "if perfect" price. The porcelain and vinyl dolls at the outlet are not signed and numbered as are the first quality dolls. Vinyl dolls are regularly $200-$250, but here you will find them for $120-$150. The porcelain dolls are regularly $200-$500, but here you can find them for $120-$300. Free tours are offered Monday-Saturday from 9-3 at the Washington Boulevard site only. Did you know that dolls are the second most collected item, preceded only by stamps? Gives refunds. Hours vary between stores. Accepts checks, MC & Visa.

MINIATURES UNLIMITED
6317 Busch Blvd., Columbus, 43229, 846-MINI (6464)

This store purchases inventories from retailers who are going out of business, discontinued merchandise and manufacturer closeouts. While the majority of the merchandise is first quality, there is some slightly damaged merchandise which is clearly marked and usually in a separate area of the store. You can save 10-40% off dollhouses, furniture, dollhouse wallpaper, building and electrical supplies for dollhouses, as well as Erna Meyer dolls. Provides layaway. Gives refunds. Tu-Sat 12-5. Accepts checks, MC & Visa.

TOYS R US
4340 W. Broad St., Columbus,. 43228, 274-3389
4285 Groves Rd., Columbus, 43232, 866-9163
1265 Morse Rd., Columbus, 43229, 268-3586
6547 Sawmill Rd., Dublin, 43017, 792-9194

This store features a large clearance section of discontinued, overstock and boxed damaged toys at savings of 30-80% off regular retail prices. Special values and reduced merchandise are also scattered throughout the store. You'll find a large selection of toys, games, children's furniture, bicycles, sporting goods, carriages, infant clothes and accessories from all major manufacturers at everyday low prices of about 10-20% less than manufacturer's suggested retail prices. Provides layaway. Gives refunds. M-Sat 10-9, Sun 12-5. Accepts checks, MC & Visa.

YANKEE TRADER
463 N. High St., Columbus, 43215, 228-1322

This store offers a large selection of paper and party goods, novelties, gags, seasonal and holiday items, decorations and carnival type prizes.   Closeouts, buyouts, discontinued stock and volume buying enable this business to offer savings of 10-50% on many items. If you purchase a dozen of the same product, you'll be entitled to a further savings of about 15%.   This is a fun store to purchase prizes for kids' parties as well as stocking stuffers. Gives refunds.   M-F 8:30-5:30, Sat 8:30-3:30.   Accepts checks, MC & Visa.

ALSO SEE

All For One, Berwick Corner Outlet, Columbus Metropolitan Library, Darby Sales, Direct Imports, Doll House, Drug World, Encore Shop, Extravaganza, Family Dollar, Garage Sales, Golden Hobby Shop, Just For Kids, Kids Quarters, Lake Erie Factory Outlet Center, Liquidations Now, 99 Cent Shops, Nearly New Shop, Odd Lots, Once Upon A Child, Only $1, Outreach Christian Books And Records, Paper Factory, J.C. Penney Outlet, Radio Shack Outlet Store, Sam's Club, Schottenstein's, Sears Outlet, South Drive In Theater, Springfield Antique Show and Flea Market, Stork Exchange, Trader Tots, Treasure Trunk, Tuesday Morning, Warehouse Club, White's Distributing

BARGAIN HUNTING TERMINOLOGY

BAIT AND SWITCH
How many times have you seen an ad in a newspaper or advertised on the radio and have gone to the store to purchase the item, only to find that it is supposedly sold out? Or perhaps you were told that the advertised product was inferior and that a different, higher priced product in the store would be a better value? This bait and switch tactic is illegal! Insist on seeing the advertised item.

BANKRUPT STOCK
A business which is in financial trouble, will sell their inventory to another business at prices below wholesale, to pay off their creditors. The business which purchases the inventory, is able to resell it to the public at far below regular retail prices. Bankrupt stock is also referred to as liquidations or liquidation merchandise. Schottenstein's buys bankrupt stock in addition to other types of merchandise.

BETTER QUALITY
Quality workmanship, durability and unique styling, characterize this merchandise.

BUDGET QUALITY
Inexpensive components, simple styling and often imprecise workmanship, characterize this type of merchandise. However, in some cases, you might be inclined to purchase these products due to their low cost or short term need.

BUYOUTS
This is a broad term which can refer to the act of purchasing all of the inventory of a business or all of a particular type of merchandise such as a buyout of bankrupt stock, a buyout of overruns etc.

CANCELLED GOODS (CANCELLATIONS)
Due to late delivery, financial difficulties or a variety of other reasons, a retailer may decide not to accept delivery of an order which was placed with a manufacturer. This merchandise, if it cannot be resold to another retailer at the regular wholesale price, becomes surplus merchandise which is sold to another retailer below wholesale. This business then resells it to the public at a percentage below its regular retail price.

CLOSEOUTS
A small amount remaining of a certain style or model is sold below wholesale in order to make room for new merchandise at manufacturer. This is sometimes also refereed to as odd lots. This term is additionally used to refer to styles or models which will be discontinued by the manufacturer. A business which purchases this inventory, will resell it to the consumer at a percentage below its retail price. It is important to consider whether parts will be available in the future for your purchase if needed.

COMBINATION PRICING
This method is used to encourage you to buy a group of related items at a fixed price, such as a patio set consisting of 2 lounge chairs, a table and an umbrella. Check to ensure that this combination price is really offering you a savings, and that it is not merely the sum of the prices for each individually marked item. Be sure that you can use all of the items in the group before you decide to make your purchase.

DIRECT IMPORT PRICES
Similar to "factory direct" or "manufacturer direct" prices in that the middleman has been eliminated by importing directly, in this case, from the overseas company.

DISCONTINUED MERCHANDISE
This term is used to refer to models or styles which will no longer be manufactured. A business which purchases this inventory, will sell it to you at a percentage below its retail price. You should inquire as to whether parts will be available for your purchase in the future.

DISCOUNT
A percentage or dollar amount off the regular retail price.

FACTORY DIRECT
You have seen this phrase many times, but does it mean a good value? Not always. To most people, the term implies that the retailer has purchased inventory directly from the factory or manufacturer and has eliminated the middleman's markup. This happens frequently in big volume purchases. This phrase also implies that you are being offered savings from regular retail prices. In many instances, this is the case. However, some unscrupulous businesses will use that phrase to mislead you into believing that you will be saving money. There are many manufacturers who always sell their products directly to retailers at traditional wholesale prices. So the phrase, factory direct, does not always indicate a good value. When in doubt, ask the store's staff.

FACTORY OUTLET OR MANUFACTURER'S OUTLET
In this business, you can purchase merchandise in a retail store which is often owned and operated by the manufacturer. Sometimes these retail businesses are located within, or adjacent to, the manufacturing facility. In another instance, there may be one or more factory outlets , owned by the same manufacturer, in other parts of town or even in other cities. The factory outlet generally provides you with the opportunity to see the manufacturer's full line of goods. This is not always possible in other stores as businesses tend to stock only those items which sell best and often like to have a variety of products from several manufacturers. The factory outlet does not always provide a discount on their first quality, current merchandise. If it does, savings can vary from 10-50% depending on the store..The outlet may also carry discontinued, past season, overstocks, seconds and otherwise blemished goods at savings of up top 90% depending on the store. Perhaps only a small portion of the factory outlet;'s stock is discounted, as is the case with Krema Products. However, since it is difficult to find their full line of peanut butters at any one grocery, the outlet store is a good option if you are loyal to the Krema brand., Many factory outlets also provide the opportunity tot purchase food products almost right out of the oven. Each factory outlet operates differently. Some businesses will use the words, factory outlet, to let you know that they are the only store in a certain geographic area to sell a certain product. The store may sell items from one or more different manufacturers. This does not imply that the store is offering you a savings off the retail price.

FACTORY OUTLET MALL OR FACTORY OUTLET SHOPPING CENTER
A group of stores under one roof, in one strip shopping center or in a specified area (such as the Aurora Farms Factory Outlets) which are supposed to be factory outlets or manufacturers' outlets (see description above). Most consumers expect that all of the stores in this shopping facility will provide good values on all of their products. But this is not always so! Often, there will be businesses intermingled among the true outlets, which do not discount at all. Sometimes the outlets which are offering a savings are only doing so on selected products, and so much of their inventory could be at full retail price.

FIRST QUALITY
Merchandise which has no visible or hidden defects or flaws in workmanship, design, material or pattern.

FLOOR SAMPLE OR "DEMO"
A demonstration model or style of merchandise which is displayed in the store. These sometimes get a little dirty or may be come scratched due to customer use. Savings on floor samples/demos vary from store to store, but are generally 20-60%. Be sure to inquire about the floor sample's/demo's warranty prior to making your purchase. Often, you will be compromising on a warranty in exchange for this lower price. Floor samples are also referred to demonstration models. Automobiles can often be purchased at substantial savings through car dealers, if they have been "demos".

FREIGHT DAMAGED OR SALVAGE
All or part of a shipment from a manufacturer may be chipped, dented or otherwise damaged in transit. The entire shipment will then be marked "freight damaged", and sold to a business way below wholesale even though there are likely to be many undamaged items. The savings are then passed on to you.

GRADED SECONDS OR SELECTED SECONDS
The merchandise has been hand sorted to extract only that which has minor flaws which will probably not affect the performance or appeal of the product.

IRREGULARS
Merchandise with minimal imperfections which are hardly noticeable and may not affect its performance or durability. Some seconds, however, are marked irregular.

JOBBER
The wholesaler who serves as the middleman between the retailer and the manufacturer. Not all manufacturers deal through jobbers. When you read the advertisements which state "factory direct" or "no middleman", the jobber is the one who is supposedly out of the picture.

KNOCKOFFS
This phenomenon runs rampant in the garment industry in which; less costly copies are created of the expensive clothes.

LIQUIDATIONS
See bankrupt stock

LOSS LEADER

This is an item which is priced very low, often at a loss for the retailer, as a way of enticing you into the store. The business anticipates that once inside, you will not only purchase the low priced item, but will also impulsively purchase more expensive items (which have a higher profit margin). The solution is to stock up on as many of those loss leaders as you will reasonably use. Don't be led into buying items which you do not need and which are not good values.

MANUFACTURER'S SUGGESTED RETAIL PRICE

Sometimes a manufacturer will pre-ticket his merchandise with the price he is suggesting it to be sold at in the stores. At other times, a manufacturer may recommend a retail price for his merchandise as depicted in a wholesale catalogue. Different sorts of merchandise have different markups or profit margins for the retailer. Some businesses will take a lower markup for a variety of reasons, and then pass the savings on to you, resulting in a good value.

MANUFACTURER'S OUTLET

See factory outlet.

MARKUPS

See manufacturer's suggested retail price

MULTIPLE PRICING

Retailers will subtly encourage you to purchase more than you need by offering several items at a single price, such as 5 for $1, instead of 20 cents each. Therefore, it may appear as a better deal to you, when in fact, it may not be. On the other hand, businesses may legitimately offer a discount for buying several of an item such as 20 cents each or 10 for $1.50. In multiple pricing, you do not always have to buy more than you need. Often you can purchase 1 of an item at a pro-rated price.

NO FRILLS ENVIRONMENT

The bare minimum of store decoration usually assists in keeping the prices low to the consumer. Such is the case with the Warehouse Club.

ODD LOT

This is a very small amount of remaining inventory in a particular style, size or color, at the wholesale level. The wholesaler will sell this merchandise cheaply to another business which in turn offers the consumer a price which is lower than the suggested retail price. The store, *Odd Lots*, is a fine example of this.

OFF PRICE OR O.P. RETAILER

These businesses generally purchase goods during the season they are to be used by the consumer, as opposed to pre-season, which is typical with most retailers. This in-season buying helps the manufacturer to unload surplus inventory which is still in the stores at the proper timing for consumer use. Off price retailers may also purchase samples, overruns, seconds or discontinued items. Sometimes the O.P. retailer will remove the labels from the merchandise so as to hide the manufacturer's name from the consumer. *Marshall's and T.J. Maxx* are off price retailers.

OVERRUNS
A manufacturer may create more merchandise than needed to account for damages and faulty construction, which sometimes can occur. These are sold below wholesale to a business which then passes the savings on to the consumer. This merchandise is sometimes referred to as surplus or overstocks.

OUTLET
Webster's New Collegiate Dictionary describes this as "a market for a commodity", "an agency (as a store or dealer) through which a product is marketed at retail". The word, outlet, is being used very frequently in a business' name and/or advertising to denote a place where there are good values or items sold at a discount. Another frequently used reason is to denote a retail operation (often a cash and carry) of a wholesaler. You may or may not be getting a savings off retail in these places. However, this allows you to have a bigger selection of that company's products under one roof and/or the opportunity to purchase freshly baked or prepared products .

OVERSTOCK
See surplus goods.

PAST SEASON MERCHANDISE
Items which have been created or manufactured for a previous season.

PSYCHOLOGICAL PRICING
A common practice is to price items at 1 penny or 1 dollar less than the next larger whole number. For example, a $99 item is only $1 less than $100, but it appears as if it costs much less than it does, although after paying sales tax and/or service charges, your item can cost over $100.

REMNANT
This term is usually used to refer to carpet and flooring, wallpaper and fabric. It refers to ends of rolls which are leftovers. Sometimes these are short lengths. The terms, mill ends or bolt ends, are used interchangeably with the term, remnant.

SAMPLE
An item which a salesperson shows to a prospective purchaser for the purpose of taking orders for the product. The sample is created as a result of a plan or a pattern. As potential problems may not be realized until the sample is actually created and/or tested, the sample item may be slightly different than the item actually shipped to a store. For instance, maybe the crotch was cut too short, or the neckline too tight, or perhaps the pocket should be on the right side instead of the left. Although samples tend to be first quality, some are slightly soiled. Some samples on the other hand, are exactly the way the merchandise will be shipped to the stores.

SECONDS
Merchandise which has more than just a minor blemish or flaw which may, in some instances, affect its performance or appeal. Some of these imperfections can be easily repaired. The Hanes L'eggs mail order company mentioned in this book, offers seconds of pantyhose which has variations in color or a different weave in the knit panty than intended. Seconds are sometimes erroneously referred to as irregulars.

SURPLUS OR OVERSTOCK
An amount of merchandise which is more than a manufacturer or dealer needs

VALUE PRICED OR GOOD VALUE
Your money is well spent by purchasing one of these items as the quality might be better than you would expect for the price, the size may be bigger than usual, the warranty may be longer than usual etc. In these cases, the merchandise is not necessarily discounted, but by comparing the cost of the product to what you are getting, the value is great. Low markups by retailers often result in good values. The MCL Cafeteria, mentioned in this book, is a fine example of value priced food.

WHOLESALE OR WHOLESALE PRICE
This is the cost which retailer s pay for their merchandise

ZIP CODES IN COLUMBUS AND VICINITY

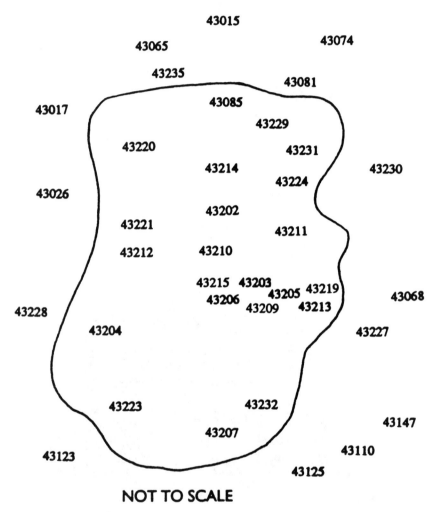

43015

43065   43074

43235   43081

43017   43085

43229

43220   43231

43214   43230

43224

43026

43202

43221   43211

43212   43210

43215   43203
43206   43205 43219
43209   43213   43068

43228
43204   43227

43223   43232
43147

43207

43123   43110

43125

NOT TO SCALE

OHIO CITIES IN THIS BOOK

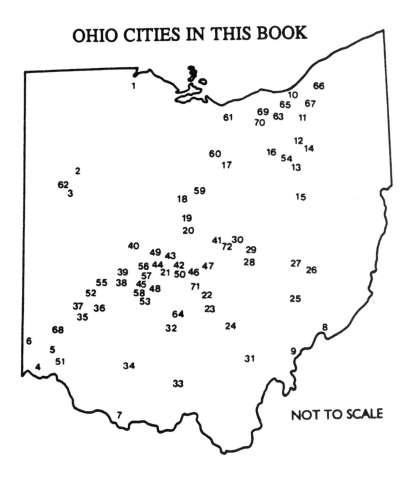

NOT TO SCALE

1- Toledo	19- Waldo	37- Dayton	55- YellowSprings
2- Lima	20- Delaware	38- Springfield	56- Plain City
3- Wapakoneta	21- Columbus	39- Urbana	57- W. Jefferson
4- Cincinnati	22- Lithopolis	40- Marysville	58- S. Vienna
5- Sharonville	23- Lancaster	41- Sunbury	59- Galion
6- Hamilton	24- Logan	42- Westerville	60- Shelby
7- Ripley	25- New Lexing.	43- Worthington	61- Milan
8- Marietta	26- Cambridge	44- Dublin	62- Spencerville
9- Belpre	27- Zanesville	45- Hilliard	63- Brunswick
10- Cleveland	28- Heath	46- Reynoldsburg	64- Ashville
11- Aurora	29- Newark	47- Pickerington	65- Brooklyn
12- Akron	30- Granville	48- Grove City	66- Willoughby H.
13- Massillon	31- Nelsonville	49- Powell	67- Maple Hts.
14- Canton	32- Circleville	50- Bexley	68- Monroe
15- New Phila.	33- Chillicothe	51- Mason	69- Brook Park
16- Wooster	34- Wash. Ct. Hse.	52- Kettering	70- Middleburg H.
17- Mansfield	35- Miamisburg	53- London	71- Groveport
18- Marion	36- Xenia	54- Canal Fulton	72- New Albany

LOTUS PRESS

The **Lotus** is attributed to Nepthys. the Egypytian goddess of tranquility. The flower represents the ideas of continuity, placidity and inner peace through meditation.

INDEX

BOOKS AND NEWSLETTERS
AVAILABLE FROM
LOTUS PRESS

see order form on next page

BARGAIN HUNTING IN COLUMBUS:
A comprehensive shopper's guide to savings and values in Columbus and central Ohio. Plus a section on bargain hunting day trips around the state. This book has over 1,100 listings. It will be updated about every two years. Cost $12.95.

BARGAIN HUNTING IN COLUMBUS ZIP CODE DIRECTORY:
All of the listings in the *Bargain Hunting In Columbus* book have been categorized by zip code which enables you to see at a glance, which stores are in which parts of town. It can save you time and money by allowing you to visit several businesses in a particular geographic area. Or, if you unexpectedly find your self in a certain part of town, you'll be prepared by knowing which businesses are nearby. This handy companion to the book can easily fit into your car's glove compartment. It is not a substitute for the *Bargain Hunting In Columbus* book, but merely a companion. The zip code directory also contains pages on which you can attach fabric swatches of clothes you want to match up accessories to and pages on which you can record sizes, personal tastes and special occasion dates of family members. Cost $2.50.

BARGAIN HUNTING IN COLUMBUS NEWSLETTER:
This quarterly newsletter will offer its first issue in January 1992. It will include information not currently found in the book such as listings of additional bargain sources, more shopping tips, mail order bargains, updates to the book and more! As the *Bargain Hunting In Columbus* book will be updated every two years, this is your best way to stay informed of the latest bargain hunting information. Cost $9 annually.

OTHER TITLES;
Several other titles of local/regional interest are now in progress and will be published over the next few months.

SEE ORDER FORM ON THE NEXT PAGE

ORDER FORM
(see descriptions on the previous page)

PLEASE SEND ME:

TITLE	# OF COPIES	COST
Bargain Hunting In Columbus $12.95 + .74 tax + $2.50 shipping/handling = $16.19 each	_____	_____
Bargain Hunting In Columbus Zip Code Directory $2.50 + .14 tax + $1 shipping/handling = $3.64 each	_____	_____
Bargain Hunting In Columbus Quarterly Newsletter $9 annually (includes tax and shipping)	_____	_____
	TOTAL COST	$ _____

TERMS

Allow 3-6 weeks for delivery. Payment may be made by check or money order made payable to Lotus Press. There will be a $20 fee assessed for each check returned by your bank for any reason. If not completely satisfied with your purchase, you may return it for a refund.

SHIP TO:

NAME_____

ADDRESS _____

CITY, STATE, ZIP _____

AREA CODE & PHONE_____

MAIL ORDER TO:

LOTUS PRESS
P.O. BOX 8446
WESTERVILLE, OHIO 43081-8446

ABOUT THE AUTHOR

Debbie Keri-Brown was born in Brooklyn, New York on January 8, 1953. She is a cum laude graduate of the Long Island University with a B.A. in speech pathology. Debbie is the former owner of the Potpourri Boutique and Fantasy Designs Gallery in the Ohio Center, Columbus. She is the founder and former executive director of Arts Alive, a nonprofit organization providing opportunities in the visual and performing arts for people with disabilities. The Columbus Dispatch has honored her with two awards for advancement in the cultural arts and Arts Alive was the recipient of another. For the past 11 years, she has been the producer and host of a weekly radio show on the arts, community affairs and bargain hunting on the Central Ohio Radio Reading Service. Debbie, a professional artist who creates jewelry using beads, handmade paper and mixed media, maintains memberships in several art leagues including the Ohio Designer Craftsmen, the Central Ohio Bead Society, the Central Ohio Weavers Guild and the Dublin Area Art League. Debbie is also on the advisory board of Columbus Parent Magazine. She has taught many classes in wearable art, bargain hunting and publicity through most area adult education programs. As a public relations/marketing professional by vocation, she is employed in this capacity by a major art facility in Columbus, Ohio. Debbie has provided consultancies in these areas to many organizations and individuals and may be contacted at: Lotus Press, POB 8446, Westerville, Ohio, 43081-8446.